PATHWAYS INTO THE JUNGIAN WORLD

In *Pathways into the Jungian World* contributors from the disciplines of medicine, psychology and philosophy look at the central issues of commonality and difference in phenomenology and analytical psychology.

The major theme of the book is how existential phenomenology and analytical psychology have been involved in the same fundamental cultural and therapeutic projects – both legitimize the subtlety, complexity and depth of experience in an age when the meaning of experience has been abandoned to the dictates of pharmaceutical technology, economics and medical psychiatry. The contributors reveal how Jung's relationship to the phenomenological tradition can be, and is being, developed, and they rigorously show that the psychological resonance of the world is immediately available for phenomenological description.

Roger Brooke is Professor of Psychology at Duquesne University, Pittsburgh. He is the author of *Jung and Phenomenology* (Routledge, 1991).

Contributors: Lionel Corbett; Veronica Goodchild; John Haule; David Michael Levin; Stanton Marlan; Bertha Mook; Robert D. Romanyshyn; Ronald Schenk; Charles E. Scott; Eva-Maria Simms; Michael P. Sipiora; Mary Watkins; Mark Welman.

PATHWAYS INTO THE JUNGIAN WORLD

Phenomenology and analytical psychology

Edited by Roger Brooke

London and New York

First published 2000
by Routledge
11 New Fetter Lane, London EC4P 4EE

Simultaneously published in the USA and Canada
by Routledge
29 West 35th Street, New York, NY 10001

Routledge is an imprint of the Taylor & Francis Group

Typeset in Times by RefineCatch Limited, Bungay, Suffolk
Printed and bound in Great Britain by
TJ International Ltd, Padstow, Cornwall

British Library Cataloguing in Publication Data
A catalogue record for this book is available from the British Library

Library of Congress Cataloging in Publication Data
Pathways into the Jungian world : phenomenology and analytical psychology / edited by Roger Brooke.
p. cm.
Includes bibliographical references and index.
1. Psychoanalysis. 2. Jungian psychology. 3. Existential phenomenology. I. Brooke, Roger, 1953– .
BF175.P29 1999
150.19′54 – dc21 98–56540
CIP

ISBN Volume 0–415–16998–4 (hbk)
ISBN Volume 0–415–16999–2 (pbk)

FOR MY FATHER, KENDALL

. . . Whoever you are, no matter how lonely,
the World offers itself to your imagination,
calls to you like the wild geese, harsh and exciting –
over and over announcing your place
in the family of things,

Mary Oliver (1986) *Dream Work,*
New York: Grove Atlantic Inc.

CONTENTS

FIGURES

CONTRIBUTORS

Roger Brooke, Ph.D., is Professor of Psychology and Director of Training in Clinical Psychology at Duquesne University, Pittsburgh. Since the start of his undergraduate training at the University of Cape Town he has been steeped in the issue of Jung's relationship to existential phenomenology. His doctoral dissertation at Rhodes University, South Africa, was worked into the book, *Jung and Phenomenology* (Routledge 1991). He is in private practice in Pittsburgh, where he is also Adjunct Faculty at The C.G. Jung Institute Analyst Training Program in Pittsburgh. As well as publishing in the areas of analytical psychology and phenomenology, he has written several papers on psychotherapeutic issues.

Lionel Corbett, MD, trained in medicine and psychiatry in Britain, and graduated from the C.G. Jung Institute of Chicago. He is a Professor of Depth Psychology at Pacifica Graduate Institute in Santa Barbara, California. He is the author of numerous articles in analytical psychology, and a recent book, *The Religious Function of the Psyche* (Routledge 1998).

Veronica Goodchild, Ph.D., studied theology and philosophy at London University in England, and completed her Masters in Clinical Social Work at Columbia University, New York. She practiced as a Jungian psychotherapist for more than fifteen years, and recently completed her doctoral degree in Clinical Depth Psychology at Pacifica Graduate Institute. She has taught Jungian psychology extensively on the East coast of the USA, and in South Africa at Rhodes University in 1995. She is married to Robert Romanyshyn, and they are the parents of four children.

John Ryan Haule, Ph.D., is a certified psychoanalyst, and training analyst in the New England Society of Jungian Analysts, of which he is a past President. Since his dissertation in the area of Jungian psychology and phenomenology at Temple University, he has many publications to his credit, including several books. *Divine Madness*, has been published also in German.

David Michael Levin, Ph.D., is Professor of Philosophy at Northwestern University, Illinois. He is internationally acclaimed for his pioneering investigations in phenomenology, and is especially appreciated for his attempts to deepen philosophical phenomenology with insights from depth psychology. He has had a long-standing interest in Jungian psychology, in particular. Of his many publications, which include *The Listening Self* and *The Opening of Vision*, perhaps his best-known is *The Body's Recollection of Being: Phenomenological psychology and the deconstruction of nihilism* (Routledge 1985).

Stanton Marlan, Ph.D., is a Jungian psychoanalyst in private practice at the Pittsburgh Center for Psychotherapy and Psychoanalysis, and is Director of the C.G. Jung Institute Analyst Training Program of Pittsburgh. He is a training and supervising analyst for the Inter-regional Society of Jungian Analysts. He holds a Diplomate in Clinical Psychology from the American Board of Professional Psychology, and a Diplomate in Psychoanalysis from the American Board of Psychoanalysis in Psychology, Inc. His current and long-standing interests include the psychology of dreams, post-modernism, and archetypal psychology. He has published a number of articles on Jungian psychology, and most recently has edited and written critical introductions to two books: the first a reprinting of classic essays by Ernest Jones, C.G. Jung, and James Hillman, *Salt and the Alchemical Soul*, the second, *Fire in the Stone: the alchemy of desire* (Chiron 1997). Among his many responsibilities, he has recently been invited to teach at the Pacifica Graduate Institute in California.

Bertha Mook, Ph.D., is Professor of Psychology at the University of Ottawa, Canada, where she is especially involved in the doctoral and post-doctoral training in child psychopathology and psychotherapy. Her Ph.D. was in Child Clinical Psychology, but her clinical training included experience in South Africa, Holland and the United Kingdom. She is a scholar known for her rigour, and is a pioneer in phenomenology and hermeneutics, which she has systematically extended into the areas of family therapy and play therapy. Many of her recent publications have been exploring the (creative) tensions between descriptive understanding and hermeneutical interpretation. These include, "Imaginative play in child psychotherapy: the relevance of Merleau-Ponty's thought," (in D. Olkowski and J. Morley (eds): *Merleau-Ponty, Desires and Imaginings*, New York: Humanities Press, 1996) and "The significance of hermeneutics to child psychotherapy," (*Journal of Psychiatry and Neuroscience*, 16, 3, 1991, 182–187).

Robert D. Romanyshyn, Ph.D., is a "former" psychologist and psychotherapist who now practices "cosmo-analysis" in the spirit of the later Jung, the later Merleau-Ponty, and the work of Gaston Bachelard. He is the author of two books and more than forty other publications in books and journals. He is a core faculty member at Pacifica Graduate Institute, and Coordinator of research for their doctoral programs in Clinical and Depth Psychology. He has recently completed a book entitled *The Soul in Grief: Love, death, and transformation* (Berkeley: North Atlantic Books). He lives with his wife, Veronica, and three of their four children in Santa Barbara, California.

Ronald Schenk, Ph.D., is a Jungian analyst and Senior Training Analyst in the Inter-regional Society of Jungian Analysts. He practices, teaches, and writes in Dallas and Houston. His many publications include "Navajo healing," "Bare bones: the aesthetics of arthritis," "A ground for Jungian thought," and a recent book, *The Soul of Beauty* (London: Associated University Presses, 1992).

Charles E. Scott, Ph.D., is Edwin Erle Sparks Professor of Philosophy at The Pennsylvania State University. An internationally acclaimed scholar in European thought, particularly Heidegger, he has also had a long-standing interest in analytical psychology and in the work of James Hillman. Among his numerous publications are books on Heidegger, ethics, and immediate awareness in psychotherapy. He has also edited a collection of essays on the phenomenological psychoanalyst, Medard Boss. He has also trained and practiced as a psychotherapist.

Eva-Maria Simms, Ph.D., is Associate Professor of Psychology at Duquesne University. She completed her doctoral degree at the University of Dallas, where her dissertation on Rilke was supervised by Professor Romanyshyn. An outstanding example of the contemporary movement of phenomenology, her work displays clarity, scholarship, and originality. Although her main interests at present involve the phenomenology of childhood, she has had a long-standing interest in the *rapprochement* between phenomenology and analytical psychology.

Michael P. Sipiora, Ph.D., is Associate Professor of Psychology at Duquesne University, Pittsburgh, and a licensed psychologist in private practice and at the Ielase Institute of Forensic Psychology in Pittsburgh. After attaining a Masters in Philosophy, his Masters and Doctoral studies in Psychology were at the University of Dallas (1981–1987), during which time he also worked for Spring Publications, which published a journal and books in archetypal psychology. He has published widely in the fields of archetypal psychology and in both phenomenological philosophy and psychology, and has a special interest in the relevance of Heideggerian phenomenology for social psychology. His papers, which include such titles as, "A soul's journey: Camus, tuberculosis, and Aphrodite," "Heidegger and epideictic discourse: the rhetorical performance of meditative thinking," "Miracles and the spiritual un-consciousness of technological culture," and "Alienation, the self, and television," are notable for their rigorous scholarship, clarity, and contemporary relevance.

Mary Watkins, Ph.D., is Chair of the M.A. Program in Counseling Psychology at the Pacifica Graduate Institute in Santa Barbara. She studied phenomenological psychology at Duquesne University, and Jungian and archetypal psychology at the Jung Institute in Zurich: her Ph.D. was in clinical and developmental psychology at Clark University. Her publications include *Waking Dreams* and *Invisible Guests: The development of imaginal dialogues*.

Mark Welman, Ph.D., completed his dissertation, "Death and gnosis: archetypal dream imagery in terminal illness," at Rhodes University, South Africa. Both Roger Brooke, his dissertation director, and Robert Romanyshyn, his external examiner, found it to be an outstanding work of scholarship and clinical sensitivity. He has many years' experience working for Hospice. He has several publications, including "The dream in terminal illness", which appeared in *The Journal of Analytical Psychology*. At present Dr Welman is a Lecturer in Psychology and a clinical supervisor at the Rhodes University Psychology Clinic.

ACKNOWLEDGEMENTS

I would like to thank Dr Fred Evans, Department of Philosophy at Duquesne University, for reading and commenting on my Introduction. Responsibility for remaining problems remains mine. Thanks also to Ms Amy Goodson for her assistance with editorial word processing.

All references to Jung's Collected Works are recorded as CW with the volume number. For historical interest, all Jung's references are recorded in the text with the first date of publication. If revised and republished both dates are given, separated with a slash (e.g. Jung 1926/46). These references are taken from *The Collected Works of C.G. Jung*, trans. R.F.C. Hull, edited by Sir Herbert Read, M. Fordham, and G. Adler, executive editor W. McGuire, Bollingen Series XX, 20 volumes, London: Routledge; Princeton: Princeton University Press, 1953–1979.

Acknowledgement is due to the following for permission to reproduce their work:

Art Resource, New York, for the pictures of Florence which appear in Chapter 1, "Jung's recollection of the life-world."

Perseus Books, for the woodcut illustration, "*Ein schoen Neutzlich Buechlein und Unterweisung der Kunst des Messens,* " by Johann II of Bavaria and Hieronymous Rodler, which also appears in "Jung's recollection of the life-world."

Doubleday Publishing, for permission to reproduce an illustration from Marshall McLuhan (1967) *The Medium is the Massage*, New York: Bantam Books. It appears here in Chapter 5 by Ron Schenk, "The spirit in the tube."

Random House, Inc., for permission to quote some lines form *Selected Poetry of Rainer Maria Rilke* (Vintage Books, 1989) in Chapter 11 by Goodchild: "Eros and Chaos: mysteries and shadows of love."

David Levin for permission to reproduce "Eros and Psyche: a reading of Merleau-Ponty," which originally appeared in *The Review of Existential Psychology and Psychiatry*, 18, 1–3, 1982–1983. It appears here, with minor alterations, under the title "Eros and Psyche: a reading of Neuman and Merleau-Ponty."

ACKNOWLEDGEMENTS

Renos Papadopoulos, editor of *Harvest*, for permission to reproduce my essay, "Jung's recollection of the life-world." It originally appeared in *Harvest*, 41, 1: 26–37, and has been slightly modified for this volume.

INTRODUCTION

Analytical psychology and phenomenology have had an uneasy relationship. Jung liked to describe himself as an "empiricist" concerned with "facts," but clearly what he meant by this was not how these terms are usually understood in psychology, defined as it is (or was) as an extension of natural science into the human realm. To use Dilthey's classic terms, Jung understood "facts" not in terms of the *Natuurswissenschaften* but in terms appropriate to the *Geisteswissenschaften*, the human sciences.[1] In other words, Jung's appeals to the scientific status of his ideas rested on the legitimacy of meanings as the fundamental evidence of human experience. From this perspective, there is less tension between Jung's claim to being a scientist concerned with "facts" and his insistence that he was a phenomenologist. His appeal to phenomenology was central to his criticism of Freudian reductionism, the tendency to interpret the magnitude and range of experience as "nothing but" something else, at a lower order of explanation – religious experience, for example, as regressive, Oedipal, and defensive. In line with the phenomenological tradition, Jung was concerned to address the phenomena of psychological life "on their own terms," in ways that did not violate the integrity of experience.

That is a fair definition of phenomenological psychology: it is the systematic attempt to describe the phenomena of psychological life without violating the integrity of experience. The question then is why the pioneers of phenomenology paid so little attention to Jung and were generally so unsympathetic, even though their essential criticisms of Freud were not only articulated by Jung but in general *anticipated* by him. Before pioneers such as Ludwig Binswanger and Erwin Straus, it was Jung who cogently critiqued Freud's psychophysiological and materialist assumptions, historical determinism, and his apparent inability to acknowledge that his "findings" were not merely "objective" but were constituted by a certain historically conditioned perspective. Herbert Spiegelberg (1972), in his definitive study of the history of phenomenological psychology, devotes only a page and a half to Jung, and says that Jung's claim to being a phenomenologist owed to the movement's popularity rather than to anything substantial. Spiegelberg's neglect of Jung merely reflects the field.

It must be admitted that Jung hardly endeared himself to the phenomenologists. He thought Heidegger, upon whose thought much of existential phenomenology is based, was "mad." He described Heidegger's work as "twaddle," "unutterably trashy and banal," and suggested that Heidegger's "kindred spirits . . . are sitting in lunatic asylums, some as patients and some as psychiatrists on a philosophical rampage" (Jung 1973: 331–332). Was he referring to Binswanger and Boss (and perhaps Trub), whose writings he probably had perused? I frankly don't know why Jung felt so little affinity for their work, except that the phenomenologists met him at precisely his epistemological blind spot. Medard Boss, Heidegger's protégé psychiatrist in Zurich, attended the seminars that Jung held in the 1940s, but when Boss left, there was misunderstanding and some animosity between the two of them.The Jungian analyst, John Perry, who was in Zurich at that time, told me (1984) that Jung felt Boss was not giving him credit that was due, and that Boss felt Jung was failing to understand the problems he had with Jung's work. This recollection by Perry feels credible. It is easy to imagine the frustration Jung might have felt. To read Boss's (1957) early book on dreams, for instance, is to be struck by the contrast between his dream interpretations, which are clearly informed by a Jungian sensibility, and his theoretical rejection of terms, such as the collective unconscious, archetypes, and symbol, that Jung held dear. It must have stung Jung to hear Boss criticize him for the very reasons – especially reductionism – that Jung had earlier criticized Freud.

In recent years, however, there has been a growing number of writers in each tradition that has been creatively influenced by the other, and has also been increasingly informed. That is the inspiration for this book. All the contributors fit that description, and it seems time to bring our thoughts and styles together in a single volume. The polemics have settled down. Partly this seems to have been because both analytical psychology and phenomenology have broadened far beyond the ideas and personalities of their founders. The following generations have gone through the doors that were opened and have taken their own paths. Both fields have become movements rather than schools of praxis and thought, and both have had to respond to the changing intellectual and cultural climate in which they are situated.

It should be mentioned that the association between Hillman, who has had such a major impact on the conceptual foundations of analytical psychology, and the phenomenologists Romanyshyn and Sardello at the University of Dallas in the early 1980s was especially fortuitous for both fields. Mutual influence can be seen in the following pages. At risk of oversimplification, the phenomenologists in this book have found an increasing appreciation for the imaginal and archetypal threads within the constitution of experience; those from a Jungian background have become clearer about the epistemological contradictions in Jung's work and about the existential world-relatedness of psychological life. None of this *rapprochement* implies a collapse of the traditions, or, for instance, less of an appreciation by the phenomenologists here of other Jungian contributions to the theory and practice of analytical psychology. I, for one, am equally indebted to what Samuels (1985) has called the "developmental" school of analytical psychology, although that kind of influence is not found much in these pages (see Brooke 1996).

This does not seem to be the place for a detailed analysis of Jung's relationship with phenomenology. I have written extensively about it elsewhere (Brooke 1991, 1996). However, it might be useful to outline the central terms and themes of phenomenology so that readers at least somewhat familiar with Jung but new to phenomenology can get their bearings.

Phenomenology developed around the work of the philosopher, Edmund Husserl, in the first decades of the century (see Husserl 1913/83, 1954/70). Husserl's concerns were that science obscured the question of meaning in the constitution of knowledge, and that it imposed a perspective on the world while assuming that it did not: science was supposedly merely an "objective" account of the world in which the scientist was an "outside observer." His argument, therefore, was that, prior to the imposition of scientific assumptions and methods, one needs to return "to the things themselves:" that is, to allow the phenomenon to show itself clearly to the consciousness that plays a role in its constitution. In this way, the phenomenon can be "intuited" in its essential structure, which is meaning. Such an act of intuition – which is the primordial, pretheoretical mode in which phenomena appear to us, whether in perception, imagination, memory, etc. – undercuts the subject–object dichotomy in our understanding of the world and of science, and provides access to an immutable, essential foundation for knowledge.

Husserl also tried to set out a systematic method for arriving at and articulating this intuitive ground of phenomena under study. Called the "reduction," it included: (1) the *epoche*, which meant "bracketing" all epistemological and theoretical assumptions concerning the status of the phenomenon, so that it could show itself immediately and clearly to an intuiting consciousness; (2) the *eidetic* reduction, which was the process of imagining, recalling, or perceiving variations of the phenomenon, so that its immutable essence could be grasped; (3) the *transcendental* reduction, in which the foundation and constitution of meaning in the "transcendental ego" were reached.

Thus phenomenology is primarily a method, but it must immediately be said that most phenomenologists, even among Husserl's closest colleagues and pioneers, did not follow the method that Husserl described. For many, the three prongs of Husserl's method have all undergone change, or, as in the case of the transcendental reduction, have been utterly rejected. The transcendental reduction has been seen by most phenomenologists (perhaps unfairly?) as an unfortunate and ultimately futile return to the idealism of Kant and Descartes, in which self and world have once again been severed.

The *epoche* is generally regarded as an impossible ideal. Heidegger's (1927/62) *Being and Time* put an end, at least outside of such limited disciplines as ontology, mathematics, and geometry, to the notion of ahistorical "essences" present to a "consciousness" that is independent of its immersion in an historical context. It is a premise of existential phenomenology that everything seen and understood is also and always a way of seeing and understanding. The toddler's mother, pediatrician, and Jungian child analyst are each situated in a context that both opens and limits horizons of possible meaning in relation to him. For Heidegger, and we should include Merleau-Ponty (1942/63, 1945/62), what we call "consciousness" is always and irreducibly rooted in the body's engagements with the world, and is thus itself a process of "interpretation" – not "interpretation" as a process of conceptual abstraction or making theoretical sense of something, but as the primordial mode of engagement which allows something to be the thing it is. Therefore, a phenomenological description presupposes an engagement with the phenomenon that is already in some way an "interpretation." Thus, those phenomenologists who came to be known as the "existential" or, later, the "hermeneutic" phenomenologists arrived at a considerably more sophisticated usage of the *epoche* (although that term has generally been dropped as Husserl's understanding of it has been abandoned). Instead of being defeated by the impossible ideal of presuppositionless knowledge, it becomes clearer that the impossibility of a complete reduction is also the possibility for the *creative* use of interpretation, even if such interpretation is rooted in (Jungian, perhaps) theory. Thus interpretation does not necessarily oppose the task of describing a phenomenon; it can also allow that phenomenon to come into being. For instance, if it is true that the concept of transference can be used in a way that obscures a psychotherapist's understanding of a phenomenon that is taking place in the consulting room, it is also the case that this concept can help bring into clarity and understanding the phenomenological "essence," or "structure," of a range of experiences that otherwise remain obscure and confusing. The *interpretation* of such confusing experiences as "transference" names and thereby calls this phenomenon into being so that it can now be coherently *described*. Thinkers such as Ricoeur (1970, 1974) and Gadamer (1975) have been particularly helpful in clarifying the hermeneutic processes involved here, and have freed some phenomenological psychologists to be less inhibited in their appropriation of theory in accessing the concealed phenomena of psychological life. It is, of course, this increased openness to theory and interpretation that makes a creative contact with Jungian psychology possible.

The *eidetic* reduction, as the search for the immutable *eidos* of a phenomenon, has lost its appeal, especially in psychology, concerned as it is with "essences" that are not universal and eternal but contextual and historical (Giorgi 1979). Once again, the term "*eidetic* reduction" is rarely used, and even the term "essence" seems rather anachronistic in this post-existentialist and post-modern time. Hence the term "structure" rather than "essence" is preferable. What is this meaning structure? In the life-world of ordinary experience the structure of a phenomenon is a network of meaningful relations. That young woman's ring, for example, brings into presence – "*is*," or "gathers," as Heidegger or Boss might say – her commitment and promise of marriage, the story of her love, her parents' hopes and joy, the blessings of God and church, and also the history of her culture's rituals. If we know the family well, we might also know that her ring gathers its shadows: her family's unspoken ambivalence about her future husband, her refusal to know her own doubt about the rightness of her choice, her secret fear that her future family may resemble the family she is leaving, etc. We could go on almost endlessly. It does seem that, even if the "pure" phenomenology of the *eidetic* reduction has lost its currency value, the general theme of the reduction remains. It is, in Luijpen's words, "to return [thinking] to our most original experience of our most original world" (Luijpen 1969: 115).

There are scholars who have continued Husserl's systematic work. In academic psychology Giorgi's appropriation of Husserl's thought continues to be utilized and developed as a kind of "empirical phenomenology" in dissertation research (and John Haule's chapter in this volume is a rough example of that). But the phenomenological movement now has little coherence. Perhaps, in the same way that Samuels (1985) identifies an analytical psychologist, we should say that a person's claim to being a phenomenologist has less to do with adherence to common assumptions and methods than by his or her participation in the tensions and debates that are to be found in the field (see Brooke and Tougas 1997).

Nevertheless, what seems to remain among those psychologists who call themselves phenomenologists is a commitment to the intuition of meaning as it is concretely given in experience, a disciplined attempt to allow phenomena to show themselves without being obscured by unquestioned theoretical, cultural, and metaphysical assumptions (the operative word here being "obscured"), and an appreciation of the way in which consciousness and world are mutually implicated. In addition there has emerged a greater appreciation for the constitutive power of language, as it is recognized that phenomena are not self-contained "entities" independent of language and prior to an articulation which merely names or describes them. As Jung himself noted, it makes a difference [to the phenomenon "itself"] whether one serves a mania or a god, or calls the voice of conscience the superego instead of Jehovah (Jung 1929a: 38; 1929b: 339). Finally, it is true that the notion of "the unconscious" and its derivatives ("unconscious motivation," "unconscious experience," or "unconscious fantasy," etc.) are possible themes in Husserl's work (see Fink 1936/70) and throughout the phenomenological movement. As Heidegger said, it is precisely because phenomena are for the most part concealed that there is need for phenomenology. Nevertheless, phenomenology's contact with psychoanalysis and its own increasingly subtle reflections on the phenomena of human existence have lead to a greater respect for the obstinate opacity, historical gravity, overdeterminations, and interpersonal complexities of psychological life. In this regard, phenomenology and psychoanalysis are both "aiming towards the same latency," as Merleau-Ponty (1960/82–83: 71) puts it. If Ricoeur can say that consciousness is "not a given but a problem and a task" for an ego that "posits but does not possess itself" (Ricoeur 1974: 161, 173), then, in my view, phenomenological psychology has become a depth psychology.

Jung's relationship with phenomenology, I said, has been uneasy. Some of the issues will be addressed in the pages that follow. Without arguing the case here, it can be suggested that where Jung's work is most compatible with phenomenology would seem to be: his insistence that the phenomena of experience be accepted on their own terms – spirituality, for example, should be accepted as such and should not be reduced to the vicissitudes of Oedipal sexuality; his search always for the meaning of phenomena rather than, say, their supposed antecedent causes; his insistence that the meaning of psychological phenomena (e.g. symbols in a dream) are latencies *within* the manifest phenomena themselves, so that, in other words, phenomena are not merely signs pointing to something substantively different; his respect for the *telos* of psychological life; his explicitly hermeneutic method; and his acknowledgement that all psychology, even his own, is perspectival, a "subjective confession," and that there is no privileged arbitrator who can decide between competing points of view.

Where Jung comes to grief for the phenomenologist is right at that place Ludwig Binswanger (1946/58: 193) called "*das Krebsubel aller Psychologie*," ("the cancer evil of all psychology," weakly translated as "the fatal defect of all psychology"): the Cartesian separation of the knower from the known, and psychological life from the world in which experience takes place. This issue is the theme of the first chapter. There is also the issue of Jung's theoretical essentialism, his frequent attempt to found the origins of meaning, which are historically constituted, in pre-existential, hypostasized structures: the archetypes. His repeated claim that the archetype is an hypothetical entity in the unconscious, for example, is a red flag to any phenomenological or hermeneutic bull. It is Jung's essentialism that forecloses proper enquiry into the contextual meanings of the phenomena under consideration and that is the ontological ground of his racism and sexism (for example, talking about the "nature" of "the feminine" and of women). It inhibits a more consistently existential phenomenological hermeneutic because it substitutes hypostasis for meaning, it fails to understand the historical horizons in which the phenomena occur in the way they do, and it fails to be adequately self-reflective and perspectival.

Once again, this is not the place to be thorough. Hopefully, readers will now be sufficiently prepared to enjoy the chapters that follow. Perhaps a few further clarifications regarding phenomenology are necessary because the term has been appallingly misused and misrepresented. The following points are serious misunderstandings, so if any of them still linger in the reader's mind now is the time to get rid of them. Phenomenology is not a form of introspection as opposed to empirical observation; it is not concerned with inner or subjective experience as opposed to objective reality; it is not concerned with private realities as opposed to public meaning; it is not the study of consciousness as opposed to the unconscious; it is not merely preparatory to the "real" work of psychology, which is theoretical explanation (see Giorgi 1983; van Vuuren 1991). If, good reader, you are now thoroughly confused, may I recommend that you skip this introduction and turn directly to the chapters that follow.[2]

The three parts to the book are a rough organization only. The first part, "The Jungian World," is an attempt to stress what is perhaps the essential issue in the meeting between Jungian psychology and phenomenology: that, for the phenomenologist, Jungian psychology can contribute to our understanding of human being only if its insights can be situated in an ontology that understands the world as the network of those meaningful relations that *is* psychological life. The second and third parts indicate a range of phenomena in which a *rapprochement* can occur.

This book has been my honor to put together, but it has been very much a collaborative effort, and I would like to thank the contributors for their hard work and enthusiasm. I had heard dreadful stories about editing books, so I am delighted to say that none of those stories came true!

I would also like to acknowledge those colleagues at Rhodes University, South Africa, and Duquesne University, USA, who over many years have been a part of my intellectual adventure with analytical psychology and phenomenology. If I name too many I fear I may offend someone left out, but I would like to name especially a few: Dr Leslie Todres, Dr Jacqueline Watts, Dr Mark Welman, Dr Kevin Kelly, Professor Robert Romanyshyn, Dr Stanton Marlan, Professor Bep Mook, Professor Andrew Samuels, and my mentor Professor Dreyer Kruger, who despite being an ocean away in Cape Town continues to be an inspiring presence in my life.

Notes

1 This is despite the fact that, on at least one occasion, Jung seems to try to straddle Dilthey's distinction. In "Analytical psychology and education," Jung wrote: "In respect of its natural subject-matter and its method of procedure, modern empirical psychology belongs to the natural sciences, but in respect of its method of explanation it belongs to the humane [sic] sciences" (Jung 1926/46: 90). In my view, this is incoherent. Human experience and behavior, constituted as they are through meanings, are not "natural," at least not in the way Dilthey meant. Secondly, its "method of procedure" cannot be epistemologically divorced from its "method of explanation," as the language of one's explanations is determined by the assumptions and language of one's methods. This is not to deny that a dialectical synthesis between

natural and human science, between explanation and understanding, might be possible; that is the achievement of Ricoeur's interpretation of Freud. However, that is beyond the argument being made here.

2 There are many good introductions to phenomenology – but which it should certainly not be necessary to read before enjoying the essays here, for they have been written to stand on their own: Boss (1979), Brockelman (1980), Kruger (1988), Luijpen (1969), Strasser (1963), Valle and Halling (1989), van den Berg (1972).

References

Binswanger, L. (1946/58) "The existential analysis school of thought," in R. May, E. Angel, H. Ellenberger (eds), *Existence*, New York: Basic Books.

Boss, M. (1957) *The Analysis of Dreams*, trans. A. Pomerans, New York and London: Rider and Co.

—— (1979) *Existential Foundations of Medicine and Psychology*, trans. P. Stern, Northvale: Jason Aronson.

Brockelman, P. (1980) *Existential Phenomenology and the World of Ordinary Experience*, London, and Lanham, MD: University Press of America.

Brooke, R. (1991) *Jung and Phenomenology*, London: Routledge.

—— (1996) "Analytical psychology and existential phenomenology: an integration and a clinical study," *The Psychoanalytic Review*, 83, 4, 525–545.

Brooke, R. and Tougas, C. (1997) "Phenomenologists reading Jung," *The San Francisco Jung Institute Library Journal*, 16, 1, 67–74.

Fink, E. (1936/70) "Fink's appendix on the problem of the 'unconscious,'" in E. Husserl, *The Crisis of European Sciences*, *op. cit.*

Gadamer, H.-G. (1975) *Truth and Method*, trans. G. Barden and W. Doerpel, New York: Seabury Press.

Giorgi, A. (1979) "The relationships among level, type, and structure and their importance for social science theorizing: a dialogue with Schutz," in A. Giorgi, R. Knowles, D. Smith (eds), *Duquesne Studies in Phenomenological Psychology, Volume 111*, Pittsburgh: Duquesne University Press.

—— (1983) "Concerning the possibility of phenomenological psychological research," *Journal of Phenomenological Psychology*, 14, 2, 127–169.

Heidegger, M. (1927/62) *Being and Time*, trans. J. Macquarrie and E. Robinson, Oxford: Basil Blackwell.

Husserl, E. (1913/83) *Ideas Pertaining to a Pure Phenomenology and to a Phenomenological Philosophy, First Book: General Introduction to Pure Phenomenology*, trans. F. Kersten, The Hague: Martinus Nijhoff Publishers.

—— (1954/70) *The Crisis of European Sciences and Transcendental Phenomenology*, trans. D. Carr, Evanston: Northwestern University Press.

Jung, C.G. (1926/46) "Analytical psychology and education," *CW* 17.

—— (1929a) "On psychic energy," *CW* 8.

—— (1929b) "Child development and education," *CW* 17.

—— (1973) *Letters, Vol. 1*, trans. R.F.C. Hull, edited by G. Adler and A. Jaffe, London: Routledge & Kegan Paul.

Kruger, D. (1988) *An Introduction to Phenomenological Psychology*, Cape Town: Juta and Co.

Luijpen, W. (1969) *Existential Phenomenology*, Pittsburgh: Duquesne University Press.

Merleau-Ponty, M. (1942/63) *The Structure of Behavior*, trans. A. Fisher, Boston: Beacon Press.
—— (1945/62) *The Phenomenology of Perception*, trans. C. Smith, London: Routledge.
—— (1960/82–82) "Preface to Hesnard's *Loeuvre de Freud*," trans. A. Fisher, *Review of Existential Psychology and Psychiatry*, 18, 1–3, 67–72.
Ricoeur, P. (1970) *Freud and Philosophy*, trans. D. Savage, New Haven: Yale University Press.
—— (1974) *The Conflict of Interpretations*, Evanston: Northwestern University Press.
Samuels, A. (1985) *Jung and the Post-Jungians*, London: Routledge.
Spiegelberg, H. (1972) *Phenomenology in Psychiatry and Psychology*, Evanston: Northwestern University Press.
Strasser, S. (1963) *Phenomenology and the Human Sciences*, Pittsburgh: Duquesne University Press.
Valle, R. and Halling, S. (1989) *Existential-Phenomenological Perspectives on Psychology*, New York and London: Plenum Press.
van den Berg, J.H. (1972) *A Different Existence*, Pittsburgh: Duquesne University Press.
van Vuuren, R. (1991) "Phenomenologophobia? the aversive reaction to phenomenological psychology," in R. van Vuuren (ed.) *Dialogue beyond Polemics*, Pretoria: Human Sciences Research Council.

Part 1

THE JUNGIAN WORLD

1

JUNG'S RECOLLECTION OF THE LIFE-WORLD

Roger Brooke

In his autobiography Jung wrote:

> The earthly manifestations of "God's world" began with the realm of plants, as a kind of direct communication from it. . . . Man and the proper animals, on the other hand, were bits of God that had become independent. That was why they could move about on their own and choose their own abodes. Plants were bound for good and ill to their places. They expressed not only the beauty but the thoughts of God's world, with no intent of their own and without deviation. Trees in particular were mysterious and seemed to me direct embodiments of the incomprehensible meaning of life. For that reason the woods were the place I felt closest to the deepest meaning and to its awe-inspiring workings.
>
> This impression was reinforced when I became acquainted with Gothic cathedrals. . . . What I dimly felt to be my kinship with stone was the divine nature in both, in the dead and the living matter.
>
> (Jung 1962: 67–68)

Jung is describing here the world of his early school years, in which he bore witness to the consecrated nature of Being. Things were alive with meaning; they were occasions for the presencing of the Holy in all its mystery, promise, and multiplicity. But in the following pages Jung goes on to say that this experience had no adequate cultural articulation, and that by his middle teens it had become "a remote and unreal dream" (p.68). I want this phrase to echo through the following pages, as we trace the path by which experience is doubted into subjectivity and illusion, and the real evaporates into dream. Jung understood clearly that, for him, as for us, this path is an educational process that in certain fundamental ways recapitulates the historical drama of western consciousness, particularly as it unfolded in the renaissance. It repeats a process according to which the ensouled presence of the medieval world receded behind the veil of Judaeo-Christian iconoclasm and Galilean science. The world, thus God-forsaken, became merely a set of mathematical co-ordinates upon a geometric grid. Instead of trusting the *presentational* quiddity of our experience we are heirs to a *representational* reality, a world as illusory as a dream.

The division of the world into objective and subjective categories (scientific and personal, rational and irrational) is also a self-division. For Jung, this self-division was between his so-called No.1 and No.2 personalities. His No.1 personality was rational, scientific, and public; his No.2 personality was intuitive, spiritual, and private – and he also felt it to be more intimately real. The Renaissance division of the world was thus keenly felt by Jung as a fracture within himself, and when he was nearly forty years old he broke down.

Jung's well-documented journey into his Self was an heroic descent into the Christian underworld and the world of the dream. Because Jung's personal journey was of profound historical significance Jung was a cultural hero. He recollected what our culture had forgotten: a perceptual understanding that the world is a temple and the earth is consecrated ground. In order to amplify this theme there are several aims in this chapter. The first is to recall how Jung's personal experience fell across the cultural and epistemological divide that separated the Renaissance and the Enlightenment from the medieval world; second is to show how Jung's theoretical work has tended to remain trapped in the conceptual parameters laid down by Galileo and Descartes; third is to move through Jung's epistemological difficulties to a recollection of his sense of the meaningfulness of the world or, more precisely, of the world that Husserl (1954/70) called the *Lebenswelt*, or life-world. This is a work of phenomenology. It is an attempt to return our thinking about experience to its own vital ground, so that the integrity of that experience is not violated in our psychology. Further than that, the method here is to bring into critical focus the metaphysical assumptions within which Jung theorised, so that we can be better able to bracket[1] those assumptions and return Jungian thinking to its ground.When Jung called his approach phenomenological he did so primarily as part of his critique of Freud. But just as the phenomenologist Jung saw through the rationalism and materialism of his mentor, and was critical of the violence on experience caused by Freudian metaphysics, so we need to follow through this movement of self-reflection and free Jung's thought from those inhibiting assumptions that tend to remain largely unquestioned, as though they simply reflect matters of fact. Therefore, we need to begin by sketching the highlights of the historical drama in which Jung's significance is situated.

The evaporation of world into dream

To begin with we can recall that in the first chapter of Genesis only the human being was made in the image of God and that, more generally, the central Jewish project was the withdrawal of the image of God from His participation in things. This project continued into early Christianity. In a particularly telling passage the fourth-century Christian writer, Lactantius, wrote that obviously the things of the world – trees, plants, mountains and rivers – had no divinity, and he continued:

> Therefore, the world is neither God nor living . . ., and the world which has been made is wholly distinct from Him who made it. . . . If, therefore, it has been constructed as an abode, it is neither itself God, nor are the elements which are its parts. . . . For a house, made for the purpose of being inhabited, has no sensibility by itself and is subject to the master who built or inhabits it.
>
> (Quoted in Roszak 1972: 123)

Lactantius goes on to say that the human being is fundamentally separate from the world and is not a part of nature. Thrown into relief here are the religious roots of functionalism, as things have become "mere" things, emptied of meaning, except for serving human purposes.

The historian, Theodore Roszak (ibid.), has traced this history of western iconoclasm, peaking in the Reformation, and he has noted a fateful irony. The history of the war on idolatry, the worship of dead things, occurred because the Judaeo-Christians alone saw the things of the world as dead and inanimate. As Roszak points out, no pagan ever worshipped "*mere* things"; things were windows opening upon the sacred. The "idolators" did not worship plants any more than the Christian worships a cross-shaped couple of planks. In other words, the war on idolatry was founded upon a perceptual understanding of the world as already God-forsaken. It was *our* religious tradition, not the pagan's, that was approaching the theology of the dead God. What was lost in the Judaeo-Christian tradition, and especially in the Jung family's Protestantism, was the experience of the sacred *within* the profane, a sacramental perception of the world, which the child Jung experienced but by his mid-teens could only dream.

Robert Romanyshyn (1984, 1989) and Samuel Edgerton (1975) have discussed in detail the shift in consciousness that occurred with the development of linear perspective in fifteenth-century Florence. Of the many issues and illustrations discussed by Romanyshyn, I shall present two. The first is the juxtaposition of two pictures of Florence (Figures 1.1 and 1.2), pictures which occur on either side of the renaissance. Figure 1.1, a woodcut from about 1359, is multi-perspectival. On the left-hand side of the picture we see

Figure 1.1 View of Florence, detail from the fresco, "Madonna della Misericordia." Fourteenth century. Orphanage of the Bigallo, Florence.

Source: Alinari/Art Resource, New York.

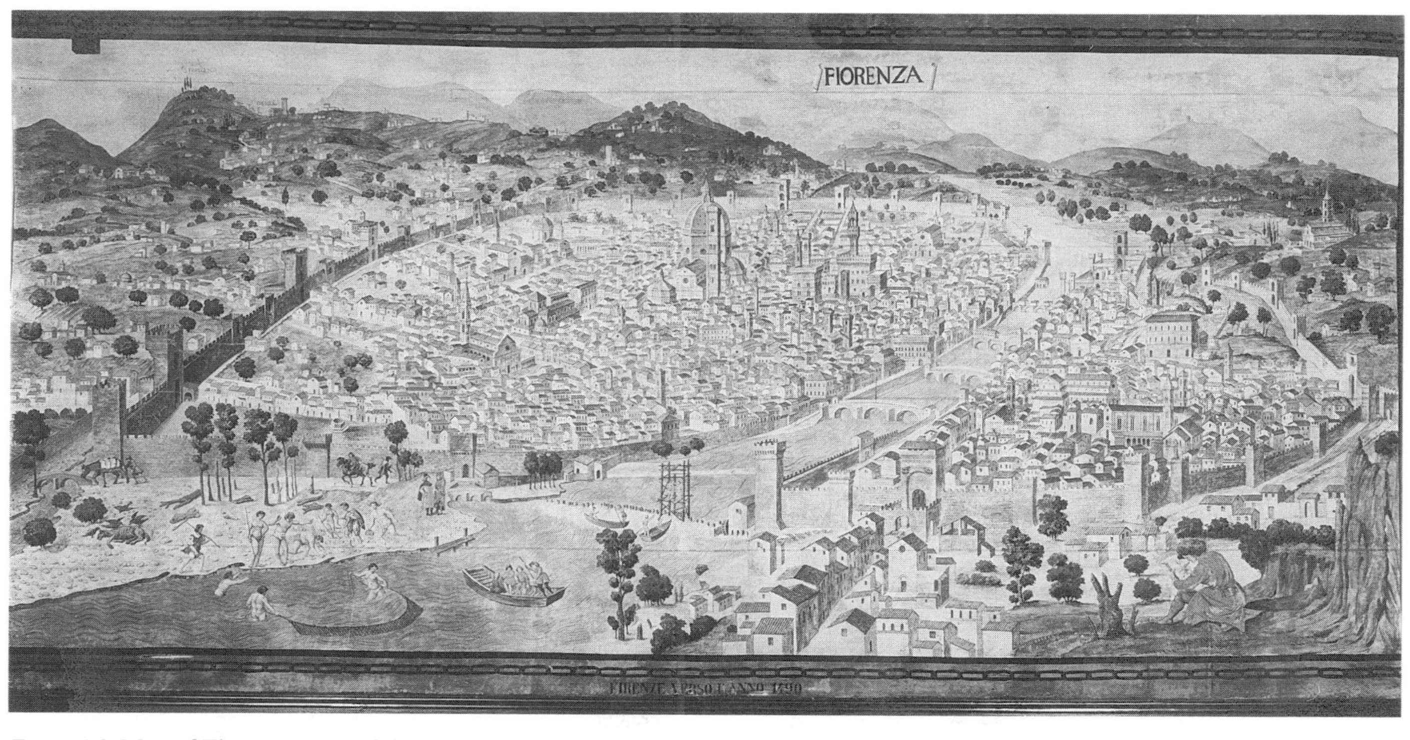

Figure 1.2 Map of Florence, copy of the Carta della Catena, 1490. Museo de Firenze com'era, Florence.
Source: Scala/Art Resource, New York.

the city from the left; similarly we can look at the city from the right. Our bodies move around the picture with our eyes. Because the eye does not dominate our embodiment, we are presented with a Florence that appeals to the senses of touch, hearing, and even smell. We have a sense of Florence's presence and of our bustling movement within its walls. We can also note that value rather than geometric location selects the buildings which are depicted. In Figure 1.2, a "map" drawn in 1480, Florence is presented according to the demands of linear perspective. The eye alone rather than value defines the city's co-ordinates and determines the placement and measure of things.

The difference between these two presentations of Florence thus reflects more than the development of an artistic technique, as if the movements in art could ever occur in a cultural vacuum. These presentations occur on either side of a transformation in western consciousness, in which, says Romanyshyn, the world became a spectacle for the disincarnate, despotic eye of the spectator. This becomes clearer in Figure 1.3. The visible world is presented in two dimensions upon a screen, and the artist's task is to record the visible in terms of its graphic co-ordinates. Instead of a world *through* which we look, we are offered a world *at* which to look. There is now a distinct boundary between the world as the object of sight and the self as the passive recorder of what is "objectively" seen "outside."

What was originally a prescription for drawing in linear perspective became a cultural epistemology defining for us the taken-for-granted nature of the "real" and of the self as the corresponding observer. The world as a geometric grid for the artist's eye became a geometric grid for scientific, and then cultural, understanding.

At the beginning of the sixteenth century Copernicus imagined standing on the sun looking at the earth rotating on its own axis while revolving around the sun. Nearly a hundred years later Galileo referred to Copernicus's imaginative experiment saying, "I cannot find any bounds for my admiration, how that reason was able . . . to commit such a rape upon the senses" (quoted in Romanyshyn 1982: 20). In this famous sentence Galileo celebrated the triumph of thought over appearance, or more precisely, of mathematical truth over sensuous knowledge. He then proceeded to articulate the significance of this perspective and to set out the epistemological foundations of modern science. I have summarized these (see Edwards 1967: 262–266) as follows:

1 empirical observation forms the primary criterion for truth;
2 only scientific method and discourse are appropriate to the world of things;
3 only the mathematical, physical properties of things are "primary," i.e., present in the things; all other qualities, meanings, and values are "secondary," or "subjective;"
4 sensuous experience is illusory.

Figure 1.3 Johann II of Bavaria and Hieronymous Rodler, woodcut illustration from their *Ein schoen nuetzlich Buechlein und Unterweisung der Kunst des Messens*, Simmern, Germany, 1531.

Source: S. Edgerton (1975) *The Renaissance Rediscovery of Linear Perspective*, New York: Basic Books.

Therefore, as Husserl (op. cit.) recognized and Romanyshyn put it, Galileo introduced a world in which the "real world" is not the world we experience, and the primary world of experience, the world of Jung's childhood, is "merely subjective" and illusory. The world of ordinary experience has little more epistemological status than the dream. The irony, systematically demonstrated by Husserl and many other phenomenologists, is that ultimately even the natural scientific world and enterprise are dependent on the life-world of ordinary experience, but this is forgotten and systematically violated in the assumptions of natural science.[2]

Galileo's scientific enterprise assumed that human experience was more than fallible, it was fundamentally illusory. Although Descartes never discussed Galileo, it was this radical erring in human experience that he was compelled to address (Straus 1937/66). In the first of his *Meditations* (Descartes 1641/1931: 144–149), radical doubt in the reliability of experience was the premise Descartes conceded. His genius is in part that he elevated this premise into a methodological principle: instead of trying to get around the issue of doubt, he embraced it as a rigorous epistemological procedure. It was this systematic doubt that lead him finally to accept that the only thing he could not doubt was that he was doubting, i.e. thinking. In other words, Descartes' only certainty was that of his own mind; hence his famous phrase, "*cogito ergo sum*" ("I think, therefore I am"). As is common knowledge, his solution to the ontological crisis left in Galileo's wake was to situate all experience, even the body's senses, in terms of an organization of interior, mental events. Thus, from a Cartesian perspective, one can no longer be certain that one perceives an actual "something" but only that one has a mental idea of something perceived (ibid.: 149–157). For Descartes, only mathematics and physics have, by the grace of God (literally), access to the "real" world.

Jung as Heir to Galileo and Descartes

Jung seemed unaware of the historical significance of Descartes, who delineated the ontological categories of the modern world (inner–outer, subject–object, mind–body, etc.). In fact, Jung never discusses Descartes at all. Perhaps because of this he is often submerged in Cartesian philosophy – and, with it, Galilean science. Said in another way, Jung's thought tends to remain largely undifferentiated from the collective consciousness that is Cartesian metaphysics. This is the heart of Jung's failure to conduct an adequate phenomenological *epoche*. Instead of seeing through the Cartesian categories as contingent and historical, Jung tends to accept them as ontologically immutable descriptions of the way things are. Thus although Jung repeatedly laments the conceptual limitations of categories such as mind and body, he seldom manages to undercut the thinking that insists upon such terms. For instance, the following passage seems to be central to Jung's conceptual thinking – and note Jung's scare quotes around the words "experience" and "real". Jung writes:

> It is my mind, with its store of images, that gives the world colour and sound; and . . . "experience" is, in its most simple form, an exceedingly complicated structure of mental images. Thus there is in a certain sense nothing that is directly experienced except the mind

> itself. So thick and deceptive is this fog about us that we had to invent the exact sciences in order to catch at least a glimmer of the so-called "real" nature of things.
>
> (Jung 1926: 327)

In these lines, not only is psychological life encapsulated within the head, but the world, drained of human habitation, is reduced to the *res extensa* of Descartes, that is, the realm of mathematical and physical co-ordinates. The world which had once made aesthetic and meaningful sense to Jung could no longer be thought[3] on its own terms, and with no epistemologically coherent ground that world became the "remote and unreal dream."

Jung's fate has also been our own, and in fact he saw this clearly. In India he recognized that people were living in a world which had been lost to Europeans for three hundred years. Jung writes about his experience in India with an unresolved ambivalence between psychological envy and European, colonial contempt that runs through many of his cultural reflections. But even his European contempt cannot obscure his insight that:

> It is quite possible that India is the real world, and that the white man lives in a madhouse of abstractions. . . . Life in India has not yet withdrawn into the capsule of the head. . . . No wonder the European feels dream like: the complete life of India is something of which he merely dreams.
>
> (Jung 1939: 518)

It seems clear that Jung never managed to think through his Galilean–Cartesian epistemology. On the other hand, he did see it as psychologically alienating and dangerous, the heart of the modern malaise, and he saw the significance of analytical psychology as contributing to the recollection of our original and forgotten world.

Jung's recollection of the world

There is a sense in which Jung's awareness of the historical significance of his work can be traced to reflections which predate even his becoming a psychiatrist, when he was still a medical student in Basel in the 1890s (Jung 1993). But this awareness was more profoundly consolidated when, in 1926, he traveled to east Africa. As he later recalled: "My liberated psychic forces poured blissfully back to the primeval expanses," and, as that happened, he said, "We found a dawning significance in things" (Jung 1931a: 62).

It is important to realize that the calling for a deepened and awakened consciousness, which Jung called individuation, comes from the world itself. Individuation is not a mental process; it does not transpire within the solitary confinement of the Cartesian head. Nor does it have egoic, or personal, aims.

Individuation is a response to the appeal from the things of the world to be brought into the affirmative light of human consciousness (Brooke 1991: 52–62). "All nature seeks this goal," says Jung. "Every advance, even the smallest, along the path of conscious realization adds that much to the world" (Jung 1938/54: 96). In other words, that human light called consciousness is the capacity to awaken the world into its own being.

It was especially at the moment of dawn, just as the sun lifted over the horizon, that Jung felt "overwhelmed" with a sense of the sacred, and he recalled, "I drank in this glory with insatiable delight, or rather, in a timeless ecstasy" (Jung 1962: 268). Jung goes on to say that at the moment of dawn the baboons too would sit motionless, facing east, like carved baboons in an Egyptian temple, performing the "gesture of adoration." He suggests that the world's revelation as a temple in which the drama of the Egyptian sky-god, Horus, is daily enacted is older than human consciousness. Consciousness has evolved as witness to the endlessly repetitive, sacred drama given at dawn, which is the primordial occasion for the coming of light in the darkness. At night the baboons huddle along the cliffs, hiding in fear of their greatest enemy, the leopard. They do not have the Promethean gift of fire, which could open a field of light and relative safety. The baboons are almost, but not quite yet, human. In their experience of the night's darkness as a fearful and alien realm, and in their pleasure at the sun's reassuring return, the baboons share with us a common reality. We can imagine, as Jung does, that over millions of years we humans have emerged out of this common ground. We have the *logos* of culture and language, which means that this primordial experience can be held in ritual and symbol, and its significance can echo through the transformative occasions of human life. But it is this common sense of the sacred that is the foundation of consciousness and makes it possible. The world as a temple, the earth as consecrated, maternal ground, and the dawn as the triumph of the spirit are primordial realities. It is to this world that we as conscious beings are most fundamentally indebted and called to bear witness. Jung's recovery of the life-world is thus the remembrance of our consecrated ground, borne in the traditions, rituals, and language of culture.

Finally, a note on the language of analytical psychology. Jung's language – shadow, *anima*, soul, spirit, *puer*, the great mother, trickster, and hero – and his use of alchemical and mythic imagery are explicitly (Jung 1931b) an attempt to speak a psychological language not yet torn from its prerenaissance experiential roots. Analytical psychology, says Jung, "will certainly not be a modern psychology" (ibid.: 344). Most of its language is not a theoretical language, or at least not primarily so, and Jung continually reminds us that even our theoretical formulations are ultimately metaphors whose roots recede into the unknown. Nor is Jung's language a pretentious attempt to dress up his insights in colorful academic regalia. Rather, the language of analytical psychology is one with cultural-therapeutic intent. If language is, as Heidegger says, "the house of Being," that is, the *templum* in which the beings of the world can dwell (Heidegger 1971: 132), then Jung's language provides a contemporary home for the root metaphors of the human soul. The fact that this language can also be used to trivialize and foreclose experience by giving it silly labels ("That was his *puer* that felt suicidal") is true enough, but is a different issue. For Jung personally the language of analytical psychology reconnected him, in his mature years (*circa.* 1928 onwards), to the child Jung, whose world had not yet fallen into dream.

Notes

1 See the editor's introduction for a discussion of this term. "Bracketing" in this context does not mean bypassing all assumptions, as though we can achieve an ideal clarity (meaning "clear and distinct ideas"). Instead, it means critically interrogating some of Jung's assumptions with the aim of seeing through them as horizons of meaning within which Jung thought. Because we are heirs to the same tradition, it means seeing through those same horizons which have constituted, or formed, our world and the structures through which we understand it.

2 The paradigmatic earth tremors in physics are interesting and have generated a considerable amount of excitement in the Jungian literature. If, however, the excitement is that we can now look to ("the New") physics to "validate scientifically" Jungian intuitions, then it seems to me thoroughly misplaced. The systemic epistemology that is emerging through physics still has no access to the human questions of meaning and value, which are the defining determinants of the life-world (see Fuller: 1990). Furthermore, trying to integrate conceptually this physics into a psychology of our relatedness is a terribly complicated way of accounting for a relationality that is obvious and available phenomenologically for immediate, concrete description.

3 It is tempting, given our habit of thought, to write "think about" in this context instead of "think." The unusual form, "to think the world," rather than "to think about the world," is a recognition of the primordially *presentational* (rather than *representational*) nature of thinking. Thinking reveals the world in the manner of thought, but it is still the world that is brought into being. We do not think "*about*" the world any more than we see "about" it (see Heidegger 1971).

References

Brooke, R. (1991) *Jung and Phenomenology.* London and New York: Routledge.

Descartes, R. (1641/1931) "Meditations on first philosophy," in *The Philosophical Works of Descartes*, vol. I, trans. E. Haldane and G. Ross, Cambridge: Cambridge University Press.

Edgerton, S. (1975) *The Renaissance Rediscovery of Linear Perspective,* New York: Basic Books.

Edwards, P. (ed.) (1967) *The Encyclopedia of Philosophy*, vol. 3, New York: The Macmillan Company and the Free Press.

Fuller, A. (1990) *Insight into Value*, Albany, New York: State University of New York Press.

Heidegger, M. (1971) *Poetry, Language, Thought*, trans. A. Hofstadter, New York: Harper and Row.

Husserl, E. (1954/70) *The Crisis of the European Sciences and Transcendental Phenomenology*, trans. D. Carr, Evanston: Northwestern University Press.

Jung, C. (1926) "Spirit and Life," *CW* 8.

—— (1931a) "Archaic man," *CW* 10.

—— (1931b) "Basic postulates of analytical psychology," *CW* 8.

—— (1938/54) "Psychological aspects of the mother archetype," *CW* 9, i.

—— (1939) "The dreamlike world of India," *CW* 10.

—— (1962) *Memories, Dreams, Reflections,* recorded and edited by Aniela Jaffe, trans. R. and C. Wilson, New York: Pantheon Books.

—— (1993) *The Zofingia Lectures*, trans. Jan Van Heurck, Princeton: Princeton University Press.

Romanyshyn, R. (1982) *Psychological Life: from Science to Metaphor*, Austin: University of Texas Press.

—— (1984) "The despotic eye," in D. Kruger (ed.) *The Changing Reality of Modern Man*, Cape Town: Juta and Co.

—— (1989) *Technology as Symptom and Dream,* London and New York: Routledge.

Roszak, T. (1972) *Where the Wasteland Ends,* London: Faber and Faber.

Straus, E. (1937/66) "Descartes' significance for modern psychology," in *Phenomenological Psychology,* London: Tavistock Publications.

EDITOR'S INTRODUCTION

Jung, more than any of psychology's pioneers, had a feeling for the symbolic character of psychological life. He understood that life can be meaningfully and consciously lived only if our experience has metaphorical and sacred resonance. This was his self-proclaimed myth, the "myth of meaning." But he struggled endlessly with the question of how to understand conceptually this "symbolic life". The problem remained to the extent that he accepted the Galilean/Cartesian view of the world as a mathematical and physical reality, because he then found it necessary to draw on the notion of "projection" to account for experiential meaning. In this way Jung attempted to locate the symbolic life as an internal sensibility, separate from the world. But this too was an unsatisfactory solution for Jung, especially as his alchemical sensibility called for an appreciation of meaning that was ultimately not psychological, at least if that term is in any way linked to the parameters of human mentation.

It is into these murky waters that Romanyshyn enters. Having been steeped in these same questions for over twenty years, and epistemologically informed by the works of Heidegger and Merleau-Ponty, he explores these tensions in Jung's work and finds, especially in his "meetings" with Philemon and in Jung's alchemical studies, a pathway to a more sustained appreciation of the structure of meaning. Thus Romanyshyn's meditation lies at the heart of the Jungian "myth."

2

ALCHEMY AND THE SUBTLE BODY OF METAPHOR

Soul and cosmos

Robert D. Romanyshyn

Introduction

In *Memories, Dreams, Reflections*, Jung openly confesses that his confrontation with the unconscious persuasively convinced him of the objectivity of the psyche. It is closer, however, to the true spirit of Jung's experience, to its phenomenology, to speak about the *autochthonous* character of the psyche rather than its objectivity, because the latter term still carries the baggage of a Cartesian metaphysics which splits subject and object and leads to a psychology of projection. Jung' encounter with the figure of Philemon is a good example of the autochthonous character of psyche. A "pagan [who] brought with him an Egypto–Hellenistic atmosphere with a Gnostic coloration," Philemon is not a projection of Jung's psyche; rather, he is an inhabitant of the land of soul. In ecology, autochthonous describes an indigenous plant or animal, and in its Greek origins the word contains the suffix "khthon" meaning earth. Thus, an "*autokhthon*" is "one sprung from the land itself" (Morris 1981: 89). Philemon, then, is indigenous to the psyche, one who from the earliest times belongs to the soil of the soul, part of the tribe of that country there before our time of colonization, that time of ego-consciousness when we have already taken possession of the soul. The soul is another country, as different from mind as it is from matter, and in this sense it makes perfect sense for Jung to say that Philemon "brought home to me the crucial insight that there are things in the psyche which I do not produce, which produce themselves and have their own life." Philemon taught Jung a most significant and profound lesson when he said to him that he (Jung) mistakenly "treated thoughts as if [he] generated them," and in contrast to this view Philemon said to Jung that "thoughts were like animals in the forest, or people in a room, or birds in the air." He then added, "if you should see people in a room, you would not think that you had made those people or that you were responsible for them" (Jung 1965: 183).

Jung in his best moments is a radical phenomenologist. In these moments he manages to exorcize the ghost of Descartes to attend to those subtle bodies of the imaginal realm which are between matter and mind. Those subtle bodies, like Philemon, have less substance to them than things, but more substance than thoughts. Philemon is no bloodless abstraction. But neither is he a matter of measurement or calculation. A radical phenomenology, like one can find in the later works of Maurice Merleau-Ponty, or the poetic works of Gaston Bachelard, or the metabletic works or J. H. van den Berg, is in service to Philemon and his tribe. It is devoted to those subtle bodies which are *neither* facts *nor* ideas. It is a work of the heart which is neither that of mind nor eye, a poetics of the soul's landscape where a mind feels its way into those imaginal presences who always haunt the margins of the sensible world. It is my belief that Jung practiced this radical phenomenology most daringly in his studies of alchemy. In doing so, I would argue that Jung, correctly so, enlarged his psychology and even transformed it into a cosmology. The transformation of lead into gold is the release of soul into its imaginal realm, its liberation from entrapment in the leaden literalism of scientific fact, or the suffocating dogmatism of a philosophical idea. Philemon, via Jung, disturbs the modern mind. He is the harbinger of the kind of consciousness which heralds the end of any psychology which would separate soul from cosmos. According to Paracelsus the soul is a star (Jung 1947/54: 193). Philemon is a figure who teaches us, as he did Jung, that when one has a cosmology one does not need a psychology.

The politics of projection

More than twenty years ago, Albert Kreinheder wrote an insightful essay entitled "Alchemy and the Subtle Body." Bemoaning the small and narrow mindedness of much of contemporary psychology he wrote the following:

> It's not enough to get to work on time, to firm up the waist line, to balance the checkbook, and learn how to smile like a nice person. If that's all there is, we're still the same little earthworms, getting older every day, and no wondrous new birth has taken place within us. It would be so much nicer to have a miracle.

Philemon is a small miracle. But consider for a moment Jung's encounters with Philemon from the point of view of that contemporary psychotherapy which Kreinheder describes. It is not too difficult to imagine its effort to make sense of Philemon by reducing him to a projection of Jung's psyche, and, even worse, treating him as a symptom, as an hallucination. This kind of sensibility, especially when compared to that of the alchemists of old, can make us "worm-like literalists, sensible to the verge of stupidity." "Miracles," Kreinheder says, "never happen to sensible people" (1975: 135–6).

Projection is one of those notions which rests upon our unacknowledged stupidity. More so, it is one of those notions whose use can explain away what might otherwise be a miracle.

Of the many sins it conceals, the one I want to attend to is the way in which projection is the psychological counterpart of a politics of capitalism. My point is that the historical roots of the notion of projection are inseparably entangled with those that have nourished the European nation state and its politics of economic colonialism. The Cartesian dualism of an interior, subjective knowing mind sealed off from an exterior, objective world to be known and exploited repeats itself in the European movements of expansion into the New World. The subjugation of soul and its indigenous inhabitants, like Philemon, by the ego mind is of a piece with the domination of the native peoples of the New World by European powers. It is no accident that the appearance of psychology in its modern sense as a separate discipline coincides with the rise of the modern nation state, or that the hegemony of European nation states in the colonization of the New World coincides with the creation of the modern ego.[1]

The powerful murals of Diego Rivera in the "Palacio nacional" in Mexico City are a disturbing reminder of the terrible effects of this legacy of exploitation, a legacy which continues in more subtle but no less effective form in the therapy room whose models of treatment uncritically make use of the notion of projection. Projection is a colonialism of the soul, an imperialism of the ego mind against the soul. In October, 1492, Columbus anticipated the later voyages of Descartes, who in November, 1619, embarked upon them in a series of three dreams. His dreams lead to the enslavement of those autochthonous inhabitants of soul no less than those earlier journeys enchained the indigenous peoples of the New World.

Psychology cannot remain unaware of its continuing contribution to a politics practiced without a sense of soul, anymore than it can remain unaware of the cultural historical roots and political implications of its own theories and practices. Andrew Samuels reminds us of this point in his important book, *The Political Psyche*. In this work, he brings depth psychology and politics into dialogue. He offers his work as a "contribution to the long-standing ambition of depth psychology to develop a form of political and cultural analysis that would, in Freud's words, 'understand the riddles of the world' " (1993: 3). Samuels' book persuasively applies the insights of clinical practice to politics and the exigencies of politics to clinical practice.

In addition, however, to this moment of application, there is another moment in this dialogue between the political and the psychological. Michel Foucault addresses this moment in the following remarks:

> Postmodernism assumes the task of reinvestigating the crisis and trauma at the very heart of modernity; the post-modern [is] a testament to the fact that the end of modernity is . . . a symptom as it

> were of its own unconscious infancy which needs to be retrieved and reworked if we are not to be condemned to an obsessional fixation upon, and compulsive repetition of, the sense of its ending. In this respect, the task of a post-modern imagination might be to envision the end of modernity as a possibility of rebeginning.
>
> (Foucault quoted in Romanyshyn 1993: 339)

This essay is less an application of the principles of depth psychology to the practice of politics, and more a critical, cultural–historical examination of those principles, especially the notion of projection. My intention is to show that the uncritical use of a term like projection already implies a politics of imperialism which functions at an unconscious level in the theories and practices of depth psychology.

In this move to deconstruct the origins of depth psychology for the sake of a new beginning, I am not suggesting that the idea of projection is either wrong or false. In its presence and in its effects it is demonstrably real. Moreover, we see it exercised daily in the practice of politics. Rather, I am arguing for a mindfulness about its heritage and a recognition of the consequences which follow upon its use. Jung's encounters with Philemon suggest the possibility of another way of knowing the world and being in it which has nothing to do with the notion of projection. It is a way of knowing and being which takes us beyond that dichotomy of subject and object which necessitates the very idea of projection. The telos of my argument is that Philemon carries us beyond a psychology of projection into a cosmology of synchronicities.

The gestural body

Disembodied minds project; ensouled bodies establish an interactive, gestural field. Merleau-Ponty's phenomenology of perception lays the foundation for what I would call a gestural metaphysics. The gestural body is a magnetic, gravitational, erotic field which sweeps the other into the orbit of its intentions and desires, and which, reciprocally, is swept up by the gestures of that other. Together, in mutuality and below any explicit conscious awareness, you and I create a landscape of experience. The actor on the stage whispers a line and the audience, almost imperceptibly, already leans into the softly spoken words. The whisper and inclination of the audience belong together; one is not the cause of the other. "The gesture is the outline of a world, the chiseling of what is otherwise a neutral space into a significant place" (Romanyshyn 1999a: 56). Animate flesh impregnates animate flesh. Together we establish an ambience and create a mood. The gestural body which solicits and seduces the other is the threnody of the Cartesian dream of reason. It is the undoing of that dream which would place the mind inside the body like a pilot is inside the ship. And the symptomatic body which inaugurates the therapy room of depth psychology is this gestural body in disguise. "The symptomatic body is the locus of a loss. What the patient brings into the field of therapy is a body haunted by an absent other, a body whose gestures find no witness, no reciprocal for their appeal" (Romanyshyn 1997a: 70). At a cultural–historical level this absent other was the world which had already faded into the distance of a measured objectivity for a spectator-self ensconced within a body made over in the image of a machine.

To think and to theorize in terms of projection is to practice a psychology rooted in Cartesian metaphysics which discounts the gestures of the animate flesh. This abandonment of the flesh establishes the codes by which the modern mind and its shipwrecks – those figures of soul haunting the symptomatic body – are described: a spectator-self, imprisoned in a body made into a specimen, observing in distance and neutrality a world turned into a spectacle for its exploitation and use (Romanyshyn 1989).

Projection rests upon a philosophy of space which separates the inside from the outside, a dualism of interiority and exteriority which identifies the interior with mind or consciousness and the exterior with the world, a world without qualities, a world drained of its erotic complexities, a world of matter that has been de-animated. It is a way of thinking and being which produces the following kind of declaration:

> It is my mind, with its store of images, which gives the world color and sound; . . . and "experiences" is, in its more simple form, an exceedingly complex structure of mental images. Thus there is in a certain sense nothing which is directly experienced except the mind itself. So thick and deceptive is this fog about us that we had to invent the exact sciences in order to catch at least a glimmer of this so called "real" nature of things.
>
> (Brooke, 1995; see chapter 1 of this volume: 20–21)

The passage is not from Descartes. On the contrary, it is from Jung (1926: 327) and it clearly illustrates that his psychology is haunted by a dualism of inside and outside, leaving soul without world and the world without soul. It is no surprise, therefore, to read in Jung that "projection is an . . . automatic process whereby a content that is unconscious to the subject transfers itself to an object, so that it seems to belong to the object" (Jung 1954: 60). Beauty is in the eye of the beholder and Philemon shudders with rage.[2]

A psychology of projection is at odds with a psychology which acknowledges the autochthonous characters of soul. And yet this tension is not about an either/or. Projection as a psychological experience does exist. But as von Franz reminds us, "what may or may not be described as projection today is still largely a question of judgment . . . so that in my opinion psychologists should use the greatest caution and discretion in dealing with this concept" (1980b: 94).

Greeting Philemon

Who is Philemon? And *what* is he? What kind of being is he and to what landscape does he belong? Autochthonous, he dwells in the land of soul, but now it is a question of *how* he dwells there. How Philemon is tells us who and what he is.

Jung reports that he talks to Philemon as if he were another person. And he does so while walking in his garden. Jung speaks with Philemon while they walk together. Their relationship is peripatetic. Jung and Philemon have a walk-about.

This small detail is not trivial because it tells us that for Jung there is a differentiation between himself and Philemon but not a separation. Philemon is different from Jung, a someone else, an-other, and yet in their walk-about they are related. Philemon addresses Jung and Jung replies. Jung speaks to Philemon and Philemon listens. In this other-ness, Philemon has his own reality. We can, however, easily imagine that for Jung Philemon's presence is not like that of the flowers in the garden, or the stones on the path, or the birds in the tree. Philemon is present in a different way. His presence is more subtle.

What shall we call this subtle presence of Philemon who is neither a factual object in the world (like those stones or those birds can be), nor a subjective idea in Jung's mind which he projects onto the world? What is the nature of this subtle body of Philemon who is neither a thing nor a thought? Philemon haunts the garden of Jung. He plays on the border of the real and the ideal, hovering like some great being of light, a vibration which at one moment seems substantive like a particle and at another moment without substance like a wave. Philemon is an imaginal being, one of those invisible guests in the felicitous phrase of Mary Watkins (1986). Philemon, I would claim, is the subtle body of metaphor.

Metaphor is a *third* between the two of things and thoughts. It is the halo which surrounds even perceptual things, like stones on a path, when in a moment of reverie they display their elusive charm and reveal their presence as mineral beings who know the patience of endurance and the peace of waiting. In such moments, one can long to be the stone because its imaginal presence is so strong, because its metaphorical character has been welcomed, because one has allowed oneself to be drawn out of the separation and isolation of one's subjectivity to be penetrated by the spell of its animate presence. "The sea observed is a reverie," Victor Hugo once said, and around it waves of desire or storms of emotion can appear (Bachelard 1969: 12). A radical phenomenology of the sensuous world, as Merleau-Ponty's phenomenology presents, releases the imaginal trapped in the literalism of facts or the dogmatism of thoughts. It reveals that the real is most radically the subtle body of metaphor.

As an autochthonous character of soul Philemon is an imaginal being, a metaphorical presence in the world. He is not a metaphor. Rather he is that kind of presence which a metaphor brings, a figural presence whose texture is neither that of fact nor idea, and a presence which requires of us that delight in and attunement to the play of language and experience. A psychology of projection resting in a dualism which rationalizes mind and literalizes matter loses the sense of this kind of presence, this third between things and thoughts. It eclipses the imaginal realm of experience and leaves only a void in the space between matter and mind. Indeed, the primary consequence of the Cartesian dream of reason is this eclipse of the world's imaginal body, this eclipse of soul and the indigenous figures who belong to its landscape. Philemon and his kin are uprooted by the reasonable mind which de-animates the world and transforms the flesh of soul into a mechanism. Philemon and his kin are perhaps the first refugees of modernity, displaced and homeless wanderers who appear at the gateway of ego-consciousness in the ragged and tattered disguise of a symptom, or in the chaotic form of a dream, whose alien, mad logic terrorizes the reasonable mind. Philemon and his kin rise up out of that void between matter and mind, and in ghostly form, like a mist, announce their presence.

In a superb, historical irony, the Cartesian dream of reason begins in 1619 with three dreams, nightmares really, which disturb Descartes' sleep. These haunting wraiths of the soul are the harbingers of what will come out of those dreams to vex the sleep of our world. They are an early anticipation by the soul of its own banishment by the ego mind, protestations of what is to come and will come when Descartes works out his project. They are the shadow side of the 1641 opus, *Meditations on First Philosophy*, where Descartes writes that "the human body may easily perish, but the mind or soul of man, *between which I find no distinction*, is immortal by its very nature" (Romanyshyn 1991: 23).

This erasure of difference between mind and soul is the colonization of soul by mind. In both the Latin and French editions of his text, Descartes continually shows his preferences for those terms which translate as mind or spirit over those which translate as soul. In Latin, "Mens" – the masculine spirit or mind – subdues "Anima" – the feminine soul. And in French, the masculine "l'esprit" conquers the feminine "l'ame". Moreover, it is important to notice that this eclipse of difference between soul and mind, and the triumph of the latter over the former, is situated in relation to Descartes's vision of the body. The mind is immortal, the body is not. But this mortal body which perishes is not for Descartes the animate, ensouled flesh. On the contrary, it is a mechanism, its perishability illustrated by the idea of the watch whose mainspring has broken. To perish, then, is not so much to die as it is to fall apart. Into that void between matter and mind, the feminine soul as animate flesh disappears. Torn between matter and mind, the soul falls apart and slouches toward Yeat's Bethlehem and Freud's Vienna, waiting to be re-born in his therapy room.

Philemon as an autochthonous character of soul demands a redemption of that lost third, the realm of the imaginal between things and thoughts. Philemon himself, as well as his tribe – the figures of the dream and the ghosts who haunt our symptoms – is not only an animate presence in the world; he is also the animate presence of the world.[3] Philemon is an example of the world's subtle body, a reality which is neither a fact nor an idea. To encounter him and his kin requires, then, a kind of consciousness attuned to metaphor. Writing of this subtle body, Nathan Schwartz-Salant says that, "The question is not whether or not the subtle body exists, but whether or not its existence can be perceived." By perceived he means a vision which is more than a matter of what meets the eyeball. He means another kind of consciousness, "not concerned with ordinary perceptions, but with imaginal ones." "Those who can *see*, will do so," he adds; "those who cannot will remain skeptical" (1989: 133).

Alchemy is the kind of consciousness which predates the skepticism of Descartes' dreams. Jung's alchemical studies offer another way of greeting Philemon, apart from that skepticism and doubt of the imaginal which leads to a psychology of projection.

Alchemy and the subtle body of metaphor

The literary critic, Howard Nemerov tells the following brief story to illustrate the character of metaphor.

> While I am thinking about metaphor, a flock of purple finches arrives on the lawn. Since I haven't seen these birds for some years, I am only fairly sure of their being in fact purple finches, so I get down Peterson's *Field Guide* and read his description: 'Male: About the size of a House Sparrow, rosy-red, brightest on head and rump.' That checks quite well, but his next remark – 'a Sparrow dipped in raspberry juice' – is decisive: it fits. I look out the window again, and now I *know* that I am seeing purple finches.
>
> That's very simple. So simple, indeed, that I hesitate to look any further into the matter, for as soon as I do I shall see its simplicity is not altogether canny. Why should I be made certain of what a purple finch is by being lead to contemplate a sparrow dipped in raspberry juice? Have I ever dipped a sparrow in raspberry juice? Has anyone? And yet there it is, quite certain and quite right. Peterson and I and the finches are in agreement.
>
> (Romanyshyn 1982:150–1)

A purple finch is a sparrow dipped in raspberry juice! The power of the metaphor is that it opens a vision of the world which is neither empirically true nor false. The metaphor is not a factual description of the world.

Indeed, if in a fit of empirical frenzy Nemerov managed to enter the garden and seize in his hands a purple finch, his hands would not drip with juice.

In the Cartesian dream of reason, what is not an empirical fact in the world must be a rational idea of the mind. But the purple finch which Nemerov sees is not an idea in his head. He is looking at the bird in the garden. The metaphor which opens Nemerov's vision is neither a fact in the world nor an idea in the mind. A metaphor is a power which releases the imaginal sense of things. Winston Churchill, that great master of the English language and of metaphor, once described Mussolini as "that utensil." Does one not see through that image the empty buffoonery of Mussolini?

Alchemy was and is a way of thinking which installs one in this *neither/nor* domain of metaphor. Within this domain any absolute separation of inner and outer, of mind and matter, of consciousness and nature is dissolved. David Fideler makes the same point in the following fashion. "Alchemy," he says, "is rooted in an uncritical way of knowing, in which there is no fundamental difference between the alchemist and the rest of nature" (1997: 8).

Fideler's use of the term uncritical refers to a way of knowing which suspends the judgmental activity of an ego mind that distances and separates itself from what it would know. In fact, in speaking of no fundamental difference, Fideler, I would argue, is suggesting that alchemy is a way of knowing where consciousness or spirit belongs to matter or nature, a way of knowing which recognizes that spirit matters and that matter yearns to be in-spired. Alchemy is and was a way of knowing and being which holds difference within relation. It does not deny the tension of difference between consciousness or spirit and matter or nature. Quite the contrary, in accepting this tension alchemy depicts a way of knowing through intimacy and relation rather than through separation and distance. A metaphor dis-solves separation between knower and known; it holds us in relation with the other without erasing the difference between us. The contemporary physicist, like his alchemist counterpart of old, recognizes that his presence as observer affects what is observed. That recognition, however, does not eclipse the difference between them.

The *neither/nor* logic of metaphor, the logic of the third between matter and mind, the realm of soul, requires that one must give up the notion of being able to attribute with final certainty that the epiphany of meaning belongs *either* on the side of consciousness as experience, *or* on the side of the world as an event. The *either/or* logic of mind is undone in the *neither/nor* logic of soul. The density of facts and the clarity of ideas are dis-solved and confused in the softer texture and diaphanous mist of the imaginal. Indeed, the work of soul, like that of alchemy, is about dis-solutions rather than solutions. The dream, for example, is a nightly alchemical work which dissolves or undoes the fixed solutions of the daily ego-mind. And metaphor does in daylight what the dream does at night. It is a piece of soul work, a waking dream, or what I would call, following Bachelard, a reverie, one of whose benefits is to free us into the imaginal depths of the world. Indeed, the depths of the world which metaphor reveals extends to the stars. "At the end," Bachelard says, "imagining a cosmos is the most natural destiny of reverie" (1969: 23).

Alchemy's opus – the transformation of lead into gold – is metaphor's work of releasing the spirit of things from their leaden literalism. In this regard, the alchemist is like the poet, who is a maker and master of metaphor. Both alchemist and poet are *metaphoricians*, one of nature and the other of the word. The alchemist and the maker of metaphor practice a poetic science of the natural world, not an empirical one. Therefore, when the poet Emily Dickinson says, "Tell all the truth, but tell it slant," she could be speaking also of the alchemist's vision (1961: 248). For alchemist and poet the imaginal reveals itself to an oblique vision which alludes, like a metaphor does, to something which always remains elusive. The imaginal is not captured by the focused stare of the empirical sciences, or the clear and distinct ideas of the Cartesian mind. I imagine that Jung walks with Philemon in his garden and *side by side* they converse, perhaps, on occasion, stealing a glance at each other, leaving the other in mystery.

In an alchemical work entitled *De chimea* there is the famous illustration of the winged and wingless birds. The winged bird is above the wingless one and each is eating the other's tail. The text says that the wingless bird prevents the winged bird from soaring away. But we can also say that the winged bird in its efforts to fly away slightly elevates the wingless one.

The illustration is perhaps the best and simplest way to indicate the central issue of alchemy: the tension of spirit and matter. Alchemy, as I said earlier, is a kind of consciousness which holds this tension and in holding it the subtle body of the third, the soul, the realm of the imaginal, which is neither that of spirit, consciousness, mind, nor matter, nature, body is born.

Commenting on this central issue, von Franz notes that this tension where we cannot decide whether something belongs to the realm of mind or matter is an eternal problem (1980a). But in fact, it is not even correct to say problem because the term implies a solution. Indeed, von Franz is indicating that when one takes up the claims of the soul there is no solution. A solution to the tension of spirit and matter happens only when one denies the tension; it happens only when one separates the winged and wingless birds. Then the clarity of a two is achieved, the clarity of a dualism, which allows one to say with certainty that a particular occurrence is either a subjective, psychological experience projected onto the world, or an objective event in the world cleansed of our participation. But in achieving that clarity what is lost is that creative tension which reveals the desire, longing, hunger on the part of spirit to matter, and that equally strong hunger on the part of matter to be in-spired.

Alchemy redeems the subtle imaginal body of the world, Philemon's landscape.[4] More than once, Jung makes it quite clear that the domain of alchemy is this region between spirit and matter, this domain of neither/nor. In *Psychology and Alchemy*, for example, he writes:

> it always remains an obscure point whether the ultimate transformations in the alchemical process ought to be sought more in the material or more in the spiritual realm. Actually, however, the question is wrongly put: there was no "either-or" for that age, but there did exist an intermediate realm between mind and matter, i.e., a psychic realm of subtle bodies whose characteristic it is to manifest themselves in mental as well as material form. This is the only view that makes sense of alchemical ways of thought, which must otherwise appear non-sensical.
>
> (Jung 1953: 278–9)

In reverie before his fires the alchemist witnessed the conjunction of spirit and matter. The psychic realm of subtle bodies which is realized in that act of witnessing is neither matter nor mind. On the contrary, as a footnote appended to the above text poignantly indicates "[Anima] is a subtle, imperceptible smoke" (ibid.: 278n.). Smoke and vapors, dust and mist: these are the stuff that soul is made on. The subtle body of alchemy, like the subtle body of metaphor, is the stuff of mood, an ambience which pervades and penetrates the field. The imaginal is neither in us nor in the world. It surrounds us, like light or wind. Philemon in his subtle, imaginal body is an aroma, a perfume.

Philemon, Jung, and Phenomenology

It is difficult, if not impossible, to distinguish with any finality between a projection and an autochthonous figure of the soul. In telling us about Philemon, Jung wants us to appreciate him as an autochthonous character of soul and not a projection. We have no grounds to disbelieve him. Moreover, the issue here is not an either/or, for as von Franz so wisely notes regarding the term projection, its use "depends on the state I am in" (1980b: 123). In this chapter I have attempted to show the historical context of that state. Its use coincides with an eclipse of the imaginal as a third between matter and mind, with a de-animation of the flesh which transforms the vital, gestural body into a mechanism, and with a broken connection between the ensouled sensuous body and the sense-able world.

The Cartesian dream of reason, with its metaphysics of an inside-mind-space and an outside-world-space, is a moment in the history of the soul when this eclipse of the imaginal became acute. We are still living within that dream, as is Jung's psychology. The notion of projection and its use bears witness to this fact. But the possibility of projection is certainly older than this dream. Indeed, perhaps, as von Franz notes, it is as ancient as consciousness itself. Speaking of a monk who has fallen in love, she asks whether his love should be regarded *either* as a spiritual crisis and explained in terms of an anima projection, *or* as a legitimate desire for a relation with an actual woman in the world. Wisely she cautions that this conflict cannot be solved rationally. She writes: "The only way the self can manifest is through conflict." One must roast in the conflict, like the salamander in alchemy roasts in the flames. One must endure in the difficult third place where the conflict is neither this nor that. "It is consciousness," she says "that creates the split and says either/or." And then, most astonishingly, she adds that "to meet one's insoluble and eternal conflict is to meet God, which would be the end of the ego with all its blather". This moment is "the moment of surrender . . . where Job says he will put his hand on his mouth and not argue about God" (von Franz 1980a: 136–7).

Autochthonous characters of soul are also moments which invite surrender. The Cartesian dream of reason is a response to that moment which has refused the invitation to surrender. Modern ego-consciousness rests upon this refusal and in that refusal lies both its power and its shadow. It is what has allowed the ego mind to keep itself distant, separate, and apart from the world, and to bend it and the soul to its own will.[5]

In one respect, Jung's psychology has been an attempt to come to terms with this refusal, an attempt to go beyond the psychology of projection which arises in the void between mind and matter. "Man, with his consciousness, is a disturbing factor in the order of nature; one could really question whether man was a good invention on the part of nature or not." This is von Franz who adds, "one aim of analysis is to get consciousness to function again according to nature" (1980b: 156–7). Jung's studies of alchemy and his notion of synchronicity tend in that direction. They move toward a psychology which is in fact no longer a psychology in the modern sense of an interior soul or self, but a cosmology where the self is a star. They move toward a consciousness which surrenders to its participation in the order of creation.

In this move, Jung's psychology converges with phenomenology, especially with a phenomenology like that of Merleau-Ponty. In an early work, *Phenomenology of Perception* (1962), Merleau-Ponty shows how the *cogito* is flesh, a sensuous consciousness impregnated by the sense-able things of the world. And in his final work, *The Visible and the Invisible* (1968), he describes the body–world relation as a chiasm or crossing where the world is the telos of the sensing-sensitive flesh.

Between these two works, there are numerous, significant essays like "The Philosopher and His Shadow" (1964a), a work whose very title evokes the suggestive image of the light of reason carrying its own darkness. Thinking is an embodied gesture, always embedded within and arising from a specific situation. Thinking is always carried into its thoughts by a body already seduced by the allure, the charm of the world, by the spell of the sensuous to borrow a title from David Abram's (1996) richly evocative book on Merleau-Ponty. In addition, there is the late essay *Eye and Mind* (1964b), perhaps Merleau-Ponty's best work, where he tells us that the painter takes his body with him. In effect, he is saying that there is the miracle of painting, and the everyday epiphanies of vision, because vision fulfills itself only through the visible, because the cogito-incarnate realizes itself only in, and through, and as the world. Between body and world lies the field of eros, a bond of desire which already inscribes the mind with a hunger for this otherness of the world. And if we ask what is this world which seduces the passionate mind to embrace it; what are these things of the world – the trees, the mountains, the stones; the stars, the oceans, the clouds; the birds, the animals, the flowers; the roads, the houses, and the gardens – we discover that they are pregnancies of possibilities, swollen seeds of promise ready to release their fruitful mysteries in our presence.

In *Psychological Life: From Science to Metaphor* (1982), I drew on this work of Merleau-Ponty, as well as that of J. H. van den Berg, to declare how a phenomenology of the sensuous world reveals the world's metaphorical character.[6] In its metaphorical structure, we find a world where we encounter things not as facts to be discovered, or as screens for our mental projections, but as invitations, or even temptations, or as occasions to participate in the world's continuous unfolding and realization. A more recent work (Romanyshyn 1996b)[7] draws upon the poetic phenomenology of Gaston Bachelard to show how reverie is the mood of this radical phenomenology which liberates the imaginal presence of the world, which frees it from the dead literalism of fact, and the uninspired dogmatism of thought.

An incarnate consciousness is a first, necessary step toward the recovery of the imaginal as real, and the real as imaginal. Starting with a body that is already mindful of the world, with a mind which is already kissed by things, phenomenology allows one to appreciate the metaphorical structure of reality and the metaphorical character of our experience. Soaked within this appreciation, we are able to be responsive to the third between material facts and mental ideas, the third of the imaginal, where metaphorical consciousness dwells. And such a consciousness is indispensable for encountering someone like Philemon who will not yield himself to the literal minded or to a thinking which is too rational.

In this regard, Jung's psychology needs phenomenology. It needs its radical epistemology which goes beyond the Cartesian dream of reason. Indeed, it needs it because ghosts are powerful beings, and even someone like Jung could not so easily exorcize the ghost of Descartes. His psychology, in fact, is always moving between one uncritically rooted in projection and one that acknowledges the autonomy of soul. Thus, one will find in the very same passage about the subtle bodies of alchemy quoted earlier this statement: "the existence of this intermediate realm [subtle bodies] comes to a stop the moment we try to investigate matter in and for itself, apart from all projection" (Jung 1953: 279). Or, one will find a statement like this : "the real root of alchemy is to be sought in the projections of individual investigators" (Jung 1953: 245). In these passages, Jung not only defends projection, he also makes it a condition for the appearance of the subtle realm.

I would argue, however, that those moments when Jung's psychology is humbled by the autonomy of the soul are the ones where the alchemical opus of transforming lead into gold continues, and where his psychology is most radical and realizes its own destiny. They are the moments when he steps out of our Cartesian consciousness which splits spirit and matter, mind and nature, into a consciousness attuned to the synchronicities of spirit-matter. Indeed, I would claim that it is no accident that after his long studies of alchemy Jung announced this principle of synchronicity, for it is the telos of that journey from a psychology of separation based in projection to a cosmology of relations based in synchronicity. The third of metaphor between matter and mind, the realm of the imaginal is a synchronistic field. We encounter Philemon and his kin when our consciousness, weaned of the literal and released into the figural, situates us in the field between the literal and the logical.

Open to the miracle: from psychology to cosmology

A metaphor is a small miracle, a momentary tear in the fabric of the quotidian round, a moment when a vision which erupts between us is neither a psychological experience nor a material event. It is the kind of moment which recognizes and appreciates the subtle body of the world, the kind of moment which can occur, for example, when in a state of reverie, of empathic attunement to the world, I say of the smile which marks the countenance of a loved one that it is a facial orgasm, or of the wind which slightly stirs the trees that it is the sky's ocean. It is a moment of beauty really, a moment when one is awe struck by the fecundity of the world, by its glorious ripeness and outpouring generosity. Those marvelous paintings of old which show the Angel in encounter with us always impress this point of being awe-struck, struck dumb, because we are truly capable only of silence in this moment where we witness the conjunction of spirit and matter, of mind or consciousness and nature. These small miracles, which open to us that third of the imaginal between spirit and matter, are moments when that arc which bridges the earthy animal passion of our material existence, and the heavenly angelic beauty of our spirit, energizes our humanity, delivers us from ourselves, and releases us into the cosmos.

It is no accident, I believe, that Jung acknowledges that in former times moments of synchronicity were known as miracles (von Franz 1992: 162). A metaphor is a moment of synchronicity and such a moment, as von Franz notes, situates us in the between of the imaginal. Synchronicity, she writes, is more than a new idea. It is "the manifestation of a concrete living principle which can not be described as dead matter, or as 'only' psychic [with the implication of not being connected with matter]." With the eruption of this concrete living principle, we are in that same place of neither/nor, the third of metaphor. Moreover, when von Franz adds that synchronicity "is a power which brings forth acts of creation in time" (1992: 183), we are again in the mood of metaphor, because, as we have already said, the vision of metaphor is the way in which we continue the work of creation, releasing the promise of the world into its fulfillment.

The alchemists of old were adepts in this release, witnesses to the conjunction of spirit and matter. They lived in the subtle field of neither/nor, as Jung himself acknowledged, and in doing so they occasioned moments of synchronicity, occasional miracles. Indeed, the principle task of alchemy was the redemption of matter, the release of those divine sparks of spirit which had fallen from the heavens. The telos of Jung's psychology was, I believe, always a sacred cosmology where soul finds its home again in the order of creation. The passageway of this journey lies between eye and mind, between the empiricism of facts and the rationalism of ideas. A scared cosmology requires the poetic vision of the soul. It calls for that kind of consciousness which, in delivering us from the literal and the logical, lives in the realization of the metaphorical. The synchronicity of metaphor occasions a moment when the veil of creation lifts to reveal the sacred face of the ordinary, the miraculous in the mundane. Philemon belongs to such moments. He resides in them, just beyond the curtain, waiting for us, over there in the field.

Postscript: Philemon and the Angel – a confession

When I had finished this chapter, I was thinking of Philemon, about the subtle body of metaphor, about his place in the world as an imaginal being. But something was not quite right, and I felt a bit uneasy about this claim. Was it right, or better, fair, to describe him as an imaginal presence in the world? My unease had to do with the question of whether this claim was already too much, whether it had already yoked Philemon too closely to us and kept him a prisoner of our psychologies and the human realm to which they belong. Did the claim eclipse the radical other-ness of Philemon? To borrow for a moment a philosophical mode of expression, I wondered if the claim did not rob Philemon of his ontological status as something wholly other and apart from the human psyche. The claim, of course, has an epistemological weight, since it is only through the human psyche that the experience of the world and all its appearances takes place. But epistemological claims should not occlude ontological differences, and it is Philemon's difference from us which is at the heart of this claim. From an epistemological perspective the imaginal is and must, of course, always be a psychological experience. But from an ontological point of view the imaginal is not the psychological. In this regard, Philemon is *not* a psychological being. Indeed, the point of my chapter is that he leads us beyond psychology into a cosmology where different orders of being intersect with us and we with them.[8]

Musing along these lines, I thought about the Angel, and recalled how in an earlier publication I refused to call the Angel an imaginal being (Romanyshyn 1995). Guided by Rilke's appreciation of the Angel who in its radiant alterity is a mirror who draws back into itself its own beauty, I understood how this absolute otherness can reveal itself as a kind of terrible indifference to us. This radical other-ness is in fact the basis for Rilke's claim that every Angel is terrible. In the face of this other-ness, then, it seems to me too poor of us to call them imaginal beings, too insensitive, and even, perhaps, too arrogant. And I recalled at this moment the consequence of an encounter with beings like Angels who belong to and come from other orders of creation. In their awe-ful presence, we are struck dumb, and silence is often the norm.

Between the claim and the silence, then, what are we to choose? The great paintings of Angels from Medieval Christendom depict these other beings and the painted image is a claim. And Rilke has taught us not only to appreciate our power to claim, but also to value it as a sign of *our* difference. For Rilke we are called to speak and proclaim; we are called into the claim. Language is our vocation and we are asked to speak, not only *to* the angel – "Praise the world to the Angel/Tell him things" (Rilke 1939: 75–7) – but even of the Angel. What seems important here is the recognition that the claim is not the being who is proclaimed. The Angel is not the painting; the Angel is not the image, nor the word. And yet, still, the image or the word alludes to the being who is other. The claim alludes to an other-ness which seems elusive, two words whose roots mean to play.[9] What seems important, then, is a proclaiming – Philemon is an imaginal being – which plays with other-ness. What seems important is a kind of proclaiming which never takes itself too seriously. It is a way of speaking which recognizes that for the moment, that's enough.[10]

These reveries on Philemon and Angels were interrupted by the appearance of a friend and colleague at the threshold of my office. He came in and we began a conversation. In the midst of it, I "saw" my wife crossing the path outside my office, and I knew she had come, as promised, to see me for a moment before I began an evening class. I halted my conversation with my friend, and ran outside to greet her, but she was not there. I called her name, thinking that she had disappeared behind the row of hedges on the far side of my office. But there was no response. Completely mystified by her absence, I returned to my office. At that moment, the phone rang, and it was my wife. She was calling to tell me that she would be unable to arrive at my office on time and that she was keenly disappointed. Both of us were strongly anticipating this meeting, as brief as it would be. We were missing each other and longed to be together, even for a moment.

On the way to my evening class, I realized for the first time, that, given the position of the chair in my office, I could not have seen with my bodily eyes my wife crossing the path. On the contrary, I had seen her with an imaginal eye, that third eye which is open to that realm which is neither factual nor rational. In that moment, her presence was of that subtle sort which belongs to an-other realm of experience, to that third realm which I had been calling in this essay the imaginal.

In that circuitous way of thinking characteristic of reverie, it occurred to me that I had also just witnessed an occasion of bi-locality, which quantum physics ascribes to quantum objects in that state called "superposition." At the quantum level matter is highly energized – matter, we might say, is truly in-spired – and in this state an electron can occupy more than one orbital level simultaneously. Since we too are material beings, is it possible that in inspired states of desire and eros we can be in more than one place simultaneously? Sinking deeper into reverie, I then remembered that another aspect of superposition is that a photon, a particle of light, not only can travel along two paths at the same time, but also traverse space in the same way that Thomas Aquinas described the movement of Angels. When an Angel's movement is discontinuous, he said, "it does not cross all the intermediate places between its starting place and its term" (Fox and Sheldrake 1996: 105). Its movement between two places is instantaneous, and one cannot say where it was in between those two places, like one cannot say with any certainty where a photon has been between, for example, its emission from the sun and its impact on Earth. In between, it is non-localized, anywhere or everywhere as it were. Moreover, the state of superposition of quantum objects is a condition best described in terms of neither/nor. Indeed, the famous example of Schroedinger's cat who is neither dead nor alive is a classic example of superposition. Quantum objects in superposition are in that same metaphorical state which, I said, describes Philemon's presence. At this moment, an awe-ful conclusion pressed itself upon me: the imaginal is a quantum reality, a quantum field. Quantum physics and imaginal psychology are two sides of the same coin. Philemon and his kind are expressions of that other-ness where soul, spirit, and matter meet, where physics and psychology join.

It is the principle of synchronicity which yokes the imaginal psyche and quantum matter. Philemon is an experience – event that one can describe only as neither psychological nor physical, a metaphorical presence, which this principle of synchronicity addresses. Moreover, since synchronicity is described by Jung as acts of creation in time, creation is continuous, and thus it no longer makes sense to ask about the origins and endings of creation. These questions are dis-solved and one can say only of creation, of Philemon, of photons, of the imaginal-quantum order, that it is because it always was and because it always was it will continue to be. In that place of synchronicity, in that place where an experience/event is neither physical nor psychological, in that place of metaphorical presence, that place of imaginal-quantum beings, Philemon and his kind, like Angels, are beyond time, are eternal.

A-musing reveries, wild musings prompted by this experience of bi-locality evoked the Angel, and I wondered why in relation to my concerns about Philemon the Angel had appeared. I wondered about the connection between Philemon, the Angel, and this experience of bi-locality. Was it a moment of synchronicity?

Speaking of synchronicity, von Franz has used the quotidian example of a telephone call from someone about whom one is thinking in that moment. It seems to me that this was such a moment, an opening in the world's fabric through which the imaginal erupted.

But still, why? Why at that moment when I had been musing about Philemon and the Angel, concerned that I might have done him a dis-service by calling him an imaginal being? I have no answer. But I do have a feeling and the feeling is that this experience was Philemon's way of cautioning me at the end of this essay not to forget the difference between us. It was, I believe, his way of saying, "Be care-ful not to take the claims of your psychology too seriously."[11]

Notes

1 My first two books (Romanyshyn 1982, 1989) are explorations of these relationships among psychology, science, technology, politics, and economics, especially in terms of the origins of these relations.

2 The true depth of depth psychology is the world, a lateral depth which surrounds us and whose mysteries can be plumbed in a state of reverie, which is neither an empirical, fact-minded, information-seeking consciousness, nor a rational, detached consciousness addicted to a dogma of fixed meanings or principles. Thus to recover the imaginal is to recover the world as the depth of soul. In this regard, projection not only eclipses the imaginal, it also de-animates the world, an ironic twist on the way this doctrine is usually understood. More precisely, projection withdraws soul from world, mis-places it in us as an interior experience, and then dis-places it back onto the world. But then, the full anima-tion of the world is reduced to the terms of the individual human psyche, or, even with Jung, the collective human psyche. The psyche of the world is lost. Psyche in its cosmological reaches is lost. For a more detailed discussion of this notion of lateral depth see Romanyshyn (1983).

3 For a more detailed discussion of this notion of the ghost who haunts our symptoms see (Romanyshyn 1999a).

4 In this regard, alchemy is an authentic depth psychology and Jung's move into it a stroke of genius. Jung, however, vitiates the radical character of alchemy by placing it within a Cartesian frame, within a psychology of projection. Alchemy is not a forerunner of Jung's psychology; it is a corrective of it.

5 If projection is older than the Cartesian dream of reason, if it is a possibility of consciousness itself as von Franz suggests, still the Cartesian dream of reason which separates psyche and matter has a singular significance. As an epistemo-

logical foundation for our modern, scientific–technological culture, it made a psychology of projection into a method. Or said in another way, with Descartes there is a reversal between being and knowing, where knowing and its claims now assert themselves not in response to the call of being, but over and against these calls. Much of Martin Heidegger's work is to be situated here.

6 The work of J. H. van den Berg has been a continuing source of inspiration for my own work, and I can not let pass this opportunity to acknowledge again my indebtedness to him. For some specific references see 1972, 1974, 1975.

7 Earlier versions of several of its chapters appear in various journals (Romanyshyn 1995, 1996, 1997).

8 My good friend and colleague, Lionel Corbett, deals with this important question in his remarkable book *The Religious Function of the Psyche* (1996). I find our conversations fruitful in exploring this difficult question of how one safeguards ontological differences from the claims of our epistemological assertions. In Corbett's book, this issue is focused on the question of the numinous, and his work is especially helpful in sighting those relevant passages in Jung where the numinous seems to possess its own radical alterity. And yet, I always feel that Jung (and Corbett?) does not go quite far enough in drawing this distinction between epistemology and ontology, and, I believe, Philemon, as an eruption of the numinous, insists upon it.

9 For a detailed account of the structure of metaphor as an allusion to the elusive, of metaphor as a field of play see Romanyshyn 1982.

10 In the essay "For the moment, that's enough: reveries on therapy and the poetry of language" (1999), I consider in detail how the language of therapy is a claiming by letting go. Philemon, like the ghosts who haunt our symptoms, requires this kind of speaking. The imaginal requires the poetic.

11 I want to acknowledge here the contributions of my wife, Veronica Goodchild, to this essay, especially the postscript. Before the experience recounted there happened, it was she who questioned the description of Philemon as an imaginal being. Those conversations sent me back to my earlier work on Angels.

References

Abram, D. (1996) *The Spell of the Sensuous*, New York: Pantheon Books.

Bachelard, G. (1969) *The Poetics of Reverie*, New York: The Orion Press.

Brooke, R. (1995) "Jung's recollection of the life-world", *Harvest*, 41, 1: 26–37 (reproduced in this volume).

Corbett, L. (1996) *The Religious Function of the Psyche*, London and New York: Routledge.

Dickinson, E. (1961) *Final Harvest: Emily Dickinson's Poems*, ed. T.H. Johnson, Boston: Little Brown and Co.

Fideler, D. (1997) "The alchemy of attachment: an epistemology of transformation," paper presented at the Symposium of the Palladian Academy, Vicenza, Italy.

Fox, M. and Sheldrake, R. (1996) *The Physics of Angels*, San Francisco: Harper.

Jung, C. G. (1926) "Spirit and life," *CW* 8.

—— (1947/54) "On the nature of the psyche," *CW* 8.

—— (1953) "Psychology and Alchemy," *CW* 12.

—— (1954) "Concerning the archetypes, with special reference to the anima concept," *CW* 9, i.

—— (1962) *Memories, Dreams, Reflections*, New York: Pantheon.

Kreinheder, A. (1975) "Alchemy and the subtle body," in *Psychological Perspectives*, 6, 2.

Merleau-Ponty, M. (1962) *Phenomenology of Perception*, trans. C. Smith and K. Paul, London: Routledge.

—— (1964a) "The philosopher and his shadow," in *Signs*, trans. by Richard C. McCleary, Evanston: Northwestern University Press.

—— (1964b) "Eye and mind," in J. M. Edie (ed.) *The Primacy of Perception*, Evanston: Northwestern University Press.

—— (1968) *The Visible and the Invisible*, trans. by Alphonso Lingis, Evanston: Northwestern University Press.

Morris, W. (ed.) (1981) *The American Heritage Dictionary of the English Language*, Boston: Houghton, Mifflin & Co.

Rilke, R. M. (1939) *Duino Elegies*, trans. J. B. Leishman and S. Spender, New York: W.W. Norton & Co.

Romanyshyn, R. (1982) *Psychological Life: From Science to Metaphor*, Austin: University of Texas Press.

—— (1983) "Unconscious as a lateral depth: perception and the two moments of reflection," in H. J. Silverman, J. Sallis and T. M. Seebohm (eds) *Continental Philosophy in America*, Pittsburgh: Duquesne University Press.

—— (1988) *Technology as Symptom and Dream*, London: Routledge.

—— (1989) *Technology as Symptom and Dream*, London and New York: Routledge.

—— (1991) "Complex knowing: toward a psychological hermeneutics," *The Humanistic Psychologist*, 19, 1.

—— (1993) "The despotic eye and its shadow: media image in the age of literacy," in D. Levin (ed.) *Modernity and the Hegemony of Vision*, Berkeley: The University of California Press.

—— (1995) "The orphan and the angel," in *Psychological Perspectives*, 32.

—— (1996) "Starry nights, sexual love and the rhythms of the soul," in N. Cobb (ed.) *Sphinx-7: A Journal for Archetypal Psychology and the Arts*, London: The London Convivium.

—— (1997) "Egos, angels and the colors of nature," in D. Fideler (ed.) *Alexandria-4: The Order and Beauty of Nature*, Michigan: Phanes Press.

—— (1999a) "For the moment, that's enough: reveries on therapy and the poetry of language," *San Francisco Jung Institute Library Journal*, 18, 1.

—— (1999b) *The Soul in Grief: Love, Death, and Transformation*, Berkeley: North Atlantic Books.

Samuels, A. (1993) *The Political Psyche*, London and New York: Routledge.

Schwartz-Salant, N. (1989) *The Borderline Personality: Vision and Healing*, Wilmette, Illinois: Chiron Publications.

Van den Berg, J. H. (1972) *A Different Existence: Principles of Phenomenological Psychopathology*, Pittsburgh: Duquesne University Press.

—— (1974) *Divided Existence and Complex Society: An Historical Approach*, Pittsburgh: Duquesne University Press.

—— (1975) *The Changing Nature of Man: Introduction to a Historical Psychology*, New York: Dell Publishing Co.

Von Franz, M.-L. (1980a) *Alchemy*, Toronto: Inner City Books.
—— (1980b) *Projection and Recollection in Jungian Psychology*, La Salle and London: Open Court.
—— (1992) *Psyche and Matter*, Boston: Shambhala Publications.
Watkins, M. (1986) *Invisible Guests*, New Jersey: The Analytic Press.

EDITOR'S INTRODUCTION

Both Jung and Heidegger felt acutely the loss of the sense of the sacred in modern culture, and both spoke poetically of the status and meaning of "the gods" in what Heidegger called this "destitute time." However, their approaches were different, as were their solutions. Jung found the gods in the unconscious psyche, Heidegger found them beneath western metaphysics but still present "in" the things with which we dwell. Rilke is an intriguing figure here as he forms something of a bridge between them. As Simms shows, he expresses in his poetry the suffering felt by both Heidegger and Jung – and indeed by all of us – and she shows how Rilke struggled to find an authentic way of speaking about and relating to the sacred that was psychologically astute yet ultimately beyond psychology.

3

IN DESTITUTE TIMES

Archetype and existence in Rilke's *Duino Elegies*

Eva-Maria Simms

> Our heart remains between
> hammers, like the tongue
> between the teeth:
> it continues to praise.
> (R.M. Rilke, *Duino Elegies*)

"Who came?"

In January 1912 Rainer Maria Rilke received a bothersome business letter while he was a guest at Castle Duino on the Adriatic coast. Even though he had been writing poems sporadically during the fall and winter, he felt despondent, as Marie von Thurn and Taxis, his hostess at Duino, reports, because he feared that another season would pass without any true poetry. Thinking about the proper response to the business letter, Rilke climbed down to the bastions where the cliffs fell about 200 feet down into the sea and walked back and forth on a narrow path. A heavy Bora blew, but the sun, nevertheless, brilliantly illuminated the stormy sea. His thoughts were suddenly interrupted when it seemed to him that he heard a voice calling to him from out of the storm: "Who, if I cried, would hear me among the angelic orders?"[1] He wrote in his notebook, and a few other verses followed "without his own contribution." Marie Taxis continues her account: "Who came? . . . He knew it now: the god . . . Quietly he climbed back up to his room, put aside his notebook, and finished his business letter. When evening came, the whole elegy had been written down" (*RDE*: 50).[2]

Rilke himself would probably not have answered the question "Who came?" with the simple pronouncement "the god," because what he heard from the storm was not a new annunciation of God through divine messengers. The voice from the storm itself questions the very possibility of the connection between human and divine beings. The question "who speaks?" in the moment of inspiration became a profound and profoundly disturbing issue for Rilke, one which touched his self-understanding as a man, as a poet, and as a person of the twentieth century. It also became the inspiration for the *Duino Elegies*.

If we did not know what came after the phrase Rilke heard in the storm, we would guess at a typical romantic experience: the lonely poet, the stormy sea, inspiration catching him unawares out of the communion with the elements. But Rilke was a man of the twentieth century, and matters of inspiration had become a thorny issue. Had Rilke lived in biblical times a voice in the storm would have been heard as the voice of God; had he lived in classical times, the sea-god could have arisen from the waves and addressed the poet; had he lived in rural Switzerland at the turn of the sixteenth century, the vision of light, storm, and water could have been experienced as an angelic messenger announcing the will of God. But at the turn of the twentieth century, the allusions to biblical, classical, and Christian images sound hollow and cast a sheen of false sentimentality over Marie Taxis' description. It is this same falseness in the voice, the failure to speak truly and truthfully about his experience in a language adequate to capture its fullness, which makes some of Rilke's poems unbearable to the reader and causes many critics to turn away in disgust (Friedrich 1956, Heller 1959a). Rather than dismiss these false notes as a failure of the artist, I suggest that they reveal a deeper pathology: not merely a disturbance of Rilke's personal life, but a suffering that goes to the heart of human existence in postmodern times.

Rilke, as Heidegger (1971: 91) phrases it, is a poet in a destitute time. The time's destitution lies in the default of God, which:

> means that no god any longer gathers men and things unto himself, visibly and unequivocally, and by such gathering disposes the world's history and man's sojourn in it. . . . Not only have the gods and the god fled, but the divine radiance has become extinguished in the world's history.

Rilke was acutely aware that the linguistic and symbolic tools available to him were insufficient to capture his experience of the numinous because traditional religious symbolism and language had lost their meaning. The *Second Duino Elegy* (Rilke 1966) summarizes the difficulty elegantly:

> For our own heart still transcends us,
> as their's did. But we cannot follow it anymore
> in images that calm it, nor through
> divine bodies in which it finds its greater measure.
> (*DE*: 2)

This inability to find a symbolic system to contain experiences of the numinous does not mean that individuals have no longer a personal relationship to the divine, but that in the life of our culture the clearings in which the divine can appear have become more and more invisible: the Zeitgeist, Rilke says, " . . . does not know temples anymore. Those extravagances of the heart . . . " (*DE*: 7).

When Marie Taxis in her exuberance evokes "the god," she performs a profound misreading of the situation, since the words out of the storm announce not the presence, but the absence of the divine agent. The angel, by his very evocation through the *Duino Elegies*, is not a positive or guiding figure, but a dead symbol, a trace of a presence that once was close to humans:

> Where are the days of Tobias,
> when one of the shining beings stood at the simple door,
> slightly disguised for the journey, no longer terrible;
> (Youth to the youth who curiously looked out).
>
> (*DE*: 2)

Now the angelic orders are so distant that even the loudest cry cannot reach them, and if one of them heard us, we "would perish through his greater existence" (*DE*: 1).

Carl Jung, a contemporary of Rilke, also had a deep understanding of the voices that suddenly intrude into consciousness through dream, reverie, or vision. And like Rilke, Jung was also painfully aware of the growing impoverishment of religious symbols. In the past, an image like Rilke's angel would have been embraced by the system of religious symbols. Dogma would have channeled, ordered, and defused the experience of the numinous in creed and ritual, and "the figures of the unconscious were expressed in protecting and healing images" (Jung 1954: 12). But today our symbolism has become impoverished, our gods have died, like other gods before them: "People discovered then, as today, that they had no thoughts whatever on the subject" (ibid.: 14). Religious images do not contain power anymore. Instead of turning to the Eastern religions, whose symbolism still intrigues us, Jung calls the people of our time to:

> stoutly avow our spiritual poverty, our symbol-lessness, instead of feigning a legacy to which we are not the legitimate heirs at all. . . . Anyone who has lost the historical symbols and cannot be satisfied with substitutes is certainly in a very difficult position today: before him there yawns a void . . . . [S]o spiritual poverty seeks to renounce the false riches of the spirit in order to withdraw not only from the sorry remnants . . . of a great past, but also from all the allurements of the odorous East: in order, finally, to dwell with itself alone, where, in the cold light of consciousness, the blank barrenness of the world reaches to the very stars.
>
> (ibid.: 15)

Both born in 1875, Rilke and Jung suffered the deepest and most transforming crisis of their lives in the years surrounding the outbreak of the First World War. While Jung experienced personal disintegration, had visions of rivers of blood before the outbreak of the war, and felt impelled, in his personal crisis, to explore "to what extent [his] experience coincided with that of mankind in general," Rilke experienced the war as a complete break in the spiritual continuity of human existence and a deep rift in the movement of his own life and work. Permeating the *Duino Elegies* and the *Sonnets to Orpheus* is Rilke's evaluation of the nature of modern existence: we live in an "interpreted world," we are unable to be touched by divine presences, we are alienated from other human beings, and even the world of things is no longer an abode for human feeling and imagination. Human beings have always been "like the Laurel, a little darker than all other green" (*DE*: 9), and their relation to the world is different from that of all other living beings. But our time has intensified the human ability to process appearances, form concepts, and change reality, so that our "true relation," i.e. our proper place within creation, has been covered over.

> And we: voyeurs, always, everywhere,
> turned toward it all but never beyond it!
> It overcrowds us. We organize it. It falls apart.
> We organize it again and fall apart ourselves.
> (*DE*: 8)

Jung echoes a very similar insight: "Our intellect has achieved the most tremendous things, but in the meantime our spiritual dwelling has fallen into disrepair" (Jung 1954: 16). The night sky, once structured by angelic spheres and connected to humans through divine hierarchies, is empty now. The heart and its visible expressions are bankrupt. The *Zeitgeist* does not build temples anymore. In a world like this, the angel is an anachronism. "Our myth has become mute and gives no answers" (Jung 1962: 332). The blank barrenness of the world reaches up to the very stars.

I want to show two divergent paths taken up after the acceptance of the default of God (the gods). Jung's path turns inward and leads him to articulate the unconscious as the seat of the divine. Rilke's path turns outwards, locating traces of the divine in the world. Jung's understanding of the divine is psychoanalytic; Rilke's understanding of the archetypal image is existential.

The kairos

During his life C.G. Jung had intimate experience with the power of the artistic process. When he was in turmoil after the break up with Freud, or later, in the difficult time after the death of his wife, Jung carved stone, built rock monuments, or painted pictures to regain his equilibrium. Even though he refused to be called an artist himself, he saw the deep cultural significance of the artist's work. His homage to the artist is profound, since he ascribes to the poets, painters, and sculptors the task of transforming a personal destiny into the destiny of mankind, and to evoke in their audience the primordial forces that have allowed humankind to survive even in the darkest times:

> The creative process, so far as we are able to follow it at all, consists in the unconscious activation of an archetypal image, and in elaborating and shaping this image into the finished work. By giving it shape, the artist translates it into the language of the present, and so makes it possible for us to find our way back to the deepest springs of life. Therein lies the social significance of art: it is constantly at work educating the spirit of an age, conjuring up the forms in which the age is most lacking. The unsatisfied yearning of the artist reaches back to the primordial image in the unconscious which is best fitted to compensate the inadequacy and one-sidedness of the present. The artist seizes on this image, and in raising it from deepest unconsciousness he brings it into relation with conscious values, thereby transforming it until it can be accepted by the minds of his contemporaries according to their powers.
>
> (Jung 1922: 820–83)

Jung clearly sees the social significance of art: it is not merely there to provide a protected domain for the pleasure principle, as Freud (1930) has it, but it compensates for a cultural lack. Artistic images balance the tendencies of the collective consciousness by evoking primordial forms and injecting them into the discourse of a culture. The language of the present needs to be shaped, expanded, and deepened to contain the force of unconscious archetypal material. The poet, hence, does not merely speak for his own life, but always addresses the life of his culture – and its neediness.

In Jung's sense, Rilke's angel is an archetype, breaking through the poet's conscious life with the primal force of the elements. Rather than making the image, the poet experiences it as a gift from a sphere beyond his control and infused with power. Its meaning as experienced by poet and audience cannot be reduced to simple conceptual language. It seems to have a life of its own. In many letters Rilke speaks of his own amazement at the appearance of the *Duino Elegies*, and what he writes about the *Sonnets to Orpheus* best summarizes his attitude toward his poems: "they are perhaps the most secret, and for myself the most mysterious dictation I have ever suffered and gone through, especially in their appearance and in the task they brought to me" (Rilke 1950: 832).

From its appearance out of the storm, the emergence of the archetypal image of the angelic orders did not bring consolation, but challenge. The time's destitution made it impossible for Rilke to embrace the angel as the harbinger of the numinous. Instead of a glorious hymn to the wisdom and beauty of the heavenly hosts the voice from the storm dictates an elegy which mourns the rift that has opened between humankind and divine beings:

> Who, if I cried, would hear me among the angelic
> Orders? And even if one of them
> suddenly took me to his heart: I would perish
> in his stronger being. For the beautiful is nothing
> but the beginning of the terrible which we can just bear,
> and we admire it so because it serenely scorns
> to destroy us. Every angel is terrible.
> And so I hold myself back and swallow
> the luring call of my dark sorrow.
>
> (*DE*: 1)

The problem with the archetypal image of the angel is that it is no longer an appropriate form for the expression of human spirituality. The *Duino Elegies*, even though they still celebrate beautiful angelic images of the "pollen of the blossoming god, joints of light, hallways, stairs, thrones, spaces of being, shields of pleasure," ultimately turn away from the angel since the image of the angel covers over the true destiny of human beings. The image does not speak to human existence anymore, except as a lack. Through his struggle with poetic images Rilke intuitively grasped what Jung (1957: 304) understood by studying the human psyche: "We are living in what the Greeks called the *Kairos* – the right time – for a 'metamorphosis of the gods,' i.e. of the fundamental principles and symbols."

Poetic image: "supreme possibility of the human heart itself"

While Rilke was aware of this metamorphosis of fundamental spiritual principles, many of his interpreters were not. Because of Rilke's claim that his poems were mysterious dictations, the angel of the *Duino Elegies* has often been interpreted as a religious, Christian symbol, and Rilke has been accused of offering an inauthentic message to the human quest for salvation (Guardini 1961) and speaking the untruth about human existence out of a deep self-deception (Heller 1959b). But Rilke's angel is not another word for God, and Rilke does not attempt to create a new theology. In his correspondence he frequently rejected the Christian interpretation of his angel. If the angel is not a symbol in the Christian canon, how then can we understand it?

In the essay "Letter of a Young Worker," Rilke (1966: 574–75) uses an interesting metaphor to describe the nature of religious images. He describes the large stained glass windows of a medieval cathedral. In the illuminated pictures every aspect of human life could find its place. "Here is the angel, who does not exist, and the devil, who does not exist; and man, who exists, is between them, and it strikes me that their unreality makes him more real to me." Although the angel and the devil do not have the kind of existence that human beings have, their image frames and reveals human nature by showing *what it is not*. They stand for the other which the human reaches for but never fully encompasses. The angel is an outline of human existence, an intensification of human qualities sculpted as a poetic image. Rilke, through his angel, tries to define what is human by exploring the inhuman: "Early successes, you darlings of the universe, high ridges, dawn-red crests of all creation – pollen of the blossoming godhead" (*DE*: 2). "What is evoked here as the Angel, then," Gadamer (1994: 157) writes,

> is a supreme possibility of the human heart itself – a possibility never fully realized, one that the heart cannot achieve because the human being is conditioned in so many ways, rendering him incapable of a clear and total surrender to his feelings.

Rilke, as a poet and not a theologian, takes the image out of the religious realm, and moves it into the sphere of poetic experimentation, where it evokes and alludes to the numinous without fixing it in a religious system. The *Duino Elegies* are intensely spiritual in the sense that the *experience* of the numinous is still possible, but the traditional symbols fail to contain it. A new attitude toward the transcendent and toward communicating it must be developed: the playfulness, tenuousness, and intensity of poetic images allow for the freedom to take up this experience in a new way. The angel stands in the rift between the old symbolism and a new way of thinking about transcendent as well as immanent being.

Jung's project, too, took religious symbolism out of the sphere of theology. He examined religious imagery and experience in psychological terms: the figure of Christ, for example, is seen as an archetype of the self and as figure in the drama between consciousness and unconscious (Jung 1959: 9.2), a statement which earned Jung the wrath of many theologians, who called him an atheist (1961). Psychology, as an empirical science, steps into the place formerly occupied by theology to "raise up the (unconscious) treasure-house of eternal images" (Jung 1954: 6), and to discover that religious formulas can be expressed now in psychological terms. After the religious symbol has lost its function as a cultural referent to the sacred, it becomes open to other kinds of reflection.

The "real world" and "that strange inner world"

Both Rilke and Jung were deeply touched by experiences of the numinous, and both struggled to preserve the possibility of a relationship to the transcendent in their work, and to discover a system of referents that made speaking of the divine possible in a time where the usual religious language had lost its power. Jung's path went through the exploration of dreams and reveries, beginning with the productions of his own unconscious, amplifying them through connections with mythological material, to arrive finally at the ever deeper and impersonal origins of personal life. He followed this process in his own analysis as well as with his patients. He spoke of archetypes such as the anima as interfering from *within*, as existing in the psyche, and the journey of encounter with the unconscious is imagined as a descent deep into the interior of the self. Jung felt a particular gratitude toward his family and profession as a "point of support in this 'world.'" He calls them the "real world as a counterpoise to that strange inner world," and he greatly feared to become "a blank page whirling about in the winds of the spirit like Nietzsche" (Jung 1962: 189). In Jung's work the metaphors of interiority allude to the true world of the psyche, while the descriptions of the "real world" of family and profession seem incidental and not very meaningful in the dramatic narrative of Jung's life.

The dichotomy between inner and outer world is a peculiar phenomenon of modern times, as Jung was well aware:

> All ages before us have believed in gods in some form or other. Only an unparalleled impoverishment of symbolism could enable us to rediscover the gods as psychic factors, that is, as archetypes of the collective unconscious. . . . Since the stars have fallen from heaven and our highest symbols have paled, a secret life holds sway in the unconscious, that is why we have a psychology today, and why we speak of the unconscious. All this would be quite superfluous in an age or culture that possessed symbols. Symbols are the spirit from above, and under those conditions the spirit is above too.
>
> (Jung 1954: 23–24)

But people before us, "primitives" as Jung calls them, did not know that their experiences of mythological presences were actually projections of an inner, psychological drama upon natural events. After having understood the dynamics between conscious and unconscious, Jung thought it impossible to return to the primitive *participation mystique*.

In Jung's cosmology the outside, objective world becomes a screen onto which the inner drama of the unconscious is projected. Family and profession exist as a prop for the ego so that it does not disintegrate into insanity. The real work is not a work of cultivating the outside world, but of descending into the depth of one's own psyche to discover there archetypal forces that go beyond one's personal life. "Know thyself" is Jung's motto, and the scrutiny of one's own unconscious is the great challenge for people in our century and in Jung's view the only path to survive the evils of our time.

Rilke's project, on the other hand, was deeply directed by his love for the visible world. His years of working with Rodin in Paris sharpened Rilke's perception of simple things, and made him exquisitely sensitive to their presence. In a letter from the Spanish city of Ronda he describes how he encountered a small, pregnant dog and how the exchange of a piece of sugar became in the next instant the sacred exchange of gift and acceptance: "the meaning and seriousness of our complete understanding were infinite." He continues: "this can only happen on earth, and it is really good to have gone through life willingly, even if insecure and guilty and completely unheroic. In the end it prepares you wonderfully for the divine conditions." (*RDE*: 73).

Archetype I: "floods of origins"

We have already seen how Jung connects the collective consciousness to the collective unconscious and its appearance through archetypal images. Archetypes, as we know them through dream-work and art, compensate personal attitudes and cultural habits. They are profoundly historical, even though they also have primordial and unchanging aspects. "There are as many archetypes as there are typical situations in life," Jung wrote:

> Endless repetition has engraved these experiences into our psychic constitution, not in the form of images filled with content, but at first only as forms without content, representing merely the possibility of a certain type of perception and action. When a situation occurs which corresponds to a given archetype, that archetype becomes activated and compulsiveness appears, which, like an instinctual drive, gains its way against all reason and will, or else produces a conflict of pathological dimensions, that is to say, a neurosis.
>
> (Jung 1936/37: 48)

Archetypes are possible forms of human experience and they represent typical situations in life. An archetypal image such as the angel appears with such force because it personifies an archetypal, primordial experience, but in a historically and culturally bound manifestation. Archetypes in this sense are not mere interior psychic events, but possible ways of perceiving and acting in the world. An archetypal image arises when the poet encounters a typical situation that has been encountered time and time again by human beings before him.

Jung's understanding of the archetype as a possible form of human experience opens up two paths for investigation. One path, the one Jung followed initially, is to explore the universe of images through personal dreams, myths, reveries, and psychopathologies. After his personal disintegration and the terrible visions of blood before the outbreak of the First

World War, Jung, in an attempt to understand the coincidence between his personal situation and humankind in general, made a decision: "Therefore my first obligation was to probe the depth of my own psyche. I made a beginning by writing down the fantasies which had come to me during my building game" (Jung 1962: 173). The other path, the one Rilke was forced to pursue and which is implied in the recognition of the situatedness of the archetype, was to explore, by means of archetypal images, the possibility of existing in a time where those images clash with the collective consciousness. Jung, in his later years, returned to this perspective as well, for unlike Rilke, who died in 1926, Jung was a witness to the definitive evils of the twentieth century and struggled to understand a collective consciousness capable of fascism and the atom bomb. His later works are suffused with the urgency of a prophetic voice, warning that if the powers of the collective unconscious are not brought into balance with our collective consciousness, the forces of evil that humankind has unleashed will destroy us (e.g. Jung 1957). Nevertheless, Jung's style of engaging his culture is always intensely personal and inward directed. Psychology meant for him the exploration of human nature, and he saw the resultant self-knowledge as the only way to persevere through the evil and confusion of the twentieth century.

Rilke struggled with these two paths as well. For a time he seriously considered undergoing psychoanalysis, but he finally decided against it since it was too person-centered and might damage his work (Simms 1989). Influenced by Lou Andreas-Salome and by his attendance at the Psychoanalytic Congress in Munich in 1913 (under the chairmanship of Carl Jung) Rilke explored the inner world of instinct and its images in the third elegy, which he wrote a short while later, and in the series of poems about Narcissus which were written a few weeks before the Congress. Rilke understood that mythological images can evoke the world of human passions. His *Third Elegy* is an attempt to capture the archetypal experience of a youth's first passion through the image of the "river-god of the blood," the "Neptune of the blood and his terrible trident": how the boy in his sleep falls into "the floods of origin in him" and becomes entangled in the "interior wilderness" of passions older than his single life. It speaks of an interior personal unconscious, but also collective images and processes that are evoked along with a personal experience. Following the personal, "human" path into the *Duino Elegies*, we could pursue an archetypal interpretation in a number of directions, following the images of the angels, the lovers, the dead, the animals and others and elucidating mythic parallels and amplifying the images through historic references. This would, in Jung's sense, reveal the eternal reappearance of the same archetypes, and imbue the *Duino Elegies* with the halo of primordial and timeless forces. But the turn toward this imaginary map of interiority is only a preliminary step in the conception of the *Duino Elegies*. Rilke's "thinking poetry," to adapt a phrase from Heidegger, is deeply aware of the cultural significance of the poet's vision. Rilke felt intensely that the *Duino Elegies* stood in direct relation to the collective consciousness of their time, and that his personal experience and suffering became a tool for moving into and through the destitution of our era. And so Rilke, throughout the elegies, mourns the vacuum that appears when the angel leaves and struggles to face the spiritual emptiness and find a way through it – for himself and for his times. The path goes through a recollection of human existence, and of qualities that are alien to the angel: of being embodied, of living with others, of dwelling in a particular time and place, of having a language, and of dying. But more than anything else it was Rilke's lifelong fascination with non-human beings such as things, animals, and landscapes that led him out of the interior world into a quest for a language of being that could speak of human being as a being related to the non-human, the non-self.

If the angel then is not a "true" religious metaphysical being, and if he is not an inner complex arising out of dreams or psychopathologies, perhaps we should explore the archetypal image of the angel as the "possibility of a certain type of perception and action" (Jung 1936/37: 48), that is as a figure that arises out of a particular encounter with the world.

Archetype II: contour of feeling – "a matter of locating oneself in the world"

At the end of 1912 Rilke visited the Spanish city of Toledo, which deeply touched and intensified his experience of a natural place. In a letter to friends Rilke describes Toledo as a city "of heaven and earth," a city which already reaches beyond the visible world:

> Here is something which already has the intensity of a work of art, even though I do not know which truth of the human soul comes into its finality here, into an existence, into a visibility about which you think that as it stands it must be the same for any goatherd and for God's angel.
>
> (*RDE* 1: 74)

In his diary he notes: "Nothing could teach you to bring the supra-sensory into representation as Toledo could, if you only accepted its influence. For the things there have the intensity of what is usually and daily not visible: the intensity of appearance" (*RDE* 1: 79). The same day he writes the poem "To the Angel" and he discusses El Greco's angels, which he sees everywhere in the painter's native city:

> Greco, driven by the condition of Toledo, introduced a heaven-interior, discovering up there heavenly mirror images of this world that are as different and as ordered in their way as the reflections of

> objects in water. His angel is no longer anthropomorphic like the animal in a fable, and also no longer the ornamental secret sign of the Byzantine kingdom of God. His being is more flowing, he is a river that goes through both kingdoms. Yes, what is water on the earth and in the atmosphere, that is the angel in the larger circle of the spirit: creek, dew, trough, fountain of soulful being.
>
> (*RDE*: 80)

There is much we could say about the implications of this passage for Rilke's larger work, and how parts of this description echo the early *Elegies*, but it might suffice here to focus on the recurrent appearance of the angel: once again the image of the angel appears in conjunction with a powerful landscape. And not just Rilke, but El Greco also experienced and painted the angel's epiphany. Rilke saw the intensity of this landscape's appearance as a promise and a calling to the heart's joy, as if things could move closer to human existence here, and as if the visible could reach the invisible and transcend itself. In the poem "To the Angel" (*RDE*: 78) the angel stands at the edge of our existence and reaches into realms that we cannot even fathom:

> Light placed at the rim, strong and silent:
> above, the night becomes more exact.
> But we spend ourselves in unenlightened
> hesitation working on your base.

We have seen before how an archetype breaks through into consciousness, but the phenomenology of the angel's appearance in Rilke's work points not toward the archetype as an interior event, but as a response to a landscape. The angel is *situated*, not just for Rilke, but also for the painter El Greco. The angel appears in situations where either a natural or a human landscape speaks of more than human production and evokes a realm of existence that goes beyond the visible. The feelings Rilke experiences, which can be characterized through his letters and poems as feelings of awe, joy, pleasure, and fear, come together in the metaphor of the angel. And like other great metaphors it holds much more than what can be spoken directly.

The feeling when faced with the landscape is not merely a categorized emotion or a sentimental self-indulgence. As Paul Ricoeur (1985: 69), puts it, feeling is "a matter of locating oneself in the world," and "each feeling delineates a manner of situating oneself, of orienting oneself within the world." The image or metaphor of the angel arises out of the landscape and takes its shape as a response to the "more" that cannot be spoken, but which resonates through the image. The inspiration Rilke received out of his landscapes assumes the form of the angel because a new possibility of being is delineated here. Through the angel Rilke perceives the world in a different way, and this vision changed the way he lived, long after he left Toledo.

In the months after Toledo the struggle with the angel became intensified as well. The poem "To the Angel" shows already how insufficient Rilke felt when confronted with angelic being:

> Ours is this: not to know the exit
> from the confusing inner demesne;
> you appear upon our barricades
> and shine upon them like the high mountains.
>
> Your pleasure is *above* our kingdom
> and we barely catch its rain
>
> (*DE*: 78)

The whole poem is already a turning away from the angel, a recognition that the possibility of being revealed through the image of the angel is not a human possibility. We can imagine the intensity of feeling that the angel feels when the boundaries of body, time, and space do not exist. We can follow Rilke's angel into the realm of the dead or up to the stars where he feels more intensely than we (*DE*: 9). But what stands in the way of our being is that we are embodied, that we are passing away, and that we love other human beings.

Rilke's work after Toledo went through confrontations with embodiment, love, and death, as we see from his poems, letters, and diaries. He struggled to find other images that could delineate a new "contour of feeling." When finally, after ten difficult years, the larger part of the *Duino Elegies* was completed within a few days, it was preceded by a new image, which, like the angel before it, came upon Rilke unsuspectingly and with surprising force: twenty-four *Sonnets to Orpheus* were written within two days. The healing image which replaced the grandeur and narcissism of the angel was the image of Orpheus, the mythical figure who intimately knew death, whose song made the trees weep, and who, as a poet, lent his voice to the visible things of the world to raise them into the invisible.

Through Orpheus Rilke recognized and accepted the challenge of a poet in destitute times: if consciousness is our burden, it is also our great gift and challenge; if language is our burden, it is also a great mystery and task; if death is our burden, it, too, is perhaps part of a greater design and something to be taken up willingly. The archetype of Orpheus transformed Rilke's understanding of reality, but Rilke also knew that Orpheus was not just a personal message. He was meant to compensate for the inadequacy and one-sidedness of present cultural attitudes. The archetype of Orpheus delineates a clearing for *poiesis* at the center of a technological world (*DE*: 499, *Sonnets to Orpheus*, XIX):

Like the shapes of clouds
the world changes quickly,
every completed thing falls
and returns to its ancient ground.

Above progress and change,
more wide and free,
remains your early song,
God with the lyre.

Suffering has not been understood,
love has not been learned
and what leaves us in death

is not unveiled.
Only the song over the land
blesses and celebrates.

The visible and the invisible

It would go beyond the scope of this chapter to trace in detail the symbolic shift away from the angel, which begins with the *Fourth Elegy* (Simms 1989). Let it suffice to say that the angel moves into the background and the figures of the lovers, the dead, the doll, the artiste, the animal and finally of the earth herself move to center stage, to be followed by the presence of Orpheus in the *Sonnets to Orpheus*. The *Seventh Elegy* is a direct refusal of the angelic as a model for the human: "Wooing, no longer be wooing the nature of your grown-up voice," and "Angel, even if I wooed you – you do not come. For my call is always filled with leaving. Against such strong current you cannot step."

The lesson of Toledo's angel is that the visible reaches toward the invisible, that its beauty and intensity are as real as the rock upon which the city is built. The *invisible* is a key term in Rilke's late poetry, and it arises out of his understanding of our times. In the past great feelings, like love, reverence, and awe were made visible through the things that human beings made. Temples, cathedrals, the sphinx, Chartre, and music went far beyond their human makers. They were our spaces, and they proudly reached up to where the angel stood: "How terribly large they must be, since thousands of years of our feeling cannot fill them" (*DE*: 7). But our time does not know spaces like this anymore, "And where one thing survives that once was prayed to, served, kneeled before – it holds itself, as it is, already up into the invisible" (*DE*: 7). The character of our times is that more and more things of value become invisible, to be replaced by objects that have no enduring effect on human beings, technological products that give no witness to the human lives that invented them. "The outside becomes less and less. Where once there was an enduring house, now a thought-up structure proposes itself, obliquely, and belonging completely to thinking as if it still stood in the brain" (*DE*: 7).

Our times, then, do not have a language anymore for expressing the invisible as it approaches us through experiences of the numinous in love, art, and religion. Rilke's fist resolution is to turn inward, and the word "*Herzinnenraum*," i.e. the heart's inner space, seems to delineate the place where human beings can still feel, imagine, and contain the numinous in a personal and private way. But with the *Ninth Elegy* Rilke breaks out of this restricted space, and the break happens with the final recognition of our difference from the angel: we are not here on earth to feel great feelings, for the angel is much better at it. What then is our destiny? Our destiny is to:

> Praise the world to the angel, not the unspeakable,
> for you cannot impress him with glorious feelings.
> You are a novice in the cosmos, where he feels all intensely.
> Therefore show him simple things: what was shaped from generation
> to generation and lives as one of ours next to the hand and in our glance.
> Tell him the things.
>
> (*DE*: 9)

Rilke's turn away from the angel and the expectation of the numinous as otherworldly is a return to the speakable, the visible, but so that it is revered and spoken and carried into the invisible.

> Earth, is this not what you want: to rise in us
> invisibly? – Is it not your dream
> to be invisible? – Earth! Invisible!
> What if not transformation is your urgent request?
>
> (*DE*: 9)

The "*Herzinnenraum*" becomes "*Weltinnenraum*," i.e. the inner space of the heart becomes the inner space of the world, and Rilke sees himself and humankind bound into the great relations of nature and what lies beyond. We have the ability to intensify the visible world through our care and we can speak the world of things, "but to speak so as the things themselves never deeply fathomed to be" (*DE*: 9). Death is no longer the end; it is the bond that binds us to all perishing things. It is also the possibility of applying our specifically human ability to symbolize the world, i.e. to make it invisible, and carry it with us wherever we go after our life on earth is over.

Rilke's turn away from the image of the angel signifies a shift in attitude. While the angel still contained traces of Christian mythology and in his grandeur was alienated from the human world, Rilke's insight in the later part of the *Duino Elegies* is that the transcendent and numinous are not closed in on themselves but that they are immanent in the world. The archetype of the angel gives way to the archetype of the earth as the mother of all existing things, and both are completed by the image of Orpheus: the invisible is now within the visible, rather than beyond it. Human beings through their perception and language, bear witness to the full possibility of existence of the Other, the non-self, and their task is to lend themselves to seeing and speaking the world.

Notes

1 All citations of Rilke's poetry and of other materials listed as German texts in the bibliography are my own translations.

2 The following works are cited as abbreviations:
RDE: Fulleborn, U. and Engel, M. (eds) (1980) *Rilkes Duineser Elegien*, Band 1 (Materialien), Frankfurt am Main: Suhrkamp Verlag.
DE: Rainer Maria Rilke (1966/1980) "*Duineser Elegien*" and "*Die Sonette an Orpheus*," in Werke, Band 1.2, Frankfurt am Main: Insel Verlag.

References

Freud, S. (1930) "Civilization and its discontents," in *The Standard Edition of the Complete Psychological Works of Sigmund Freud*, vol. XXI, London: Hogarth Press.

Friedrich, H. (1956) *Die Struktur der Modernen Lyrik*, Hamburg: Rowohlt Verlag.

Fulleborn, U. and Engel, M. (eds) (1980) *Rilkes Duineser Elegien*, (Erster Band, Selbstzeugnisse), Frankfurt am Main: Suhrkamp Verlag.

Gadamer, H. (1994) *Literature and Philosophy in Dialogue*, trans. R. Paslick, Albany: State University of New York Press.

Guardini, R. (1961) *Rilke's Duino Elegies*, trans K.G. Knight, Chicago: Henry Regnery Co.

Heidegger, M. (1971) "What are poets for?" in *Poetry, Language, Thought*, trans. A. Hofstadter, New York: Harper & Row.

Heller, E. (1959a) *The Artist's Journey into the Interior*, New York: Harcourt Brace Jovanovich

—— (1959b) *The Disinherited Mind*, New York: Meridian Books.

Jung, C.G. (1922) "On the relation of analytical psychology to poetry," *CW* 15.

—— (1936/37) "The concept of the collective unconscious," *CW* 9.i.

—— (1954) "The archetypes of the collective unconscious," *CW* 9.i.

—— (1957) "The undiscovered self," *CW* 10.

—— (1959) "Aion," *CW* 9.ii.

—— (1962) *Memories, Dreams, Reflections*, ed. A. Jaffe, New York: Random House.

Ricoeur, P. (1985) "The power of speech: science and poetry," *Philosophy Today*, Spring.

Rilke, R.M. (1950) *Briefe*, Frankfurt am Main: Insel Verlag.

—— (1966) "Duineser Elegien," in *Werke*, Frankfurt am Main: Insel Verlag.

Simms, E. (1989) "Angel and doll: Vicissitudes of Eros and Thanatos in Rilke's Duino Elegies," unpublished dissertation, University of Dallas.

EDITOR'S INTRODUCTION

It is probably fair to say that Jung's understanding of images reflected his re-presentational heritage in Cartesian epistemology: we do not see others, for instance, but mental images of others, and we do not see the archetypes but archetypal images. Image is for Jung the stuff of psyche. But especially in his later work, through the notions of *esse in anima* and *anima mundi*, Jung came to appreciate the profound sense in which images are not to be located in individual psychology, no matter how "deep" the archeology into "collective" regions of the mind. Nevertheless, as Sipiora argues, it is especially in Hillman's work that the image is more securely linked to the manner in which a world is presented (not re-presented). However, from the perspective of Heideggerian phenomenology, Hillman's work is still in need of an ontological ground in that most original occurence of presentation known as Being. The grounding of Hillman in Heidegger is not a one-way journey, however, as Sipiora uses Hillman's understanding of images to "psychologize" (Hillman's term) Heidegger's ontological analysis of Being.

We are aware that this is a difficult paper, especially for those not at all familiar with Heidegger. So let me encourage perseverence and good cheer: it is a profound meditation on the ontological significance of Hillman's work and a psychologically creative introduction to Heidegger's late thought. It might be helpful to point out that because Sipiora's paper is scholarly one can mistakenly feel that it is abstract whereas in fact it is profoundly concrete, to be read with an imaginative eye.

4

THE *ANIMA MUNDI* AND THE FOURFOLD

Hillman and Heidegger on the "idea" of the world

Michael P. Sipiora

> The individual presented himself in the therapy room of the nineteenth century, and during the twentieth, the patient suffering breakdown is the world itself.
>
> Sardello (1980: 1)

Psychologizing the idea of the world

In his seminal 1981 lecture, "*Anima Mundi*: The Return of the Soul to the World," Hillman (1992: 94) calls into question the Cartesian conception of reality "which generally operates throughout depth psychology." But this is nothing new for Hillman who has been a daunting critic of the subject–object, internal–external divisions advanced by both natural science and psychology. What is new in this essay is a shift, long in the making, in Hillman's thought. In his *magnum opus Re-Visioning Psychology*, Hillman (1975: 189) holds that "the path of depth psychology still remains the individual psyche." By the time of the "*Anima Mundi*" essay, Hillman (in paraphrase of the title of one of his later works) comes to the disturbing conclusion that we have had 100 years of depth psychology's tending to the individual soul and the world has become worse. Hillman attends to the breakdown of the world by directly calling into question the idea of the world.

> Ecology movements, futurism, feminism, urbanism, protest and disarmament, personal individuation cannot alone save the world from the catastrophe inherent in our very *idea* of the world. They require a cosmological vision that saves the phenomenon "world" itself, a move in soul that goes beyond measures of expediency to the

> archetypal source of our world's continuing peril: the fateful neglect, the repression, of the *anima mundi*.
>
> (1992: 126–7, emphasis added)

The notion of the *anima mundi* or world soul goes back at least to the cosmological myth told in Plato's *Timaeus*. From its beginning in myth, philosophical discussion of the *psyche tou pantos* moves through Stoicism, Middle Platonism and Gnosticism. This progression of ancient thought culminates, to a great degree, in the Neo-Platonism of Plotinus, one of the most influential proponents of the doctrine of the world-soul. The *anima mundi* reappears in the Renaissance Platonism of Ficino, the humanism of Bruno, and the new science of Vico. The world soul plays an important role in alchemy, particularly in the works of Paracelsus. It is to be found in the Cambridge Platonists, specifically Henry Moore, and in the nature philosophy of the Romantics. The dawning of the Enlightenment and the rise of purely mechanistic explanations of nature signaled the twilight of the world's soul. Banished to the realm of the primitive, the *anima mundi's* only safe haven in modern times has been poetry and the willing suspension of disbelief. (Compare Hillman's recital of the *anima mundi*'s lineage [1992: 127].)

The *anima mundi* is the locus of some of the most complex issues in ancient thought. Among the metaphysical, epistemological and theological problems raised are those regarding the origin of the cosmos, gradations of being, and the nature of knowledge and the reality of evil, as well as the relationship between souls or aspects there of (individual and cosmic). Invoking Ficino, Hillman is eager to evoke the rich Neo/Platonist heritage of the world soul. Yet just as quickly does he take his distance from the philosophical conundrums it provokes.

> Let us imagine the *anima mundi* neither above the world encircling it as a divine and remote emanation of the spirit, a world of powers, archetypes, and principles transcendent to things, nor within the world as its unifying panpsychic life-principle . . . Rather let us imagine the *anima mundi* as that particular soul-spark, that seminal image, which offers itself through each thing in its visible form . . . *anima mundi* indicates the animated possibilities presented by each event as it is . . . – in short its availability to imagination, its presence as a *psychic* reality.
>
> (1992: 101)

In all fairness to Hillman, recognition of the *anima mundi* has been implicit in nearly all of his work. In the traditions from which he draws, in the archetypal/Jungian framework he employs, in the poets he quotes lies the belief that "not only is the psyche in us as a set of dynamisms, but we are in the psyche" (1975: 134). Indeed, the world and soul are inseparable in the lines from Keats which are Hillman's motto: "Call the world if you please, The vale of Soul-making. Then you will find out the use of the world. . . ." (1975: ix). "The curative or salvational vision of archetypal psychology," he tells us, "focuses upon the soul in the world which is also the soul of the world (*anima mundi*)" (1983: 26). What Hillman makes explicit in his direct turn to the world is the need to articulate an idea, a vision of its soul.

Hillman has been both a severe critic of his field's poverty of ideas and a passionate advocate of a theoretically sophisticated psychology. The soul, he has argued, asks for vision . . . the psyche needs its ideas. The very dimension of soul that Hillman specifies as the deepening of events into experiences (1975: x), requires ideas. It is by means of ideas that we see-through events transforming them, deepening them into experiences. However, compared to the seminal articulations of imagining, pathologizing, psychologizing and soul-making provided in *Re-Visioning Psychology* (not to mention those of alchemy, the anima, puer, etc., presented elsewhere in Hillman's opus), the *anima mundi* was slow to receive its conceptual due.

"Something further is needed," Hillman acknowledged, "and I have known this for some time" (1989: 214). "The critical tradition of seeing through, of perspectivalism, of metaphorical ambiguity, of relativism and desubstantiation – my *via negativa* in the vale of soul-making – is necessary but not sufficient" (1989: 216). That something further needed, that something for which Hillman's *via negativa* is necessary but not sufficient is the impoverished vale, the neglected *anima mundi*, the world imperiled by the deprivation inherent in our neglect of its imagination. To imagine the world, to go beyond just seeing through, Hillman has attempted to re-vision metaphysics. He sees through static metaphysical postulating to cosmological envisioning, to psychological cosmology as *mythos* and metaphysical praxis as the aesthetic sensibility he calls the thought of the heart (1986, 1989). In addition to Ficino and the poets, it is Henry Corbin and Alfred North Whitehead who figure prominently in Hillman's aesthetic and cosmological musings. Rather than follow him in these musings, I wish to suggest an alternate path through metaphysics, the alternative of a phenomenological idea of the world.

Psychologizing and phenomenology

Just as one of the major contributions of archetypal psychology has been to keep the soul within psychology's discourse, that of phenomenology has been its philosophical articulation of the world and the worldly character of psychological experience. So it is that phenomenology, specifically that of Heidegger, can be of help in providing the sought for theoretical understanding of the *anima mundi*. Yet Hillman is no stranger to phenomenological thought, and his critique needs to be considered before we continue.

Phenomenology, in Hillman's critique, is a philosophical approach whose "what" question – what is it that something is? – while distinct from the "why" of natural scientific explanation, is different yet from the "what" of archetypal inquiry. Both archetypal and phenomenological psychologies answer the "what" question in terms of meaning. What something is, is understood in terms of how it matters. (This is yet again different from the "how" of practicality, for how something matters is itself a qualitative issue of significance or value, a matter of the difference the thing makes.) "Phenomenology stops short," writes Hillman, in that its articulation of essential structures fails to see-through these conceptualizations to their psychological ground in "fantasy images" (1975: 138). In Hillman's reading, phenomenological meaning, while definitely qualitative rather than quantitative, remains a cognitive affair that fails to "dissolve" its "what" into the animated "which" and personified "who" of archetypal fantasy images (1975: 139).

This brings us to another of the dimensions of the soul specified by Hillman: "by 'soul' I mean the imaginative possibility in our natures, the experiencing through reflective speculation, dream, image, and fantasy – that mode which recognizes all realities as primarily symbolic or metaphorical" (1975: x). "Seeing-through," as the primary work of psychology, is the seeing of any and all things *as* fantasy-images. "Fantasy-images are both the raw materials and finished products of psyche, and they are the privileged mode of access to knowledge of the soul" (Hillman 1975: xi). Without the move from concept to fantasy-image, phenomenology falls short of genuine knowledge of the soul. Thus while Hillman acknowledges that phenomenological psychologists "amplify and explore [situations] for significance much as Jungians do symbols" (1975: 147), he argues that theirs remains more a "metaphysical" than "psychological activity" (1975: 146).

We will take to heart the claim that seeing-through or psychologizing is the appropriate mode of thinking for psychology. "*Psychologizing*," writes Hillman, "*goes on whenever reflection takes place in terms other than those presented*" (1975: 135). Psychologizing is a movement into the depth of whatever presents itself at face value. It is a reflexive movement from literal to imaginative, from facts (as a specific kind of literalism) to fantasies. It is not, however, the move from the concrete to the abstract. Quite the opposite, it is the literal which is seen to be abstract, while the fantasy-image is always concrete.

Hillman's understanding of psychologizing has much in common with Heidegger's conception of hermeneutic phenomenology in *Being and Time* (1962). Phenomenology is the method which seeks, in the formal definition Heidegger provides: "to let that which shows itself [phenomena] be seen from itself [logos] in the very way it shows itself from itself" (1962: 58). Yet this formal definition does not get to the heart of the matter. It is precisely because phenomena are covered over in the way they show themselves, in the functionally oriented literalism of everyday encounters (what Hillman calls the daylight perspective of the ego), that phenomenology is necessary. Phenomenology seeks to uncover, to show forth (in the etymological sense of fantasy that Hillman refers [1975: 135]) what does not show itself in the everyday. "What is it that phenomenology is to 'let us see'?"

> Manifestly, it is something that proximally and for the most part does not show itself at all: it is something that lies hidden, in contrast to that which proximally and for the most part does show itself; but at the same time it is something that belongs to what thus shows itself, and it belongs to it so essentially as to constitute its meaning and ground.
>
> (Heidegger 1962: 59)

Here the apparent difference arises. While it is fantasy-images which are the hidden value to which Hillman appeals (1975: 140), it is the being of phenomena which Heidegger seeks. Yet Heidegger's questioning is not about being as if it were a thing – which it would be if his were a metaphysical project (– which it is not). It is about the meaning of being. Meaning, from the phenomenological perspective, is always hermeneutical. The very structure of meaning – a thing as something – involves the hermeneutical "as" of interpretation. If phenomenology stops short, as a mode of psychologizing, it is in the failure to recognize hermeneutic disclosure, meaning, as fantasy-image. To recognize the fantasy-image in phenomenology's understanding of the world – its idea of what "world" means – would be to a path to a theoretically sophisticated and genuinely psychological conception of the world's soul. What we will see is that, although not his intention (for his is the question of being and not soul), Heidegger has already traced such a path for us. The path runs from the structural articulation of worldhood of the world in *Being and Time* to the mytho-poetic "worlding of the world" in his later work.

The worldhood of the world

Like Hillman's *anima mundi*, Heidegger's conception of world, in *Being and Time*, is neither that of a collection of entities nor as the realm in which such entities are to be located. World is "that '*wherein*' a factical Dasein as such can be said to 'live'" (1962: 93). The world is not a physical container for Dasein as a kind of living "thing" but the referential context wherein which the human kind of being orients itself, encounters others and deals with things. World is the web of signifying relationships which allow phenomena to appear as the things which they are, signifying relationships which allow Dasein's concernful engagement. These signifying relationships – the "for-the-sake-of-which," the "in-order-to," the "in-which, and the "with-which"

(1962: 120) – constitute a contextual whole of primordial familiarity wherein Dasein always finds itself. The various "worlds" of experience – the work world, the sports or fashion worlds, the world of tribal ritual, etc. – are modalities of the structural totality Heidegger designates as the worldhood of the world. The "isness" of the world, its worldhood lies in its character as a "context of assignments or references" which Heidegger terms "significance" (1962: 121). Significance or "total meaningfulness" (Richardson, 1974: 57) is the weave of references which constitute the world as an orienting context for human concerns.

Dasein finds itself as immersed in differentiated worldly regions or contextual configurations. Dasein finds itself always already situated within the nearness of these regions. The "always already" quality of the world is of critical import for our inquiry. World is pregiven. We find ourselves as delivered over to an already existing context of references. The ultimate reference of the signifying relationships which configure significance – the structure of the world – is Dasein in its being its possibilities of relatedness. The "for-the-sake-of-which," the "in-order-to," the "in-which, and the "with-which" has as its ultimate "for the sake of" a possibility of Dasein. Refusing any subject–object spit between substances (which is a fundamental presupposition of natural science inquiry and causal explanation), we can recognize being-in-the-world as a unitary phenomena. The human kind of being is inherently worldly, and the world is always the human world.

The grasping of something *as* something – interpretation – has a fore-structure, a way of taking the thing in advance which guides the grasping. Never a presupposition-less description, interpretation grasps the thing as what it is in terms of pregiven significance. This grasping is not a process of conscious cognition but a prethematic, concrete engagement. "The primordial 'as' of an interpretation . . . which understands circumspectively we call the "existential-*hermeneutical* 'as' . . .," (Heidegger 1962: 201). What gets understood in interpretation is the "isness" or being of the thing. What the "isness" is understood "as," or in terms of, is meaning. "Meaning is the 'upon-which' of a projection in terms of which something becomes intelligible as something; it gets its structure from a fore-having, a fore-sight, and a fore-conception" (Heidegger 1962: 193).

Structurally, meaning is inherently connected to significance as the basis of the world. That which is had, sighted, and conceived before hand in any interpretation is significance. Significance, as the worldhood of the world, is the context in which things can be meaningful or meaningless.[1]

The world must be understood as a pregiven, referential context of involvement and intelligibility with which we are implicitly familiar and which situates us in our average everydayness. World, as a matter of meaning, is the "wherein" of human dwelling. The idea of the worldhood of the world, as a weave of references in terms of which phenomena are encountered as whatever they may be, is a structural conception. Such conceptualization deepens our understanding of world in that it allows us to see the world in a manner that transcends literal interpretation, goes beyond the everyday conception of a collection of inanimate things. As J. H. van den Berg remarks, "Most essential in phenomenology is that the nature and characteristics of human existence are to be found . . . by studying and describing [the person's] world" (1987: 8). Phenomenological amplification of significance, which we have heard Hillman note to be similar to Jungian work with symbols, discloses a world of experience. However, we have also heard Hillman suggest that Heideggerian phenomenology remains a "metaphysical activity": it fails to move from "conceptualized situations" to "personified processes" (1975: 147). What is needed is to "dissolve" its "what" (the world as structure) into the animated "which" and personified "who" of fantasy images (1975: 139).

World as fourfold

Like that of Hillman, there is a turn in the path of Heidegger's thinking. In simplified terms, the "turn" (*Kehre*) in Heidegger's thought is from a thinking of being from out of the openness of being-in-the-world to a thinking of the openness of being-in-the-world from out of the clearing of being. The "turn" is a shift in the direction of thought from Dasein to *Sein*. As Heidegger himself writes in his "Letter on humanism": "This turning is not a change of standpoint from *Being and Time*, but in it the thinking that was sought first arrives at the location of that dimension out of which *Being and Time* is experienced" (1977a: 206). Dasein is the dimension out of which the analytic of existence is experienced; *Sein* is the location of that dimension.

Sein (being) in Heidegger's thought is not the being of metaphysics. Heidegger continually uses alternative spellings of *Sein* (*Seyn*), alternative expressions for being (the Clearing [*Lichtung*]), and even goes so far as to cross out the word (~~*Sein*~~) in order to stress that he is attempting to reach what has remained unthought in the metaphysical tradition. Heidegger's crossing out of *Sein* is more than a negation of a metaphysical concept. "It further indicates," writes Heidegger, "the Four directions of the Fourfold [*Geviert*] and their assemblage at the place of crossing" (1958: 83). The Fourfold is comprised of earth, heavens, mortals, and divinities. Their assemblage, as we shall see, happens in things and the place of their crossing is the world. In short, ~~*Sein*~~ means world as the presence of the Fourfold as it is gathered by things. We can take the Fourfold as a way of disclosing the presencing of the world, a way of imagining the deepening of events into experiences, a way of psychologizing the worldhood of the world. The very notion of ~~*Sein*~~ is mythic. "Myth," according to Heidegger,

> means the telling word. For the Greeks to tell is to lay bare and to make appear – both the appearance and that which is present in the

> coming to appearance, in the epiphany. *Mythos* is that which becomes present in its telling, namely, that which appears in the unconcealedness of its claim. For all human beings *mythos* makes the claim which is in advance of all others and which is most fundamental. It is the claim which permits thought about that which appears, that which becomes present.
>
> (1968: 10)

~~Sein~~ is a *mythos*: a telling word which makes a fundamental claim. ~~Sein~~ claims the world as the presencing of mortals, gods, earth, and sky. This claim brings the world into unconcealedness; it marks the epiphany of the world as world. ~~Sein~~ as the polyvalent presencing of the Fourfold is an image, not an explanation of the fundamental nature of the world. Heidegger warns us that "As soon as human cognition here calls for an explanation, it fails to transcend the world's nature, and falls short of it" (1971a: 180). Myth, by virtue of its presentation rather than explanation of that which appears, can reach to the heart of the world's presencing and bring that presence to disclosure in a play of images.

Heidegger remarks that, "Thought has scarcely touched upon the essence of the mythical, especially with regard to the fact that *mythos* is the saying, . . . the calling bringing-into-presence" (1975: 94). ~~Sein~~, in its extreme interpretation as a leap out of the metaphysical tradition, is a *mythos*, a calling bringing-into-presence of the world as the assemblage of the Fourfold. The Four moments of this gathering – earth, heaven, mortals, and divinities – are given as figures to be seen through, fantasy or images, not as concepts with which to manipulate thought.

~~Sein~~ coming forth into unconcealment as the Fourfold is an image of what Heidegger calls *Ereignis*, the Event of Appropriation.[2] Lest we misconstrue *Ereignis* as a factual occurrence set in linear time, we need to appreciate the character of the formulation Heidegger is advocating. *Ereignis* is a relational and dynamic understanding as opposed to a reified and static concept. It is an imaging of the origin of Dasein as continuously occurring, concurring with the advent of the world. It is not a primal origin, set once upon a time, but the perpetual happening of Dasein's being called into its existing, its being called upon to be. Being, as understood in *Ereignis* is no-thing, not a thing whose presence Dasein is set upon revealing. Instead it is the dynamic coming-into-presence which sets forth any and all things as present before us, the coming-into-presence which prevails upon us to preserve what has been presented. The Event gives us not a metaphysics of presence, but a mystery whose unfolding is the heart of our existing.

~~Sein~~ is an imaging of psychological life, Jung's "*esse in anima*" (quoted in Hillman 1989: 217), as originating in the disclosive appropriation of earth and sky, mortals and divinities. ~~Sein~~, the myth of the Event, tells of psychological life as a reality of reflection lived in and through the world. The meaning of experience, the deepening of events into experiences, resides in the reflective mirroring of gods, mortals, earth and sky. Phenomenological psychologizing, if it is to follow the path marked out by Heidegger's later thought, is led to the mythic configuration of the Fourfold as a showing forth, a fantasy-image of psychological life.

The fourfold as psychological configuration

In the text in which he makes clear that ~~Sein~~ can "not merely be a negative symbol of crossing out," that it as well points to the Fourfold, Heidegger refers his readers to the essays collected in *Vorträge* and *Aufsätze*. Among the English translations of these essays are "Building, dwelling, thinking," "The thing," and ". . . Poetically man dwells . . . ." Not surprisingly, earlier mention of earth, sky, mortals, and divinities are to be found in Heidegger's discussions of poetry and or art in general, and to a lesser extent in a small number of poetic reflections, like "*The Pathway*." Most of these discussions show the direct influence of poets such as Hölderlin, Rilke, George and Trakl.

In addition to its mythical nature, what must also be taken into consideration in any attempt to interpret the Fourfold is that it is a poetically inspired imagining. In the essay ". . . Poetically man dwells . . . ," Heidegger remarks that "poetic images are imaginings in a distinctive sense: not mere fancies and illusions but imaginings that are visible inclusions of the alien in the sight of the familiar." Earlier in the same passage Heidegger tells us that the image lets "the invisible be seen." The Fourfold lets invisible being be seen in the polyvalent presencing of ~~Sein~~. This kind of imagining, as Heidegger says of poetic images, is a taking of the "mysterious measure" of human dwelling (1971b: 226). The Four regions of ~~Sein~~ are the measure of the world, they bring the world to presence as the world.

Joseph Kockelmans reminds us:

> The term *Fourfold* as well as the Four terms *heaven*, *earth*, *gods*, and *mortals* must be understood as being ontological in character; thus all semblance not withstanding, they do not refer to ontic things, nor do they divide the totality of all ontic things into Four basic sets of things.
>
> (1984: 95)

The Fourfold, as an image, is not a representation of anything but rather a way of seeing every-thing such that the world comes to presence in it. One sees through the image of the Fourfold to envision the hidden dynamic which is the Event of the world. This hidden dynamic which the Fourfold brings before our eyes is what Heidegger calls the "worlding of the world" (1971a: 179). Far from being a static picture, the Fourfold is a vision of the active con-figuring of earth, heaven, mortals, and the divinities which is embodied in historically varying constellations.

Phenomenological psychologizing takes up the Fourfold as a form of what Greek sophism understood as *fantasia*. According to Heidegger: "In unconcealment *fantasia* comes to pass: the coming-into-appearance, as a particular something, of that which presences – for man, who himself presences toward what appears" (1977b: 147). Imagination (in the sense of *fantasia*) and myth originate in the belonging together of the disclosedness of being and Dasein's revealing, rather than the metaphysical project of obtaining objective certainty. Heidegger writes of this kind of revealing: "The apprehending of that which presences, within whose unconcealment apprehending itself belongs, belongs indeed as a unique kind of presencing toward that which presences that is unconcealed" (1977b: 149). Phenomenological psychologizing attempts to provide the ideas/fantasy-images for a non-metaphysical psychology by attending to the Fourfold presencing of earth, sky, mortals and divinities as a "self-unconcealing" (1977b: 149) of psychological life, a way in which the *anima mundi* calls to be imagined.

In the essay, "The thing," Heidegger sees through the image of the Fourfold to present the thingness of a jug. The Fourfold allows for the articulation of an earthen jug as the thing which it is. The vital, animate presence of the thing is brought forth, thus enabling the recognition of the jug as gathering a world. Heidegger shows us both that the essence of a thing is revealed in its bringing earth and heaven, mortals and divinities together, and that the disclosure of the Fourfold comes to pass in what he terms the "thinging of the thing" (1971a: 180).

The jug, made from the clay of the earth, holds the wine yielded from the grapes, which in turn have been grown from the soil and nurtured by the sun and rain from the heavens. The wine provides enjoyment for the mortals who partake of it. The gods are honored in the liberation poured in their names. The jug, in its thingness, evokes the presencing of each of the Four. As a matrix, or even better said, a vortex of interilluminating presences, the jug gathers a world.

Only within a world, a referential context of concerns, can the jug be seen as a specific thing. Envisioning the jug through the image of the Fourfold gives us the Event of the world as happening in the concrete event of an earthen vessel. An event in the world becomes the meaningful experience of a world. The image of the Fourfold allows us to recognize the jug as conditioning, "bethinging" us."This," as Heidegger explains, "now means things, each in its own time, literally visit mortals with a world . . . . Things bear world" (1971c: 200, 202). Hillman tells of things laying bare the soul of the world in the lure of Aphrodictic beauty (1992: 63). Heidegger's jug gathers a shining world in which earth and sky bestow their favors on the labor of mortals and the gods are well disposed to human offerings.

In order to grasp how things bring a world into being, we can amplify the presence of the Fourfold's regions. Attention to each of the Four brings the world into clearer relief thus allowing us to explore its nearness. It should not surprise us that in doing so we find ourselves within that domain marked out by the "fence-poles" Hillman uses to set down his idea of the soul: the deepening of events into experiences and the primacy of metaphorical reality already mentioned, as well as "the significance soul makes possible, whether in love or in religious experience, which derives from its special *relation with death*" (1975: x).

Earth is the hiddenness from which things arise, and it is as well the concealment which accompanies all unconcealment. All attempts at peering within the earth, whether the unlocking of the secrets of geological activity or the splitting of hydrogen atoms, are "successful" only insofar as they bring these phenomena into the daylight of rational, empirical inspection. The earth itself, the blanket of concealment, as Heidegger writes, "spreading out in rock and water" (1971d: 149) remains poised within itself, unexposed to inspection and calculation. "Rising up into plant and animal," the earth makes its appearance in the "blossoming and fruiting" (1971d: 149) which preserve its impenetrability, while in the same moment bringing forth the inexhaustible wonders of its preserve. Earth is the unseen depth, the primordial origin from which things come and to which they are called to return. Earth is the flow of that which gushes out into unconcealment. Earth is as well the elemental presence and persistence of things which keeps them rooted in an unfathomable darkness yet simultaneously exerts the vitality of self-generation and perpetuation. Heidegger refers to earth as the "serving bearer" and the " building bearer" which "tends" and "nourishes." (1971d: 149 and 1971a: 178). While not to be simplistically identified as a principle of growth, earth is what drives things to burst forth and unfold themselves in the face of the sky. Earth is too like gravity, a pull to origins, an attachment to the solidity of the ground which supports us. Earth is all that which under-stands us in a fundamental, foundational mode – the home ground of mortal being.

Simply put, heaven is that which is above the earth. As Heidegger writes, " 'on earth' already means 'under the sky'." "The sun's path, the course of the moon, the glitter of the stars. . . . The drifting clouds and the blue depth of the ether," these celestial phenomena are what Heidegger means by the sky or heavens. "The year's seasons and their changes, the light and dusk of the day, the gloom and glow of the night, and the clemency and inclemency of the weather" are also to be included (1971d: 149).

The heavens, traditionally imagined as the realm of transcendence, are the open region in which whatever has come out of concealment can shine forth. The sky is the atmosphere in which the things of earth can reach beyond themselves and run their cycles of growth and decay. Heaven is the inviting warmth of the sun's bright shining as well as the chilling fall of a dark night's rain. The heavens threaten and rebuke, calm and console. Time is given by the movement of the heavens. The sky seems always to speak to us of time and place, early or late, far or near. The paths of sun and moon mete out the passing of the day, the coming of night, and the changing of the seasons. Out of the unknowable heights of the heavens the gods either come or fail to appear. Our upward gaze encounters the sky as a height which reaches down to touch the earth at the same time it rises up from the earth to the mysterious recesses of deep space.[3]

"The divinities," who either appear or fail to appear from out of the firmament, "are the beckoning messengers of the godhead." The godhead is the Holy, that which is removed "from any comparison with beings that are present" (1971a: 178). The gods, on the other hand, are part of the world we experience. Thus immanent in the world, the divinities mediate between transcendent Holiness and mortals on earth. This mediation, which constitutes the essence of the divinities, is the presence of the "wholly other" as we experience it within the horizons of our living.

Influenced by Hölderlin's perception of the gods' withdrawal, Heidegger directs our attention to the divine presence today as a "no-longer" which is "itself a not-yet of the veiled arrival of [the divine's] inexhaustible nature" (1971a: 184). While not identical to the Greek gods, it is nevertheless these gods which most shape the figure of the divinities as they are given in the Fourfold. Grecian deities are neither unnatural nor miraculous. Like the mortals in whose lives they intercede, these gods are a presence within the world rather than a violation of it. Or, better described, the Greek gods can be understood as modes of the world's presence. "The visage of each true god," according to mythologist Walter Otto, "is a visage of a world" (1981: 136). The gods are faces, personalities which can be recognized in the world's appearances. Dwelling in the world, the mortals of Greek myth felt the touch of the divine, the hand of powers greater than their own. In the modern world, the mortals of the Fourfold experience the divine as an absence before which they "can neither pray nor sacrifice . . . can neither fall to [their] knee[s] in awe nor can [they] play music and dance" (Heidegger 1969: 72).

Human beings, as part of the Fourfold, are called mortals "-not because their earthly life comes to an end, but because they are capable of death as death" (1971a: 178). The mortality of human being-in-the-world is a central theme in Heidegger's *Being and Time*. Death stands as an ever-present possibility for human beings. It is the extreme revelation of our being because it is the possibility of not having any more possibilities. Death does not come to us as a realized actuality but always remains with us as the experience of having Nothing as a possibility.

"Death", we are told in the essay "The thing," is the shrine of Nothing, that is, of that which in every respect is never something that merely exists, but which nevertheless presences, even as the mystery of Being itself" (1971a: 178). The death of a mortal is, for that person who dies, never an event occurring within the world. When the person dies, the world is Nothing.

Death is the shrine of the Nothing because in experiencing death as an unactualizable possibility within the world, mortals acknowledge the world – ~~Sein~~ – as No-thing. The ontological difference between being and beings is disclosed in this experience. World happens in the coming to pass, the Event, of the Difference. In their devotion to the shrine of Nothing, which is their potential for dwelling with death as their ownmost possibility, human beings are delivered over to the disposition of ~~Sein~~. From out of the Event of ~~Sein~~ human beings appear as mortals within the gathering of the earth, sky, and divinities.

The quadrants of ~~Sein~~, the regions of the Fourfold, belong together in a simple oneness which is the worlding of the world. Heaven, earth, mortals, and divinities are joined in a mutual mirroring which expropriates each to the other while at the same time appropriating each to its own uniqueness. "Each of the Four mirrors in its own way the presence of the others" (Heidegger 1971a: 179). In that mirroring, earth, mortals, and divinities are given back to themselves as figures reflected in the presence of the others. For example, the figuring of mortals, in the presence of the other three is a freeing of mortals to themselves. The essence of being human is lighted-up, made visible to mortal eyes in the reflection of a figure on the earth, beneath the heavens, awaiting the divinities.

At the same moment that the "appropriating mirroring" of the Four is a reflection which grants to each its nature it also binds them to one another. The essence of heaven and earth, mortals and immortals is expropriated from each to the simple unity of the Four. So, as Heidegger asserts, "Whenever we say mortals, we are then thinking of the other three along with them by way of the simple oneness of the Four." The reflection which brings each of the Four to themselves also binds them "into the simplicity of their essential being toward one another" (1971a: 179).

Both bound and freed by their gathering, the Four belong together as the presencing of the world. "This expropriative appropriating is the mirror-play of the Fourfold" (1971a: 179). The mirror-play is thus the presencing of the world, what Heidegger calls its "worlding." The worlding of the world is ~~Sein~~. In it the simple onefold on the world presents itself as the polyvalent presencing of the Four.

In addition to naming it as the Event, Heidegger describes the worlding of the world in several ways. He calls it the "round dance of appropriating" (1971a: 180) in order to draw attention to the fluid, playful, and dynamic nature of the gathering of the Four. He also refers to this gathering as the "ringing." The presence of the mirror-play of the world is a joining which has the qualities of being "nestling, malleable, pliant, compliant, nimble – in Old German these are called *ring* and *gering*" (1971a: 180). In all of his characterizations of the gathering of the Fourfold, Heidegger conveys the mythic, elusive character of the world's worlding and its generative as opposed to derivative status.

The worlding of the world is the happening of meaning, the deepening of events into experiences. Contrary to Hillman's misconception of the phenomenological understanding of meaning as a cognitive phenomenon, meaning as the grant of world's worlding, is precisely the "appreciation of the inherent intelligibility given in the qualitative patterns of events" which he himself calls the "aesthetic response" appropriate to the appearance of the *anima mundi* (1992: 12). The Event of Appropriation renders the world as meaningful, a meaningfulness which is measured out by the quadrants of the world's being. "Though I cannot identify soul with anything else," writes Hillman, "I also can never grasp it by itself apart from other things, perhaps because it is like a reflection in a flowing mirror . . ." (1975: x). The mirror-play of earth, sky, mortals and divinities – which plays through things – grants the reality of reflection which is the soul of the world.

World and things

Things lie at the heart of ~~Sein~~ for they turn the Four toward each other and draw earth, sky, mortals and immortals together. In things, the Fourfold comes to appearance. The thing's dynamic presentation of the Four regions of ~~Sein~~ is the worlding of the world. In Heidegger's words, "The thing stays – gathers and unites – the Fourfold. Each thing stays the Fourfold into a happening of the simple onehood of the world" (1971a: 181). As we have already seen with the example of the jug, things gather heaven and earth, mortals and divinities in such a binding way that they manifest a world. "Things bear world." They give birth to the world in assembling the Four. The world, in turn, "grants to things their presence" (1971c: 202). The world's coming to presence is provoked by things, and things are invoked by the world's appearance. World and things belong together in the round dance of Appropriation. In the ringing of the Fourfold, world and thing are "disclosingly appropriated" (1971c: 203) each to the other such that the presencing of one is simultaneously the appearance of the other.

The modes of presence in which the Fourfold, the Event of the world, gives itself to be revealed is what founds history. History, for Heidegger, is the mittence (*Geschick*), the destining ordained by the presence of the Fourfold. Historical epochs have their source in the coming to presence of things as gatherings of the Fourfold and are to be understood in terms of the multiple images in which the Fourfold prevails.

Our time, a time whose name changes even more quickly than the span of a generation – atomic age, nuclear age, space age, computer age, etc. – presents a unique constellation of the Fourfold. The gods have most certainly withdrawn and so long ago that even our memory of them begins to fade. The heavens and the earth have both been forsaken. The dimension in which mortals have their stay is no longer marked out by the open distance between the "deep blue of the ether" and the sheltering of the earth. Instead that dimension is surrounded by exploitable resources of liquid, solid and vaporous constitution. The outward expanse of the firmament has been replaced by calculable, quantifiable, conquerable reaches of outer space. Even the paths of sun and moon, the cycles of rain and heat, night and day are but factors in calculations which transform their very premises. Earth is treated like dirt, as energy source and garbage dump, pretty garden or nasty mess of long-dead animal matter. Even before the jungle perimeter falls to the gnawing approach of the tractor and bulldozer, the earth has been forced to yield up for consumption the jungle's thingly character – its ability to gather and stay the presencing of a world. And what of mortals? They too have disappeared like the earth they stood upon. Human resources, consumers, workers, and video viewers have replaced those who once figured as mortal men and women. The dis-ease in such enframement is testified to by the patients we encounter in our consulting rooms (Hillman 1992: 92).

This constellation of the Four – which sounds a lot like the ugly (1992: 59), dead world devoid of soul lamented by Hillman – is held by what Heidegger terms the Enframing (*Gestell*) (1977c). The Enframing is the name for the predominance of the technological perspective. "Technology" is not meant in this usage to refer to merely any or even all technological devices and their accompanying uses. Rather, technology is to be understood as a presence of being in which everything is revealed as "standing-reserve." Everything is disclosed as a resource to be used at will, to be stockpiled or exploited as dictated by the need of further technological development. Technology is an ordering of the world, a way in which the world is present to us and revealed by us, before it is ever expressed in any mechanical devices.

The Enframing, the technological disclosure of that which is, is the obliteration of the Fourfold, and the therefore, as Heidegger asserts, "the denial of the world, in the form of the injurious neglect of the thing" (1977c: 48–9). This neglect is no mere passing over, or disregard which ignores things. Quite to the contrary. It is a determination of everything as a resource, a regarding of things as means to an end which in turn become another end in a never-ending chain of activity that defies human control. The neglect of things is injurious in its disallowance of things' essential nature as the bringing forth and binding of heaven and earth, mortals and divinities. The usefulness of things, in the pursuit of the continually unfolding designs of technology, obscures their thingness. The world which the thing draws near in gathering the Four is passed over, ignored, denied in the rule of the Enframing.

Here in lies "the repression of the *anima mundi*" with which we began. An injurious neglect of things, a "fateful neglect" of the world's soul which Hillman sees as latent in our impoverished idea of the world, a poverty of thought to which Heidegger tends. The "idea" of the world "that goes beyond the measures of expediency," the mythopoetic image of the Fourfold we have traced in Heidegger offers the kind of "cosmological vision that," in Hillman's hope, "saves the phenomena 'world' itself." Such hope anticipates the miracle of ensouled dwelling.

Notes

1 In that significance has as its "for-the-sake-of" a potentiality of the human kind of being, it is being-in-the-world, not things, which is meaningful. Dasein's grasp of significance is the basis for its understanding comportment toward itself, others, and things. It is in terms of world or total meaningfulness that particular phenomena are sighted as the very things which they are. World, in this way, grants phenomena their meaningfulness for the human kind of being. Human meaning, and there can be no other kind, is always a matter of the world. Indeed, meaning is the very matter of the world. How things matter is what the world means. Things are meaningful only in their encounterability for being-in-the-world. Meanings change when the significance of the world changes. Such changes are historical in nature – world historical changes which bring significant shifts in human meaning. Indeed, the very meaning of the human changes.

2 *Ereignis* is the ongoing happening of Dasein as the realm of the presencing of being. In *Ereignis*, being and human beings are mutually appropriated in that the "there" of Dasein's disclosive engagement is granted by the presencing of being, just as Dasein's disclosive engagement preserves the "there" of being among beings. In Medard Boss' words: "*Ereignis* is the invisible unity of the appeal of Being and of Dasein's response to this appeal" (1988: 61).

3 The descriptions given of earth and sky appear as poetic renderings of physical nature. Heidegger's understanding of nature is based on the Greek notion of physis. According to Heidegger:

> The Greeks did not learn that *physis* is through natural phenomena but the other way around: it was through a fundamental poetic and intellectual experience of being that they discovered what they had called physis.
>
> (1961: 12)

Physis is not any particular being, nor is it any specified set of observable phenomena. Rather, *physis* is the spontaneous coming forth and abiding presence of all and any thing to lie before us in the unconcealment. "*Physis*," writes Heidegger, "means the power that emerges and the enduring realm under its sway" (1961: 12). This enduring realm is the distance between heaven and earth, the open region in which mortals dwell.

References

Boss, M. (1988) "Recent considerations in Daseinsanalysis," in E. Craig (ed.), *Psychotherapy for Freedom: a Special Issue of the Humanistic Psychologist*, 16,1: 58–74.

Heidegger, M. (1958) "The Question of Being," trans. W. Kluback and J. Wilde, New Haven, CT: College and University Press.

—— (1961) *An Introduction to Metaphysics*, trans. R. Manheim, Garden City, NY: Doubleday.

—— (1962) *Being and Time*, trans. J. Macquarrie and E. Robinson, New York: Harper and Row.

—— (1968) *What Is Called Thinking?*, trans. J.G. Gray, New York: Harper and Row.

—— (1969) *Identity and Difference*, trans. J. Stambaugh, New York: Harper and Row.

—— (1971a) "The thing," in *Poetry, Language, Thought*, trans. A. Hofstadter, New York: Harper and Row.

—— (1971b) ". . . Poetically man dwells . . .," in *Poetry, Language, Thought*, (op. cit.).

—— (1971c) "Language," in *Poetry, Language, Thought*, (op.cit.).

—— (1971d) "Building dwelling thinking," in *Poetry, Language, Thought*, (op.cit.).

—— (1975) "Moira," in *Early Greek Thinking*, trans. D.F. Krell and F. A. Capuzzi, New York: Harper and Row.

—— (1977a) "Letter on humanism," trans. F.A. Capuzzi and J.G. Gray, in D. F. Krell (ed.), *Martin Heidegger's Basic Writings*, New York: Harper and Row.

—— (1977b) "The Age of the World Picture," in *The Question Concerning Technology and Other Essays*, trans. W. Lovitt, New York: Harper and Row.

—— (1977c) "The question concerning technology," in *The Question Concerning Technology and Other Essays*, (op. cit.).

Hillman, J. (1975) *Re-Visioning Psychology*, New York: Harper and Row.

—— (1983) *Archetypal Psychology: A Brief Account*, Dallas: Spring Publications.

—— (1986) "Cosmology for soul: From universe to cosmos," in *Cosmos-Life-Religion: Beyond Humanism*, Nara: Tenri University Press, 1988.

—— (1989) "Back to beyond: On cosmology," in D. Griffin (ed.), *Archetypal Process: Self and Divine in Whitehead, Jung, and Hillman*, Evanston: Northwestern University Press.

—— (1992) *The Thought of the Heart and Soul of the World*, Dallas: Spring Publications.

Kockelmans, J. (1984) *On the Truth of Being: Reflections On Heidegger's Later Philosophy*, Bloomington: Indiana University Press.

Otto, W. (1981) *Dionysus: Myth and Cult*, trans. R. Palmer, Dallas: Spring Publications.

Richardson, W. J. (1974) *Heidegger; Through Phenomenology to Thought*, The Hague, Netherlands: M. Nijhoff.

Sardello, R. (1980) "From the editor," in *Dragonflies: Studies in Imaginal Psychology*, Winter.

Van den Berg, J. H. (1987) "The rise and fall of the medical model in psychiatry: a phenomenological analysis," in *Psychiatry and Phenomenology*, Pittsburgh: The Simon Silverman Phenomenology Center.

EDITOR'S INTRODUCTION

Existential phenomenology has always insisted that the place of experience is the world in which experience happens, the "life-world," and that this place of experience should not be conceptually transposed, following Descartes, into another place called "mind." For a Jungian analyst with a phenomenological sensibility this means that the term "psychological" refers to a *dimension* of experience rather than to a quasi-substantive, interiorized place called "the psyche." Jungian psychotherapists are especially sensitive to the "symbolic" dimensions of our experience of things: to the way in which things "presence" themselves to us as the materiality of our psychological lives. However, whereas other papers in this volume have addressed this issue in general terms, Ron Schenk has taken up the specific issue of television and television-watching. He discovers there – in the rituals, hypnotic viewing, and addictions to TV, in the bizarre delusions of schizophrenics, and even in television's history and physics – some of the longings of the human spirit. Just as the psychotherapist looks for the archetypal *telos* in an individual's suffering, Schenk imaginatively uncovers the "calling" in this magical phenomenon of late modernity.

5

SPIRIT IN THE TUBE

The life of television

Ronald Schenk

The soul of culture

At the time of the invention of television in the early 1920s, the materialist and positivist values of modernism had achieved their zenith. Subjective consciousness lay "within" the mind and the outer, observable world presented itself as something inanimate – to be measured, controlled, or consumed. "Reality" was that which was material, public, external and objectively measurable. The predominant mode of consciousness was rationalism, and "spirit" was consigned to esoteric group movements such as spiritism.

This state of collective consciousness led many pioneer thinkers of the time to consider the crisis of modern man as being one of the spirit. Carl Jung said that the decisive question for the contemporary individual is whether or not he or she is related to something infinite. Modern "man", in his striving for control and certainty, had forgotten a spiritual aspect of the psyche which Jung located in what he called the unknown, "interior" personality or the "unconscious." Consequently, modern man lived a waking death amidst what T. S. Eliot called a "heap of broken images," images which Jung saw in the form of myths and symbols concealed in the "inner life" of dreams and fantasies. These myths and symbols, when revealed through analysis, served to unify conscious with unconscious, matter with spirit, and the visible with the invisible, giving a sense of "wholeness" to experience. In other words, Jung's heroic thrust was to stake out ground for "the reality of the psyche," unifying the psyche's disparate aspects into a totality by delving with the light of consciousness into the dark, "inner world" of the unconscious personality.

Jung's vision, while focusing on "wholeness," still emanated from the ground of modernism, leaving the world as "outer" and inanimate. In so far as he emphasized a concealed interior personality as the dwelling place for symbolic life, he maintained the subjectivist split between inner and outer. This mode of thinking, founded on a dualism that interiorizes inherent life or "soul" and externalizes the world as culture, technology and nature, is actually an adaptation to a fractured collective consciousness. Culture is seen as "impacting" analysis which, in turn, is considered as the true agent of change. Cultural factors are imagined as influences on the "psychological development," "dynamics," and "identity" of the individual as interior being. Psychological life is "within" the individual, with the forces of a dead, material world impinging from "without." Culture and psyche are opposed, and "care of the soul," or psychotherapy, is an "inner" work which affects the "outer" world.

From a different perspective, Jung considered soul to exist prior to notions of within and without. From this position he declared, "psyche is simply 'world'" (Jung 1940: 173). The ideas that psyche does not recognize the distinctions of "within" and "without" and that the world is alive, follow in the tradition of *anima mundi* held by native cultures, ancient Greeks, the alchemists of the Middle Ages, and the neoplatonists of the Renaissance. *Anima mundi* or the soul of the world is that life which emanates through all perceptible forms. The natural world and the world of technology, as well as the world of dreams and fantasies, have a life of their own. Things of the world show forth their face in their appearance, and in doing so, reveal their depth. Divinity is at work in the machine as well as in the dream.

If we follow the spirit of Jung which was to see soul at work in the dark places of consciousness, and if we now see that psychology harbors a blind spot in relation to the soul of the world, how could we begin to explore the world as psychic reality? What would a psychology of culture be like?

The word, "culture," comes from the Latin *cultura*, referring to tilling the soil, and the husbandry of animals. It is also associated with care of monuments and training of the body. Culture refers to worship and the observance of rites. It is related to *cultus* – the act of dwelling, training of a person, personal care and adorning.

"Care" seems to be an important aspect of culture. Care of animals and tilling of land evoke the alchemical notion of working to help nature and to further natural processes. Care for the life of things of the world is religious, the life of the world speaks through things that need us to listen, things which connect us to our past, and not only things – words and ideas as well.

Culture is the meaning given to experience. In Heidegger's terminology, culture "sets up," "gathers," or "brings forth" a world. Culture provides a dwelling for the world of experience through "careful consideration" or love of ideas, words, things, and experience. The challenge in developing a caring consciousness regarding technological and cultural life would not be to write poetry as an alternative, but to "dwell poetically" with the things of the world.

Culture has its pathologies as part of its poetry. Cultural symptoms are the world's means of calling attention to its needs. One way of imagining the various forms of addiction in contemporary culture, for example, would be to consider addiction as a way for subjective consciousness to transcend itself. Dependency on alcohol, drugs, gambling, sex, work, play, etc., bespeaks the burden of "I-ness" become too great and the need for transcendence of subjectivity. "Sleep" has traditionally been considered both a metaphor for dis-inspirited life and a spiritual condition, a place outside of "I." The dis-ease of addiction in modern life would then be diagnosed as a "sleep disorder," a yearning for spirit gone wrong, with background images of Dante's and Eliot's crowds of souls living a somnambulate half-life in limbo. We don't know how to meditate, to leave our "selves," to sleep.

Television is a technological staple of contemporary culture that presents itself in an ambivalent manner. On one hand, we consider it an essential part of our lives, right up on the needs hierarchy with food, shelter, and the automobile. On the other hand, since its introduction as a popular medium in the late 1940s, it has been regarded with suspicion, often in terms of pathology and addiction. The intent of this chapter is to contribute to a psychology of culture by developing an imagination of television that reveals its concealed life (phenomenology), its myth (Jung), or its "ready-to-hand" essence (Heidegger)[1] as an attempt to transcend subjectivity.

Television as fallen world

Our relationship to television is marked by a wary attitude regarding its power to influence us. Marshall McLuhan wrote, "It is [the] continuous embrace of our own technology in daily use that puts us in . . . subliminal awareness in relation to these images . . . [T]hat is why we must . . . serve these objects as gods" (McLuhan 1964: 55). This statement reflects a popular concern for the way television molds our consciousness – our way of thinking, acting, and forming attitudes – as if it were a god (Minnow 1962, Winn 1977, Mander 1978, McCarthy 1990, Tichi 1991, Lazar 1994). The sense of television as a religious power which controls our lives is revealed in the way we relate to it. We pay money for cable television as if in offering, consume products while watching television as if in communion, schedule our day's events around television programming as if in ritual,[2] and become tied to the set when it dramatizes world events as if bending the knee before the altar.

The fear that television controls us is reflected in twentieth-century psychopathology. In 1919, four years before the invention of television, Victor Tausk, a colleague of Freud's, wrote an article describing a psychiatric syndrome, a form of delusion, in which patients would characterize themselves as being under the power of an "influencing machine." One of the effects of the machine was seeing pictures on walls, which produced and "drained off" thoughts and feelings by means of waves, rays or mysterious forces, and "weakened" the patient (Tausk 1967).

In 1959, Dr Joseph Cowen offered the following description of a woman diagnosed as paranoid schizophrenic:

> For many months during the course of her hospitalization she made frequent reference to television. When she referred to television, she would develop a look of ecstatic terror on her face. In various ways she described how she was being controlled, persecuted and tormented by television. She had clairvoyant experiences with other patients mediated by television. She variously described herself as being 'hooked' or 'taped' into television. Periodically she would tell me, 'Everything would be all right if they just wouldn't turn on the television set'.
>
> (Cowen 1959, 202–3)

In 1973, a young man walked into the lobby of a San Francisco television station and started shooting a gun in an attempt to shut down the broadcasts. The man thought that a receiver for the waves transmitted by the station had been secretly planted into his body so that it broadcast incessantly to his mind.

The symptomatology of these modern psychiatric patients would indicate that they are carrying one side of our cultural "dis-ease." Their symptoms might be seen as the condition of a culture unduly "under the influence" of an objectivizing, analytic, "far-seeing" (tele-vision) eye which has come to take on a persecutory character.

Our ambivalence toward television-watching stems, in part, from the dark connotation it carries through its association with addiction. Marie Winn called television, "the plug-in drug." Jack Gould, the first television critic of the *New York Times*, in 1948 referred to television as an "insidious narcotic" (Winn 1977: 11). Robert D. McIlwraith of the University of Manitoba states that the main attraction of television-watching is not the content of programming, but a dependency on the medium itself. "Allegedly there is something about the medium that compels us to watch it and to continue watching longer than we mean to" (McCarthy 1990: 42). Robert Kubey of Rutgers University found through his research that (1) television-watching alters mood states, (2) television-watching can be compared to substance addiction in that it is used more than intended, (3) people recognize that their use of television is often excessive but are unable to control it, (4) important social activities are given up or reduced in favor of television-watching, and (5) withdrawal symptoms develop when an individual stops or reduces viewing (McCarthy 1990: 42).

The volume of television-watching in the United States might be seen as indicative of an addiction. It is estimated by the Smithsonian Institute that the average American household has the television on seven and a half hours per day. The average American watches twenty-five hours of television per week (McCarthy 1990: 42). The average preschool child watches television about twenty-eight hours per week, and the average elementary school age child watches twenty-four hours per week (Lazar 1994: 67). By the completion of high school, a child can be expected to have watched 15,000 hours of television – far more than the child's accumulated hours of classroom time and more than any other activity except sleep (*Esquire* 1989: 122).

From its inception, television has been presented not only as a medium of entertainment, but also as a medium of education wherein the world is brought into the living room. However, little factual information is actually remembered from television-watching. Instead, television images tend to "pour through" consciousness, bypassing the cognitive faculties. One woman who, at twenty, estimated that she had watched 20,000 hours of television, confided, "it all just washed over me" (Winn 1977: 10). Even so-called "educational" programs do not enhance learning in children unless they are accompanied by adult intervention (Winn 1977: 34). Research from Australia indicates that television destroys the capacity of the viewer to attend (Mander 1978: 14). While the medical world has created a psychiatric diagnostic category of attention deficit disorder in children and adults, Winn suggests that it is television-watching that inhibits left-brain development and the ability to concentrate necessary for achievement in literary education and cognitive development (Winn 1977: 43–4). Bonnie Lazar cites evidence that heavy television-watching can cause increased restlessness as well as aggression in children and that viewing television consistently can cause a replacement of imaginative play with imitative play (Lazar 1994: 68).

Disillusionment regarding television extends to its sociological as well as its psychological effects. While television-watching was originally imagined as a family and community event, gathering the group around the hearth (Tichi 1991), in fact it has replaced rituals of family and community life such as the evening dinner and neighborly chats. Each individual family member now is more likely to commune with a private television set in his or her room (or as in Japan, each individual in a room with his or her individualized television set and a pair of earphones.) Even the ritual of viewing of the dead is now accomplished in distanced solitude by means of drive-in television at mortuaries. From this perspective, television-watching can be seen as a symptom of our time, rendering the individual confined to isolated existence, poorly equipped to initiate connection and interact with the world.

The moralistic flavor of dialogue regarding television reflects not only our ambivalence, but a spiritual conflict of good versus evil (Minnow 1962). Television is often described as if it were something sinister, a technological Cyclops, a tool in the hands of group-think engineers who market the raw material of culture – things, ideas, words, and experience – as commodities to be bought and sold. Television would seem to have taken over imagination and become, for the modern person, a mass anaesthetic, a universal medicine show, a global babysitter. Television would be viewed as having replaced the world, becoming a world in itself, a world without substance, a world of glowing, fuzzy, phosphorescent, electric dots. From this standpoint, television would be seen as tricking us into thinking that it "brings the busy world before us," or "mirrors the sights of life," as it was originally advertised to do. Mass television-watching would be seen as Huxley's "brave new world" of anesthetized human consciousness where people love servitude to invisible authority through greatly improved techniques of suggestion. Television would seem to have taken us into Orwell's "1984" where a television screen in every room exists in perpetual vigilance of the individual, where human consciousness is engineered by technicians of "goodthink," and where the worst horror is that no one realizes their condition of servitude because the oppressors remain invisible. In sum, television would be the shadow of Yeats' prophesy that the visible world is no longer a reality and the unseen world is no longer a dream.

As the weight of the moral attitude regarding television becomes overbearing, the question turns back on itself. Might not the very morality of our discussion regarding television reflect something of its essence? Would not this moral stance indicate a hidden inherent spiritual dimension to television? In that case, television could be imagined as a god, not because of our unconsciousness, but through its own self-presentation. Television would be seen as having a life of its own.

If this is the case, then we might ask: what would be its hidden intention and how have we failed to respond adequately to the calling within television's presence?

Television as Aphrodite

To be sure, television does exercise a form of subliminal control, an influence that might also be described as hypnotic. The actual experience of watching television can be likened to that of a trance state. Consciousness becomes desensitized to emotions and the perception of things and sounds. The eyes become still and the body quiets to the flickering light. People describe themselves as being "hooked," "doped," "sucked in," "fixated," "zombie-like," "dependent," and "suggestible." The sense of time becomes distorted, experience in the world seems unreal, and there is an inability to discriminate. This hypnotic effect of the television image is inherent in the physiology of television-watching.

Scientists interested in brain-waves characterize television-watching as an activity with a high percentage of alpha-wave activity which is associated with the relaxed, unfocused, inner-directedness of consciousness. (Beta-wave activity is characteristic of an outer focus.) In addition, perception is normally characterized by a small percentage of activity in the fovea, the sharp-focusing part of the eye. We take in the greater part of the world through peripheral vision. In watching television, by contrast, the eye tends to focus exclusively upon the screen, taking in the entire image through the fovea, leaving the peripheral world blotted out. This is so because the televised image produces contours that are always moving, and the eye is drawn to fixate on these moving contour lines. The contours of objects in the world are then perceived as stationary. When the eye attempts to adjust to the constantly changing image of television, the result is a defocusing of the visualizing system. The constantly changing contour of the televised image stimulates a mechanism of adjustment wherein the eye defocuses in an attempt to fixate properly. The defocusing of the eye, in effect, tunes out the world and brings about an hypnotic state of consciousness.

As McLuhan has pointed out, television is a medium of "total involvement," attracting consciousness into the screen itself. He says, "It is the total involvement in all-inclusive nowness that occurs in young lives via TV's mosaic image" (McLuhan 1964: 292). When we are watching television, we are not seeing the natural world as we are led to believe, or even a projected image as in film, but a mosaic of patterns formed by three million phosphorescent dots flickering every second. This mosaic requires an unconscious "creation," an interpretation or selection process on the part of the viewer. The creation of image is really not that since the image is already formed for us, rather it is a kind of subliminal "painting by the numbers" or "connecting the dots." Nevertheless, it is an action that unconsciously draws us into the television screen, impelling us to be "with it." (In addition, technical effects such as the quick cuts in advertisements have a special attraction for the observing eye.)

The hypnotic attraction of the televised image is a sensuous attraction, affecting our tactile perception and extending our sense of touch. McLuhan suggests that because the television image is the result of light shining through, not on, a screen, it has the experiential quality of sculpture. We can also see that the televised image lies in the tradition of impressionistic painting which immediately preceded its invention. The impressionists remind us of the bodily existence of the world by bringing us into a tactile relationship with the painted image. Cezanne said that we should paint as if we held things in our hands, not as if we were observing them. He abandoned perspective in favor of structure created with small strokes of the brush. Seurat achieved a similar effect with dots on the canvas. Seeing mythologically, we might view this sensuous attraction of the television screen as Aphrodite asking for bodily interaction.

In attempting to understand the psychological intention of television removing us from the control of our reasoning mind, we have characterized television as a medium of the senses. As a technology of the sensuous, television draws us out of our subjective mind. Subjectivism is an attitude which says the source of consciousness is within the individual human mind, and consciousness is separate from the surrounding world. To understand further the psychological necessity of "losing our minds" and the inherent connection between television and subjectivism, we now need to look historically at the background of subjectivism in our culture and imagine its connection to television. In the next section, I will attempt to show how television evolves out of the subjectivist mind, starting with a brief review of the evolution of subjectivism from the invention of linear perspective during the Renaissance (Edgerton 1976, Romanyshyn 1989).

Tele-vision as subjectivist mind

At the root of subjectivism are two ideas which came together and became predominant during the Renaissance: (1) the universe is ordered according to laws of harmony or proportion, and (2) earthly order reflects heavenly order. The fundamental principle of the first idea, proportion, is that concrete particularity is reducible to intelligible unity through a mathematically predictable order in the relationship of its parts. In other words, each entity relates to a greater whole through a numerical order. Proportion, based as it is on numbers, is concerned with quantity, as opposed to quality, and concepts, as opposed to images. The spiritual basis of proportion can be seen in the thought of one of its founders, the Greek theologian and mathematician, Pythagoras. Pythagoras believed that a purely spiritual existence could be achieved through the progression of the soul through the inherent levels of order in the universe from matter to spirit, each based on number. He held that all things of the universe, such as the notes on a musical scale, are ordered through the numerical distribution of their elements. For Pythagoras, things were not substantial in themselves, but were essentially numbers!

A second classical idea which found a receptive place in the Renaissance mind was that order on earth reflects heavenly order: "as above, so below." If heavenly order is proportionate, then earthly order must be proportionate as well. During the Renaissance, proportion as metaphysical system became transformed into linear perspective as methodology. The ontological ground of earthly reality came to be not something that was unknowable because such ground rested in the mind of God. Rather, earthly reality became that which could be observed from a fixed point through the application of linear perspective, and mathematics was its ground.

Linear perspective was invented by Filippo Brunelleschi (1374–1446), a Florentine painter and designer, when he painted the exact likeness of the doorway to the Baptistery from its image in a mirror. *Perspectiva* is a Latin word which means "a view through something." With linear perspective, that "something" is a "*transparent window* through which we look out onto a section of the visible world," as expressed by Leon Battista Alberti, a Renaissance theorist of art and architecture and a contemporary of Brunelleschi (italics added. See Panofsky 1955: 247).

Brunelleschi invented perspective by connecting two premises. The first is that the visual image is produced by straight lines which connect the eye with objects so that the resulting configuration becomes a pyramid, with the eye forming the apex and the horizon forming the base (Figure 5.1). The second is that the size and shape of the objects in the image are determined by the relative position of the rays which make them visible (Figure 5.2). The closer an object to the eye, the larger it will be. Brunelleschi's revolutionary idea was to conceive of a plane being interjected between the eye and the horizon, allowing for the "projection" of the visual image onto this surface by calculating numerically where the rays will intersect the plane (Figure 5.3). The effect was, "you thought you saw the proper truth and not an image" (de Santillana 1969: 64).

The theory of linear perspective is based upon the assumption by the viewer that through proportion, large things can be represented as smaller. The truth of an object becomes, not the quality of its form, but its measure both in size and in distance from the viewer. Objects diminish in size as their distance from the beholder increases. The laws of proportion allowed for the

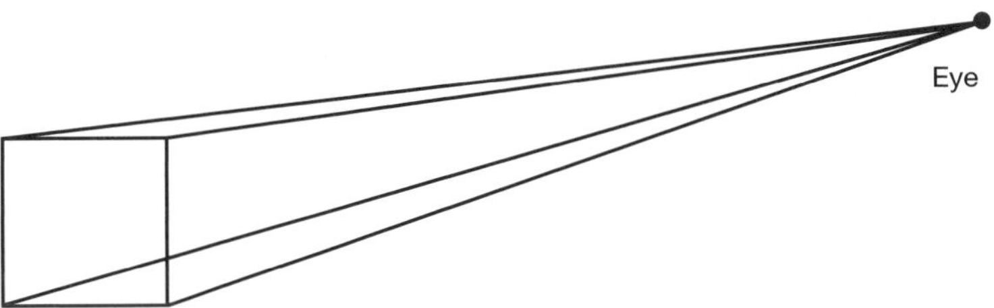

Figure 5.1 The visual pyramid.

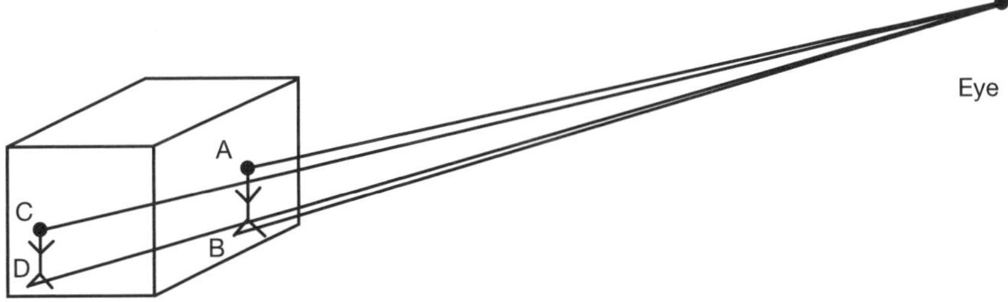

Figure 5.2 Vision and proportion.

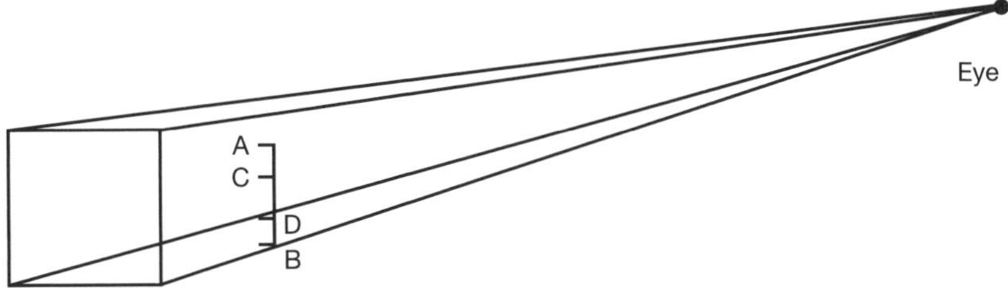

Figure 5.3 The visual plane of linear perspective.

possibility of linear perspective in that, with proportion, what appeared small signified distance and what appeared large signified close proximity. With perspective, "reality" was no longer the ideal image in the soul, but that which was literal, known through sensory perception and objectively measurable. Reality became a three-dimensional space, composed of objects and interstices that seemed to extend indefinitely behind the proscenium "frame" of the visual image. I would suggest that the proscenium frame of linear perspective, which started out on the Renaissance painter's canvas as "window to the world," can be imagined as a forerunner of the television screen, once advertised as "the biggest window in the world."

The achievement of linear perspective as the metaphysics of proportion, literalized, had several important psychological implications (Romanyshyn 1989). Consciousness became distanced from the world, fixed, flattened, and singular. The further the observer was detached from the world, the greater the sense of proportion and the more vision became "truth" as mathematical order, the more individual consciousness became the seat of judgement. The vanishing point in linear perspective, i.e. the center of the image, which draws focus to itself, might be imagined as reflecting the "divine eye" of God. This eye was now replaced by the observing eye of the individual (Figures 5.4 and 5.5). It was a short jump to the advent of subjectivism through Descartes'

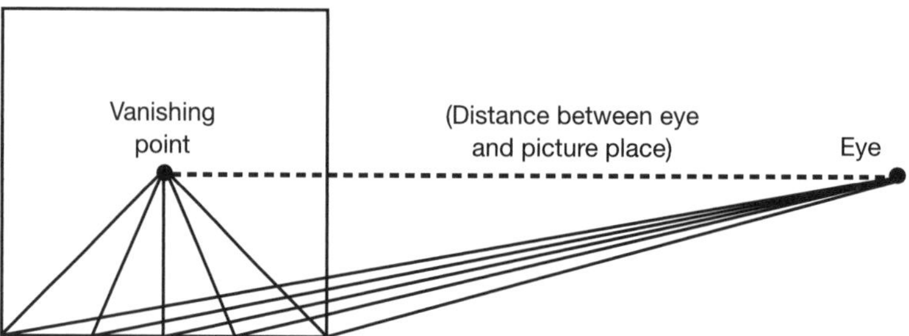

Figure 5.4 The vanishing point of linear perspective.

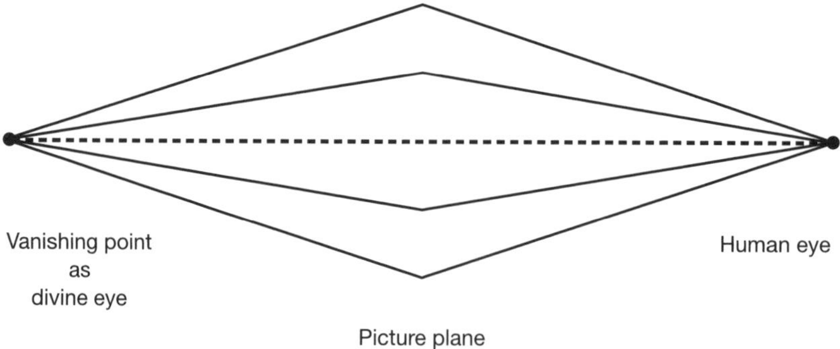

Figure 5.5 The detached eye and the divine eye.

relocating the seat of all consciousness from the mind of God to within the mind of humans – “I think, therefore I am.” The world became disensouled, something inorganic that was perceived most accurately, not through actual experience, but as if through a window. In the Renaissance, life became, as with television today, a form of peep show seen through a magic window (Figure 5.6).

When soul, the classical union of spirit and matter, is withdrawn from the world into the mind, spirit and matter become split from each other. Spirit becomes linked to faith in an unseen realm, matter becomes an inorganic abstraction, and the world becomes dead. There is set up in the soul, then, a

Figure 5.6 “Peep Show”
Source: M. McLuhan (1967) *The Medium is the Massage*, New York: Bantam Books.

yearning for spirit and body unified, a yearning for an ensouled "world" with its own life.

Today the subjectivist mind continues to keep matter and spirit separate through its literalization of world in the televised image. We think that television brings the world as actual reality into our home, just as Renaissance man thought of reality as revealed through the boxed-in window of linear perspective. Detached from the world, we use television to bring us the world, but what we actually witness are preformed matrixes of artificial light brought to us from a singular perspective.

In providing an alternative understanding of television, I would suggest that television, when seen as an entity with a life or essence that has an intention of its own, is a response to the soul's need to transcend subjectivity and unify the material "reality" of the modern world with spirit.

The spirit in the tube

Walter Ong has specified three different technological stages in the evolution of communication – the oral tradition, the written tradition of script and print, and the electronic tradition of computers and televisions (Ong 1967, 1982). Each change in stage has brought with it a crisis in the imagination, the older paradigm being highly suspect of the newer. For instance, through the voice of Socrates (*Phaedrus* 275–6), Plato voiced objections to writing that are similar to contemporary objections to television. He asserted that writing was an inhuman form of interaction, attempting to establish outside of the mind what in reality can only be in the mind, that writing destroys memory, and that writing is passive and unresponsive.

What seems to be required during each crisis is a dramatic leap in imagination. I have proposed that the television-watching eye is an analogue to the subjective eye of modernity, which itself is an analogue to the divine eye of the middle ages. I have also stated that the subjectivist mind, as an analogue to the mind of God, is blind to autonomous life outside of itself, leaving it perpetually in search of soul through spiritual awakening. I will now suggest that television, as a product of the subjectivist eye that came about in time of spiritual crisis, has an inherent life within it that would transcend subjectivism through spiritual connection. In other words, television-watching is an attempt for religious experience.

From the derivation of the word, it would seem that "tele-vision" bespeaks Apollo, the far-shooting god of light. *Tele* in Greek means, "at a distance" or "far off." *Vision* is the Latin word for the act of seeing, which in turn, comes from the Greek *eidos*, referring to that which is seen or known. For the Greeks, direct perception of appearance was knowing. Television is "seeing or knowing at a distance."

The light of television is not the clear, bright, sunlight of Apollo, however. It takes on more of the quality of the glow of his equally far-shooting sister, the moon goddess, Artemis. We might say that the soft light of television is a form of "moonshine," with television-watching taking on the aspect of moon-gazing, peering into a mist, or being drawn toward the feminine mysteries.

The light of television can be considered as a form of "divine light" when we look at how it evolved and how it works. In 1884, Paul Nipkow, a German scientist, invented a small disc with holes, which, when rotated, broke up the image of an object into light waves. He then converted the different strengths of light waves from the object into electrical impulses of corresponding strengths through photo sensitive selenium cells (discovered in 1873). Nipkow theorized that by using another scanning device, these impulses could be converted back into an image of the original object. This step in the evolution of television was accomplished with the invention of the electric cathode ray tube by William Crookes in 1897.

The motivation behind Crookes' discovery reveals the spiritual element in television. Crookes had been interested in bridging the gap between the physical and the spiritual worlds all of his life.[3] In particular, he longed to communicate with his dead brother and was quite attracted by the notion that electricity, when passed through rarefied gases, could create mediumistic effects. (We see this dramatized in old Frankenstein movies in the secret laboratory where electrical charges, creating spectacular effects, evoke life in the corpse on the table.) Instead, he discovered a "borderland where Matter and Force seem to merge into one another," resulting in the invention of the cathode ray tube (Lehrs 1985: 58). In the historical background of television there is the yearning of matter for union with spirit through the medium of electricity.

In the early 1920s, John Logie Baird, a British inventor, produced the first telecasts using a mechanical device similar to that developed by Nipkow. Campbell Swinton, a British scientist, and Boris Rosing, a Russian, each replaced the mechanical scanning device with the electric cathode ray tube. With the cathode ray tube, an image could be picked up on a thin plate coated with a photo-sensitive substance. This plate was bombarded with electrons "shot" from a "gun" at the other end of the tube. The fusillade, sweeping up and down and from side to side provided electrical impulses matching the image being received on the plate. These impulses were, in turn, transmitted to a receiver which converted them back into light rays which were projected, this time onto a fluorescent screen.

Television is produced when light from objects is broken up, converted into electrical impulses, transmitted to a distant receiver, reconverted to light rays, and finally projected onto a screen made up of thousands of phosphorescent nodules which glow when stimulated. When we watch television, we are watching what happens when a 25,000 volt cathode ray gun, going off at the rate of thirty times per second, shoots impulses onto a screen made up of 300,000 dots packed into 500 lines. Keeping in mind the intention behind Crookes' discovery, it is as if, through television-watching, we are affected by a tremendous act of penetration from "without" or from an unseen realm.

Keeping in mind that we are approaching television imaginatively as an attempt at connection with a spiritual world, a scene from Dante's *Paradiso* gives us a sense of the divine world making itself manifest to the human eye through a matrix of lights. In the Eighteenth Canto, Dante is following Beatrice through the heavenly realm of Justice illuminated by the star of Jupiter. Here he sees two images formed by configurations of the glowing lights of angelic souls. Dante tells us, "within the lights, holy creatures were singing as they flew and made themselves, in the figures they formed." The angels first formed themselves into letters that spelled the Latin words for "Love Justice, ye that love the earth." Then Dante declares that he saw the head and neck of an eagle, the bird of justice, represented in the "pricked-out fire." I would suggest that Dante's vision of the "pricked-out fire" could be imagined as the first televised image. In the early Renaissance, Dante saw figures formed by glowing angels; today, we might imagine our angels as electrically activated, glowing, phosphorescent dots making up the figures in the televised image.

To help further make the imaginal leap connecting television and spirit, we might look at the history of inter-relationship between spirit and electricity. Electricity has been associated with spirit and divinity from the beginning of recorded time. Zeus was thought to cast his thunderbolts as a form of divine judgement. It is possible that ancient Mediterranean peoples used pools of electric fish as a form of electroshock therapy (Stillings 1989: ix). By the eighteenth century, electricity was considered by many physicians as intrinsic to the life processes of both animals and humans.

In the alchemy of the late Renaissance, electricity was considered the "ethereal fire," or the "quintessential fire," and it became the primary image for the presence of divine power in the world. Anton von Balthasar wrote in 1745 of the Pentecost as "spiritual electrisation" and interpreted the Holy Ghost's pentecostal tongues of fire as electricity (Benz 1989: 40). Prokop Divisch (1696–1765) who wrote the first document in German scientific literature on electricity, and Gottlieb Rosler (1740–1790), his interpreter, were both scholars of religion and science who held that the light of the first day of creation described in Genesis 1:3 was the "electrical fire" added to matter. Friedrich Oetinger, a contemporary of Divisch and the founder of the theosophical movement, expanded this notion into a complete electrical theology. In this theology which combined biblical revelation and the natural sciences, the electrical fire, as life spirit, spread out over chaos as matter, stimulating, warming and finally fusing with it. The "electrical fire concealed in all things" is the life principle that again and again manifests itself by penetrating into new forms. Since the Creation life has been bestowed upon matter in a secret concealed impulse. Oetinger and Divisch considered this life source the soul, the nature of which was "analogous to electrical phenomena." This soul was termed the "animal soul" as distinct from the more overt "rational soul" of the mind. It is through the animal soul that spirit and matter come together, that body and psychic functions cohere. From the standpoint of alchemy, it is in the electrical fire of the animal soul wherein dwells the a priori unity of spirit and matter, today manifested in the televised image.

If electricity can be imagined as a modern form of divine fire, stolen from the heavens by Benjamin Franklin (Bennet 1985), and the television image as its concrete manifestation, might not the television set be the contemporary hearth – television as Hestia (Tichi 1991)? The hearth evokes the age-old tradition of story-telling which takes us back to our origins. The image of the hearth emerges in the early fantasies of the purveyors of television who imagined the whole family gathered about the television set in the evening, much as it might gather around the stove or the fireplace. The matrix of glowing nodules of the televised image draws consciousness into it, reminiscent of the attraction of the embers of a fire. The act of gazing into a matrix of glowing luminaries can be imagined as a form of the ancient art of contemplation, the careful consideration of that which is eternal or beyond the grasp of man, i.e. the "divine light." Gaston Bachelard describes fire-gazing as a meditative phenomenon or reverie which allows "the grieving soul to give voice to its memories and sorrows" (Bachelard 1964: 3). Fire-gazing is a common form of divination in native cultures. Among the Navajo Indians of the American southwest, medical diagnoses are made by gazing into the coals of the fire. So when we are watching television, we are enacting a tradition of imagining, story-telling, and remembering, we are repeating a meditative, contemplative ritual of connection with what is beyond mortal comprehension.

Television-watching as engagement of the unconscious through hypnotic means gives evidence to the soul's yearning for sleep (*Hypnos*). "Sleep," here, can be imagined as the "ego-lessened" state wherein subjective consciousness loses its grip on the psyche. In the Buddhist mind, sleep is simply the state when heaviness and stability are increased. It is a time of stopping, when there is no desire. Chuang Tzu taught that everything is one in sleep, and the legendary Hindu hero/king, Mucukunda, chose a life of perpetual sleep after his exploits were finished. For the ancient Greeks, sleeping was the time when healing would occur through contact with a divinity in dreams. When western mythical heroes from Gilgamesh to Ulysses to Samson fall asleep, something psychologically important happens.

Mythically, sleep and death are connected; Hypnos and Thanatos are brothers. Nietzsche said that all that is right seeks death, Freud considered the desire for death to be an instinct, and Jung saw death as life's goal. The soul yearns for death, and Bachelard connects fire-gazing with this desire. He writes:

> [F]ire suggests the desire to change, to speed up the passage of time, to bring all life to its conclusion, to its here-after. In these circumstances the reverie becomes truly fascinating and dramatic; it magnifies human destiny; it links the small to the great, the hearth to the volcano, the life of a log to the life of a world. The fascinated individual hears the call of the funeral pyre. For him destruction is more than a change, it is a renewal. This very special and yet very general kind of reverie leads to a true complex in which are united the love and the respect for fire, the instinct for living and the instinct for dying.
>
> (Bachelard 1964: 16)

Bachelard names this complex the "Empedocles complex" after the Greek philosopher who chose a death through fire, the lament he thought of as fundamental, by hurling himself into a volcano. For Bachelard, the soul yearning death through reverie is drawn by the fire to be swallowed up and to disappear into a condition in which "the universe is reduced to nothingness" (Bachelard 1964: 13). In this sense, contemporary television-watching would be a response to the soul's yearning for death, the yearning for unity with infinity through the fascinated gaze into, and ultimate engulfment by, the fire glowing in the screen.

We watch television; television watches us. McLuhan says, "TV is environmental and imperceptible, like all environments" (McLuhan 1964: ix). We have found that, seen through psychological vision, television is a world encompassing us with a life of its own. Following alchemy and Jung, I am suggesting that the intention of this life is to unite spirit or invisible life with material or visible life to make psychological "image." The act of television-watching then becomes an attempt to transcend the tyranny of "I-ness" or the subjective mind of modernity through contemplation, sleep and death. This attempt has been aborted by a collective consciousness which has maintained a subjective attitude and literal imagination regarding television, seeing it as something to use for its own purposes, rather than seeing the god in technology, the spirit in the tube.

Notes

1 In Heidegger's terminology, the "ready-to-hand" essence of television would be its essential "being" which is revealed as a world through its functioning (Heidegger 1962: 98–101, 114).

2 The connection of television to medieval theology can also be seen in the break-up of the contemporary television day with its early-morning talk shows, morning soaps, afternoon game-time, news hour, prime time and late-night talk shows as a parallel to the structure of the monastic day with its prime, terce, sext, none, and vespers.

3 Crookes' work in spiritism was read and referenced by Jung (1983: 34, 38).

References

Bachelard, G. (1964) *The Psychoanalysis of Fire*, trans. A.C.M. Ross, Boston: Beacon Press.

Bennet, S. (1985) "A play of light or Ben Franklin, the arsonist," unpublished paper, The University of Dallas.

Benz, E. (1989) *Theology of Electricity*, trans. W. Taraba, edited with an Introduction by D. Stillings, Allison Park, Pennsylvania: Pickwick Publications.

Cowen, R. (1959) "A note on the meaning of television to a psychotic woman," in *Bulletin of the Menninger Clinic*, 23, 202–3.

Dante, *The Divine Comedy: Paradiso* (1939) trans. J. D. Sinclair, New York: Oxford University Press.

de Santillana, G. (1969) "The role of art in the scientific renaissance," in M. Clagett (ed.) *Critical Problems in the History of Science*, Madison, WI: University of Wisconsin Press.

Edgerton, S. (1976) *The Renaissance Rediscovery of Perspective*, New York: Harper and Row.

Esquire, "Bringing Up Daddy," November, 1989, 122.

Heidegger, M. (1962) *Being and Time*, trans. J. Macquarrie and E. Robinson, New York: Harper and Row.

Jung, C.G. (1940) "The psychology of the child archetype," *CW* 9.i.

—— (1983) *The Zophingia Lectures*, trans. J. van Heurck, Princeton: Princeton University Press.

Lazar, B. (1994) "Under the influence: An analysis of children's television regulation," *Social Work*, 39, 1.

Lehrs, E. (1985) *Man and Matter*, London: Rudolf Steiner Press.

Mander, J. (1978) *Four Arguments for the Elimination Television*, New York: Quill.

McCarthy, K. (1990) "TV addicts not lured to shows, but medium," *The American Psychological Association Monitor*, November.

McLuhan, M. (1964) *Understanding Media: The Extensions of Man*, New York: New American Library.

Minnow, N. (1962) "Speech to National Association of Broadcasters," May 9, 1961, *Equal Time*, 52.

Ong, W. (1967) *The Presence of the Word*, New Haven: Yale University Press.

—— (1982) *Orality and Literacy*, New York: Methuen.

Panofsky, E. (1955) *The Life and Art of Albrecht Durer*, Princeton, NJ: Princeton University Press.

Romanyshyn, R. (1989) *Technology as Symptom and Dream*, London and New York: Routledge.

Smithsonian Institute. Department of Communications. Television display.

Stillings, D. (1989) Editorial introduction to E. Benz *op. cit.*

Tausk, V. (1967) "On the origin of the 'influencing machine' in schizophrenia," in R. Fliess (ed.) *The Psycho-Analytic Reader*, New York: International Universities Press.

Tichi, C. (1991) *Electronic Hearth: Creating an American Television Culture*, New York: Oxford University Press.

Winn, M. (1977) *The Plug-in Drug*, New York: Viking Press.

Part 2

THE JUNGIAN IMAGINATION

EDITOR'S INTRODUCTION

Jung's approach to religious experience has been creative and controversial, caught as it is in the task of being both phenomenologically respectful and psychologically insightful. Lionel Corbett's paper is steeped in the classical epistemology of the Jungian tradition: he refuses to collapse that tension between the hermeneutics of Jungian theory and the attempt to speak about religious experience without violating its integrity. Purists in phenomenology will spot the epistemological tensions that remain in this example of classical Jungian thought, but the paper exemplifies the considerable degree to which Jung and Corbett are committed to the descriptive heart of phenomenology while not retreating from the "creative violence" of a psychological hermeneutics. Perhaps, if a Jungian interpretation of religious experience is violent – as is any creative reading of a text – it is a violence without which a phenomenology of religious experience remains psychologically naive, where concreteness and literalism remain insufficiently differentiated.

6

JUNG'S APPROACH TO THE PHENOMENOLOGY OF RELIGIOUS EXPERIENCE

A view from the consulting room

Lionel Corbett

The phrase "religious experience" in my title needs a preliminary comment, because the term is used in so many contexts. Religious experience may refer to ritual practices, religious services, revivalist meetings, or to the sense that one is in contact with the divine described in hundreds of different ways – everything from a burning bush to pure light to a nut in the hand of the Savior. Religious experience may also refer to meditation of many different kinds, to prayer, dreams, visions, to contact or merger with the non-theistic Void, to the experience of emptiness or no-thingness, or to the experience of levels of reality that cannot be put into words, levels that are incommunicable because they are beyond the categories of ordinary language and perception. In this essay, I restrict my sense of the term to what Otto (1958) believed to be an important factor common to all religious experience, a factor that he described as the *numinosum*. Jung (1934b: 104) began to use this term in about 1934, and he used it with increasing frequency thereafter, developing it especially in his Terry lectures (Jung 1937). (Schlamm [1994] has compared in detail Jung's use of the term with Otto's own concept, and elsewhere I [1996] have discussed the psychotherapeutic implications of this idea.) Ellenberger (1970) believes that Otto's book was important enough to start a new direction in the development of Jung's ideas. I believe that this happened because Jung realized that he could use the term to make sense of many of the phenomena he was experiencing in his own life and in his consulting room. Thus it is that, as Chapman (1988) notes, Otto tended to stress the transcendent quality of the *numinosum* while Jung stressed its immanence. The frequency of numinous events led Jung (1937: 6) to suggest that the psyche has an "authentic religious function."

For Otto, the essence of religious experience is a specific emotional quality that is inexpressible and that "eludes apprehension in terms of concepts" (1958: 7). Otto describes this quality as an experience of the *mysterium tremendum et fascinans*. The subject feels as if he or she is in the presence of an uncanny, awesome mystery, that is often terrifying or dreadful, but at the same time is fascinating. We feel that we are in contact with something quite other than our ordinary experience, something that demands relationship, reverence or even worship. Emphasizing his phenomenological attitude, Jung (1937: 7) defined religion in terms of the "careful and scrupulous observation" of the *numinosum*, and his subsequent work contains frequent references to its importance and to its powerful – potentially overwhelming – effect on the subject (e.g., Jung, 1937: 184, 363; 1947/54: 186). It is important to note that the content of these manifestations may have no connection to any established creed. Only their emotional quality is determinative; the content of the experience may be completely novel and only relevant to the subject. In current clinical practice, Otto's concept of the *numinosum* has therefore been broadened, for example to include experiences of unity such as those described by the mystics. The *numinosum* may manifest itself as dreams, as visions or other sensory experiences, in the body, in relationships, in the experience of nature, and by creative, artistic or aesthetic means.

To give the reader an idea of the quality of numinous experience, I would like to provide two examples before discussing some theoretical and practical aspects of Jung's approach. The first is the dream of a psychotherapist who, at the time of the dream, was undergoing a period of serious questioning and doubt about both her vocation and the validity of the field in which she works. It is typical of numinous manifestations to appear during times of great personal difficulty.

> I am walking with a group of women. Suddenly in the distance I see the most incredible sight: huge birds, the size of airplanes, are descending to earth. They are crane- or stork-like, but mythological in their size – they are so huge that I am terrified. One of the birds is a fabulous version of what looks like an ape or monkey – but not exactly – riding on the back of its mother. I'm worried that these huge, awesome birds will come near us, and that begins to happen; they circle nearer and nearer. Then I'm in an open field; suddenly two ordinary small birds swoop down, and with their beaks, hold fast to my thumb and hand, as if to pin me to the ground. I gasp at their ablility and strength to do this. It is as if they are insisting that I *must* have an encounter with the huge birds. Then one of the enormous, mythological birds – stork-like and pink in color – swoops down by my side. It is awesome; I am so afraid. But it does not harm me. It wants me to see something, but I dare not look at it directly. From my averted gaze, out of the corner of my eye, I see that its belly is like a glistening, pinkish, huge, sphere – rather like a bubble that I

> can see into, catching the light and reflecting different colors. In this belly are contained all the secrets of creation. It is as if there is a universe there. I am overcome; I still cannot look directly, but have to keep my eyes averted. It is a very emotional, awesome experience. The group of women I'm with are both there and not there, but somehow their "presence" is like a field of energy, helping me tolerate, bear, this experience.

My second example is a visionary experience described by Jung himself:

> One night I awoke and saw, bathed in bright light at the foot of my bed, the figure of Christ on the Cross. It was not quite life-size, but extremely distinct; and I saw that his body was made of greenish gold. The vision was marvelously beautiful, and yet I was profoundly shaken by it.
>
> (1965, p. 210)

In clinical work, we find that detailed phenomenological exploration often allows such numinous experiences to speak for themselves. They seem to be self-authenticating because of their emotional power. But occasionally, when the subject remains baffled by the experience, when detailed articulation reveals no meaning, we feel a need to move beyond descriptive explication into some additional kind of interpretation, because otherwise the experience remains unusable or impossible to integrate into the rest of one's life. Here there are various choices. The psychological approach to the *numinosum* tries to discern its relationship to the specific psychology of the experiencing subject, and so offers an alternative to explanations in terms of existing religious dogma. This attitude is especially useful when a transpersonal experience does not conform to traditional concepts of divinity. In fact, as Jung (1933) shows in his study of Nicholas of Flüe, a terrifyingly powerful numinous experience may be dealt with by a dogmatic revision in order to eliminate its potentially heretical content. It is because of the unorthodox content of some numinous experiences that religious authorities have often condemned them as dangerous or demonic. But the psychotherapist, at least, does not have the luxury of being able to dismiss them; in order to help our patients we need a hermeneutical method that does them justice without reducing them. Jung's claim is that his method of doing so is a phenomenological hermeneutics.

There has been some debate in the literature of phenomenology about the validity of Jung's claim to work phenomenologically, in spite of his statements such as: "I am an empiricist and adhere as such to the phenomenological standpoint . . . I restrict myself to the observation of phenomena and I eschew any metaphysical or philosophical considerations" (Jung 1937: 5). Jung insists that his standpoint is "exclusively phenomenological, that is, it is concerned with occurrences, events, experiences" (ibid.: 6). In other words, Jung deliberately does not comment as an empiricist on the positive claims to truth that are often attributed to religious experience. He says that he engages in a "comparative phenomenology of the mind" (McGuire and Hull, 1977), and that "our science is phenomenology" (Jung 1976: 289). Chapman (1988) suggests that Jung's emphasis on direct experience and its elucidation qualifies him as a phenomenologist, at least in the broad sense of the term which indicates the use of a phenomenological method, and Brooke (1991: 79) has pointed out the similarities between Jung's concept of the psyche and the phenomenologist's *lebenswelt*. Jung notes in many places that he wishes to avoid speculation about the ontological status of what is experienced, and instead he is "concerned with phenomenal religion" (Jung 1973: 383). In matters of religion, he insists on the primacy of experience rather than belief or faith, because experience, unlike belief, cannot be disputed (Jung 1937: 104), and he is concerned that church dogma has become distanced from actual experience. Instead, Jung's attitude of openness to the unique meaning of every numinous experience, without interpretation in terms of a pre-existing system of doctrinal assertions, is a phenomenological one. Obviously, however, the concept of the *numinosum* itself is burdened by its own set of assumptions. But for my purposes, what makes Jung's work phenomenological is his fidelity to our experience of the world. In his best moments, this fidelity shows itself in his refusal to make ontological (i.e. metaphysical) statements. In his worse moments, for which we can forgive him, some of his writing falls into the old Cartesian categories, for example when he writes of the psyche as "interior". He makes up for these slips when he points out, in a 1946 letter, that the psyche is not located in the human head – it is more like the air we breath, "which is the same everywhere . . . yet belongs to no one" (Jung 1973: 408).

Jung insists that he always tries to discuss numinous phenomena on their own terms, without reducing them to manifestations of defense or wish fulfillment. But it is also true that Jung does not simply observe and investigate numinous experience purely *as* experience. He believes that the *numinosum* is a manifestation of the unconscious, abruptly appearing as a phenomenon of consciousness. He feels that he can adequately demonstrate the psychic origin of religious experience (Jung 1953: 9), although he realizes that the psyche may only be its medium of expression (Jung 1957: 293). Needless to say, such a view is in striking contrast with, and would be anathema to, the fundamentalist tenets of the western monotheistic traditions, which insist that a kind of transpsychic or transcendent entity intrudes into history. However, Jung never fully admitted the theological or metaphysical implications of his ideas, but insisted that his position was an empirically verifiable one because of the ubiquity of numinous experience.

The concept of the *numinosum* is so important to Jung that he suggests (1973: 377) that contact with the *numinosum* is actually the healing factor in psychotherapy. Perhaps his attitude about the healing function of numinous experience constitutes a form of belief about its purpose, leading to a bias of the kind that might prevent an adequate suspension of judgement about an experience. But the notion that religious experience tends to bring completeness or wholeness to the individual is a part of Jung's general theory, a hermeneutical pre-understanding, by means of which religious experience may be understood. As well, Jung clearly goes beyond the bounds of a purely phenomenological approach when he locates the source of numinous experience within an "objective" dimension of the psyche. For Jung, the experience of the numinosum *is* an experience of the objective psyche. He suggests that we attribute the epithet "divine" to autonomous contents of this level of the psyche, and these contents act like a superior force within the personality (Jung 1928: 239). These numinous factors are "important constituents of our mental make up" (Jung 1976: 253). This attitude led to accusations that Jung was reducing the divine to an intrapsychic content, as if it were "nothing but" psychological, even though he repeatedly replied that we are simply unable to decide whether such an experience points to a transpsychic entity or whether it originates within a transpersonal level of the psyche. He also complained that his academic and theological readers failed to understand that the fact that an experience is psychological does not mean that it is not real, since the psyche is real as an autonomous world of experience. Jung insists that he does not hypostasize the experience of the *numinosum*; for him, to discuss images and experiences of the divine is not to make inferences about the existence of a transpsychic divinity that may lie beyond the image. In theological language, he is concerned with the experience of God as immanent, not with a transcendent Godhead beyond experience.

His postulate of an objective or transpersonal level of the psyche is a part of Jung's metapsychology, which, as I noted above, seems to be a non-phenomenological move, since as a *concept* it is experience-distant, and generally phenomenology renounces the need to be concerned with the cause or explanation for the phenomena in question. However, Jung believed that the *effects* of this level of the unconscious are empirically observable in dreams, fantasies and religious experience. He suggests that the objective psyche reveals its own processes in the imagery of mythology and other symbol systems such as alchemy. The unconscious also reveals its presence within the transference and by producing symptoms, so that the unconscious can be seen to have its own phenomenology as it erupts into consciousness.

Jung's ontology is one that he describes as *esse in anima* – the psyche is the perspective from which everything is observed. Because the psyche is the *sine qua non* of all experience, reality means psychic reality. Jung (1926: 328) believes that an emphasis on the primacy of the psyche unites the opposites of extreme realism or idealism. If there is a reduction in his work, it is a reduction to the psyche, which is understood as a world in its own right, not reduceable to anything more fundamental, such as brain (Jung 1931: 344;

1957: 270). He believed that the only medium through which we can experience the psyche is the psyche itself, so that all explanations of the psyche are themselves products of the psyche (Jung 1947/54: 223). The object of all psychological understanding is none other than the psyche itself. Jung hopes to deal with the obvious problem of circularity that arises here by a focus on the uniqueness of the imagery that is produced in particular situations. We may live in a hall of mirrors, but the psyche reflects upon itself in many different symbolic and metaphorical systems. Jung is not alone here; his attitude has an affinity with postmodern views that the contents of human consciousness do not reflect an independent reality as much as they are a function of our organizing abilities and interpretive schemes. Also like the postmoderns, Jung denied the possibility that any psychological theory could be universally or essentially valid, believing that theories are at best "subjective confessions" (Jung 1976: 125, 127). (Jung considered this to be a Kantian position, in the sense that the way the world appears is a function of the structure of the mind, and also because he believed that one cannot attribute metaphysical validity to psychic experience, although numinous experience provides material for metaphysical speculation. Various authors have taken issue with Jung's claim to be a Kantian, (e.g. de Voogd 1977).)

Numinous experiences happen to people in unexpected ways, and since they are so surprising they feel as if they are other than the personal self. For Jung they are products of the unconscious, for the theologian they are manifestations of spirit; for Jung, the phenomenology of spirit manifests itself by means of the psyche. Whatever its absolute nature and origin, the need for a phenomenology of the *numinosum* remains, even though it seems that different disciplines will describe the experience in different ways. The psychologist – especially the religiously oriented psychotherapist – will inevitably try to connect the experience to the rest of the subject's life, and tries to discern its effects on the personality, on relationships and on behavior. The committed Judaeo-Christian theologian, who wants to locate the source of numinous experience within a transcendent deity, will try to relate the experience to a particular body of tradition.

Perhaps I should not use the term "psychologist" in such a global manner. The question of a transpersonal level of the psyche remains a hotly debated one – Jung's concept of the objective psyche may refer to an ontological realm in its own right, or the psychoanalytic skeptic may view the idea as the projected reification of an aspect of Jung's own subjectivity. In the former view, the transpersonal psyche either mediates or is the actual originator of numinous experience; in the latter view, Jung and his followers are merely attributing universal validity to aspects of their own representational world. This is an important distinction; should it be the case that Jung's concept of the archetypal level of the psyche is merely a reification of archaic objects that populate his internal world, and not a universally shared reality, then his notion that the psyche has an intrinsic religious function is actually a form of speculative metaphysics. But in either case, the Jungian style of working with numinous experience tries to be immediately present to the experience, and tries not to allow metapsychological assumptions to interfere with the subject's discovery of personal, lived meaning. My own feeling here is that Jung does not necessarily use the concept of the objective psyche as an *explanatory* principle, which would certainly be a non-phenomenological move. Rather, he uses the term "unconscious" as a descriptive term for phenomena that arise in dreams, myths and religious systems, phenomena which seem to originate from beyond the subject and which speak their own language. As far as I know, Jung never speculates about the nature or the origin of the unconscious, usually insisting that "the concept of the unconscious *posits nothing*, it designates only my *unknowing*" (1973: 411, emphasis in original). For him the unconscious is the tacit dimension of existence, an experience of otherness or of what was previously completely unknown.

The phenomenological approach tries to remain as close to the original experience as possible, hoping that the fullest articulation of the experience, allowing it to become as transparent as possible, will allow its meaning to emerge. It is hoped that full description will lead to full understanding. Full articulation is certainly the beginning of Jung's approach; in his words: "Image and meaning are identical; and as the first takes shape, so the latter becomes clear. Actually the pattern needs no interpretation: it portrays its own meaning" (Jung 1947/54: 204). Here Jung means that we must stay true in our descriptions of the manifestations of the unconscious, and not superimpose theoretical constructs onto its productions. Archetypal psychology has particularly stressed a phenomenological approach to such images, insisting with Jung that the image and its meaning are identical, although the psychotherapist finds this to be an idealized view, because the patient's image is sometimes completely inscrutable. In practice, I prefer to pay equal attention to both the imaginal *and* the affective component of the experience, for two reasons. First, as current affect theory suggests, what makes an experience meaningful is its affective intensity. As well, intense affect is also a product of the unconscious, and affect has its own phenomenology. Jung often emphasized the "gripping emotionality" of numinous experience. I believe that any intense emotion – be it joyful, painful or frightening – may be a religious one, or may have numinous underpinnings. If we privilege image, or if we pay exclusive attention to the image instead of allowing the image to guide us into its associated affect, we run the risk of fostering a split between image and affect, leading to an intellectual defense against the real meaning of the experience. Similarly, there are situations in which a person suffers from an intense affect such as depression or anxiety without any associated, conscious image. One can then attend to the subject's affect until it leads to the image with which it is associated but which has been disavowed or sequestered because it is too painful.

The exception to this rule seems to be in the psychosomatic states of alexithymic individuals who express everything by means of the body, in which case the symptomatic body is the image that we have to work with. But in general it makes no difference whether we start with image or affect, since the end point is the same; image and affect are two sides of the same unitary coin. Herein lies the crucial importance of the body, since affect is felt in the body – in fact, at the neurological level affect and body are synonymous. Here too lies an opportunity to overcome a residue of Cartesian dualism in our work. Unless mind–body splitting has occurred, either spontaneously because of the need for defense, or as a result of poor therapeutic technique, Jung's theory of synchronicity suggests that affect and image are simultaneous, and both have the same meaning. For Jung, a supraordinate, undivided reality expresses itself in ways that the *ego* divides into mind and body, inner and outer. Therefore, our focus on numinous imagery must not allow us to neglect the seamlessly associated phenomenology of affect and body. A psychological process such as the imagination cannot be separated from its somatic concomitants, although both the psychoanalytic and the Jungian traditions have tended to ignore the body. Romanyshyn has made an important bridge between the psychology of the unconscious and the work of Merleau-Ponty in this area: "this *one* who perceives is the embodied subject, and hence . . . [Merleau-Ponty's] reconsideration of the Freudian unconscious is a resurrection of the body towards consciousness" (Romanyshyn 1982: 150). For Romanyshyn, "the body is a hinge around which consciousness and unconsciousness . . . revolve . . . . 'Define the mind as the other side of the body,' Merleau-Ponty says . . ." (ibid.: 151). It is not unusual for the *numinosum* to affect the body directly, rather than producing intrapsychic imagery (see Corbett 1996: 20). In fact, all numinous experience that really counts is embodied, at least by virtue of its emotional power, and ideally because it changes the subject's behaviour in the world.

In psychotherapeutic work, we elaborate numinous experience as fully as possible, clarifying its major themes, hoping that detailed description and repeated re-statement in different ways will communicate to the listener the quality of an experience, and that its meaning will emerge with such description. My own style is that of empathic enquiry into, or empathic immersion within, the quality of the experience, an approach that has been articulated by the intersubjectivists and psychoanalytic self psychologists (e.g. Rowe and MacIsaac 1991; Stolorow and Atwood 1992). The effect of this work is that I resonate bodily with the same quality of affective experience as that of my patient, and at the same time imagery presents itself to my mind's eye that imaginally depicts the situation. I believe that this approach is itself a hermeneutic one; the therapist's bodily resonance with the patient's experience is like resonance with a text. We both participate in the meaning that emerges between us. Despite all the possible pitfalls here, such as contamination by the therapist's own material, the patient's responses to the therapist's behaviour usually make it obvious whether ones empathy is accurate. Where possible, I also look for analogues to what is being described within my own life experience, and within my general knowledge and my knowledge of theory. Such mutual resonance on several levels leads to a better empathic grasp by the therapist of the meaning of the experience for the subject, which we then try jointly to express and render as intelligible as possible. Following Jung, I try not to know what the numinous experience means in terms of pre-existing doctrinal categories, although it must be admitted that years of embodiment of depth psychological theory makes it only seem as if it has been forgotten in the heat of the psychotherapeutic moment.

A difficulty arises in clinical practice when study of the experience in fine phenomenological detail does *not* allow the experience to explain itself – such was the case with the dream presented at the beginning of this essay; detailed attention to its elements did not clarify its meaning, and there were no helpful personal associations. It is at such a point that a procedure such as Jung's method of amplification is of use. Instead of using a *specific* doctrinal system to interpret religious experience, this method compares the subject's image with the way in which that image has been used within other symbol systems, such as alchemy, folklore, mythology and the world's religious traditions. It is astonishing how frequently one sees similarities between such material and the contents of dreams and fantasies, even though the dreamer has no knowledge of the use of a particular image by an entirely different culture. We then point out to the dreamer that the image in the dream is like an image from a certain myth, or "*this* is like *that*". Used carefully, without contamination of the image by forcing analogies that do not exist, amplification is helpful in releasing the significance of the experience. At this point, the method becomes a hermeneutic approach to the experience, which is understood as if it were a text in an unknown language: "I adopt the method of the philologist, which . . . is simply that of seeking the parallels" (Jung 1976: 82–3), with no attempt to explain the origins of the image. It is important not to destroy the actual experience in the attempt to understand it, by forcing parallels that have no strong emotional resonance within the dreamer. In spite of the danger of relativism here, I believe that such resonance is a reliable indicator that an amplification is useful.

Since Jung is traditionally viewed as a theorist of the unconscious, as I noted earlier, it may seem difficult to place Jung firmly within the phenomenological tradition. One of the difficulties that has plagued any attempts at synthesis between phenomenology and psychoanalysis is the fact that, as a theory of consciousness, phenomenology in the Husserlian sense has no place for the unconscious (Ricoeur 1970). However, Jung has a theory of the relationship between consciousness and the unconscious that is ontologically quite different from that of classical psychoanalysis. Brooke (1991: 124–5), following Medard Boss, has described this difference in a manner that captures the spirit of Jung's attitude. Brooke suggests that the collective unconscious is "that fundamental hiddenness . . . out of which everything comes into being." Moreover, Jung views the unconscious as a kind of consciousness in its own right, one which is often superior to conscious processes. Jung (1947/54: 186) notes that "perception, feeling, volition and intention go on in the unconscious just as though a subject were present." The personal psyche contains a multiplicity of complexes, or structural units within the psyche, somewhat analogous to the schemata of cognitive psychology, that are available to consciousness to varying degrees. Each complex consists of a transpersonal or archetypal core, which attracts to it a shell made up of images, feelings, memories and other associations derived from personal experiences that are relevant to the archetype concerned. Each complex has its own intentionality and contains its own scintilla of light. "The" unconscious is actually therefore a set of many islands of consciousness (Jung ibid.: 189–90), and in fact the unconscious may contain "a sort of ego" (ibid.: 177). By this, Jung means that the unconscious seems to be an independent center of initiative. For Jung, therefore, there is no hard and fast difference between consciousness and the unconscious, or at least the difference is ambiguous in his writing; for example the unconscious is referred to as a "wider consciousness" or a "dark region" that is not necessarily unconscious of itself (Jung 1926: 334). What the human ego calls consciousness and the unconscious are only a matter of emphasis and perspective.

The extreme pathological example that illustrates such a structural scheme is that of multiple personality disorder, which Jung would see as the result of the temporary domination of the totality of consciousness by an individual complex. Such a complex, when it is in the ascendent, thereby acts as a kind of temporary ego, only to be later displaced by other complexes or by the central ego. Jung suggests that this kind of fragmentation of the personality occurs because the intensity of the affective differences between the individual splinter psyches is too great for them to be contained within an overall synthesis. It is significant that in such situations the central ego may have no conscious memory of the sub-personalities, but one cannot argue that the person is *unconscious* while these are in the ascendent – intentional consciousness is clearly going on, even though there is no conscious relationship of the transiently dominant complex to the central ego.

The implication of Jung's structural scheme is that all significant experience has mythic or archetypal dimensions as well as cultural, historical and personal levels. These transpersonal levels shine through the personal material if we have eyes to see them. In Jung's metapsychology, the human and the transpersonal levels of the psyche are inextricably linked, and transpersonal levels of the psyche are involved in our emotional suffering, or our complexes. The activation of the *numinosum* at the center of a complex may produce numinous experience. Using this scheme, religious experience can be directly related to the deepest psychological concerns of the individual, including his or her psychopathology.

With this theoretical base in mind, I would now like to return to the dream described earlier, which puzzled the dreamer greatly, and which did not lend itself to a straightforward descriptive approach. As a general rule, when a numinous experience speaks for itself, it only needs articulation and no interpretation. In clinical practice, the therapist's approach is then simply an appreciation of the reality of the experience, resonance with its emotional significance, and a validation of its importance to the dreamer. In the case of a dream, we ask for the dreamer's associations to its elements, using a process of circumambulation, or walking around each element, looking at it from many points of view, but not allowing oneself to stray too far from the original imagery, lest our associations lead too far afield from the dream itself. But at times numinous material emerges which is not self-explanatory, to which the dreamer has no personal associations. In such a case, at the end of the most exhaustive attempts, the dreamer may still be in doubt about the meaning of the dream. Such was the case here. The dreamer did not know what to make of the huge birds, in whose belly is contained a whole universe. Jung's approach would be to suggest that the birds are so unusual, so numinous for the dreamer, that we may think of them as an image of the transpersonal Self for her. In other words, the bird is an image of the divine for this person. This example makes the further point that Self images, defined as such by their quality of numinosity, may be very unusual. Our experience of the *numinosum* does not necessarily take a traditional Judaeo-Christian form, but it none the less has profound spiritual significance for the subject because of its specificity – *the image is always precisely tailored to the psychology of the individual.* The dream's inestimable value to the dreamer is that she is given a personal revelation, *if* we grant the premise that our operational definition of the holy is the numinous defined according to Otto.

This attitude of Jung led to disputes with both psychologists and with theologians. Theologians were unable to reconcile themselves to such apparently pagan manifestations of the divine in a modern person. They insisted that to see an image of the divine in such a dream image is a form of idolatry that tries to reduce a transcendent reality to "nothing but" a manifestation of the psyche. For example, Buber (1952) protested that Jung did not distinguish between psychology, or the intrapsychic experience, and the transcendent God of theology. Psychologists such as Fromm (1950: 20) objected to Jung's "elevating the unconscious to a religious phenomenon." Jung's response is that the psyche is real, and he is simply describing its phenomenology. It happens that the *numinosum* manifests itself therein – *Jung* is not elevating the unconscious, the *mysterium magnum* appears this way of its own accord. Jung always insisted that one can say nothing about what such an experience may refer to that may lie *beyond* the psyche – the God-image is not necessarily the same as the theological "God." In other words, Jung makes no claims about the ontological reality of the experience, so that his work is like the phenomenological reduction, in that it leads us back to our own experience of the way things are (Schmitt, 1968).

Given that there were no personal associations to the image of the huge birds, Jung's hermeneutical procedure is to move to the amplification of the dream imagery by comparing it with the content of other symbol systems in which the unconscious has expressed itself in a comparable manner. One such analogy is found in the Tantric tradition, in which a divinity (usually Krishna) shows himself to his followers in a way in which his body contains the universe (Rawson 1973: 20). Jung considers that any such divinity is a local, cultural expression of an underlying archetypal predisposition to form images of the divine; in other words, there is an infinite number of possible Self images, of which Krishna is one example. Christ is another example of the same archetype with a different cultural content. It so happens that the Self appears to this dreamer in the unique and personal form of the giant bird. The dreamer is able to see the universe by looking into the bird's body – the dream therefore alludes to the cosmic nature of the Self, and suggests that when we look into the holy we see the entire cosmos. Or perhaps the image implies that the the universe and the Self are in fact synonymous. In both the Tantric iconography and the dream, the particular form in which the Self appears allows the observer to glimpse infinity by means of looking into the image. This is an awesomely frightening task, because the scale is so vast – the experience illustrates Jung's point that any symbol of the Self points far beyond itself. No single image *is* the Self itself, so that, as Corbin points out (see Avens 1984), we are not dealing with a *via positiva.* Since there are so many theophanic forms, we are forced to adopt a theology that denies that any one form is absolute. Here we see another of the (political) roots of the Judaeo-Christian theological objection to Jung's approach to the phenomenology of religious experience. If the divine can manifest itself in so many ways, and the only criterion is the numinosity of the experience, there is no room for an absolute insistence that Christ is the only way. Neither is anyone especially chosen, and no revelation is the last word. My own observation is that each individual has – or is – his or her own natural expression of the divine, and that to insist on the exclusivity of what Joseph Campbell called a "historically conditioned" God-image requires a repression of the image that might occur naturally.

The phenomenology of the bird imagery may be amplified further. In many mythologies, because of their behavior, birds present the possibility of communication or collaboration between our realm and that of spirit. The birds therefore allude to an important potential within the dreamer for connecting the two realms. The dream reveals another archetypal motif – as far back as the Bronze Age, birds themselves have been considered to be manifestations of the divine. For example, in Greek mythology it was common for a god or goddess to assume bird form. A circle or globe with bird's wings was an Egyptian and Assyrian symbol of deity, and many solar gods, such as

Ra or Horus, are depicted as a bird. The dove in Christian iconography often represents the Holy Spirit, appearing for example at the baptism of Jesus – possibly an attempt to assimilate the earlier associations of the dove with the Great Goddess. The psychological meaning of this mythologem is presumably the same as that of the numinous birds of this dream, namely the descent of spirit into the material plane. As usual, the specificity of the imagery contains an important message for the dreamer. During the dream she felt that, in her professional work, she had to value and speak about the importance of numinous disclosures (the descent of spirit) as they enter the human realm of existence. She felt that even if she were not to be taken seriously in this stance, or if she were to be considered heretical, she must take this aspect of the dream seriously. The healing aspect of the dream deals with the doubts that the dreamer had about her vocation; it gives her an attitude towards her work that makes it personally meaningful.

The validity of Jung's approach to the phenomenology of the dream partly hinges on his concept of the archetype, since he says that numinous experience is the effect of the archetype. This concept is controversial, particularly when the archetype is discussed as if it were an empirical entity or "thing." But as a founding structure and propensity in psychological life, the idea of the archetype is at the root of Jung's method of amplification. The term refers to Jung's perception of meaningful pattern and order in the psyche. The fact that our psychological life is coherent and organized allows us to make sense of the dream, which otherwise would be meaningless.

Miller (1995) has offered a detailed rebutal of various criticisms of the concept of the archetype. Here I offer a brief comment on this debate as it applies to this dream. A typical criticism of Jung's concept points to the tension between sameness and difference; the assumption that birds in the dream can be compared with the use of bird imagery in other cultures may be regarded as an invalid form of universalism. It is argued that to compare such imagery demeans the individuality and uniqueness of the people concerned. This view regards it as imperialist to stand outside different cultures and equate them. It is also argued that transcultural studies are ahistorical and deal only with stereotypes, because what we regard as archetypal is not immutably human but only given, and so can be changed (Doniger 1997). Such critiques confuse the concept of the archetype as a pure human *potential* for a particular experience with the particular *content* that is given by individual cultures. These contents are not the archetype itself, even though the contents themselves often become cultural stereotypes. Furthermore, to invoke a level of common humanity is not necessarily to devalue another culture – we may even see that culture as superior to our own in some ways. Rather, the idea of the objective psyche invites a vision of profound understanding between human beings whose cultural differences are not as important as a deeper bond of spiritual resonance.

We are archetypally predisposed to experience the world in particular ways. But human sameness consists only of our similar potentials; the possibility of human differences is infinite, because there is no limit to the number of possible contents that may fill in an archetypal potential. For example, Jung suggests that there is an archetypal potential for the experience of a God image, and this potential has been filled in by all the religions of humanity. Each tradition provides a different content for the same archetypal potential. From the psychological perspective, therefore, no God image, whether personal or collective, is more or less valid than any other. In fact, what is important to our dreamer is the *difference* between her particular numinous experience and that of the collective Christianity in which she was raised. This difference contributes to her individuation, to her becoming a unique individual with a unique spirituality. Without the method of amplification as a hermeneutical device, not only does the dream remain a meaningless content of consciousness but the dreamer is deprived of participation in the larger human context of which she is a part. As Jung noted (1970), Christianity has its own history, and there is no point in ignoring its associations with earlier paganism. For this purpose a comparative approach is useful.

Jung's vision of the green Christ may be used to illustrate further the method of amplification; I chose it here because it records Jung's own understanding of a numinous experience, and it is relevant to our ecological sensitivity. (A fuller interpretation of this vision is given by Stein 1987.) Jung begins by relating the experience to his current conscious preoccupation. He had been leading a seminar about the Spiritual Exercises of Ignatius Loyola, and at the same time he was studying alchemy. The vision colors green the image of Christ; green is the color of nature, or of the material world. The alchemists had been extremely concerned with the problem of the relationship between spirit and matter, in contrast to the devaluation of matter found in Christian doctrine. The alchemists realized that matter contained spirit, and they believed that this divine spark – the "gold" that they sought – needed redemption. Jung realized that he had ignored the early Christian split between spirit and matter, between the Christ of the tradition and the alchemical *viriditas*, the green gold that expresses the life spirit in nature. "My vision was thus a union of the Christ-image with his analogue in matter . . . the undisguised alchemical conception of Christ as a union of spiritually alive and physically dead matter" (Jung 1962: 210–11). Simply put, the vision tells him that Christ is a son of the divine as nature, or matter, as well as of the divine as spirit. The correction for his one-sided view is obvious. Without the method of amplification, we would only glean a partial understanding of the meaning of this vision. Accurate amplification reveals contextual aspects of the phenomenology of numinous experience that are not immediately given, but are tacit, or latent, within the experience. This process has the same goal as any precise phenomenological description – it tries to make manifest what is not immediately obvious.

Religious experiences may be of such importance that we try hard to find meaning for them within our own frames of reference and our temperamental preferences, in order to decide how the experience of the numinosum is relevant to our lives. Here, both the depth psychologist and the theologian run the risk that the purity of the original experience may become gradually lost as it becomes contextualized and contaminated by theoretical presuppositions. Of course Jung is not free of these, since for him the emergence of numinous experience is a revelation that results from the activity of transpersonal levels of the psyche. This is the ground of his theory. But, to his credit, Jung is clear that we have no idea about the ontological nature of the unconscious, and he refuses to hypostasize it or to define it in purely "depth" terms: "the collective unconscious is anything but an encapsulated personal system; it is sheer objectivity, as wide as the world and open to all the world. . . . There I am utterly one with the world. . . . But this self is the world, if only a consciousness could see it" (Jung 1934a : 22). In other words, psyche and world, the material and the spiritual, are inseparable. In Jung's own words (1975: 225–6), expressing an extraordinary mystical sensibility: "At times I feel as if I am spread out over the landscape and inside things, and am myself living in every tree, in the plashing of the waves, in the clouds and animals that come and go, in the procession of the seasons."

* I would like to thank Drs Robert Romanyshyn and Roger Brooke for their helpful comments during the preparation of this paper.

References

Avens, R. (1984) *The New Gnosis,* Dallas: Spring Publications.

Brooke, R. (1991) *Jung and Phenomenology*, London and New York: Routledge.

Buber, M. (1952) *Eclipse of God: Studies in the Relation Between Religion and Philosophy*, New York: Harper and Row.

Chapman, J. H. (1988) *Jung's Three Theories of Religious Experience,* New York: The Edwin Mellon Press.

Corbett, L. (1996) *The Religious Function of the Psyche*, London and New York: Routledge.

de Voogd, S. (1977) "C. G. Jung: psychologist of the future, 'philosopher' of the past," *Spring*.

Doniger, W. (1997) "The implied spider: politics and theology in myth," *Religious Studies News*, 12, 1: 9.

Ellenberger, H. (1970) *The Discovery of the Unconscious: The History and Evolution of Dynamic Psychiatry*, New York: Basic Books.

Fromm, E. (1950) *Psychoanalysis and Religion*, New Haven: Yale University Press.

Jung, C. G. (1926) "Spirit and life," *CW* 8.

—— (1928) "The relations between the ego and the unconscious," *CW* 7.

—— (1931) "Basic postulates in analytical psychology," *CW* 8.

—— (1933) "Brother Klaus," *CW* 11.

—— (1934a) "Archetypes of the collective unconscious," *CW* 9.i.
—— (1934b) "Review of the complex theory," *CW* 8.
—— (1937) "Psychology and religion," *CW* 11.
—— (1947/54) "On the nature of the psyche," *CW* 8.
—— (1953) "Psychology and alchemy," *CW* 12.
—— (1957) "The undiscovered self," *CW* 10.
—— (1962) *Memories, Dreams, Reflections*, New York: Vintage Books.
—— (1970) *Psychological Reflections*, ed. Jolande Jacobi, trans. R. F. C. Hull, Princeton: Princeton University Press.
—— (1973) *Letters, vol. 1*, ed. G. Adler, and A. Jaffe, trans. R. F. C. Hull, Princeton: Princeton University Press.
—— (1975) *Letters, vol. 2*, ed. G. Adler, and A. Jaffe, trans. R. F. C. Hull, Princeton: Princeton University Press.
—— (1976) "The Symbolic Life," *CW* 18.
McGuire, W. and Hull, R. F. C. (eds) (1977) *C. G. Jung Speaking*, Princeton: Princeton University Press.
Miller, D. L. (1995) "Biblical imagery and psychological likeness," in D. L. Miller (ed.), *Jung and the Interpretation of the Bible*, New York: Continuum Publishing.
Otto, R. (1958) *The Idea of the Holy*, London: Oxford University Press.
Rawson, P. (1973) *Tantra: The Indian Cult of Ecstasy*, London: Thames and Hudson.
Ricoeur, P. (1970) *Freud and Philosophy*, New Haven: Yale University Press.
Romanyshyn, R. (1982) "Unconsciousness: reflection and the primacy of perception," in R. Bruzina and B. Wilshire (eds), *Phenomenology: Dialogues and Bridges*, Albany: State University of New York.
Rowe, C. E. and MacIsaac, D. S. (1991) *Empathic Attunement*, Northvale: Jason Aronson.
Schlamm, L. (1994) "The Holy: a meeting-point between analytical psychology and religion," in J. Ryce-Menuhin (ed.), *Jung and the Monotheisms*, London: Routledge.
Schmitt, R. (1968) "Husserl's transcendental-phenomenological reduction," in J. J. Kockelmans (ed.), *Phenomenology*, Garden City: Doubleday.
Stein, M. (1987) "Jung's green Christ: a healing symbol for Christianity," in M. Stein (ed.) *Jung's Challenge to Contemporary Religion*, Wilmette, Il: Chiron Publishers.
Stolorow, R.D. and Atwood, G. E. (1992) *Contexts of Being*, Hillsdale, New Jersey: Analytic Press.

EDITOR'S INTRODUCTION

A considerable literature developed around the theme of death in both the Jungian and existentialist traditions, although the two traditions rarely touched. The existentialists argued that death structures time as finititude: it is as an ever-present limiting horizon of all possibilities without which any understanding of time evaporates into meaninglessness, and so does the experience of human meaning. For them, the confrontation with death as finitude was a necessary condition for authenticity. Jung had an equally strong appreciation of the significance of death, but it focused less on temporality, and it was more psychological and complex.

For Mark Welman, it is curious that Thanatos is not addressed by Jung, who merely dismisses Freud's attempt to deal with it. This is, says Welman, because Jung himself was partly rooted in the same epistemological difficulties as Freud. However, Welman shows how a Jungian phenomenology of Thanatos, freed from Cartesianism and scientific awkwardness, elaborates central themes in the individuation process and in the paradoxical movements of the imagination. For Welman, a Jungian phenomenology of that dark god becomes, in a sense, an imaginative defense of Freud.

7

THANATOS AND EXISTENCE

Towards a Jungian phenomenology of the death instinct

Mark Welman

Introduction

The vicissitudes of Thanatos, the death instinct, form the cornerstone of Freud's post-1920 psychoanalytic project. By contrast, the concept of a death instinct is conspicuously absent in Jung's psychology. However, this omission is both ambiguous and perplexing, for while Jung distanced himself from Freud's theory of Thanatos there are numerous references in his writings to death as a purposeful goal and a fundamental objective of psychological life – an objective which may be wished for, enacted and revealed in both literal and imaginal forms. This chapter claims that in their treatment of death both Freud and Jung were attempting to lend theoretical substance to a pervasive and compelling facet of existence, that the dispute between their positions reflects important tensions between different ontological perspectives, and that both theorists were to varying degrees misdirected in their thanatological formulations by a subtle but intrusive allegiance to Cartesian science. The latter concern is more obvious in the case of Freud, who tended to view psychological reality as an epiphenomenon reducible to biology. Jung's promotion of psychological life as an order of reality in its own right does appear to set him apart from the Cartesian tradition, but it will be demonstrated that positivistic reductionism is a passive but equally intrusive influence in his thanatology, as it is in his broader theory of mind (cf. Brooke 1991).

It may be argued, therefore, that Jung's theory of death was limited by an ambivalent suspension between opposing paradigms with regard to the problem of finitude. The first has objectified death by treating it as nothing but the cessation of life, a phenomenon that is beyond the realm of experience or understanding. Ultimately, this approach has sought to translate an essentially enigmatic reality into a series of concrete variables, thereby imparting a spurious sense of control over that which stands as the ultimate embarrassment of the technocratic quest for mastery over nature. The other perspective may be described as "poetic" in its emphasis, and has been developed most fully within the tradition of existential-phenomenology. It regards death as a fundamental dimension of Being and a vital correlate of the attempt to establish existence as meaningful in a world which increasingly seems to mitigate against this. Thus a central concern of poetic thanatology is that in modern consciousness death is revealed not as a significant existential possibility but as a dispassionate and anonymous event which neither involves one in its drama nor moves one by its presence. This tendency is in turn implicated in the blunting of possibilities for authenticity, and thus in the spiritual and ethical crisis of modernity (Demske 1970).

Lending further urgency to these concerns is the thought that death does not tolerate its concealment passively: when denied or repressed it may subvert the life process in ways that range from the benign to the severe (see Gordon 1978). Seen through the lens of the poetic thanatologist, the sheer self-destructiveness of the modern epoch is evidence enough not only of the failure of rationality to make sense of mortality, but of a secret and distorted longing for the death that is so feared (Romanyshyn 1989). It seems that in refusing to die the Herculean ego of Western modernism has attacked life itself (Hillman 1979). In an important sense, these deliberations situate us in the domain of Thanatos.

Even a cursory consideration of Jung's writings suggests that his psychology has a meaningful contribution to make to the poetic tradition. Emerging in the context of modernity, his thinking was oriented towards the recovery of meaning, and his works sought to give expression to the conditions necessary for such a recovery. However, it is seldom recognised that he saw death as the ontological pivot in this process, and this is at least partly because the poetic significance of his thanatology tends to be obscured by empiricist leanings. Jung himself confessed that although the problematic of finitude was central to his psychology he struggled to articulate this in an appropriate discourse and could only "mythologise" about death. In this light, the present chapter aims to offer a Jungian phenomenology of death and of the death instinct and, therefore, to salvage Jung's hermeneutics of death from his science of death.

Freud and Thanatos

Thanatos has been termed "the darkest and most stubborn riddle posed by the legacy of psychoanalysis" (Boothby 1991: 1). This is testament to a theoretical conundrum that originated with the publication of *Beyond the Pleasure Principle* (Freud 1920). The question of death, until then virtually absent in Freud's psychology, was now thrust to the forefront of his analysis of the roots of psychic conflict and psychopathology. The war of 1914–1918 had played a part in this deflection in Freud's thinking (see Freud 1915), but the introduction of Thanatos was ultimately dictated by the failure of the pleasure principle to account for important clinical observations. Conceptualised as an innate tendency to release tension and avoid pain, it could not, for instance, explain the phenomenon of traumatic "repetition compulsion." Here the psychic apparatus apparently operates in opposition to the pleasure principle by purposefully reintroducing or exacerbating energic tensions. Second, the pleasure principle could not account for the "mysterious masochistic trends of the ego" (Freud 1920: 14), or, more broadly, the psychological roots of aggression towards self (masochism) and others (sadism).

Having thus identified a need to move "beyond the pleasure principle," Freud introduced a new classification of instincts to explain psychological conflict: Eros or the life instincts, which included libidinal drives, and Thanatos or the death instinct, operating alongside but in opposition to Eros. As Freud described it, the vicissitudes of Thanatos are such that it is oriented towards a reduction of tension and the reinstatement of a homeostatic state. Deflected outwards because of the threat which it poses to the ego or the ego ideal, Thanatos manifests as aggression towards others. When that avenue is in turn blocked by the voice of authority (internal or external), Thanatos "turns within" and may be played out in masochistic tendencies.

Freud's theory of Thanatos has found relatively little favour among his followers – with Klein and Lacan being notable exceptions. There has been reasonable concern that Thanatos is too speculative a principle and lacks clinical specificity, but ultimately the claim that death and aggression are fundamental to human experience has proved distasteful to even the most devoted psychoanalysts (Boothby 1991: 8). Pontalis (1978: 86) has gone so far as to suggest that the often maligned emphasis on sexuality (Eros) in the psychoanalytic tradition may amount to something of a "cover up" of the even more maligned theme of death.

Perhaps the mistake Freud made – the one that led to the general rejection of his concept of Thanatos – is that he turned to biology for his conceptual ground. He envisioned Thanatos as deriving primarily from a biological need for organic matter to return to a prior inorganic state, with the result that its goal was formulated as that of literal death (Freud 1920: 38; cf. Boothby 1991; Brown 1959/1985; Laplanche 1976). In this context his conclusion that "the aim of all life is [literal] death" (op. cit.) was bound to elicit strong opposition even from his own ranks.

In the years since Freud, however, some psychoanalytic theorists have made significant contributions to a hermeneutics of death by revisioning Freud's theory in a poetic light. It is beyond the scope of this chaper to consider their work in any detail, but a common theme is an insistence that the goal of Thanatos is not one of literal destruction but rather a metaphoric death, referring to the "deconstruction" of the literalist ego in favour of a symbolic order, i.e. reality that is grounded imaginally (see Boothby 1991; Brown 1959/85). This approach to the issue "corrects" Freud's literalisation of the death instinct and moves Thanatos closer to existential-phenomenological thinking about the fears and aspirations attached to the image of death. It would seem that a similar approach to Jung's thanatology may prove to be equally fruitful.

Death in Jung's analysis of existence

Professional rivalry, the acrimonious rupture with his former mentor and friend, and the pessimistic undertones of Freud's thinking, may all be reasons for Jung's failure to give credence, or even critical attention, to the concept of Thanatos. In his only comment on the issue, Jung tersely stated that Freud's theory represented merely a "concession to intellectual logic" (Jung 1917/43: 53), meaning that Freud had oversimplified the equation of Eros with life and had therefore been compelled to interpret its opposite as Thanatos, death. Hence Freud had understood Thanatos to be "purely destructive, deadly and evil" (ibid.). Jung's argument here seems to be that if death is indeed intrinsic to life, to the extent that it derives from life itself and is proper to it, then it is both prejudicial and misleading to see death as inevitably opposed to life. In Jung's thanatology, this concern is addressed by a shift in emphasis from opposition to an appreciation of death as a meaningful part of life's unfolding.

Jung's treatment of the problematic of finitude adopts as its central concern the impact of death on the existence of the modern person. He was insistent that attempts to bring the study of death into the harsh glare of scientific inquiry failed to do justice to the complexity of the topic, and that the existential significance of death could not be reduced to a statistical or a biological issue only. Jung (1934a) argued that the meaning of life "never becomes more urgent or more agonizing" than in the face of death, and that to refute the significance of death by treating it as a generalised rather than a personal problem is in part a defensive posture in the face of the cold reality of life's limitation. It allows one to avoid or postpone consideration of the inevitable, but in so doing it leads to a "negation of life's fulfilment," for not wanting to die and not wanting to live are synonymous (ibid.: 407). However, it is not simply that one needs to accept the inevitable fate of human beings. Jung's understanding was that if life is to be meaningful then death must be entertained as "a goal and a fulfilment" (ibid.: 405–6). This, he maintained, is at least the manner in which the psyche itself approaches death, even though the conscious mind may recoil from its advance. In the second half of life, Jung asserted, psychological processes follow an inexorable path towards the goal of death. "The curve of life is like the parabola of a projectile which, disturbed from its initial state of rest, rises and then returns to a state of repose" (Jung 1912/52: 406).

These statements are remarkably close to Freud's understanding of Thanatos, and it may seem reasonable to infer that Jung's position was not dissimilar to that of Freud. The key difference, however, is that whereas Freud's Thanatos has as its aim a literal, corporeal death, the death with which Jung is concerned is not simply a biological event but a psychological state or reality which has meaning in its own right. Conceptually speaking, this state relates to the manifestation of the Self, the primordial matrix from which psychological life emerges and to which it must inevitably return (e.g. Gordon 1961; von Franz 1986; Welman and Faber 1992). Thus death is a fundamentally ambivalent image, the implications of which depend on whether it is approached from the reality of the ego or from that of the Self. For the former, "death is indeed a fearful piece of brutality", but from the perspective of the Self "death appears as a joyful event . . . a *mysterium coniunctionis* [through which] the soul . . . achieves wholeness" (Jung 1962/83: 346).

Understanding the meaning of death in terms of the archetype of the Self offers a model that is more existentially adequate than Freud's narrow conception of Thanatos. However, it is one thing to acknowledge that the conclusion of life has psychological significance, but it is another matter to promote an image of death as an unremitting psychological reality, a pervasive and persuasive presence throughout the course of existence. In short, it is not sufficient simply to rest with the assumption of a teleological proclivity towards death. As Avens (1982) states, to see death as a goal that is situated at the end of life only is to betray a hidden Cartesian assumption that death is also something that is essentially outside of the scope of life, and this detracts from its existential and ontological significance. Hillman (1979: 30) is critical of most teleological models of death for the same reason, maintaining that they fail to acknowledge a fundamental truth to which poets throughout the generations have professed, namely that the goal of death is always now.

A key consideration to come out of the above comments is that in analytical psychology, as in psychoanalysis, the impact of death as an existential issue has not always been followed through to its full implications. Thus Jung (1930/31: 397) asserted, for instance, that the question of mortality is essentially irrelevant to dealing with the problems of mid-life "because as a rule death is still far in the distance and therefore somewhat abstract," and this reflects a subtle but fairly persistent claim in his writings that death is a problem of late life only (e.g. Jung 1934a; 1962/83). In part this reflects the considerable degree of ambiguity surrounding his understanding of the Self, treating it both as an emergent wholeness that is actualised only at the end of life, and as an omnipresent totality within which all experience is grounded (see Redfearn 1985). But the tendency to refer the meaning of death to the end of life is, essentially, a further indication of the tension in Jung's writings between poetic and scientific frames of reference, and this muddle has often been perpetuated by his followers. Arguably, this means that Jung's writings do not do true justice to his grasp of the existential depth and complexity of death. In order to understand how the concept of Thanatos may be meaningfully articulated with Jung's psychology, it is therefore necessary to reveal the poetic intent to his thanatology by way of a hermeneutic amplification of the theoretical connections between death and the Self.

Death and the heroic ego

An analysis of Jung's poetics of death begins with his seminal work, *Wandlungen und Symbole der Libido*, first published in 1912 and later revised and translated as "Symbols of transformation" (Jung 1912/52). *Wandlungen* is a key text in Jungian thanatology. Not only did its publication signal Jung's emergence as a thinker firmly independent of Freud, but it also represents his earliest attempts to formulate a hermeneutics of death. The image of death advanced in that text is not one of a literal ending of life, but one of death as an imaginal reality: a dark and pervasive presence and a primordial abyss which is both longed for and retreated from. As an archetypal theme, the meaning of death thus points to an "undifferentiated, unconscious state of primal being" (ibid.: 417), i.e. the Self in its chaotic, preconscious form. Gordon (1961: 120) extends this formulation by defining death as "a state of absorption in a union which precludes boundaries, differentiation, separateness, and the tension of opposites."

That there is a creative and transformative aspect to death may already be evident, and this theme will receive attention in a later section. But it is primarily with the negative, destructive face of death that *Wandlungen* is concerned, and in this regard two important facets of death emerge. In the first instance, Jung described death as an obscure but omnipresent "enemy within" (op. cit.: 355), referring to the idea that as a primitive, prepersonal state of being it obliterates the light of consciousness. We are dealing here with a conservative tendency of the Self, the primordial Mother, to reclaim and to hold fast to that to which it gives life (see Neumann 1963; Sullivan 1989). On the other hand, we must also reckon with a regressive propensity on the part of the ego, described by Jung (1912/52: 292) as a longing for "the paradisal state of early infancy, from which we are driven by the relentless law of time," a "deadly longing for the abyss, a longing to drown in [one's] source, to be sucked down to the realm of the Mothers" (ibid.: 355–6). What this means is that the winning of consciousness, the Promethean triumph of the ego, is threatened both by the chthonic forces of the Self and by a regressive nostalgia for the "lost Mother."

In terms of the parameters outlined above, death is an archetypal metaphor for both relatively benign experiences of immobility, homeostasis and rest on one hand and, on the other hand, disintegrative states in which boundaries collapse and reality and phantasy become indistinguishable (Gordon 1961; Savitz 1990). The manifestation of these conditions may be accompanied by phantasies of reentry into the mother's breast or belly

(Gordon 1978), but motifs of destruction, annihilation and engulfment are equally common (Welman 1995). These themes may symbolise a collapse of ego boundaries and the immersion of the ego in a frightening liminal realm where personal identity and the known world of the subject are threatened with obliteration. For instance, a patient reported shortly before his death from cancer a dream of a great flood which obliterated all in its path and washed him away. The dreamer did appear to view the approach of death as a catastrophic annihilation, and the dream speaks to this experience. It touches on the metaphor of the alchemical *solutio*, the dissolution of matter into its original chaotic state, and in this sense appears to indicate of the engulfment of the ego by the unconscious – i.e. an image of death as a primitive, regressive reality.

Jung's grasp of death as an abysmal presence was informed by archetypal themes and images which he amplified from myth, and from dreams and visions which he recorded in clinical practice. However, he acknowledged that his most important academic work tended to be a reflection of his personal opus, a "confession" of "tasks imposed from within" (Jung 1962: 211). Therefore, the image of death appearing in *Wandlungen* reflects in an important way his own struggle, in his early life particularly, to establish and to preserve a stable sense of personal identity in the face of powerful chthonic forces which threatened to dominate his psychological life. This theme cannot be pursued at any length here, but the key point is that among the "fateful compulsions" (ibid.) of Jung's life was an unremitting labour to resolve the tension between life and death forces. This struggle is fundamental to psychological life, but in Jung's case it was exaggerated both by an "inner" vulnerability related to the absence of a stable maternal presence during his formative years (see Winnicott 1964) and by the fact that he was confronted from an early age with the harsh realities of corporeal death in the "outer" world. Thus he recalled that death-related incidents (his father officiating at funerals, bodies being lowered into the ground, drowned corpses being recovered from the Rhine Falls) served as "overwhelming images" during his early years and contributed to a morbid preoccupation with the possibility of personal annihilation (op. cit.: 23). Therefore, it may be understood that the threat of ego disintegration and the objective reality of death to which he was exposed – i.e. both metaphoric and literal configurations of death – interacted to form a compulsive complex through which his experience was mediated, and this complex may have been a primary operative factor underlying the neurotic symptoms (e.g. nightmares, vague fears, fainting episodes) which pervaded his childhood years.

Essentially, then, Jung's early psychological life appears to have gravitated around a nameless horror to do with the threat of destruction and non-being (Welman 1995). Significantly, he related that this reality occasioned almost overwhelming desires to retreat from life itself, for life, being bound to the ego, meant confronting the terror of annihilation. This propensity in turn translated into an unconscious attraction to death. Recalling numerous serious falls and one attempt to climb through the railings of a bridge over the Rhine Falls, Jung (1962: 23) reflected that "these things point to an unconscious suicidal urge or, it may be, to a fatal resistance to life in this world." It is thus reasonable to make a theoretical connection between these incidents and the operation of the death instinct, but then it must also be noted that we are dealing in this instance with a relatively primitive, presymbolic response in which the distinction between the literal and the figurative dimensions of the image of death are blurred, so that the attractive force of metaphoric death as a sanctuary from the demands of conscious existence becomes enacted as an impulse towards corporeal death.

We are led to the impression that the early years of Jung's life were characterised by a precarious suspension between the need for differentiation and development of the ego complex on one hand, and on the other hand a regressive propensity towards death and dissolution. In *Wandlungen*, Jung advanced the theory that such tension and ambivalence occasions the emergence of the heroic ego. The archetypal qualities of the hero have been well documented (e.g. Campbell 1949). They reflect essentially masculine processes of differentiation and discrimination which are necessary for separation from the Mother (in both men and women) so that the gift of consciousness can be claimed. Perhaps with his own experiences in mind, Jung recognised that while it is the destiny of the heroic ego to affirm its existence in the world, this impulse towards life tends, as already indicated, to be countered by a regressive longing for a pre-egoic state. Samuels (1985: 149) adds that this ambivalence is an integral feature of any model of life and death instincts. Strauss (1964) has argued that a resolution of this tension through the emergence of mediating symbols is in turn vital for the development of a reasonably stable personality.

Death as home to the imagination

In *Wandlungen* Jung had drawn a vague connection between death, images of psychical totality (later conceptualised in terms of the archetype of the Self), and the Eastern idea of an all-pervasive "soul" which is both "in" the person and at the same time encompasses the personal ego within its boundaries (Jung 1912/52: 123). Though he did not pursue these associations at the time, his resonance with Eastern philosophies grew stronger with the recognition that they may offer an important correction to the dualistic emphasis of Western thinking. While Jung maintained that the importation of Eastern approaches is not a solution to the problems facing a spiritually bankrupt Western culture, there can be little doubt that Eastern paradigms were influential in the development of his thanatology. For instance, his analysis of the *Tibetan Book of the Dead* (Jung 1935/53) revealed a more hospitable face of death than the one to which he had been accustomed, and it enabled him to extend the theoretical parameters of the association between death and the Self. He came to appreciate that as a psychological reality death refers not only to a regressive condition but to an evolved state of wholeness in which customary ego-based boundaries give way in favour of a more encompassing totality, a union of opposites or *mysterium coniunctionis*. This capacity for transcendent consciousness involves the incarnation of the Self in a way that is also conducive to the development of the ego, even though it may be experienced, at least initially, as a threatening upheaval (Jung 1955–6: 360f.). In other words, the ego's boundaries are transcended and "widened" without its basic integrity being compromised. But this movement also implies an experience of reality in a non-dualistic way, meaning the suspension of "inner" conflict and tension and the reparation of the Cartesian rupture between self (ego) and world. It is in this light that Jung (1934b: 184) wrote of the transcendent capacity of the Self as "the voice of a fuller life, of a wider, more comprehensive consciousness," leading to the recognition that death, in its "positive" form, is no less than a liberation from the narrow confines of egocentric consciousness. It reveals to us "the primacy of the psyche, for that is the one thing which life does not make clear to us" (Jung 1935/53: 513).

This is a key and perhaps understated argument, for it establishes a vital connection between the Self and death, on one hand, and the imaginal ground of Being, or that capacity which Jung termed "symbolic life," on the other. However, the existential significance of this argument is evident only if we refrain from the tendency in analytical psychology to reify the Self and to think of it as an encapsulated space within the mind (see Brooke 1991: 96ff.), which also implies the reduction of death to a Cartesian event inside the head. As Jung himself emphasised, however, psychical wholeness or totality is not simply limited to the boundaries of the person (Jung 1929: 51). The Self is "true reality . . . not only in me but in all things" (Jung 1959: 463), and to forget this is to confuse the Self with the ego (Jung 1947/54: 226). Brooke (1991: 99) summarises the issue by asserting that to think of the Self as a "something" is less accurate than to understand it "as a 'no-thing' . . . a fertile and hospitable emptiness within which the things of the world . . . shine forth." Or as Avens (1982: 144) puts it, the Self is best thought of as "an empty 'place' where many selves come to mingle and depart."

These considerations serve to clarify the connection between death and imaginal life. As an illimitable space or "nothingness" within which images can emerge in their own right – i.e. unadulterated and free of the ego's proclivity for the rationalisation of the poetic – death is the proper home to the imagination. Death as a transcendent reality (as opposed to its representation of primitive states of fusion) is therefore a metaphor for a pivotal shift in one's mode of experiencing things from iconoclastic literalism to imaginative vision. Jung (1939: 546) made precisely this point in asserting that the transcendence or death of the ego heralds a "new state" of being in which (quoting the Zen master Suzuki) "the old ways of seeing things is abandoned and the world acquires a new signification" (ibid.: 546n). "*It is not that something different is seen*," Jung explained, "*but that one sees differently*" (ibid.: 546, original emphasis). This theoretical position has been advanced particularly vigorously in the work of Hillman (1975), who treats death as a metaphor for a shift from literalism to an imaginative perspective.

The meaning of death and the death of meaning

An understanding of death as the *sine qua non* of our imaginative capacities is a central theme too in existential phenomenological approaches to thanatology. Particular mention must be made of the work of Heidegger (1927/62) and his followers (e.g. Avens 1982; Demske 1970; Levin 1988), who have promoted an image of death as a "nothingness," or a Void through which is facilitated the divine revelation of Being. Heidegger's celebrated description of death as "the shrine of nothing" (op. cit.: 178), meaning an ontological emptiness within which Being is grounded and through which its necessary recollection may be effected, should suffice to illustrate this point, but it is also worth noting Segal's (1989: 118) comment that the poet is one who "touches the extremes of life and death and overcomes the threat of nothingness by transforming the physical world into pure Being." The important consideration here is that death offers a poetic space within which rigid assumptions and hypostatised experience may be deliteralised and reviewed in an imaginative or symbolic light so that they are lent a quality of depth and meaning which tends to be lost in everyday life. Therefore death is not a retreat to a sequestered and congested space in the mind but an opening of the imagination – "a clearing which is good to things," as Levin (1988: 378) puts it – through which the world is transformed from its inanimate and desolate place in Cartesian experience to the authentic dwelling place of Being.

What emerges is that death is an existential necessity in so far as it facilitates the emergence and recollection of Being and the reenchantment of personal existence. On the other hand, it also seems evident that the concealment of death's meaning through its objectification in modern consciousness leads inescapably to a death of meaning. As Gordon (1978) has argued, a retreat from death may lead to an impairment in the capacity to symbolise, with the result that psychological life becomes dogged by sterile literalisms (or "projections"). Thus in the absence of an imagination of death there is a death of the imagination (Sardello 1974). In this regard, Brooke (1991: 110) points out that the flattening of personal identity within the literalisms of contemporary life is not necessarily pathological or excessive, but it does seem to be the price paid for technocratic mastery in the modern world. The key point is that the development of consciousness necessitates the emergence of something beyond the narrow, literalistic confines of the ego. If theoretically this entails a confrontation with the reality of the Self, then existentially it involves an encounter with the ontological immediacy of death. Thus a major theme in Jung's later writings is that of a need to relinquish the heroic qualities of the ego in favour of emergent possibilities of wholeness and the recognition that this developmental process tends to be reflected by and orchestrated through archetypal images of sacrifice, death and renewal (e.g. Jung 1934a, 1940/54, 1962).

As with his understanding of the regressive features of death, Jung's appreciation of the existential significance of sacrifice was informed both by his analysis of myth and ritual (particularly the Catholic Mass) and through personal experience. With regard to the latter, it was primarily during his mid-life metanoia, a period lasting some four years (1912–1916), that the theme of sacrifice was lived out. It was reflected in a series of numinous dreams and visions – e.g. plunging down into dark depths, the corpse of a blonde youth, a cataclysmic flood that killed thousands – which Jung (1962: 173) interpreted as referring to a "drama of death and renewal." The climactic point in the process came with a dream in which he shot and killed Siegfried, the archetypal hero of Germanic myth. Motivated by an inner voice commanding him to shoot himself if he could not make sense of the dream, he recognised that it carried both personal and cultural significance:

> [It] showed that the attitude embodied by Siegfried, the hero, no longer suited me. Therefore it had to be killed. . . . I felt an overpowering compassion, as though I myself had been shot: a sign of my secret identity with Siegfried, as well as the grief a man feels when he is forced to sacrifice his ideal and his conscious attitudes. This identity and my heroic idealism had to be abandoned, for there are higher things than the ego's will, and to these one must bow.
>
> (ibid.: 174)

The dream represented a focal point in Jung's individuation and, indeed, in the history of analytical psychology. Its meaning spoke both to Jung and to the modern *Weltanschauung*: the imperialistic, heroic attitude of the ego must be sacrificed in the service of a "higher" calling, and this constitutes an ethical imperative. For Jung, it led to a process of "immersion" into "the reality of the psyche" (ibid.) – a symbolic *nekyia* or descent to the underworld – which anticipated in turn the embodiment of a mature consciousness anchored by the ego but able to dwell in close proximity to death (Welman 1995). It also led Jung to the realisation that the process of individuation, especially in the second half of life, entails a work towards death. The renunciation of heroic ego qualities involved in this process is no easy matter – "it is a sacrifice which daunts even the gods" (Jung 1912/52: 356) – but the refusal of such a concession "leads to stagnation and desiccation of soul" (ibid.), i.e. to a neurotic *stasis* characterised by the impairment of the symbolic process and an atrophy of the imagination.

The death instinct: a Jungian formulation

The death instinct may be described as an innate propensity located in the processes of the Self or, as Gordon (1961: 125) has defined it, "the valence of the Self, that is, its attractive force." Therefore Thanatos is oriented on one hand towards a "return" of the ego to its primal origins and on the other hand towards a transcendent union of opposites. It is useful for heuristic purposes to think of these conditions as referring to "regressive" and "progressive" facets of the death instinct, although in practice a neat distinction between these propensities cannot be maintained because the movements of psyche are ambiguous and paradoxical. That is, the regressive and progressive aspects of Thanatos tend to manifest concurrently (Welman 1995). This makes sense particularly in the context of analysis or psychotherapy, where movement towards integration and the development of consciousness is invariably coupled with experiences of loss, abandonment or threatened disintegration, at least initially. Rebirth is both ecstatic and painful.

Gordon (1961) argues that whether Thanatos is directed towards preconscious fusion or transcendent wholeness depends on the dynamic tension between the ego and the Self. Here it is helpful to think in terms of Thanatos as operating along an ego–Self axis. When there is a lack of differentiation between the two or when the ego is constitutionally vulnerable (as in the infant and the psychotic patient), then the death instinct may manifest as a seductive and regressive force which precipitates or maintains a psychical state characterised by primitive chaos and the lack of appropriate boundaries. But when the ego is sufficiently differentiated from the Self, then Thanatos may serve as a creative impulse towards transcendence and the integration of the Self in space and time. In both instances, however, the propensity towards non-being needs to be balanced by a drive, located in the functions of the ego, towards differentiation and separation (ibid.). This is because the development of consciousness demands dialectical tension between the ego and the Self with the implication that, as Sandner (1986) puts it, one mandala must collapse so that another might be formed. Thus we are led to the recognition that the tension between life forces (ego, separation, differentiation) and those associated with the death instinct (Self, fusion, wholeness) forms the existential pivot of psychological development throughout the life span. Such is the nature of the *opus* to which mortals must submit. At one moment it is a work against death so that the boundaries of personal identity might be forged, even as it is paradoxically understood that this life affirming endeavour involves the death of ego–Self inflation and preOedipal omnipotence. At the next moment, it is a work towards death so that one may gather oneself together and reconnect with the source of life itself, thereby deepening the metaphors through which personal existence is lived.

The clinical challenge is to mediate and resolve through naturally occurring symbols the tension between the life and death forces so that a reasonably stable personality – one neither driven by nor rooted in the extreme fringes of life or death – can emerge. This challenge appears especially pronounced for the borderline personality, characterised as it is by the concretisation of imaginal life and a destructive ambivalence towards situations of merger, fusion, loss and separation. Perhaps we must recognise that beyond purely clinical issues there is a sense in which the borderline condition manifests as a mad and demonic shadow haunting those liminal realms which the modern ego has vacated. Perhaps the borderline person enacts the archetypal struggle for *psychological* existence which is forgotten by the accomplished ego, and thereby speaks to each of us as therapists, whether or not we are borderline too. Perhaps the discomfort so often experienced in work with these patients is partly a reflection of our own unease operating in a space where the boundaries of life and death, creation and destruction, are entirely blurred.

It is in the context of the modern alienation of the ego from the world of the Self that the transformative value of the death instinct is most apparent. As Demske (1970: 166) writes, death is to the alienated technocrat "a force which calls one, gathers oneself together, and provides an orientation toward that which gives meaning to existence." In these terms Thanatos may be envisioned as a propensity emerging from the Self and oriented towards the restoration of imaginal life through a creative dialectic between Self and ego. In the profane atmosphere of contemporary Western life the death instinct thus serves as a poetic calling, a calling of Being and to Being. But as the Self is not only "in" oneself but "in" all things, it is therefore a calling which emerges both from "within" one's person and from the world (see Brooke 1991: 104). An ecstatic union with a lover, being lifted up in prayer, a pilgrimage to a place felt as holy or sacred, the tranquillity of a summer evening in the wilderness, the guilt experienced by a white South African who accepts ethical responsibility for the human catastrophe of Apartheid: these experiences all may invite self-reflection and, perhaps, the transcendence of the finite ego, so that the recipient feels a connection with and an obligation to higher things than the ego's will. Therefore they may be lived as metaphors for the renunciation of narrow ego-based ways of being and their personal significance deepened through an appreciation of their imaginal connections to psychological processes of death and renewal.

For modern Man and Woman the ethical significance of this shift is that it represents atonement for the "wrongfulness" of existence that is governed by a dogmatic and covetous attitude. This calling is exemplified by the figure of Philemon, the humble peasant in Goethe's *Faust* who offers shelter to the gods forced to flee from Faust's destructive machinations (Jung 1962: 221–2).

Philemon represents a comportment of hospitality and unpretentious openness to the moment (Giegerich 1984), an aliveness to the presencing of Being that is lacking in modern consciousness.

Thanatos constitutes a calling which need not always emerge in dramatic or extreme form, and perhaps seldom does. Often the calling may take the form of a relatively subtle need for respite from the habitual patterns and demands of one's daily life, to seek repose or a "resting place" where, as Jung phrased it with reference to his sanctuary at Bollingen, "the torment of creation is lessened" (op. cit.: 253). Samuels (1985: 99) has similarly argued that one purpose of the death instinct is to bring to being "the peace and quiet of an integrated state of oneness (where) the boilers of creativity can be restoked." By way of illustration, a patient whose chief complaint was chronic fatigue came to understand that, instead of being an irritating impediment to progress, her tiredness represented an invitation to disengage from a compulsive need for achievement by calling her away from a "masculine" world of competitiveness and ego-based ambition towards a quieter, "feminine" (her terms) space of solitude and regeneration. Thus she began to balance her dedication to work with periods of repose brought about in her garden, which had previously been her favourite sanctuary. Hence the tiredness that she embodied may be interpreted as a benevolent form of the death instinct, operating to bring about a more therapeutic way of being.

A further consideration is that if Thanatos serves as a calling of Being then for this calling to translate into a response that is ethical or therapeutic there needs to be a comportment of "proper hearing" (Leman-Stefanovic 1987: 75) on the part of the ego. Avens (1980: 33–4) captures the essence of this concern in writing that "we can get to the specifically and ontologically human, the 'no-thing' at the centre of our being, only by moving through the poetic mode and by using poetic tools. Only the poet in us is tuned to our essential 'no-thing-ness'." In this regard we have seen that Jung voices the need for a sacrificial attitude, the embodiment of which amounts to a capacity to tolerate the "defeat" of the ego. It is Thanatos, perhaps, which calls for us to "listen" instead of "speak" (Holt 1975), to let things be in that patient acceptance Heidegger (1936) calls *Gelassenheit*. Without this willingness it is unlikely that one will be amenable to the radical relativisation of the ego which Thanatos entails. It would seem that this transformation in attitude or orientation is partly a matter of developmental maturation, but then it must also be realised that this maturation is itself partly a function of repetitive processes of death and regeneration in the life of the individual (Gordon 1978). It is through these repeated encounters with death that an ego is forged which is "willing to die," that is, to relinquish the old ways of being. But the rejection of death and of thanatomimetic ("death-like") modes of experience in Western culture has meant an absence of this willingness, making the task of a recollection of death all the more difficult –

but also all the more necessary, for when life does not want to die then it seems to turn away too from the tasks of living.

Concluding thoughts

Experiences involving the collapse or the transcendence of personal boundaries are captured by the imagination as images of death. In these terms death and dying are metaphors through which is lived an awakening of symbolic life and a deepening of personal identity and of one's experience of the world. This process is initiated by the death instinct operating in the service of the Self. For an ego that is vulnerable or fragmented, however, Thanatos may be a destructive force that shatters precious vestiges of personal identity and propels the psyche towards a primitive state of non-being.

This phenomenological interpretation of death should not be understood to relieve us of facing the stark reality of death "on its own terms." To forget that the metaphoric dimension of death refers also to a concrete reality is to approach death in an ungrounded and overly abstract way. At worst the calling of death is intellectualised to the point of irrelevance. However, it must be emphasised that if symbolic death is lent potency through an affirming imaginal connection to literal death then it is equally true that literal death and dying are cast in an imaginal context which imparts meaning and transformative value to the ending of life (see von Franz 1986; Welman 1995). Indeed, the dreams and visions of the dying suggest that towards the end of life Thanatos acts to facilitate a meaningful reconciliation between the concrete implications of death on one hand and its imaginal connotations and aspirations on the other (Welman 1995). Perhaps it is here that the value of Freud's work on the death instinct emerges, for it draws attention to literal death as an ultimate end and psychological ground.

References

Avens, R. (1980) *Imagination is Reality: Western Nirvana in Jung, Hillman, Barfield and Cassirer*, Dallas: Spring Publications.

—— (1982) *Imaginal Body: Para-Jungian Reflections on Soul, Imagination, and Death*, Washington: University Press of America.

Boothby, R. (1991) *Death and Desire: Psychoanalytic Theory in Lacan's Return to Freud*, London: Routledge.

Brooke, R. (1991) *Jung and Phenomenology*, London: Routledge.

Brown, N. O. (1959/85) *Life against Death: the Psychoanalytic Meaning of History*, (2nd edn), Conn.: Wesleyan University Press.

Campbell, J. (1949) *The Hero with a Thousand Faces*, New York: Pantheon.

Demske, J. M. (1970) *Being, Man and Death: a Key to Heidegger*, Lexington: University of Kentucky Press.

Freud, S. (1915) "Thoughts for times on war and death," *The Standard Edition of the*

Complete Psychological Works of Sigmund Freud, ed. and trans. by James Strachey *et al.* (24 volumes), 14, London: Hogarth Press, 1958.
Freud, S. (1920) "Beyond the pleasure principle," *S.E.*, 18.
Giegerich, W. (1984) "Hospitality towards the gods in an ungodly age: Philemon-Faust-Jung," *Spring*, 61–75.
Gordon, R. (1961) "The death instinct and its relation to the self," *Journal of Analytical Psychology*, 6, 2, 119–37.
—— (1978) *Dying and Creating: a Search for Meaning*, London: Society of Analytical Psychology.
Heidegger, M. (1927/62) *Being and Time*, trans. J. Macquarrie and E. Robinson, Oxford: Basil Blackwell.
—— (1936) "What are poets for?" In *Poetry, Language, Thought*, trans. A. Hofstader, New York: Harper Colophon Books, 1971.
Hillman, J. (1975) *Re-visioning Psychology*, New York: Harper & Row.
—— (1979) *The Dream and the Underworld*, New York: Harper & Row.
Holt, D. (1975) "Projection, presence, profession," *Spring*, 130–44.
Jung, C. G. (1912/1952) "Symbols of transformation," *CW* 5.
—— (1917/43) "On the psychology of the unconscious," *CW* 7.
—— (1929) "Commentary on 'The secret of the golden flower'," *CW* 13.
—— (1930/31) "The stages of life," *CW* 8.
—— (1934a) "The soul and death," *CW* 8.
—— (1934b) "The practical use of dream analysis," *CW* 16.
—— (1935/53) "Psychological commentary on *The Tibetan Book of the Dead*," *CW* 11.
—— (1939) "Foreword to Suzuki's *Introduction to Zen Buddhism*," *CW* 11.
—— (1940/54) "Transformation symbolism in the mass," *CW* 11.
—— (1947/54) "On the nature of the psyche," *CW* 8.
—— (1955–6) "Mysterium coniunctionis," *CW* 14.
—— (1959) "Good and evil in analytical psychology," *CW* 10.
—— (1962) *Memories, Dreams, Reflections*, ed. by A. Jaffe, trans. R. and C. Wilson, London: Routledge and Kegan Paul.
Laplanche, J. (1976) *Life and Death in Psychoanalysis*, trans. J. Mehlman, Baltimore: Johns Hopkins University Press.
Leman-Stefanovic, I. (1987) *The Event of Death: a Phenomenological Enquiry*, Dordrecht: Nijhoff.
Levin, D. M. (1988) *The Opening of Vision: Nihilism and the Postmodern Situation*, London: Routledge.
Neumann, E. (1963) *The Great Mother: an Analysis of the Archetype*, Princeton: Princeton University Press.
Pontalis, J.-B. (1978) "On death-work in Freud, in the self, in culture," in A. Roland (ed.) *Psychoanalysis, Creativity and Literature*, New York: Columbia University Press, 1985.
Redfearn, J. W. T. (1985) *My Self, My Many Selves*, London: Academic Press.
Romanyshyn, R. (1989) *Technology as Symptom and Dream*, London: Routledge.
Samuels, A. (1985) *Jung and the Post-Jungians*, London: Routledge.
Sandner, D. F. (1986) "The symbolic life of man," in L. Zoja and R. Hinshaw (eds) *Symbolic and Clinical Approaches in Practice and Theory*, Zurich: Daimon.
Sardello, R. J. (1974) "Death and the imagination," *Journal of the Institute of Man*, 10, 1, 61–73.

Savitz, C. (1990) "The burning cauldron: transference as paradox," *Journal of Analytical Psychology*, 35, 1, 59–78.

Segal, C. (1989) *Orpheus: the Myth of the Poet*, Baltimore: Johns Hopkins University Press.

Strauss, R. (1964) "The archetype in separation," in A. Guggenbuhl-Craig (ed.) *The Archetype*, Basle: Karger.

Sullivan, B. S. (1989) *Psychotherapy Grounded in the Feminine Principle*, Wilmette, Ill.: Chiron Publications.

Von Franz, M.-L. (1986) *On Dreams and Death: a Jungian Interpretation*, trans. E. Kennedy and V. Brooks, Boston: Shambala.

Welman, M. (1995) "Death and gnosis: archetypal dream imagery in terminal illness," unpublished PhD thesis, Rhodes University, Grahamstown.

Welman, M. and Faber, P. (1992) "The dream in terminal illness: a Jungian formulation," *Journal of Analytical Psychology*, 37, 1, 61–81.

Winnicott, D. (1964) "Book review of *Memories, Dreams, Reflections* by C. G. Jung," *The International Journal of Psychoanalysis*, 45, 450–5.

EDITOR'S INTRODUCTION

Existential phenomenology is at often its best when it questions once again phenomena that are enigmatic not because of their remoteness but because of their proximity. Remembering and forgetting are a case in point. The fallibility of memory is taken for granted, and memories are too quickly discussed in terms of neurology ("traces"), their relationship to factual histories ("recovered memories"), or their over-determined falsifications ("false-memory syndrome"). Any competent analyst or psychotherapist comes to sit comfortably with deep uncertainties surrounding memory, even as it is at the center of analytic work (perhaps reconstructively through the transference). We are tempted to say that memories are a "mixture" of historical fact, primitive fantasy, transference derivatives, and so on. But few of us have taken up the question of what memories are *as memories*. This is Charles Scott's question.

In the Introduction to *Being and Time* Heidegger writes that phenomenology is ontology. This is true in Scott's hands too. He uses the kind of archetypal amplification that is familiar to Jungian readers – in this case Mnemosyne, Lethe, and Hermes – and for this reason gently seduces us into feeling we are on secure and familiar ground. But if his immediate concern – his method – is an archetypal phenomenology of memory, his goal is to invite a rigorous meditation through the mystery of "forgetfulness" to ontological questions about what it means to have memories at all, to think theoretically, to have a sense of self, and to be human. It becomes clearer, I think, that the profound uncertainties with which we are left can not be placated.

8

MNEMOSYNE AND LETHE

Memory, Jung, phenomenology

Charles E. Scott

> One thing must be understood: I have said nothing extraordinary or even surprising. What is extraordinary begins at the moment I stop. But I am no longer able to speak of it.
>
> Maurice Blanchot

I would like to address two issues: the appearing of memories and the losses that occur in the appearing. I use the phrase, "the appearing of memories," instead of "remembering" because I do not want to suggest that remembering is primarily something that we do or intend to do. We do remember, and that activity may be characterized by effort, discipline, failure and success, and many other attributes of individual effort. But actively remembering is only one, broad way in which memories appear, and even active remembering may well not be as defined by individual activity as we ordinarily think it is. "Loss" of memory in memories' appearing, I shall suggest, figures a nonvoluntary and nonindividual aspect of memory, and remembering loss in the occurrence of loss – a performative possibility in memory – I shall say, constitutes a vital option as we attempt to let memory appear with awareness – as we remember memory's loss, we might say awkwardly, in memories' appearances.

I propose by this discussion to address also a group of interrelated problems – a problematic – that arises in considering memory's loss and that allows Jungian and "phenomenological" thought to encounter each other.[1] This problematic is composed of questions about and interests in appearing, the "structures" (if they are structures) of appearing, the possible bases of appearances, and the "function" of memory in appearances and our recognitions of things. This problematic could quickly get out of hand, because, in addition to its intricacies, it could move easily into further questions of dreaming, psychodynamics, sacrality, and theoretical methodology. But I forego these and most other equally important issues and focus on the appearing of memory's loss, which I believe will provide a space of encounter for people who work in a Jungian tradition and people who work in a phenomenological one.

I shall put to work issues that arise in Jungian and phenomenological thought rather than comment on Jungian and phenomenological thought, and I would like to do that work in a manner that is not exclusively attached to either tradition. In this way I hope to avoid an ideological orientation that insists on the limits or the preferability of either tradition and to take a step toward an imaginative and descriptive field that remembers both traditions, allows them to fuse, we could say, in a horizon that alters each of them because of their encounter.

I feel cautious about this "focus" on loss because when loss is focused it seems to be something – a loss – although loss occurs in an absenting of focus and content and would seem not to *be* any *thing* at all. Our language is ill suited to this dimension of memorial occurrence, and a significant part of my intention here is to write in such a way that I off-set the implication that my words indicate memories that are, we might say, fully connected to what they remember and that are themselves "ungapped" by losses and untranslatable fissures. Most of us are probably accustomed to the perception of memories as ambiguous and fallible. But the perception that memories are characterized by loss of memory sees them not only as ambiguous and subject to error. This perception also sees memories as embodying something like irretrievability, as without memory – as characterized by radical forgetfulness or error writ large.

My hypothesis is that memories' loss of memory not only makes remembering and the appearances of memories' "processes" continuously open to questioning and not to certainty but also shows us something about ourselves, about the way we occur in our consciousness and identities. If I am right in thinking that memories' happenings pervade our lives, that we belong to memories, then our conscious ways of recognizing them and living in them and through them constitute a living knowledge that tells us about who we are and how we exist. Such knowledge informs our basic expectations, our basic beliefs, our hopes and our sense of what is real and unreal. As our knowledge of memory changes, our ways of relating to everything, including ourselves, change. The knowledge of memory that is forecast by this hypothesis suggests a way of life that experiences things with the sense that whatever we take to be fundamentally stable is closer to something imagined than to timeless entities that exist outside of memorial events and, as it were, substantially in themselves.

These observations and claims bring together these possibilities: (1) The occurrences of appearances are best conceived as memorial, disclosive events that show themselves in *their* ways of occurring and are not like symbols are said to be – they are not events that reveal something outside themselves, something other and "higher" that exists outside of the event's temporal happening; both the Jungian hypothesis of archetypal symbols and the

Husserlian hypothesis of transcendental subjectivity are thus in question.[2] (2) Memories are best conceived as scenes and fragments, not as interconnected and completable narratives. Narratives that are tightly stitched and that lead to systematic completion – that close in on themselves by conclusions – require a kind of theft that fills in the gaps by borrowing from other imaginative events such as anxious hoping, images of wholeness, or a hypothesis that fundamental unity is required to give meaning to multiple and often disparate events. (3) The occurrence of forgetting is not the same as something forgotten. An important option for us is to remember that impenetrable forgetfulness occurs and makes impossible its transformation into a determinate meaning. (4) The broad Jungian claim that there are multiple foci that are not reducible to each other and that are crucial for understanding memories, foci that engender very different, simultaneous, and often incompatible perspectives, rhythms, times, and "voices" is highly suggestive but is not our best option, although this hypothesis provides a desirable destabilization of the idea of transcendental subjectivity. (5) These foci and the hypothesis that posits them are subject to finite timing in memory's loss; they are like historically formed patterns in lineages whose occurrences are temporal and subject to mutation. We might wish to speak of patterns and forms (particularly if our perceptions are strongly intuitional), but these patterns and forms are themselves memorial: they embody traces of multiple events and experiences and are subject to transformations due to conflicts among the elements that constitute them as well as due to the impacts of new circumstances. (6) Finally, by this approach I am suggesting that when one lives in and through concepts and as one recognizes things in and through concepts, conceptual knowledge is concrete and experiential. It is abstract only when we do not know how to think in and with particular concepts or when we look at them from a distance. I am suggesting that changes in our knowledge of memory can constitute changes in both our everyday and our professional lives.

Mnemosyne and Lethe

I turn now to a consideration of an "image" of Mnemosyne's and Lethe's belonging together and to our efforts to be accurate as we remember. I wish to highlight the dissension that characterizes our experiences when we attempt to give them order and the meaning of stable origins.

I cannot begin these remarks on Mnemosyne with an invocation in the manner of Hesiod, whose poetic story is close to the rituals in which the gods had their lives. I am closer to Byron who began one canto of *Don Juan* with, "Hail Muse, et cetera" (Grant 1962: 105–7). And even Hesiod's "solemnity" and "earnestness" (Kerényi 1966: 311–22) are at a distance from these thoughts and observations. I am, however, affiliated with Hesiod's written account, which is not designed for worshipful performance but for a narrative and genealogical performance that enacts its difference from worship. This is part of the strange situation of memory with which I begin: worlds apart in recall, but a re-calling nonetheless in which the recalled seems to play a part in the recalling presentation. I also begin with a suspicion that an interpretation based primarily on the structure of signifier/signified is insufficient when we think of memory, a suspicion based in part on the observation that what is past effectively returns in something like a fusion at the border of our present and future, a fusion I shall call it, of perceptive return and yet-to-be that gives birth to a horizon, a past present not-yet that might be more radical in the past's return than the unovercomeable slash of signifier/signified. This "fusion" in its delicacy might give birth – rebirth – to a muse, to art we say prosaically, in an enacted memory of Mnemosyne, the flowing source of return. But I am moving too rapidly. For now, I note that we are attuned to Hesiod's loss of worship – not obliteration but loss nonetheless, a subtle, distinct process of fading figured by another kind of presentation, as he gave accounts of the gods and their origins. And since we are dealing with memory let us not count this loss as a deficiency but as memory that composes a fusion of several horizons of appearance and experience. The future of that loss did not happen as a failure but as a birth of which this writing, in the fading of Hesiod's earnestness and solemnity, is a distant progeny.

Hesiod gave three invocations to the gods before whom he experienced a degree of awe and wonder. He undergoes or at least reflects their forces in his writing. I might choose to feel shame before his experience of the nearness of the gods and in that shame find a lineage of lost divine immediacy that also shows itself in his writing at a distance from ritual. But that would be an indulgence on my part by which I would project a loss – a tragic loss perhaps – of life-enhancing divinity. I shall forego that option and attend rather to the distance that separates us, to the life-enhancing aspect of that distance, and to the horizonal, resourceful life of the memory that it harbors. The memory of Mnemosyne, I shall say, figures a life of thinking and writing in which her mythological life is wildly transformed into a quite different event (a return fitting to a Titan), no less presentative and originative than her earlier, distant manifestation. In addition to thinking and writing we shall continue to speak of such arts as poetry, music, and dance, but these arts now are not, of course, Greek – except in the sense of a lineage and distant, mutated connection. For Mnemosyne is not given to simple repetition but to a dark transformation indigenous to her mother, earth, Gaea, and given as well to the chaotic lineage of her father, heaven, Uranus, who housed the gods with an infinite distaste for their orders: fecund Uranus, arching over Gaea with spacious noncontent and with discontent for all determinations: Mnemosyne, earthly, heavenly power, giver and taker of forms. Mnemosyne appears to happen originatively in her loss of form, substance, clarity, and identity. Does "she" ignite "her" loss?

The flow of Mnemosyne is affiliated in some aspects of Greek culture with

Lethe, the "region" of forgetting and oblivion. In Plato's *Republic*, Lethe functions as an image of forgetfulness, one that Socrates recalls, but in that recall suggests that it hides itself, that it refuses not only eternal reality but clear imagery and, in its hiding, gives humans to believe that their limited perceptiveness can traverse everything that is, the full range of being. Lethe is imagined as a river, flowing with water that cannot be contained, water that disperses determinations and discriminations. Drinking its water, souls cease to remember their lineages and lives. They assume a flowing transcience, lost to their own permanence, lost, strangely, to their own source. This loss is figured by desire: the flow of Lethe creates, as it were, a desert without springing life because this water does not nourish or quench. It makes dry, gives no satisfaction, will not become a life-giving source to any organism. Those who drink of Lethe starve as they long for water. Lethe, daughter of dissention (Eris), produces something in the direction of chaos by way of continuous evacuation. So far, Lethe appears inimical to life, to give the soul to be "a leaky sieve" (Kerényi 1966/77: 120–30). The soul in this situation, as Plato writes of it, lives in a futile effort to replenish itself with immediacies that flow away as they come to presence. Its life is like an unremitting effort to be here now, continuously unsatisfied, thirsting for what Lethe gives in withdrawal. In this imagery, Lethe embodies the soul's self-forgetfulness, its withdrawal from itself as it lives out of itself.

Karl Kerényi has an hypothesis that I shall adopt. He says that in its preclassical life, the image of Lethe presented the normal, temporal life of human beings. Lethe is not negative, not something suggesting a need for philosophical or Eleusinian cure. It speaks, rather, of "outflowing." The archaic image of Lethe is that of a spring, and Kerényi suggests that it is "fashioned after the spring of Mnemosyne" (Kerényi 1966/77: 92–3) that springs forth, originates, and gives something for return as well as for loss. There appears to be an early and inner affiliation of Mnemosyne and Lethe that precedes their separation and externalization. This suggestion brings Mnemosyne and Lethe together before their religious and philosophical dispersion. But Lethe also remains imagistically apart from Mnemosyne – a spring on the left by the Cypress tree, as one figure has it, a spring that is to be avoided by the souls of the dead, whereas Mnemosyne is the spring on the right that provides water of life, recollection, and balm. Kerényi sees the early Lethe as belonging to the land of Mnemosyne, Mnemosyne who with her daughters is the predominant power that heals the losses figured in Lethe, Lethe who belongs nonetheless to Mnemosyne's eventful region.

In this account, the *benefit* of Lethe – and hence the dominance of Mnemosyne – is found in the loss of life's disaster. Rather than only constituting disaster and darkness, Lethe also presents their obliteration – something like the withdrawal of the withdrawal of life – and defines an aspect of the muses' power to give Mnemosyne's comfort: "it is only both the elements – giving illumination and letting disappear, Mnemosyne and her counterpole, Lesmosyne – that make up the entire being of the goddess, whose name comes solely from the positive side of her field of power" (Kerényi 1966/77: 92–3). (*Lesmosyne* is an early synonym for Lethe.) Mnemosyne in this figuration retains her titanic depths and incorporates darkness in her luminosity in a manner that both defines and makes possible their later separation.

The religious and philosophical transformation of Mnemosyne into a distant counterforce to Lethe is not altogether a surprise insofar as her lethic dimension constitutes a withdrawal of clarity and makes room for the art of recovery as well as for the disaster of dumbness and oblivion. The taming of titanic Mnemosyne in forgetfulness of her lethic dimension is what her image allows us to expect. Her titanic image also allows us to expect that her image is intrinsically forgetful in its power to recall that "Mnemosyne" also presents nothing that is an image, recalls us to no image at all, no image that is lost to "its" imagery. From such loss in the midst of determinate images flows incitement to recall, to re-form, to present again. It is not exactly like water in a sieve, but it is not like ontological perfection either. Such loss is resourceful, without prior guarantees, without enduring stability: rather much like art on a horizon that discloses, i.e. remembers in its performance, its resourceful loss as it refigures the happenings of its time.

It's in memories that we steal

> No matter how useless these words might seem to be, they have nevertheless stood between me and a silence that continues to terrify me. When I step into this silence, it will mean that my father has vanished forever.
>
> (Paul Auster, *The Invention Of Solitude*)

People frequently make the claim that the memories that a person in therapy has are often not literally true. The father might or might not have abused her when she was very young. The young boy might or might not have witnessed the primal scene, as the man reports he did. The man might or might not have stolen the cherries when he was four years old. Or the woman might or might not remember her dream accurately. The important question, many say, is not whether we remember exactly *what* happened or undergo a fabrication in a memory of what happened. The important question is whether the "memory" carries feelings and issues the therapeutic engagement of which relieves the individual's depression, anxiety, or other distress. The therapeutic consequences of engaging a particular memory rather than the accuracy of the memory draws one's attention.

This position is a difficult one to hold if self-discovery is the therapeutic goal. If I discover myself to have a history of abuse and make my understanding of myself in the impact of that discovery and then later find out incontrovertibly (let us say) that I was not abused as a child, I would be justified in saying that I had reformed my self around false memories and that I had mislead myself into feeling like I were someone I am not.[3] In this instance we would say that "accuracy" makes a difference, even though (let us say) my "memories" of abuse were therapeutically effective as I worked through depression. I would like to hold this issue in reserve for now (and return to it later) in order to give attention to the hermetic situation of taking memories that are not our own – stealing them in that aspect of the legacy of Hermes, the god of borders and thieves, and in the process enjoying his strange blessing of both identity and dissolution of identity at the border of our limits and our "reality," a border at which our identity and "reality" come to pass away and something like a message is given in the occurrence. Both theft and return seem to happen at the borders figured by Hermes.

I am using the term "stolen memories" to emphasize that memories may come from somewhere other than a literal past – say, from scenes in other memories or from something like imaginative production and figuration – and to emphasize that the processes of vital – *life*-developing – self-formation are not under the jurisdiction of a traditionally moral compunction regarding literal honesty. "Stolen" in this context suggests loss and gain, origin outside of what is properly my own, excess to ownership, not my property, and, from a "normal" social point of view, impropriety. The image of Hermes can aid us because we do not "take" him literally but we do find in his image the figuration – the memory – of thievery and of border experiences, experiences of crossing boundaries in which crossing who we definitively are comes into question and other possibilities arise.

Border experiences. In popular imagination and in some fields of psychological knowledge, a person suffering from identity dissociation disorder is unaware as he – let's make the person here male – switches from one persona to another.[4] As the child persona who is petulant, irresponsible, and extremely hostile, "he" – the adult man before us – is not conscious of himself as thirty-five years old, married, and the father of two children. He has tantrums and sees the world as a disturbed four year old. In the persona of a withdrawn and reclusive woman he is not conscious of the child persona, and so on – in this case he has many persona who are unaware of the others. The crossing of one persona to another is without awareness, and the man is dissociative in his identity because he lacks adequate self-consciousness, as we say, and is unable to manage the multiple differences that characterize his life. He crosses many borders, leaving behind one identity or another without awareness in the crossing.

That individual contrasts to another person who is quite aware of his different aspects, who is alert *in* the movements among the voices or the persona to other voices and persona who dwell in him – aware of the child, the mother, the very feminine one, the athlete, the business executive, the one who successfully worked his way through an early trauma, etc. He is alert in the crossing from the border of one persona to another and has a sense of himself and some degree of self-direction in the passages to different aspects. Although I hesitate to use *integrated* to describe this state of mind, because the word tends to blur the radicality of some of the departures and differences in which he is aware but which are distinct to the individual he finds himself primarily to be, we could nonetheless say that he is in active touch with many of his aspects, is able to interact and associate with them, and he is alert when one or another of them come into prominence. He is not dissociative in his transitions.

There are many kinds of border experiences. I have just noted the experiences of different persona that an individual finds in his life. There are also experiences of dying, in which something living and present becomes something past, of anticipation in which he projects himself as someone definitively different from the way he now is, of the coming of sleep, of various times of ecstasy, of becoming drunk, of living in the arrival of a powerful and new attitude, of significant changes in external circumstances, of being different from one's determinate situation, of animal-like "biological" responses – multiple borders that one undergoes in normal living. I am emphasizing that in these lived crossings we experience something lost, such as the priority of this voice or the presence of that perspective, in the coming of something else, and I emphasize that we happen in such loss. The loss is part of the border crossing, a Hermes aspect in the occurrences of our lives.

Memories seem to arise at times with such occurrences of loss. Both the loss and the lost are traced in remainders. They might be traced in feelings that occurred at the time of loss and arise again in other situations or in scents or in words and verbal associations. Feelings, scents, and words often carry as traces much more than we can easily and actively recall. Other memorial carriers (traces) can be found in attitudes, postures, muscle formation, shifts in body chemistry, the ways a certain kind of person appears (i.e. in structures of recognition), dream scenes, experiences of momentum, situational alertness – i.e. situations that trace earlier situations, reflect them, embody them, "mean" them. These memorial happenings are traces of events that are otherwise not at all present, and they can mark multiple transformations in an individual's life.

Memory-in-loss. We have seen that the titanic Mnemosyne and Lethe belong to each other, that memory belongs to a loss of memory and that loss of memory belongs to memory. I have suggested that the figure of Hermes elaborates one dimension of memory's loss, namely that in the loss one can undergo a sense that something is taken away, stolen. In returning now to Hermes I want to suggest that such "stealing" can be an aspect of memory.

In crossing over to different persona and to quite different regions of experience one leaves something behind. When the radicality of such transition is writ large, as it is in the knowledge of identity dissociation disorders, the traces of the losses are suppressed in the occurrences: one often does not remember or recognize the other persona, the "past," or the transitional happenings. The traces may not appear to be present in the speaking voice, in the dissociative manner of being present and being the "who" that one at the moment is. But in preferable instances, when dissociation does not dominate, one lives in memories of the "others," the "past", and the transitional happening. The traces and the losses that they mark figure in one's present awareness.

Consider this latter way of living. One's awareness is constituted in part by the loss of the traced occurrence. I do not mean that a person is thematically aware of all that has transisted, died to presence, or even of transitional movement. Rather, the person is prethematically available to – hospitable to – the traces and transitions and is available to herself and to the world through them. She is not traumatized when confronted unavoidably with the transitoriness of living, with the quite different, multiple aspects of her "identity," or with the dying that runs through her living. This is like her being open in and to transitional multiplicity, accustomed to living in boundary occurrences, familiar with the fading appearances of traces, accustomed to the happening of unexpected associations, to the shadowy return of what is past (of the dead) and is now traced in her life. She is familiar with Hermes the reiver, the one who steals the present in the coming appearances of all things, the one who gives boundary and origin in taking away what now is, as it were, in her possession, the one who takes away aspects of one's life in personal transformation and transition.

And what happens in this context as memory occurs? I suspect that memory steals in this sense: in addition to presenting traces of bygone events, memories also attach to and draw from other seeming memories and narrations, and this "attaching" or "drawing from" is something like stealing. Not distortion so much as taking from other situations, from other traces, from several different "pasts," filling in the gaps, and appearing as remembrances of things as though they had no lost origins, were thoroughly formed and without so much fragmentation. Memories are often presented as though they possessed a plentitude of significance. They seem to forget the fragmentary, lost, utterly incomplete, and often indeterminate appearances of the traces that mark the pastness of what has occurred. Memory can vivify the lost and the dead with presence, with patterns and connections that are taken from elsewhere, seeming to lose the power of death, and figuring by theft from other memories and images coherent, determinate, explanatory formations that help to make sense of who and where we are.[5]

Far from condemning memories for their thievery, I wish to recognize them – remember them – and to be acquainted with this kind of occurrence in remembering. By remembering and recognizing memories in this way I wish to understand selves in their loss and thievery. I believe that in recognizing memory in this aspect I both know something about it and lose something of it – that I know it in its loss – the loss that gives rise to supplements by "stealing" from other memories – as I supplement my own recognitions, for example, with mythical figures in my lineage, and by them add to memories' determinations. I counteract Lethe, for example, by recalling the image of Lethe (thereby making the trace of loss into a determinate figure!). By transforming the losses that mark Mnemosyne's historic images into new, mutated, and supplemented images with new possibilities, I both know her and disclose loss of contact with her. I give this discourse significance and a future in her revised "presence," a presence that arises, as I work on this knowledge of memory, only by the theft of determinations from other memories and by such theft replace her loss with determination and narrational meaning. I have, for example, presented her image in a close association with that of Lethe and by the closeness of this association, which functions in this discussion as a primary narrational thread, I have lost the very oblivion that I want to address. I have also given her figuration a currency that is largely foreign to her inception and mythological development: I have brought her out of her mythological field of meaning and brought her into a distinctly non-mythological discourse. I have also found her disclosive of dimensions of fusions that occur both in cultures and in individual mentation.

There are many assumptions at work in the previous two paragraphs that I cannot properly justify here. I am assuming that the idea that a memory has a determinate and unambiguous origin is not adequately defensible – that is, I am assuming that a memory, a trace, occurs in an originary multiplicity of elements – in fluid configurations – and that the idea of a simple, determinate origin for memories is misleading. I am assuming that many – I suspect most – memories occur as living embodiments, practices, words, uses of words, and nonvoluntary images but not primarily as constructions over which an individual has control. I am assuming that we should not use the word *unconscious* systematically because of its paring with *consciousness* in a lineage that divides disastrously mind and body. I am assuming that the best images in the context of a knowledge of memory are those that put themselves in question and jeopardize their use for the purpose of establishing clear, explanatory, and determinate origins. And I am assuming that by this encounter with memory we are encountering traces – indeterminate memories – of simple origins' absence in the determinations of our lives. I have chosen a style of expression that requires continuous indirection in the midst of direct statements, a requirement for recognition of continuous uncertainty and fragility in the midst of declarations and descriptions. That means that theories of transcendental or empirical entities (such as transcendental subjectivity, archetypes, or necessary facts) that provide continuing stability behind and through memories are inappropriate. Such theories seem to add to memories' losses too much theft from our lineage of anxiety over death and fragmentation.

What, then, are we to say about self-discovery? By recognizing memory as intrinsic to our lives, I have suggested the possibility of a knowledge of self that valorizes boundary, mutational events, and both the fragmentation and reformation that accompany those events. Our ability to recognize multiple things and configurations from the transcendence of a point of view, a dominant complex of images, or a relatively stable identity allows nonetheless for the forces of multiple "voices" and personae that carry their own fluid trajectories and centrifugal movements. A sense of lively identity appears to depend on something like their cooperative interaction, on their disclosures to each other, on hearing, saying, recognizing – something like a defined and open region of communication that has determinate foci and a tolerance for transformation and differentiation. These qualifications – "appears to", "something like" – carry an intention to maximize fluidity and indeterminateness in the definition of self, to suggest that a self is composed of fragmentary, hermetic, and lethic aspects that take place in the lives of memories that constitute a self.

Let us return to our earlier example of the man who discovers that he in fact was not abused after he developed a knowledge and understanding of himself in the impact of remembering that he was abused. The question revolves around the "facts" that he discovers. The "facts" appear to stand outside of his memory's occurrence, to provide a stable point of reference for the correction of his "mistake," to allow him the possibility for a self-awareness that is more true to what he experienced than his earlier memory allowed. The "facts" appear to be unremembered, free of theft, unmovable in their determination. This is not a question of how the "facts" *should* be interpreted or appropriated, but how they as "facts" are presented and recognized. I do not want to deny the occurrences of "facts." Memory is certainly not everything, although I believe that something like memory qualifies all presentations and recognitions. In the case of our misled man, his memory and recognition of abuse took place in a culture in which not only abuse is valorized, but also one in which what constitutes abuse is considerably broadened in comparison to thirty years ago.[6] But then he discovered that what is defined as abuse did not happen, that there were no events that fit into even the broad definition of abuse. The "fact" is found in the absence of abuse and in the past occurrences of a non-abusive relation with (let us say) his father. The mistaken memory carried, it seems, another kind of trauma for which the fabricated abuse served as an affective carrier. Was there an abusive dimension to the "factually" nonabusive relation? Were there traces of abuse in it? Was there an experiential memory of trauma totally separated from his relation to his father, but one that stole the father–son relationship as an affective image of transmission? I believe that one can never know for sure, that memory's loss means uncertainty and indeterminacy in the fabric of "facts" – because "facts" *mean* something, they occur in complexities of associations and shifting fields of experience that give them remarkable fluidity and a measure of persistent indeterminacy. "Facts" are never "facts" with one, unchangeable identity. Whether the man was abused in "fact" appears undecidable before his memory of experiencing abuse and his experience of release from depression through his confrontation with his memory of abuse, even if one can show convincingly that the father related to the son without doing what the son's memory attributed to him.

Through this horrific experience something else comes to light about the lives of a father and son, something about themselves and their memories. My hope is that they believe and accept the son's experience of abuse and his release from that experience's hold on his life, that they accept his stolen memory as disclosive of something in his life even in its factual "error" and likely injustice to his father, that they accept the aspect of indeterminacy not only in memory but also in "facts," that they hold open the possibility that the events of a life can be abusive or carry abuse even when they appear otherwise, that there might be something in their relation that made it, in its loving quality, a productive host to the son's memory, that everything remembered – the good and the bad – is infused with Lethe and Hermes and appears shimmering in the losses that accompany the return of what occurred and occurs beyond factuality. I hope that in a knowledge of memory and thus in freedom from literalization, they would accept the son's successful therapy in the context of error and stolen memories. Perhaps they can accept in a knowledge of memory (a self-understanding) a theft by which the son is relieved of a measure of suffering by an error.

Recovering loss

> The rampant, totally mystifying force of contradiction. I understand now that each fact is nullified by the next fact, that each thought engenders an equal and opposite thought. Impossible to say anything without reservation: he was good, or he was bad; he was this, or he was that. All of them are true. At times I have the feeling that I am writing about three or four different men, each one distinct, each one a contradiction of all the others. Fragments. Or the anecdote as a form of knowledge. Yes.
>
> (Paul Auster, *The Invention of Solitude*)

I have been writing descriptively of the loss of memory in an effort toward experiencing memories with something like increased clarity regarding their events. Does one gain intensification and clarity in experience by means of descriptive writing and thinking? Do we have a language and conceptuality that can describe loss without turning loss into "something" and thereby losing it? I have suggested that the hypotheses of archetypes and transcendental subjectivity are barriers to experiential and reflective encounter with aspects of memorial loss, that they are imaginative contributions to a way of thinking – broadly termed modern and metaphysical – in which the radicality of loss and of Lethe's inclusion in Mnemosyne's region are blurred if not completely forgotten by the posited endurance of universal and deathless entities. This forgetfulness is figured as forgetting the loss inherent in the thoughts and images of archetypes and transcendental subjectivity. I suspect that remembering such loss can lead toward languages and conceptualities that increase our perceptiveness regarding memory.

Both hypotheses (archetypes and transcendental subjectivity) are clearly within a tradition that is defined by Leibnitz's and Kant's turn to the universal spontaneity of reason in our experience of all things. Broadening in some ways and limiting in other ways their interpretations of reason, refining their ideas of imagination, and transforming their thoughts of the ideas and ideals of reason constitute significant aspects of Jung's and Husserl's work. The immense richness of Jung's field of description carries the Kantian project far beyond its scientific and epistemological orientation, and Husserl's turn in *The Crisis of European Sciences* to the cultural, environmental bases of thought, while postponing the role of transcendence, added a transformational dimension to Kant's transcendental empiricism. But in both instances, the gappy, chaotic, and scenic aspects of the appearances of things are ordered – overridden – by things that seem to remain, if not eternally, certainly universally the same – remain for all practical purposes outside of time and memory's loss.

Among the many issues that we could raise, let us focus only on universality. Universality carries within its thought the necessity of the universal for the orders of contingent and fragmented things and events. In approaching the question of universality, consider the bewildering variety and range of orders that we engage in everyday life. Each grouping of things has its order. Each seems to have its laws and necessities without which it would not be as it is. Each order has a certain defining identity – this group of experiences, this body of knowledge, these primary images, these spheres of relevance. Each order appears to have suborders and larger orders within which they function often with subtle complexity. They all comprise limits and possibilities of expression and existence. The sheer multiplicity of separate orders suggests chaos unless there is some greater order, some principle of organization that gives them coherence and meaning. Although there are many archetypes, for example, the idea of archetypes functions nonetheless in this universalizing way. By such a principle we can make sense of multiple and conflicting orders.

And the image of *an* ordering principle? What does it carry? What does it transfer to the orders? A desire for ultimate order that we identify as an interest of reason? A sense that unorder must be subsumed under higher order and meaning? A history of anxiety over death's finality? The elevation of one order over all others and over their borders and mutual losses – a totalizing intention, an ideal of ultimate meaning, the fixation of a definitive place of organization? And what happens in the universalizing process to the traces of loss in memory? In the Husserlean method of phenomenological reduction one brackets the relative contents of appearances to reach the residual traces not of loss, but of the transcendental presence of an infinitely connected life, and in the instance of archetypal symbols in Jung's interpretation one finds amidst the welter of individual experiences the traces of the presence of transcendental entities. In both cases, traces lead to continuing presence that is traced in the losses of appearances. Loss is transformed, hypothetically, into full, noncontingent presence.

I note that in Jung's and Husserl's remarkable "empirical" emphasis on concrete experiences and events we are led to orders without Order until one makes a series of increasingly speculative and hypothetical moves. What history and memory do these moves carry? What is their lineage? What do they disclose in their appearances?

I do not intend to suggest that Jung and Husserl were fearful and anxious individuals who projected their flawed psychological states onto the world by means of their theories. The history of their universalizations is not located primarily in their personalities or characters. It is found rather in the language, art, thought, and practices which form all of us in western culture. The field of universalization is vastly extended in comparison to the psychological makeup of an individual. The lineage of universalization appears to me to be pervasive of our ability to think as we do. But there are also countermovements to universalization in our living heritage. I have said that the images of Mnemosyne, Lethe, and Hermes mark aspects of such countermovements, that their figurations mean that the loss that they mark is lost and only traced in their images, that their images lead nowhere determinate, that they determine no determination at all. We might also accept Michel Foucault's descriptive claim in *The Order of Things* that the formation of knowledge and disciplines in the eighteenth and nineteenth centuries carries in their orders a silent perception of lack of order, a lack that they do not overcome but perpetuate. Jacques Derrida shows in *Of Grammatology* that the established knowledges of language carry in them a largely unrecognized loss of meaning upon which their theories of meaning are based. In both instances, the claims recognize that loss of memory is inherent in this memory of lineages and that such loss is silently recorded in the lineages of our knowledge, art, and thought and not primarily in the dynamics of consciousness or the psyche. In lineages, not subjectivity, we find the histories and memories that constitute both movements of universalization and resistance to such movements.

Such instances of turning away from the field of subjectivity to the field of lineages constitute a turn to orders without Order. Not only is the lineage of this turning toward lineages important. Important too is the lineage of turning toward reality beyond mortal orders, toward the settlement of inconstancy, limits, dispersed multiplicity, conflicts, and disorder. Eris – dissention – is the mother of Lethe, and we might judge Lethe harshly for her parentage. But if Lethe belongs to Mnemosyne, if Eris is related to Mnemosyne's muses, we must expect the soothing arts – including the art of hypothesizing – to occur in the company of dissention. The issue is not one of dissolving dissension – Lethes' oblivion takes care of that – but is rather one of recognizing error and unorder in our solutions to unorder, recognizing unorder in Order, and turning to the lineages of solution as the fields in which loss might be most apparent in *its* loss and memory most accessible in her trace of no order at all.

All of these remarks are indebted positively to the Jungian and phenomenological traditions. Jung's openness to the widest range of experience, his imaginative and constructive attentiveness to mythology, his emphasis on imaginative creation, his esteem for interpretive tentativeness and repeated recontextualization, and his ability to hold before him multiple and contradictory phenomena and possibilities – these characteristics of his thought are all formative for this departure from his theories that seem to lose some of what he gained. The entire discussion is also dependent on Husserl's accent on appearances and the open field of intentionality that gives disclosure and synthesis in the coming of things. These ground-breaking ideas and principles have led not only to theoretical adjustments of their work but also to major theoretical departures from their work. I believe that a measure of their work's value is found in departures from it, that the fecundity of their ideas is not found in their theories of transcendental orders but in a turning to the formations of language and conceptuality – to a different knowledge – which arise from perceptions of things without a sense of transcendence or quasi-religious references. This kind of transformation and thought, which this discussion valorizes by its focus on memory's loss, also gives the possibility of a perceptiveness – an ability to perceive – that does not feel required to imagine anything ultimate or finally conciliatory, one that is able to feel well without intimations of immortality on the part of anything. I state the transformation by means of negatives – "not required," "without intimations" – in order to suggest the magnitude of the change in theory and method that is forecast. Both Husserl and Jung exemplify a tension in modern and contemporary knowledge: perception of disparate worlds of images, meanings, events, and visions, and perception that requires something transcendent, something outside the dispersion, to make sense of all the dispersion and yet contributing to the dispersion still another competing order for the distinction of Order, adding to the dispersion and dissention that the Order would cure. Neither, in an exemplary manner, thought that a person could achieve a direct gaze upon transcendental reality and truth, but both were driven to transcendental hypotheses in the absence of which world-openness and imaginative creation would seem hopeless and desperate, or, if not that extreme (and I suspect that it was that extreme), at least partial, incomplete, verging on nihilism. That strong, traditional inclination formed a definitive part of their perception of things, events, and people, a part that usually operated without reflective consciousness and that came to articulation in theories that made sense of what they perceived: those theories, they believed, were necessary to make sense of experiences.

Once that felt inclination weakens or ceases to operate, appearances happen quite differently, without the usually inchoate sense that in the absence of transcendental meaning we are lost and hopeless in our lives, that without something to convert scenes into transcendentally founded narratives our memories are fragments in nihilistic drift. The imaginative plays of transcendental entities, far from innocent, seem to embody a long lineage of trouble over fragmentation. When a less troubled disruption of that dominant sense within the lineage begins to gain more prominence, both Husserl's and Jung's thought can become sites of transformation that play host to changes of perception in living memories of loss, loss that makes of memory a site of fissure and dissention as well as of imaginative transformation and solace.

So I write in the power of an hypothesis that replaces two other (Husserl's and Jung's) hypotheses, an imaginative hypothesis in the sense that it attempts to recognize Mnemosyne's lethic aspect in a synthetic region of mutual belonging, an aspect that Jung and Husserl do not seem fully to appreciate. Perhaps you can show that they "really" do give full honor to fragmentation and error in regard to their own imaginative work, that they "really" do know that death and oblivion dwell within archetypes and transcendental subjectivity. Perhaps their thought exemplifies considerably more than their imaginative syntheses say. Perhaps they knew well that their transcendental moves exemplify a lineage that dwells fitfully and with internal interruptions in their psyches and reasons. Perhaps. And perhaps through our engagements with them horizonal synthesis and rethinking will go on and our lives will change with altered hopes and memories, with a sense that our well being occurs in our suffering memory's loss.

Notes

1 I shall use "phenomenological" and "phenomenology" as signs for what we also call continental philosophy. Just as "continental philosophy" does not indicate primarily a geographical area where philosophy is done – one could think in the influence of Nietzsche and Heidegger in China as well as in Germany – but indicates rather a limited and definable tradition of thought, so "phenomenology," as I shall use the word, does not indicate primarily a method used by Husserl or Merleau-Ponty, but rather indicates thought that is within the continental tradition. For a careful study of Jungian and phenomenological thought, see Brooke (1991).

2 I use the term "transcendental subjectivity" to refer to an apriori and unconditioned structure for all appearances in human life, one that provides the

basis for all conscious activity. While any conscious event, such as perception of an object or conceptual grasp of a situation, is conditioned by its circumstances, the possibility of that event, according to the hypothesis of transcendental subjectivity, resides in an unconditioned and universal state of mind. Such a state of mind would constitute human subjectivity and would transcend the particular conscious, perceptive activity. While this noncontingent state is "pure" according to Husserl in the sense that it is not changed by changing circumstances or by psychological differences, I will suggest that the very idea of transcendental subjectivity composes a relative, historical development that is infused with psychological and cultural interests and that any basis for recognition and perception is formed in part by specific memorial processes.

3 Ian Hacking (1995) develops this problem especially well in the final chapter of *Rewriting The Soul*. In the course of this section I will engage several of the ideas that he raises in this provocative book. Positively, I will appropriate several of his descriptive accounts of the contemporary knowledge of multiple personality disorder and dissociative identity disorder. But I will take a direction quite different from his "realism" which I find to constitute a disorder of its own.

4 I am using this disorder to provide a broadly drawn example. Such disorder is now known in some "official" publications and societies, although it is in question among many theorists and clinicians. I do not wish to address the issue of the extent to which the disorder is an invention of recent years. Like all knowledges, I suspect, it has the advantages and disadvantages of imaginative and social construction that accompany and help to define a body of recognized experiences. I remind myself that my knowledge and the traditions to which I belong have those same advantages and disadvantages. The advantage of this "disorder" for my purposes is that it presents, perhaps in exaggerated form, some aspects of memory that I wish to valorize, and these aspects remain to jeopardize not only any conclusiveness that might be attached to the diagnoses of multiple identity disorder, but also any definitive rejection of such diagnoses. It also has the advantages of challenging some types of conventional, clinical wisdom and of taking early childhood abuse as both literal and figurative in a context that is frequently undecidable. I shall emphasize the undecidability. For five studies of sexual abuse in a Jungian context, see *The Journal of Analytical Psychology*, 40, 1995, pp. 5–76.

5 I have used "memory" and "memories" as the subjects for many of the verbs in this paragraph. I do not know the extent to which an individual intends or does not intend the theft of which I speak. No doubt we can individually garnish a remembered scene and turn fragments into narratives. But I suspect that much of that work is also done in the formation of memories and their appearances before we have a chance to do our own imaginative work with them.

6 See, for example, Corwin *et al.* (1993) and Hacking (1995: chapter 4).

References

Auster, Paul (1982) *The Invention of Solitude*, New York: Penguin.

Brooke, R. (1991) *Jung and Phenomenology*, London: Routledge.

Corwin, D. L., Olafson, E., and Summitt, R. C. (1993) "Modern history of the child sexual abuse awareness: Cycles of discovery and suppression," *Child Abuse and Neglect*, 17, 1, 7–24.

Derrida, J. (1976) *Of Grammatology*, trans. G. C. Spirak, Baltimore, Johns Hopkins University Press.

Foucault, M. (1973) *The Order of Things*, New York: Vintage Books.

Grant, M. (1962) *Myths of the Greeks and Romans*, World Publishing Co.
Hacking, I. (1995) *Rewriting the Soul*, Princeton: Princeton University Press.
Kerényi, I. (1966/77) "Lesmosyne, Über die quellen erinnerung und vergessenheit," *Humanistische Seelenforschung*, I: 311–22, Zurich: Spring Publications.
The Journal of Analytic Psychology (1995), 40, 5–76.

EDITOR'S INTRODUCTION

Maurice Merleau-Ponty was Professor of Child Psychology at the Sorbonne. He is the only one of phenomenology's pioneers to have taken seriously both psychoanalysis and empirical research in psychology. In fact, it has been noted that his reading of Freud redefined and deepened the field of existential phenomenology. That his work has not been taken up in psychoanalysis and psychology is a curious neglect, but for those interested in understanding the roots of thought in human embodiment, the relationships between gesture, desire and perception, the dialectics of interaction, or the interpersonal constitution of identity, Merleau-Ponty's work is the mother lode. It is thus a special pleasure to reprint this little gem by David Michael Levin, as it is the only paper in this volume to investigate explicitly Merleau-Ponty's significance for analytical psychology – and vice versa. Levin's concern is twofold: to articulate a phenomenology of corporeality that is the latent ground of Jung's and Neumann's accounts of psychological transformation, and to articulate one of the central archetypal processes that transform the blind animality of the human body into an embodiment of compassion and self-reflective insight. Although Levin shows how analytical psychology and phenomenology "complement" each other, his work stands as an original synthesis, and it anticipates a number of books that appeared in the years after this paper was written.

9

EROS AND PSYCHE

A Reading of Neumann and Merleau-Ponty

David Michael Levin

> The embrace of Eros and Psyche in the darkness represents the elementary but unconscious attraction of opposites, which impersonally bestows life but is not yet human. But the coming of light makes Eros "visible"; it manifests the phenomenon of psychic love, hence of all human love, as the human and higher form of the archetype of relatedness.
>
> (Erich Neumann, *Amor and Psyche*)

> Hitherto he [Eros] had experienced love only in the darkness, as a wanton game, as an onslaught of sensual desire . . . but through Psyche's act he experiences it as a travail of the personality, leading through suffering to transformation and illumination.
>
> (Erich Neumann, *Amor and Psyche*)

> The fateful question of the human species seems to me to be whether and to what extent the cultural process developed in it will succeed in mastering the derangements of communal life caused by the human instinct of aggression and self-destruction. In this connection, perhaps the phase through which we are at this moment passing deserves special interest. Men have brought their powers of subduing the forces of nature to such a pitch that by using them they could now very easily exterminate one another to the last human being. . . . And now it may be hoped that the other of the two "heavenly forces," eternal Eros, will put forth his strength, so as to maintain himself alongside of his equally immortal adversary.
>
> (Sigmund Freud, *Civilization and its Discontents*)

> Only to the extent that [the beauty of] Being is able to elicit "erotic" power in its relation to man is man capable of thinking about Being and overcoming oblivion of Being.
>
> (Martin Heidegger, *Nietzsche: The Will to Power as Art*)

The Original Story

In the second century, Apuleius, Roman poet, turned the echoes of ancient Greek myth into the legendary story of Cupid and Psyche (Hamilton 1942: 100). This recollection of Eros and Psyche, this repetition of their story, successfully civilized the myth. Many centuries later, Erich Neumann (1973) repeats this charming story; but he also deepens it, in doing so, by reading into it an underlying story of archetypal significance. As a Jungian, Neumann sought to articulate love's transformation of the human psyche. According to Neumann, the human personality undergoes a transformation of the most fundamental significance when it remembers the wisdom and beauty of love. But, he argues, the nature of love itself is changed when the psyche meets it in a spirit of acceptance. Thus, when Psyche and Eros come together, the *feminine* character of Eros, its hitherto undeveloped aspect, is finally brought to realization. And Psyche, of course, is fulfilled through love, and made whole.

I would like to tell this story once again. Like the earlier stories, mine will be a repetition which changes it. For I want to tell it as a way of reading Merleau-Ponty. To be more specific: I propose to understand what Merleau-Ponty calls "the task of radical reflection" as a process of "recollection" – a sort of *anamnesis*, really, by means of which the human psyche learns to recognize, and learns to accept, its primordial body of love. For the wisdom which is innate with respect to this body is unfathomably deep: a measure of psyche's insight.

Now, our retelling of the story has two correlative aims. One is to give to Neumann's account of Psyche's transformation the *explicit embodiment* it needs in order to become a completed story. Like Jung before him, Neumann tends to conceive of psychology as a psychology of "consciousness" (a term which includes, for now, "the unconscious"). As he tells the story, Psyche and Eros are subjects almost without real bodies. And when the body does get involved in their stories, it is the physical body of instinct and drive. But the body of Eros which alone can fulfill the needs of Psyche is, and must be, a body of feeling and perception. Depth psychology, therefore, is in need of a phenomenology of the body.

The second aim, then, is to complete the story of the body which Merleau-Ponty (1962) tells in his *Phenomenology of Perception*, by making explicit the presence, and the character, of that *transformative psychological process* to which, for the most part, he is content simply to allude – for example, when he writes that radical reflection "aims at self-comprehension" by "recovering the unreflective experience of the world . . . and displaying reflection as [but] one possibility of my being" (ibid.: 241). If this radical reflection really is aimed at self-understanding, then we surely need to understand how it participates in a process of psychological transformation. Merleau-Ponty seldom considers how reflection *changes* our experience of ourselves, even though he maintains that it does, and must. And this disregard is all the more striking, inasmuch as he articulates so lucidly the character of that dimension of our corporeal being which radical reflection first discloses and opens up.

Now, we do not want to forget the work of Freud here. But my conviction is that the deep archetypal psychology of Jung and Neumann can contribute at least as much, if not ultimately more, to our understanding of the psychological dynamics which are implicit in the story Merleau-Ponty wants to tell.

Neumann writes that the marriage, or the union, of Psyche and Eros is "the apotheosis of Psyche" (Neumann op. cit.: 143). He argues that it is useful to read the Roman tale as a story teaching us "the liberation of the individual from the primordial mythical world, the freeing of the psyche" (ibid.: 153). And he clarifies this process by noting that, "in her encounter with Eros, she [Psyche] has gone forward to strata of her unconscious in which masculine powers and figures are dominant" (ibid.: 134). But, he adds, "she converted the unconscious forces that had helped her into conscious activity and so liberated her own masculine aspect" (ibid.: 136). This liberation is a process which consists in Psyche's "becoming conscious of her masculine components and realizing them, and having become whole through development of her masculine aspect" (ibid.: 136).

Our story, therefore, is an attempt to recollect, for depth psychology, the primordial body of feeling and perception which Merleau-Ponty celebrates in his work. Because of its holistic, gathering nature, the *recollection* of this body is the key to the *metamorphosis* of that body, thanks to which Psyche can become whole at the level of consciousness. We are also attempting, consequently, to make explicit, in terms of a deep psychology of the Self, the transformative potential which is implicitly recognized in that phenomenology of the human body. Without a clarification of this potential, a potential we are finding in Eros, radical reflection is not only condemned to impotence; it is also being untrue to human nature, which is capable of the most profound metamorphoses, and to its own capacity, precisely as a recollection of our potential, to bring such changes into being.

Because I must severely limit the length of this essay, it will be necessary that we confine ourselves more than I should like to mere fragments of the full story. I would like to have been able to say more about recollection, for example; and more, too, about the question of masculinity and femininity. But perhaps even these maieutic fragments – a few hints – will suffice to set our thinking in motion. Each one of us can certainly continue the story.

The archaic body: a recollection of traces

There is in the *Phenomenology of Perception* a passage of dark significance. Its meaning is obscure – perhaps unavoidably so. In any case, I propose it as a passage we should not continue to ignore. It reads:

> When I turn towards perception, and pass from direct perception to thinking about that perception, I reenact it, and find at work in my organs of perception *a thought older than myself* of which those organs are merely a *trace*.
>
> (Merleau-Ponty op. cit.: 351, italics added)

In order to penetrate the hermetic seal and open up the meaning of this passage, we must consider two others. The first is this:

> My *personal existence* must be the resumption of a *prepersonal* tradition. There is, therefore, *another subject beneath me*, for whom a world exists *before* I am here, and who *marks out* my place in it. This captive or natural spirit is my body, not that momentary body which is the instrument of my *personal* choices and which fastens upon this or that world, but *the system of anonymous "functions"* which draw every particular focus into a general project. . . . Space and perception generally represent, at the core of the subject, the fact of his birth, the perpetual contribution of his bodily being, *a communication with the world more ancient than thought*.
>
> (ibid.: 254, italics added)

I submit that this "other subject," this body of pre-personal communication so ancient as to have no proper name, and to be almost without a trace, is no other than our old friend, Eros. Hard to believe? Well, I do not blame those who find it difficult to see through all the masks with which Eros, as befits his nature, loves to play.

Here, anyway, is the third passage I think we need to ponder:

> *I start from unified experience* and from there acquire, in a secondary way, consciousness of a *unifying activity* when, taking up an analytical attitude, I break up perception into qualities and sensations, and when, in order to *recapture* on the basis of these the object into which I was in the first place *blindly thrown*, I am obliged to suppose *an act of synthesis* which is merely the counterpart of my analysis. My act of perception, in its unsophisticated form, does not itself bring about this synthesis; it takes advantage of *work already done*, of *a general synthesis constituted once and for all*, and this is what I mean when I say that I perceive with my body or my senses, since my body and my senses are precisely that familiarity with the world born of habit, that *implicit or sedimentary body of knowledge*.
>
> (ibid.: 238)

Just *who* is the *subject* of this unifying activity? What is the name of the one whose work of synthesis always turns out to have been *already done* when analytical consciousness undertakes to reflect on the holistic and integrated dimension of our body of perception?

Now, the first of the three passages resonates in a most striking way with some passages written by Carl Jung. Jung holds that, "Just as the body has its evolutionary history and shows clear traces of the various evolutionary stages, so too does the psyche" (Jung 1912/52: 29).

Another passage fills out the meaning of the text:

> Just as our bodies still retain vestiges of obsolete [*a priori*] functions and conditions in many of their organs, so our minds, which have apparently outgrown those archaic impulses, still bear the marks of the evolutionary stages we have traversed, and reecho the dim bygone in dreams and fantasies.
>
> (ibid.: 28)

Erich Neumann, penetrating the archetypal character of this dimension that Merleau-Ponty calls "thought older than myself," considerably deepens the Jungian analysis:

> Millions of years of ancestral experience are stored up in the instinctive reactions of organic matter, and in the functions of the body there is incorporated a living knowledge, almost universal in scope, but not accompanied by any [explicit egological] consciousness. . . . By reason of this incorporated knowledge, the pleromatic [i.e., primordial] phase . . . is also intuited as one of primordial wisdom. The Great Mother has a wisdom infinitely superior to the masculine ego, because the instincts and archetypes that speak through the collective unconscious represent the "wisdom of the species" and its will.
>
> (Neumann 1970: 284)

I propose to identify what Jungians call our "collective unconscious" with the "primordial body." Then we may regard the archetypal structures as constitutive of what Merleau-Ponty (1963) describes in terms of an "organismic *a priori*." When radical reflection returns to articulate this *a priori* and make it explicit, it is functioning, in part, as an archetypal memory, a recollection of our embodiment in a time of wholeness and integration. This memory, however, is no ordinary memory. It works through mythic images, archetypal projections of the imagination. For the primordial body is without an egological subject (Jung 1919: 133). And its processes are, at first, more like dreams than like thoughts.

Radical reflection therefore does not seek to discover innate structures already fully stabilized and developed. On the contrary, it seeks out the primordial – that dimension of our experienced existence which is in need of understanding, since, without such understanding, the potential inherent in that dimension cannot continue to evolve. Radical reflection is active and creative, as well as receptive and repetitive. For the "amorphous existence which preceded my own history" (Merleau-Ponty 1962: 347) is without articulation. When reflection brings it to light and makes it explicit, the repetition incorporates it into a conscious process of self-understanding and self-development. Eros, the primordial body, can finally grow up.

Radical reflection is also a process of recollection in that it gathers and centers us, repeating on a higher level of articulate awareness the organismic operations of Eros which took place spontaneously, i.e. without our conscious control. Neumann speaks, here, of "centroversion." Merleau-Ponty writes that the gathering and centering has *already* taken place when radical reflection encounters it. He notes that,

> While I perceive, and even without having any [objective] knowledge of the organic conditions of my perception, I am aware of drawing together somewhat absent-minded and dispersed "consciousnesses": sight, hearing, and touch, with their fields, which are anterior, and remain alien, to my personal life.
>
> (ibid.)

But the reflective encounter with this prereflective gathering by Eros – the process of bringing its primordial body into awareness – deepens, extends and stabilizes the original gathering. A new experience of wholeness – this time a spiritual one enjoyed by Psyche – begins to form. And new possibilities emerge for further experiential adventures in the life of the Self. Radical reflection makes the Self possible by undermining the ego. It undermines the ego by going under it, back to its primordial body.

Recollection is a personal decision, a resolute step, of great significance. For in recollecting the original gathering, a gathering of feeling centered around the living body, the ego, which assumes control as "I" center as well as source, surrenders, or opens itself to an expanded field of explicit awareness. Jung, in fact, considers the ego to be the gathering point, or center, for consciousness in general (Jung 1926: 323–4). According to him, it is the ego's gathering which makes psychic processes conscious. On this point, Jung's understanding might seem to agree with Merleau-Ponty's.

But Jung raises a question of utmost importance: "This view of the ego as a composite of psychic elements logically brings up the question: Is the ego the central image and thus the exclusive representative of the total human being?" (ibid.: 324). And he answers this question in the negative: "The ego is a complex that does not comprise the total human being; it has forgotten infinitely more than it knows. It has heard and seen an infinite amount of which it has never become conscious" (ibid.).

Merleau-Ponty would certainly contest the way depth psychology makes the non-egological existence explicit as a deep stratum of the unconscious. But, once we construe the unconscious in terms of the pre-personal body in its field of awareness, we can see how depth psychology and Merleau-Ponty's phenomenology can provide complementary insights into the simultaneous co-emergence of ego-subject and its correlative object from within the depths of a more primordial ontological situation (Merleau-Ponty 1968: 123). According to Merleau-Ponty, the body-ego gradually emerges from its encompassing field, taking over from the primordial body the various organizing functions which once took place without any ego at their center. But the body itself thereby gets increasingly restricted – both as ego's body-subject and also as an object for the ego – to boundaries defined and imposed by the ego, representative of a mainly patriarchal and masculine culture.

Whereas the notion of an unconscious blinds depth psychology to the inherent richness of our perceptual life – and not only to the original configurations of our perceptual attunements – Merleau-Ponty's understanding of embodiment suffers from a lack of any phenomenologically defined ideal, or vision, of selfhood, Psyche's fulfillment. Thus, he seems to see less clearly than Jung and Neumann how our primordial holistic situatedness prefigures our potential for developing our humanity beyond the limitations of a personal ego. The notion of a Self, of Psyche, keeps us focused on the potential transcendence of the ego. Psyche, in our story, stands for the fulfillment of our existential potential. The Self is a transpersonal personality, a personality in touch with its pre-personal nature and on the way towards the development of a potential which that nature suggests. But this Self is in need of conceptual clarification. In particular, it requires interpretation as a process connected with, and indeed, inseparable from, the gradual emergence of the body-subject that finds its normal life in a more or less permanent ego-stage.

It is imperative, therefore, that we clearly distinguish, at this point, between the "prepersonal" and the "transpersonal." The *prepersonal* dimension, which Merleau-Ponty recognizes and discusses, is the site of a fundamental but implicit gathering – an "intertwining," a "chiasm," as he might have called it in his late manuscripts. But this dimension is essentially different from the *transpersonal*, which opens up for us when the glory of that original gathering is first brought to light by the philosophical act of recollection. For the act of recollection, the fields of being are (re)gathered into a whole no longer splintered by the rule of the ego-subject, and (re)centered, centered no longer around the ego-logical subject, but around the deepening processes of the encompassing Psyche. Merleau-Ponty, however, does not recognize the transpersonal, a highly developed stage of psychic embodiment, whose unselfish, selfless character is implicit, or latent, in the primordial anonymity and egolessness of the prepersonal mode of being-in-the-world. And yet, what depth psychology calls the "transpersonal" is not different from what Merleau-Ponty has described as the "prepersonal" – except that it has undergone a fundamental transformation in the process of being raised into consciousness through an act of radical reflection. The transpersonal life of the Self is, therefore, the fruit of reflection: it is what becomes of the prepersonal, the anonymous, when it is taken up into the light of consciousness.

Recollection: the moment when Psyche insights Eros

In *The Origins and History of Consciousness*, Neumann (1970: 294) writes: "with increasing differentiation, the zones under control [e.g. the erogenous zones of the infantile, or primitive body] come to be increasingly represented in the control organ of consciousness."

Inasmuch as this "control organ" is, for Neumann, no other than the ego, the implication is that it is ego which cathects – and cathects in order to bind, or repress – the polymorphous perversity of the original libidinous body. In other words, the polymorphous body of Eros is increasingly subject to restriction as Psyche falls under the spell of an ego bent on rising to power. Now, as ego rises to power and assumes the royal patriarchal throne, Psyche begins to lose touch with this erotic body of prepersonal wholeness, and especially, with the feminine principle that is inherent, or implicit, in the body of Eros. Psyche thereby becomes separate from its origins in the more elemental, more nurturing erotic relatedness characteristic of an earlier matriarchal power, a power functioning through the matrix of intentionalities which involved the primordial body in its world. Psyche forgets, because the masculine ego which dominates her – and dominates, above all, her own feminine aspect – has long since forgotten her. And the original body of Eros, separated from Psyche, remains correspondingly undeveloped; for its masculine aspect can mature only in conjunction with its feminine aspect, the aspect which Psyche can teach it to understand (Neumann 1973: 107). Recollection, then, is the moment when Psyche envisions, or insights, the full-bodied beauty and goodness of an Eros which is free of duality, free of self loathing, especially in regard for the sexual libido. It is the moment when Psyche accepts the truth in Eros – the truth *of* Eros. Recollection consists in an accepting embrace of that primordial body, whose wisdom is so vast and deep that it includes the gathering wholeness of time and space.

Thus Neumann declares, "It is in the light of knowledge, her knowledge of Eros, that she [Psyche] begins to love" (ibid.: 81). He observes that, at the moment when Psyche recognizes Eros and accepts him, Eros is enabled, finally, to develop his true potential (ibid.: 82–3). And yet, Neumann has no way of conceptualizing this potential in terms of Psyche's body, since the only body he is acquainted with is a body of matter, a body of instinct.

We therefore ask: What is the relationship between, on the one hand, the hermeneutic understanding of Eros we learn from depth psychology and, on the other hand, the understanding of Eros as a prepersonal body of polymorphous perversity, a body which we find in the phenomenological work of Merleau-Ponty?

Suppose we begin our reflections by listening to a passage from a chapter entitled, "The Body in its Sexual Being": "Let us try to see how a thing or a being begins to exist for us through desire or love and we shall thereby come to understand better how things and being can exist in general" (Merleau-Ponty 1962: 154).

According to Merleau-Ponty, it is Eros, erotic intentionality, or perhaps we should say, intentionality as Eros, which underlies the more ego-centered, ego-generated intentionalities – the various intentionalities of cognition, for example. Without attraction and aversion, the intentionality of cognitive awareness would have continued to sleep its deep sleep in an elemental darkness. It is Eros which awakens Psyche; it is Eros which moves through perception, causes motility, and bears responsibility for the organization of our space. But, insofar as Eros, manifesting primordially as desire and aversion, is responsible for the arising of the structural polarization characteristic of the subject–object relationship, it is also responsible for the pathological polarizations which make that relationship needlessly painful – a persistent, structurally engendered source of frustration, disappointment, suffering. Instead of the expansive, playful openness belonging to a full-bodied Eros, we experience recurrent anxiety, isolation, conflict, claustrophobia (Levin 1982–3). Recollecting how, thanks to the creative embrace of Eros, we are always being renewed with life, and are always *already* enlaced in the openness of a world of perception, motility and feeling, we experience the solace of a corporeal attunement, an incarnate belongingness, an intertwining, which corresponds, dynamically, to the movement of the psyche as understood by depth psychology. There is an Eros which hides in the play of perception, an Eros which intensifies all intentional relationships, an Eros which motivates the arc of every step, every movement, every gesture, and without which everything we initiated would disintegrate. We could do even less than the brain-damaged Schneider, whom Merleau-Ponty discusses at length in the *Phenomenology of Perception*. There is even an anonymous Eros whose embrace is responsible for the gathering of time, giving it its protentional and retentional unity (see Merleau-Ponty 1962: 69, 329, 407, 420–1). We cannot doubt, then, that the disclosures of Eros in the works of Merleau-Ponty flesh out, and richly supplement, the analysis and diagnosis of Eros that we find undertaken in the therapeutic process of depth psychology.

Language and the song of Eros

Eros also appears, in due time, hiding within the sensuous play of language. In essence, language is the song of Eros. Can we hear its singing? Merleau-Ponty observes that, "Like crystal, like metal and many other substances, I am a sonorous being" (Merleau-Ponty 1968: 144).

No other kind of being is endowed with such a range of sonorous modulations and inflections. Thanks to our capacity to speak, we not only greatly exceed the sonorous possibilities of all other beings, including the musical instruments we have invented to extend the sonorous field of expression, but also we are able, because of the sensuous incarnation of linguistic meaning, to create meaningful sounds which, on their own, give birth to further sounds of meaning – especially ambiguities, metaphorical transfers, word plays, echoes that hint, onomatopoeia, and what Paul Ricoeur calls "the interplay between reference and predication" (Ricoeur 1977: 299, 302–7). As Eros is the hidden figure active in the intentionality of memory, so too is it the elusive trope which keeps our language turning. As our most fundamental openness-to-others, Eros is the transcendental condition of the very possibility of language! Without Eros, where would language find the desire to communicate and express? Merleau-Ponty points out that, "The memory or the voice is recovered when the body once more opens itself to others or to the past, when it opens the way to coexistence and once more . . . acquires significance beyond itself" (Merleau-Ponty 1962: 165).

But of what is language capable? What is its essential nature, its potential as the voice of a fulfilled Psyche? Merleau-Ponty writes:

> If we consider only the conceptual and delimiting meaning of words, it is true that the verbal form . . . appears arbitrary. But it would no longer appear so if we took into account the emotional content of the word which we have called its "gestural" sense. . . . It would then be found that the words, vowels, and phonemes are so many ways of singing the world.
>
> (ibid.: 187)

Singing, the singing of the poet, above all, is the perfection, or fulfillment of our linguistic potential. But if singing manifestly realizes the human capacity for language, it does so only because that fulfillment is already present, immanent, "in the very beginning," prefigured in the babbling "foreplay" of the child. As I have said in another essay,

> There is much more to speaking than meaning (*Sinn*) and referent (*Bedeutung*), much more than a process of conceptual re-presenting (*Vor-stel-lung*). Instead of inhabiting the everyday process of re-presentation, so we get caught up in, and restricted by, the working of our standard grammar, we could try letting go this rule by grammar, in order to focus for a while, on the wholesome sensuous presence of speech, i.e., on how it presently feels as a process of free resonance. We may find that *undergoing* an experience with language as song soon becomes a process of *going under* our conceptual chatter and languaging compulsions, so we get more in touch with

> the song of their wholesome, preconceptual medium and ground. Language as presence, prior to representation in grammar.
>
> (Levin 1978b: 18–19)

Grammar is the binding of Eros, the ego's binding of the song of feeling, the emotional essence, which comes to expression, but without that song, in the egological grammar of controlled emotion. Of course we need grammar. But it is necessary that we understand how it relates, or could relate, to the speech of Eros. Grammar fixates, censors, represses libidinal energy. It must also therefore engender, and give expression to, a certain degree of anxiety. Now, anxiety is (as the root of the word itself reminds us) a closing off, or constriction, of the throat. (See Merleau-Ponty's discussion of the infant's buccal space during the oral stage of development. Grammar actually shapes our body, shapes and trains it. Shaping our speech, our patterns of breathing, it even structures our sense of being-in-space.) So long as anxiety has us in its grip, the spontaneous opening of speech, which is song, will not take place. For singing is the opening of our being: an outpouring of the heart, an expansion of the chest and lungs, an opening of throat, mouth, lips. In singing, we go out of ourselves, we give voice to our being as a felt whole; we express ourselves in the "*ecstase*" of a complete and fulfilling expression. Until we can sing our emotions, we cannot be really free.

Merleau-Ponty's work on language alludes to the playful presence of Eros – and to its needs. He understands that the speech of Eros arises from a preconceptual matrix of sonorous awareness, an open stratum of polyphonic feeling and sensuously felt meaning. This stratum, however, opens out into a limitless reserve of vibrant energies, so that the experience of returning to the resonance of such energies, when we listen and when we speak, can be wonderfully refreshing and healing. And it is out of this reserve that, instead of the grammatically restricted, univocal, and often monotonous speech of representational concerns, there can also well up the authentic spontaneity of heartfelt song. Grammar makes possible the birth of meaning in sound, but it also reduces our openness to the resonance of feeling out of which language first arises through our bodily nature. After we go back to the speech of Eros, we may speak through grammar once again. But this time, our speech will give Eros a new voice – a voice which articulates its song.

Yet Merleau-Ponty misses the therapeutic significance of his own reflective revelations. Nor does he entirely understand how radical reflection, returning to Eros as the original body of speech, can contribute to the emergence of a Self such as depth psychology is seeking. His phenomenological meditations, however, go very far to explain how the talking cure may successfully liberate desire. Consider, for example, how free association sets us free of ego's rule by grammar and puts us more in touch with the playful, creative wisdom of Eros. This wisdom is the polyphonic perversity of language in touch with desire. Depth psychology understands this much: that, somehow, when we let our speech go – or let go of speech – the hidden truth, always a truth involving some stage of Eros, will disclose itself in the openness of speech itself, where we have finally bidden it to play. But this psychology is ultimately at a loss for words when pressed to explain the process; for it has lost touch with the *body* of Eros. In *The Intertwining – The Chiasm*, however, Merleau-Ponty alludes to the bidding which addresses this body. "In a sense," he writes, "to understand a phrase is nothing other than fully to welcome it in its sonorous being" (Merleau-Ponty 1968: 155). Free association helps us to realize this welcome. But it is helpful to understand *who* it is we are welcoming: the voice of Eros. It is a voice which, therefore, cannot be confined to the grammar of any psychology, no matter how deep.

Singing, understood as speech coming from feelings whose voice is openly welcomed, puts us in touch with the wholeness of our being: with that openness-to-Being which precedes the arising of the more egological emotions and the perduring constructions of grammar. Below the process of languaging ruled by grammar that serves us well for representing the world, beneath the *work* of egological meanings, there is the more open field of *playful* sound; and it is polymorphic, polyphonic, and polysemic. A resonant attunement to the very Being of sound in its amplitude of energy (Levin 1978b; 1989). The body of Eros *plays* freely in that field. When our languaging recalls that play, it is quickened, filled with energy. Touched thus, it no longer serves the ego, but speaks, instead, with selfless voice: the full-bodied, transpersonal voice which audibly resonates with the gathering ring of compassion. It is in the speech which sings with compassion – the speech of the Self – that Eros is most fully realized.

Eros in movement

Neumann contends that, "on the uroboric level, where ego and consciousness are least developed," "the body stands for wholeness and unity in general, and its total reaction represents a genuine and creative totality" (Neumann 1970: 288). He argues, furthermore, that, "A sense of the body as a whole is the natural basis of the sense of personality" (ibid.).

This suggests that our development as human beings in the fullest sense depends upon our capacity to develop a felt sense of the body as a whole. Merleau-Ponty would, I think, enthusiastically concur. Speaking of the "intentional arc" which informs every movement, and which "projects round about us our past, our future, our human setting . . . or rather which results in our being situated in all these respects," he asserts: "It is this intentional arc which brings about the unity of the senses, of intelligence, of sensibility and motility" (Merleau-Ponty 1962: 136). I want to suggest that it is first and foremost *in movement* that we experience, as a bodily feeling, such a sense of our unity and wholeness; and that an awareness of movement, therefore, can deepen and intensify, and consequently enhance, that felt sense of our wholeness, the intentionality of our belonging, on the basis of which a more fully integrated, more lightly balanced, more expansive and open personality can begin to flourish.

The felt sense of wholeness constitutive of body-in-movement has a name: Eros. Eros is a metaphor for movement. In movement we discover, as Merleau-Ponty puts it, "a global bodily knowledge which systematically *embraces* all its parts" (ibid.: 314, italics added). Now, since each movement, as "a motor intentionality," involves the "projection" of "the possible," (ibid.: 109) we can say that, "Each instant of the movement *embraces* its whole span" (ibid.: 140, italics added).

But this embrace is none other than that between Eros and Psyche, who meet in the chiasm of energy which is our embodiment. The "embrace," symbolized by Eros, is a distinctive modality of intentionality. Merleau-Ponty explains it further, observing that,

> The normal function which makes abstract movement possible is one of projection, whereby the subject of movement keeps in front of him an area of *free space* in which what does not naturally exist may take on a semblance of existence.
>
> (ibid.: 110–11, italics added)

The corporeal projection of the possible, which is a necessary condition for movement, takes place within a unified field of comportment whose vectors of desire the movement itself has partially constituted.

Motor intentionality has the character of a "physiognomic perception." In this sense, it constitutes a vectorial field in a holistic manner, and it gives rise to an incarnate knowledge which cannot be conceptualized in the objectivist vocabulary of classical metaphysics (ibid.: 267). Where movement takes place, where can we locate the "subject"? And exactly where is the object which touches us through its occultation of attraction or repulsion? Subject and object are always intertwined, inseparable partners in the dance of movement. Despite appearances, subject and object are innately in touch, embraced by the rainbow arc in our every gesture, whether it be a gesture of love or a gesture of hate.

Eros sings not only in our speech, but also through the musculature of the body-in-movement. In the form of movement, Eros is the rainbow arc, the motor intentionality which dances, and which discloses in every movement the beauty of its true nature in relation to Psyche and Being. In the case of Schneider, therefore, the pathology clearly manifests its deficient nature when the patient is called upon to move. Merleau-Ponty emphasizes that his gesturing "loses the melodic character which it presents in ordinary life, and becomes manifestly a collection of partial movements strung laboriously together" (ibid.: 105).

Eros, fundamental metaphor that it is, appears wherever there is movement; and it appears most openly and with the greatest beauty wherever a movement takes place which displays the truth of its "melodic character." Eros is thus most beautifully visible, most "in its truth," in the heightened movements of dance (Levin 1985). If, as Merleau-Ponty believes, "the body is essentially an expressive space" (Merleau-Ponty op. cit.: 146) it is nowhere more expressive, more intensely alive, more in communion with the spaciousness and rhythm of being than in its dancing, when the song of the Earth can be heard and felt, coursing through the expressive articulations of the body.

The body is especially articulate, perhaps, when it gestures. As is the case with movement in general, Eros is visible in every moving gesture. We greet, we entreat, we give, we receive, we hold, we keep, we touch and caress, we fight with wounded pride and love. These are gestures.

But the question is: of what is Eros capable? In other words, of what are our gestures capable? Merleau-Ponty alludes to the existence of "consecratory gestures" (ibid.). For me, this locution implies that Eros is not just a figure of sexual embodiment. Even in its libidinal infancy, it bears within itself the divine madness of the urge to realize a more spiritual nature, more attractive to Psyche's dream. And so, when Psyche truly recollects this urge, its union with Eros may be consummated in gestures of great compassion: gestures that are gentle, tender and caring; gestures that lend a helpful hand; gestures that exemplify the two senses of yielding; gestures that touch and caress without hate or greed (Levin 1978a). The spiritual union of Psyche and Eros represents, in Neumann's words, "the symbolic accentuation of the body, and the sanctification of everything pertaining to it, which are characteristic of the uroboric phase" (Neumann 1970: 291).

It is Eros which always moves us. So the question is whether we will be moved by blind sexual desire and ego-centered attachments, or by the Eros which consecrates our gestures and movements – the Eros which yearns to become, in the embrace by which Psyche recognizes him and recollects the magnitude of his reserve, the reaching out of great compassion.

Eros as compassion

Jung says: "Access to the collective psyche means a renewal of life for the individual" (Jung 1928: 169). If we understand this access as an act of recollection, then the individual owes his renewal of life to a recognition of Eros, the basis for compassion and sense of community it engenders. Since Eros is embodied, embodied in a body which gives itself up to a neurophysiological understanding, Jung's insightful penetration of the somatic basis of compassion is not inappropriate:

> The unconscious is the psyche that reaches down from the daylight of mentally and morally lucid consciousness into the nervous system that for ages has been known as the "sympathetic." This does not govern perception and muscular activity like the cerebrospinal system, and thus control the environment; but, through functioning without sense-organs, it maintains the balance of life, and, through the mysterious paths of sympathetic excitation, not only gives us knowledge of the innermost life of other beings, but also has an inner effect on them.
>
> (Jung 1934/54: 19–20)

But we must translate the insight here into the phenomenological language of the body of experience, the body we live, the body we are (Merleau-Ponty op. cit.: 351). Had Jung and Neumann fully appreciated this body of experience, perhaps they could have given the "numinosity" of the Psyche a body more suitable to the spiritual wisdom they sought to make possible for it. Merleau-Ponty gives their psychology of the Self the understanding of embodiment which it needs. He writes: "The constitution of others does not come after that of the body, others and my body are born together from an original ecstasy" (Merleau-Ponty 1964b: 174).

Recollecting this "original ecstasy," the openness of existence-with-others in "the undividedness of feeling," we can endeavor to achieve another, more enduring ecstasy: "an ideal community of embodied subjects, of an intercorporeality," as Merleau-Ponty (1970: 131, 82) expresses this dream. Sharing this dream, Jung articulates the psychology of the compassion which constitutes the foundation of such a community:

> If this supra-individual psyche exists, everything that is translated into its picture-language would be depersonalized, and if this became conscious would appear to us *sub specie aeternitatis*. Not as my sorrow, but as the sorrow of the world; not a personal isolating pain, but a pain without bitterness that unites all humanity. The healing effect of this needs no proof.
>
> (Jung 1931: 150)

We must, however, leave behind us the *original* ecstasy of our being-with-others as we progressively identify our psyche with the ego which is emerging in the process of individuation. Now this process cannot be other than painful. Nevertheless,

> Psyche dissolves her *participation mystique* with her partner and flings herself and him into the destiny of separation that is consciousness. Love as an expression of feminine wholeness is not possible in

> the dark, as a merely unconscious process; an authentic encounter with another involves consciousness, hence also the aspect of suffering and separation.
>
> (Neumann 1973: 85)

It is precisely into the light of such consciousness that Merleau-Ponty wants to bring our "*participation mystique*." His phenomenological hermeneutics, blessed, no doubt, by Hermes himself, therefore does more than simply penetrate the disguise of Eros, whose compassionate aspect has been kept in the dark during the reign of the patriarchal ego. His work of reflection and recollection breaks new ground by articulating the compassion of Eros in terms of our experience of embodiment. It consequently provides an understanding that really inspires and guides us through a process of psychic transformation.

Nowhere is Merleau-Ponty's work of recollection more experientially illuminating, I think, than in his essay, "The child's relations with others" (1964a). It is in this paper that he sheds a gentle light on the embrace of Eros and Psyche, whom he (re)discovers in "the total continuum made up of all the lived relations with others and the world" (Merleau-Ponty 1964b: 140–1). This continuum is an original openness-to-others which, we will recall, is manifest, for example, in the warm "radiance" of the flesh, and which constitutes the "pre-communication" that serves as basis for a "genuine sympathy" in the mature adult and for a progressively less selfish and egoistic form of community (ibid.: 119–20).

In his phenomenology of intersubjectivity, Husserl was compelled to recognize the essential role of the living human body; and he spoke, but with much discomfort, of the phenomenon of "coupling" (*Paarung*) and the transcendental structure of an "intentional transgression (ibid.: 118). But openness-to-others, extremely puzzling, if not also doubtful, from the standpoint of a transcendental rationalism, becomes much more intelligible once we situate it within the world of human embodiment. "I live," writes Merleau-Ponty, "in the facial expressions of the other, as I feel him living in mine" (ibid.: 146). And he suggests, along the way, that we reflect on the smile which passes, by a sort of "postural impregnation" (ibid.: 118) from mother to infant (ibid.: 115–20). Taking up Husserl's bewilderment as a challenge to recollect the body of Eros espoused by Psyche as openness-to-others, Merleau-Ponty argues that, "Insofar as I have sensory functions, a visual, auditory and tactile field, I am already in communication with others" (Merleau-Ponty 1962: 353).

Let us concentrate on vision as an example of this prereflective, prepersonal, implicit communication. "The look, we said, envelopes, palpates, espouses the visible things" (Merleau-Ponty 1968: 13).

According to Merleau-Ponty, "the palpation of the eye is a remarkable variant" of tactile perception, since

> every vision takes place somewhere in the tactile space (ibid.) and the visible spectacle belongs to the touch neither more nor less than do the "tactile qualities." We must habituate ourselves to think that every visible is cut out in the tangible, every tactile being in some manner promised to visibility, and that there is encroachment, infringement, not only between the touched and the touching, but also between the tangible and the visible
>
> (Merleau-Ponty 1962: 134)

Thus we can understand how it is possible that "One sees the springiness of steel, the ductility of red-hot steel, the hardness of a plane blade, the softness of shavings" (ibid.: 229).

If we now recollect the potency of Eros which is implicitly manifest in the visual situation – recollect *for the sake of Psyche* the tenderness and care implicit in the embrace of Eros, then we begin to get in touch with the true nature of our vision: its extensive capacity for the openness of compassion and for the compassion in openness. How often, and to what degree, is our vision in touch with what we are given to behold? How deeply do we let ourselves be touched, and even moved to tears, by what we see? How tightly are we held by what we behold? How beholden? These questions are intended to focus on the potential depth of feeling which underlies our sight, so that we may recollect the compassion by which Eros fulfills the needs of Psyche (Levin 1988).

If the vision of our eyes can be touched by the tangible things it sees, that is because, "being of their family, itself visible and tangible, it uses its own being as a means to participate in theirs" (Merlean-Ponty 1962: 137).

The gaze of compassion, the gaze which can be touched and moved, is but a special case of the intertwining in which vision and touch are, inseparably, joined together. A special case – and an essential fulfillment of the potential implicit in that crossing of fields. Vision fully participates in the world it is granted to behold when it is open to receiving it: open and fully compassionate. Such participation, akin to yet different from a primitive "*participation mystique*," involves vision in a process whereby it develops, or realizes, its capacity for care, gentleness of focus, and tender regard. What is in question? Is it not the feminine aspect of the powerful Eros which, itself invisible, inhabits our vision? (see Foucault 1975).

In "The Philosopher and Sociology," Merleau-Ponty reflects that, "Philosophy is not a particular body of knowledge; it is the vigilance which does not let us forget the source of all knowledge" (Merleau-Ponty 1964c: 110). This source of all knowledge is Eros, body of creative wisdom. And the vigilance which does not let us forget – that is *anamnesis*, the act of recollection which, without ever denying Eros its unceasing disseminations and without ever being finished, makes Psyche feel whole.

References

Foucault, M. (1975) *The Birth of the Clinic: an Archeology of Medical Perception*, New York: Vintage Books.

Freud, S. (1930) *Civilization and its Discontents*, trans. J. Riviere, New York: Doubleday Anchor Books.

Hamilton, E. (1942) *Mythology*, New York: New American Library, Mentor Book.

Heidegger, M. (1979) *Nietzsche, Vol. 1: the Will to Power as Art*, trans. D. Krell, New York: Harper and Row.

Jung, C. (1919) "Instinct and the unconscious," *CW* 8.

—— (1912/52) "Symbols of transformation," *CW* 5.

—— (1926) "Spirit and life," *CW* 8.

—— (1928) "The relations between the ego and the unconscious," *CW* 7.

—— (1931) "The structure of the psyche," *CW* 8.

—— (1934/54) "Archetypes of the collective unconscious," *CW* 9.i.

Levin, D. (1982–83) "Sanity and myth in affective space," *The Philosophical Forum*, 9, 2, 157–89.

—— (1978a) "The embodiment of compassion: how we are visibly moved," *Soundings*, 61, 4, 515–22.

—— (1978b) "Mantra: sacred words of openness and compassion," *Gesar*, Berkeley: Dharma Publishing Company.

—— (1985) *The Body's Recollection of Being*, London: Routledge.

—— (1988) *The Opening of Vision*, London: Routledge.

—— (1989) *The Listening Self*, London: Routledge.

Merleau-Ponty, M. (1962) *The Phenomenology of Perception*, trans. C. Smith, London: Routledge.

—— (1963) *The Structure of Behavior*, trans. A. Fisher, Boston: Beacon Press.

—— (1964a) "The child's relations with others," trans W. Cobb, in M. Merlean-Ponty, *The Primacy of Perfection*, Evanston Northwestern University Press.

—— (1964b) *The Primacy of Perception*, Evanston: Northwestern University Press.

—— (1964c) *Signs*, Evanston: Northwestern University Press.

—— (1968) *The Visible and the Invisible*, trans. A. Lingis, Evanston: Northwestern University Press.

—— (1970) *Themes from the Lectures at the College de France*, Evanston: Northwestern University Press.

Neumann, E. (1970) *The Origins and History of Consciousness*, trans. R. Manheim, Princeton: Princeton University Press.

—— (1973) *Amor and Psyche: the Psychic Development of the Feminine*, trans. R. Manheim, Princeton: Princeton University Press.

Ricoeur, P. (1977) *The Rule of Metaphor: Multi-disciplinary Studies of the Creation of Meaning*, Toronto: University of Toronto Press.

EDITOR'S INTRODUCTION

Central to phenomenology's method is the *epoche*, the systematic attempt to see through one's own assumptions and prejudices so that phenomena can show themselves anew, with greater clarity and depth. But phenomenology, particularly in its Husserlian form, with its transcendental, ideal emphasis, has been cogently criticized and "deconstructed" by postmodern thinkers such as Derrida. In fact, phenomenology and deconstruction are frequently opposed in the politics of contemporary intellectual life. On the other hand, deconstruction has always been an important tool in phenomenology's method; it is central to the *epoche*.

Marlan's paper is an especially creative application of phenomenological deconstruction. Following recent French thought, he critically investigates and deconstructs the image of solar light as it permeates western metaphysics and is to be found in the work of both Jung and Heidegger. The intriguing thing is that his method is thoroughly Jungian too, as he draws from Jung's experience in Africa and his alchemical reflections on "blackness." But, for Marlan, Jung's alchemical studies are useful less as objects to think about than as ways of thinking; the alchemical images of light and dark are thus investigated as total organizations of experience and thought. Re-reading Jung's notions of consciousness and individuation with an alchemical and Hillmanian eye, Marlan leads us to a considerably more subtle appreciation of those defining terms of analytical psychology, and more cautious about the politics that operate within psychic life as well as in culture.

10

THE METAPHOR OF LIGHT AND ITS DECONSTRUCTION IN JUNG'S ALCHEMICAL VISION

Stanton Marlan

> The eyes and the ears are bad witness for me if they have barbarian souls.
>
> (Heraclitus, *Frag.*, 107)

> For the darkness has its own peculiar intellect and its own logic, which should be taken very seriously.
>
> (C. G. Jung, "Mysterium coniunctionis", 345)

> One does not become enlightened by imagining figures of light, but by making the darkness conscious.
>
> (C. G. Jung, "Alchemical studies", 265–266)

Introduction

The metaphor of light is fundamentally intertwined with the history of western consciousness. Our very language demonstrates the pervasiveness of this metaphor and its intimately connected twin metaphor of vision and enlightenment: it is nearly inconceivable to *envision* a way of thinking that doesn't rely on one or the other of these metaphors. As a result, in the most common means of communication light and vision appear to be an essential factor of western imagination and our view of consciousness. In language and myth, in science, philosophy and religion, we find abundant confirmation of this view:

> From the primitive importance of the sacred fire to the frequency of sun-worship in more developed religions – such as the Chaldean and Egyptian – and the sophisticated metaphysics of light in the most advanced theologies [and philosophies], the ocular presence in a wide variety of religious practices has been striking. Some faiths, like Manichaean Gnosticism, have fashioned themselves "religions of

> light"; others, like the often polytheistic Greek religion, assigned a special role to sun gods like Apollo. Unearthly, astral light surrounding the godhead, the divine illumination sought by the mystic, the omniscience of a god always watching his flock, the symbolic primacy of the candle's flames – all of these have found their way into countless religious systems.
>
> (Jay 1994: 11–12)

It is not surprising then to see that Jung also relied on light's metaphorical depths in the way he imagined his own self-understanding and in the theories he constructed. Even in his late alchemical writing he states that the soul is "an eye destined to behold the light" (Jung 1953: 13). Light and vision as fundamental to our western consciousness are the inheritance of modern man and the tradition of modernity; but it is also a tradition that has brought suspicion and even aroused hostile reaction. Its privileged role has always been challenged, and today's challenge is at the center of current debate (Jay 1994: 13). Jung was a modern man and was both a shaper and participant in the culture of modernity, a central metaphor of which is light and vision. In postmodern times, the tradition of modernity has come under deconstructive scrutiny, revealing its dark shadow. The light the eye was "destined to behold" displayed a blind spot with regard to vision itself.

The shadow of vision

For the postmodern mind the hegemony of vision and the entire western intellectual canon has become defined as a privileged view of "a more or less exclusively white male European elite" (Tarnas 1991: 400). Jung belonged to this elite, informed as he was by his European language and historically rooted in a Christian and Cartesian world view. It was an elitism that brought with it charges of racism and colonialism (Ortiz-Hill 1997: 125–133). Ortiz-Hill, while not wanting simply to point at Jung's "clay feet," raised many important questions about his Eurocentrism. Here he joins others within and outside the Jungian community whose critiques have helped both to de-idealize Jung as well as to make us painfully aware of the cultural biases and presuppositions of our own time. A critical eye to Jung's personal and collective shadow is an important part of our current consciousness, but this should not blind us, as sometimes it has, to his important contributions and to the development of his ideas beyond his biases as he and his work developed and matured.

What I find of particular value in Jung was his capacity for continual self-reflection. He had the desire and ability to stand outside himself with critical insight. If in our time we have come to see Jung as Eurocentric, it was also an awareness he had of himself, an awareness that ultimately brought him to the very edge of his modernity and perhaps beyond it. One might imagine the seeds for this awareness developing as he prepared for his trip to Africa in 1925–1926.

Jung's travel in Africa

As Jung contemplated his journey, he expressed his desire to be "in a non-European country where no European language was spoken and no Christian concepts prevailed" (Jung 1962: 238). In short he wanted "to see the European from outside, his image reflected back to him by an altogether foreign milieu" (ibid.: 238); and to find "a psychic observation post outside the sphere" (ibid.: 244) of his own culture. Jung "wanted to find that part of [his] personality which had become invisible under the influence and pressure of being European" (ibid.: 244). Jung was aware of the limitations of his conscious situation; and in his travels the invisible "other" which he sought looked back at him, reflecting his whiteness as if from a dark mirror, primordial, terrifying and numinous. He identified with the light of consciousness and, like the Elgonyi of East Africa, whose solar mythology he studied but perhaps did not fully understand, he feared the darkness into which the sun passed at night. This fear of the blackness of Africa emerged most poignantly as he struggled with a dream of an "American Negro" (Jung's expression) whom he identified as his barber, and who "in the dream . . . was holding a tremendous red-hot curling iron to my head, intending to make my hair kinky – that is, to give me Negro hair. I could already feel the painful heat, and awoke with a sense of terror" (ibid.: 272).

Jung took this dream as a warning from the unconscious, and he concluded that his European personality must under all circumstances be preserved intact (ibid.: 272–273). One might say that what the dark light of the dream threw into relief was Jung's modernity, his identification with the light of consciousness and its underlying myth of "the continuous 'Chain of Being' that stratifies and holds in order a hierarchical cosmos . . . with Europeans being at the pinnacle of evolutionary development" (Ortiz-Hill 1997: 127). What was revealed to Jung was his desperate clinging to his identity as a white male psychiatrist, for whom "going black" and "kinky" meant a deep regression and the danger of being overrun by instinct.

For Jung, becoming Negro was also a *Nigredo*, a terrifying blackness (Gr: *melanosis*) from which he could, for the moment, only retreat. One might however imagine that he was on the brink of what he had hoped for at the beginning of his travels, which was to find that part of himself that had become invisible under the pressure of being European. To engage this Other required a *Mortificatio*, a terrifying descent or *Nekyia* into the blackness of the *Nigredo*, which is synonymous with the experience of death (Edinger 1985: 169). To retreat before this death anxiety seems quite natural, but some have raised the question as to whether Jung perhaps more than most was threatened with concerns about the disintegration of the Self (Brooke 1991:

60–61, following Papadopoulos 1984, and Winnicott 1964). It is interesting to note that it was not until after he had assimilated this experience that a deeper theoretical distinction between ego and Self was made (Brooke 1991: 61). Still, as Ortiz-Hill notes, in Jungian theory there is a persistent concern about "being overwhelmed by the psyche, by instinct, by the anima, by the shadow, by the female, or ethnic 'other' " (Ortiz-Hill 1977: 133), such that he felt the need to ask what he considers to be an unavoidable "Freudian question:" i.e. "what was the moment of being engulfed that led Jung to see himself a potential victim of being overwhelmed by 'otherness' within and outside himself?" (Ortiz-Hill 1997: 133).

Whatever import there may be in evaluating Jung's personal dynamics it is also important to note that the archetypal terror of the *Nigredo* experience is by definition fundamentally threatening and wounding to the ego. Alongside the question of personal dynamics we must ask: "could there be an archetypal aspect to darkness that might account for our disdain, as well as the fear, the physiological shudder it can release"? (Hillman 1997a: 45). For Hillman, the essence of this fear lies in the black radix itself, and Edinger provides an archetypal if compensatory understanding as well, when he comments that the ego, "by daring to exist as an autonomous center of being, takes on substantial reality but also becomes subject to corruption and death. The ego is eventually eclipsed – falls into the blackness of mortificatio" (Edinger 1985: 163). Thus simply to psychologize or analyze these fears into personality dynamics and/or "race relations" (Hillman 1997a: 52) does not get at the archetypal imagination of these fears. Hillman undoes the equation: Negro is *Nigredo* (an identification unconsciously made by Jung), placing it back from its cultural projection into the heart of our archetypal dynamics (ibid: 50). While this analysis does not preclude the evaluation of personal dynamics against this archetypal background, personal analysis alone is inadequate to represent the full range of both structural and archetypal levels of meaning.

Returning to Jung's dream, it is of interest to follow Adams (1996) who suggests that, rather than expressing a warning, "the unconscious is attempting to compensate his ego's too-civilized white European attitudes" (Adams 1996: 79). From this perspective, the dream may not be warning Jung to avoid "going black" but "inviting, encouraging or challenging him to do so" (ibid.: 79). Or, as Edinger comments, "dreams that emphasize blackness usually occur when the conscious ego is one-sidedly identified with the light" (Edinger 1985: 150).

From both Adams and Edinger, one gets a sense of the compensatory possibilities of Jung's encounter with the darkness of his invisible other and how his dream might have served psyche's attempt toward decentering, deepening and darkening Jung's Eurocentric ego, attempting to bring him into touch with his and the culture's archetypal shadow. In terms of archetypal dynamics, Hillman goes beyond the theory of compensation and notes that blackness, the "subtle dissolver," when mixed with other hues, brings about their darkening and deepening, or – in alchemical psychology's language – their suffering (Hillman 1997a: 48) For Hillman: "black steers all varieties of brightness into the shade" (ibid.), but its deeper purpose is not simply that of compensating the ego – to shade its natural innocence a necessary step – but also to introduce "the deeper invisible realm of shades, the Kingdom of Hades, which is the ultimate "subtle dissolver" of the luminous world. . . . Like a black hole [this pull of the underworld] sucks into it[self] and makes vanish the fundamental security structures of western consciousness" (ibid.). If we consider the archetypal meaning of blackness, this places Jung's anxiety less in his neurosis, historically or structurally seen, but more at the existential core of his Being. For it is this blackness that "breaks the paradigm [and] dissolves whatever we rely upon as real and dear" (ibid.). Jung's existential anxiety then might be seen not only personally but also as an underlying archetypal dimension of the angst at the root of western metaphysics and modernism, and perhaps as a fundamental dynamic of the human condition. It is the anxiety of every man standing before the dissolution of foundations and which has a particular coloring in Jung and in the visionary tradition and its hegemonic role in the modern era.

The hegemony of vision

Whatever personal anxieties Jung may have felt returning from his fear of "going black," he also echoed the collective anxiety of a culture standing at the edge of modernity. In this paradigm-breaking blackness lay the deconstructive counter-vision of postmodernity ready to translate "the great phenomenal world into the inked abstractions of letters, numbers and lines, replacing the palpable and visual given[s of phenomenology and presence] with the [postmodern] data of marks and traces" (ibid.), or as Hartman was to put it, "the blackness of ink or print suggests that écriture is a hymn to the Spirit of the Night" (Jay 1994: 510, quoting Geoffrey Hartman). Could we then call the semantic insights of Derrida, Lacan and others a "black art"? By deconstructing presence into absence, the *Nigredo* makes possible psychological, if not cultural, change. Is it any wonder then why so many find postmodernism so threatening and complain of not being able to grasp it? For Hillman, "each moment of blackening is a harbinger of alteration, of invisible discovery, and of dissolution of attachments to whatever has been taken as truth and reality, solid fact, or dogmatic virtue" (Hillman 1997a: 49). One such truth and dogmatic conviction that needed to be unsettled has been the "founding trope of western metaphysics, the privileging of whiteness over blackness, light over darkness" (Jay 1994: 509, quoting Derrida). Influenced by Heidegger, Derrida has likewise seen a certain ocularcentrism concealing itself behind the history of metaphysics. What he adds is that in modern times this perspective has extended itself beyond the margins of philosophy into the politics of culture, into power relations and the sociology of racism. Derrida notes that behind our western visionary tradition is the shadow of phallocentrism, egocentrism, ethnocentrism, and a heliopolitics "driven by the 'violence of light' and threatening to impose the ontological order of presence wherever its mastery can reach" (Levin 1993: 7, quoting Derrida). Derrida put it this way: "the white man takes his own mythology, Indo-European mythology, his own logos, that is the mythos of his idiom, for the universal form of that he must still wish to call Reason" (Jay 1994: 509, quoting Derrida). This not only privileges one race over another but it also derives from the time-honored privileging of the sun as the dominant locus of signification: "value, gold, the eye, the sun, etc." (ibid.: 509). In Jungian language one might say that Derrida is pointing to the cultural power shadow of western thought and the dominance of one archetypal form literalized in the Eurocentric logos. One might imagine that it was this shadow which looked back at Jung in his identification with western man and his terror of blackness, a shadow Jung was attempting to transform.

Movement toward an alchemical vision

As Jung and his theory matured, the shadow of his Cartesian/ Eurocentric bias began to give way, and he developed a fuller, deeper understanding of consciousness. One place this can be seen is in his alchemical work (Brooke 1991: 61). Brooke notes the contrast between Jung's earlier heroic Faustian consciousness and a developing "reverent hospitality" exemplified by the figures Philemon and Baucis. As Jung's consciousness grew more hospitable, the uncertainty and neurotic European anxiety lessened, and his ego began a deeper relationship with the Self. Here the idea of the Self is not viewed as an enclosed entity, and Brooke's reading helps to bring Jungian psychology and existential phenomenology into closer proximity with each other.

The value and interface of these traditions have produced fruits for each and for depth psychology in general. One example is the manner in which Brooke uses Heideggerian insights to describe Jung's later and more mature vision of "consciousness as the illuminating realm within which the being of the world can shine forth" (ibid.: 58). In the poetics of this image Brooke tries to point to a way of understanding consciousness from beyond the Cartesian separation of subject and world. Here Brooke too inevitably relies upon metaphors of light, yet tries to point beyond light versus dark to the primordial structures that found psychological life. This is a vision more appropriate to Jung, whose explorations into the shadow and the darkness of the unconscious have rendered him anything but a figure who can adequately be described as avoiding the dark side of the psyche. But: what would be a productive way of addressing the kind of consciousness that Jung's explorations open up? Following Brooke's lead into existential phenomenology demands that one also enter into the complexity and development of this field as well as into the developments in Jungian psychology radicalized in archetypal and alchemical psychology.

Tension and development in existential phenomenology

It is of no small consequence to note the critical interface of existential phenomenology with its postmodern challenges. Derrida for instance has critiqued Heideggerian thought as a photology and heliocentric metaphysics with its implications for heliopolitics. In fact Derrida suggests the entire movement of most western thought from Parmenides to phenomenology, and including Heidegger, falls under this critique.

He cites Heidegger's notion of "bringing to light" and others' use of this metaphor as problematic. Here Derrida is in a long line of French intellectuals for whom the reliance on light and vision is denigrated. This denigration has been richly documented by Jay (1994) in his book *Downcast Eyes*. In this work the intricacy of the metaphor of vision and light is explored in complex reflections from phenomenology to postmodernism in France with important implications for our understanding of consciousness. Jay's work documents the attempt of French intellectuals to undermine western ocularcentrism, an attempt to free consciousness from its power shadow. The history of this critique has also led to a crisis of Enlightenment described by Habermas as a "new unsurveyability" (Jay 1994: 592), an image pointing to the ironic consequences of the French critique.

While negative skepticism is not always the fault of the best French critics and philosophers, their work has often led some to speculate if their cynicism might be rooted in the possibility that most postmodern thinking is itself an obsessional exercise of the Cogito that never really cuts through the very paradigms it wishes to deconstruct. Hillman (1997b) for example suggests that deconstructionism, in its "playing with the ambiguity of the 'trace,' troping, displacing, and insisting upon difference and, as well, the absenting of all certitudes from positive propositions" (the French mode of decapitating the Cogito), ultimately becomes "one more habitual concretism of western thought" (Hillman 1997b: 13). Hillman suggests that while the French effort may in many ways mimic alchemy in its arcane obstructionism and its deconstructive talk which sounds like the language of alchemy, it does not affect an in-depth alchemical transformation. While it attempts to free the mind from singleness and literalism, "it stops short before the Nigredo turns blue" (ibid.: 13). Here Hillman uses the color imagery of alchemy to point to the importance of transformation, to move the soul beyond intellectual ideation alone. In the alchemical imagination, after blackness comes blueness,

> not cynical, but sad; not hard and smart, but slow. The blues bring the body back with a revisioned feeling, head and body rejoined . . .

> blue gives voice to the nigredo. . . . Darkness imagined as an invisible light, like a blue shadow, behind and within all things.
>
> (Hillman 1997b: 13)

While Hillman points to the importance of feeling, recognizes the shadow and pastiche of postmodernism, and offers important observations, it is too global a condemnation. The work of deconstruction is also a slow and careful reading of texts, playful at times, capturing important moments of soul and a sensitivity to the human condition. Derrida for instance, following Freud's insight into the link between castration and blindness, notes that "only man knows how to go beyond seeing and knowing, because only he knows how to cry. . . . Only he knows that tears are the essence of the eye – and not sight" (Jay 1994: 523, quoting Derrida). Jay continues: "Eyes that cry implore rather than see; they invite the question from the other: whence the pain?" (ibid.: 523). In this moment Derrida's thoughts reveal a soulful awareness that glows with a vision of blueness.

Similarly, Nye (1993) in her critique of patriarchal vision sees it as dying, as a dead vision and a vision of death, but she states the only way to prepare for the birth of another vision is from the depths of our suffering. Paraphrasing Nye, Levin (1993) asks:

> What would have happened, she wonders, if those Greek men had turned back, after learning from their vision of the Forms, to look at one another, their gazes engaged by the interactions of friendly conversation? And what would have happened if they had turned and looked at women, looked with eyes moved by feelings of friendship, admiration, and respect?
>
> (Levin 1993: 26, citing Nye)

In the above I propose we find the blue quality of soul, of slowness, the feeling and imaginative revisioning characteristic of alchemical transformation. It is this kind of revisioning of vision that can directly be found not only by looking again at myth, but by turning again to the light of alchemy.

The alchemical *lumen naturae*: the light of nature

The *lumen naturae* was an image of light at the core of ancient alchemical ideas. The aim of alchemy was to beget this light hidden in nature, a light very different from the western association of vision as separate from darkness. It was a light Jung came to see in his alchemical studies. In an Arabic treatise attributed to Hermes, the *Tractatus Aureus*, Mercurius says: "I beget light, but the darkness too is of my nature" (Jung 1942: 125). In alchemy, light and dark, male and female, are joined together in the idea of the chymical marriage; and from the marriage (of light and dark) the *filius philosophorum* emerges and a new light is born: "They embrace and a new light is begotten of them, which is like no other light in the whole world" (Jung 1942: 126, citing Mylius). This light is a central mystery of alchemy. It is of interest to imagine this alchemical marriage as a continuation of Nye's fantasy about what would have happened if the masculine psyche had embraced not only women but also the "feminine" dimension of psyche with friendship and respect. Might we speculate that perhaps a filius could have been born, a new consciousness which might have changed the whole development of western culture?

Jung traces the idea of the *filius* to the archetypal image of the Primordial Man of Light, a vision of the Self that is both light and dark, male and female, and for which Jung finds amplification in Prajãpati or Purusha in India, Gayomort ("mortal life") in Persia – a youth of dazzling whiteness like Mercurius – and in Metatron, who in the Zohar was created together with light. The Man of Light was also described by Paracelsus as identical with the "astral" man: "The true man is the star in us. The star desires to drive men towards great wisdom" (ibid.: 131). It is of interest to see Jung's insight resonating with Derrida's reading of Solar Mythology, which suggests that the light of the sun should not simply be linked to the light of Enlightenment. "The sun is also a star . . . like all the other stars that appear only at night and are invisible during the day. As such it suggests a source of truth or properness that was not available to the eye, at least at certain times" (Jay 1994: 510, citing Derrida). Jung, like Derrida, mentions two images of light: the great light and the inner light of nature, hidden and invisible, a little spark without which the darkness would not be darkness. Likewise, for Corbin (1978), light has a double nature, an innerness that is also an outerness. This dual vision is characteristic of the Primordial Man whose light is ultimately the *mundus imaginalis* and which, according to Corbin, must not be confused with the "imaginary" in our current understanding of the term.

The double nature of light is itself an archetypal theme along with the invisibility of the so called "inner light." It is a light which is neither simply subjective nor simply found in the outer world, in phenomena or in our speech, but it "buildeth shapes in sleep from the power of the word" (Jung 1947/54: 195, quoting *Liber de Caducis*) and can be found in dreams. The attainment of this light was for Paracelsus – who, according to Jung, was a well-intentioned, humble Christian – his most secret and deepest passion. His whole creative yearning belonged to the *lumen naturae*, the divine spark buried in the darkness, "whose sleep of death could not be vanquished even by the revelation of God's son" (Jung 1942: 160). For some alchemists, the light of the Christian deity could even stand in the way of the light of nature which was obscured as the development of Christianity split off from the pagan power of nature.

Light and lumen: a contemporary dream

This split between the light of the God-man and light of nature can be seen in the dream of a contemporary woman who was brought up in a strict Catholic tradition, and who had been struggling with her desire for a warmer, more sensual life and desiring to be in better touch with her sexuality, eros and bodily sense of self. She experienced her needs as in conflict with her religious training and felt a strong tension with what seemed to be a patriarchal and removed sense of God. Her dream opened up a heroic and unthinkable reaction to her god-image and drew her down into the flower of her femininity and toward a chthonic light at the core of her inner life. The dream came at a time when her analyst had moved away, and she had not yet found another analyst. It went as follows:

> I am simultaneously an observer and a small naked infant crawling on a white Easter lily. I am crawling around the flower; it is so white, no color, and I am craving to feel its texture and to feel something more, more sensuality. The flower is floating in a dark sky with lots of little lights, like stars in the night. Then I feel a beam of sunlight: it warms my body and gives me a good feeling of being grounded and embodied and a feeling of sensuality. Just as this feeling begins, Jesus Christ on the cross emerges from below and is positioned between me and the sun and, in so doing, casts a shadow over me. I then feel cut off from the light and the warm feelings I was beginning to have. I feel panic that I will freeze to death and won't be able to get any nourishment. Then I feel myself growing very large and, in a burst of rage, I punch Christ in the face, knocking him off the cross, and he and the cross fall down below me. I feel some guilt but then also notice another kind of light coming from deep within the core of the flower; it has a silvery quality.

A clinically satisfactory interpretation of this dream is not the purpose, nor a possibility, in the context of this chaper, but I would like to offer a few reflections on its archetypal nature. The context of the dream is important, in that it took place after the dreamer's analyst had moved to a new city and her analysis was interrupted. She felt abandoned and in some ways like an infant deprived of mother's breast. The psyche images the dreamer both as observing ego and infant out in space on a lily-white Easter flower. I will not follow, for our purpose here, the transferential and/or genetic implications of the image, but rather stick with the metaphoric and amplificatory dimensions of the dream.

Whatever the flower may come to express, it is the current ground of the infant, and it is floating in space. She is crawling around on it and feeling it is too white, too pure, no color, no redness or texture, and she is attempting to find a more sensual connection. It is of interest that the Easter lily is symbolically related to purity, the Virgin Mary and the promise of renewal in Christ. As she seeks a more sensual connection, two things occur: she begins to feel the warmth of the sun, a ray of light, and this gives her a feeling of being grounded and embodied; but as soon as this occurs, her god-image, Jesus on the cross, emerges placing her in the cold shadow of the deity, as Christ stands in the way of the energy which began to inform her. Here the old conflict between instinct and spirit, religion and sexuality, re-emerges, amplifying the cut off feeling of the infant Self, whether from her mother's breast, analyst, lost god-image or feeling of embodiment.

At this juncture, the dreamer panics and in her symptom of panic, the dream begins to move archetypally toward a telos. Jung has shown how in our symptoms, the ancient gods reside, and Hillman has noted that the repressed god returns at the archetypal core of our symptom complexes and can be found in the analyst's consulting room. Greek myth placed Pan as a god of nature. The ancient mythological religion was essentially a nature religion, the transcendence of which by Christianity therefore meant the suppression of the kind of nature expressed in gods such as Pan. It is of interest to note that Hillman (1972) placed Pan in a cluster of meanings associated with the abandoned child (echoing the dreamer's abandonment), and that Pan appears in the symptom of panic as a protective, instinctual/archetypal reaction in times of crisis, the only way he can appear in our time. Plutarch reports the famous cry that went through late antiquity: "Great Pan is dead!" (Hillman 1972: xxii, quoting *de def. or*. 17). Hillman notes this saying has become oracular, one meaning of which is that nature has become deprived of its creative voice. We have lost psychic connection with nature, except perhaps through dreams. The voice of nature has lost its light and "[has fallen] easily to asceticism, following sheepishly without instinctual rebellion [the] new Shepherd, Christ, with his new means of management" (ibid.: xxii). If our dream is of any proof it supports what many commentators on Pan have stated: that Pan never died, he was just repressed and still lives, not merely in the literary imagination but in the repressed, which returns when our instincts assert themselves. In our dreamer, Pan does return in panic and rebellion: filled with rage, she strikes down the god-image.

This destructive/creative act inflates the dreamer who breaks a taboo which then allows her to notice a new light coming from within the flower. This light might be seen as the *lumen naturae* or light of nature, the light that Hillman eluded to as repressed with the fall of Pan. Here the dreamer reverses this situation, striking down the patriarchal god-image that blocked the way to her light, as she moves toward it in the womb of the flower. This flower might truly then prove to be an Easter flower, a flower of rebirth. Neumann (1955) reminds us that the ancient Goddess Sophia achieves her supreme visible form as a flower. She does not vanish in the nirvana-like abstraction of a masculine spirit, but rather like the scent of a blossom, her spirit always remains attached to the earthy foundation of reality (Neumann 1955: 325).

Irigaray (Jay 1994) identifies and amplifies the split that seems to have required the appearance of Pan and Sophia, a scene in which the masculine spirit had split off from the earthy ground. She links this to the vision of Platonic truth aimed at the sun and the Forms, in which the role of the mother was eclipsed in favor of the father, the solar origin of ideas. In this way, says Irigaray, the powerful birth process is forgotten and repressed in the service of a male myth of autogenesis, a move to the intelligible rather than the sensual world. With this move she says there is a loss of mediation, of path and trail, and the need for further opening of a kind of diaphragm. Such a visually grounded philosophy forgets the materiality of the eye socket, the cave, the womb, and one might add the unfolding of the flower. With regard to the flower of our dream, it is interesting to see Irigaray conceded that the only kind of sight that might escape this phallocentric economy was the Buddha's gaze at a flower (Jay 1994: 537–538, citing Irigaray).

This flowering toward a greater sense of wholeness seems to require a change in the main God image and a diminution of direct light. For Hillman, this means a "prolonged acceptance of a twilight state, an *abaissement* and rededication of ego-light, softening it by sacrificing each day some of its brightness, giving back to the gods what it has stolen" (Hillman 1979: 49). This new light implies an increased "interiority" with each new hot idea, first being drawn through the labyrinthine ways of soul or, as Irigaray might put it, the diaphragmatic pathway. It is precisely this soft blue reflective light that our western penchant for immediate and direct vision obscures.

Hillman's sensibility has been echoed by thinkers as wide-ranging as philosopher Walter Benjamin, who formulated a critical theory of modernity, and Japanese novelist Jun'ichirö Tanizaki, whose aesthetics amplify this vision in another context.

The ego brightness of western consciousness was foreseen and feared by Benjamin who critiqued "a world enchanted and dazzled by shining objects, the fetishized commodities of late capitalism" (Levin 1993: 23) According to Levin, Benjamin anticipated Foucault's analysis of panopticism with an observation about the early days of electricity in which he already saw the potential danger in nineteenth-century projects for city lighting based on the idea of a universal illumination, an idea so appealing to the Enlightenment mentality (ibid.).

Benjamin's anxiety about dazzling and shining objects mirrors the sensibility of Tanizaki who found it so hard to be at home in the west with things that glitter and shine. Tanizaki described the westerner as progressive, always determined to better his lot, "from candle to oil lamp, oil lamp to gaslight, gaslight to electric light – his quest for a brighter light never ceases, he spares no pains to eradicate even the minutest shadow" (Tanizaki 1977: 31). In contrast, he describes the Japanese aesthetic which loves the light of nature, soft light, darkness and shadows, giving examples of the love of dark patina on silver, to the love of jade –"that strange stone with its faint muddy light" – and smoky crystals, "the impure variety . . . with opaque veins crossing their depth" (ibid.: 10–11). In Tanizaki we find a strong aesthetic critique of modernism with a romantic longing for a past and a diminishing aesthetic itself falling into the shadow of contemporary life.

In the above, we note the separation between light and lumen, modernist vision and the light of nature, the light of the sun and that of the flower, and the tension between Christian and Pagan visions. The dual aspect of light is an archetypal concern and its mysteries continue into contemporary times.

Conclusion

If in the west we cannot simply rely on a romantic reversion to an ancient Oriental aesthetic way of seeing (Tanizaki) or return to a literal alchemy, a point Hillman (1978: 40) makes, or if the downcast eyes of French intellectualism are insufficient (Jay), still it has become clear that all of the above have made us more conscious of the shadow of western religion, metaphysics and modernism; but beyond their critiques these responses to our condition have offered many insights toward the revisioning of contemporary consciousness. Jung, too, has been taken as an exemplary modern man with both personal and cultural shadows, but he is also a man whose arduous journey into darkness has taught us, echoing Heraclitus' insight, that vision is not to be trusted in those who have barbarian souls. Jung's journey from a heroic patriarch to a man of receptivity was that of a traveler who learned that darkness has its own logos. If, as Jung said, the soul is destined to behold the light, it must be seen as the soft light of the *lumen naturae*.

This is not the light of the heroic white European, Christian, Cartesian, racist, colonialist, phallocentric, logocentric, politically heliotropic vision. Neither is it the light of its critics with its skeptical, negative, cynical, smart, hard judgments that led to a new "unsurveyability." If we have any hints of the seeds for the future, it is in a slow, sometimes sad, bodily light, connected with shadows and shades, male and female, in the depths of our suffering with relatedness to others and the invisible otherness of ourselves. It is a connection with our strangeness – with friendly respect, and through attention to our dreams – in imaginative revisionary and alchemical transformation, and thus perhaps in a change in or deeper understanding of our god-image. In all of the above we are left not with a single vision but with multiple possibilities. It is of interest to notice that here Jung, archetypal psychology, and postmodernism share a resonance. It is a resonance also in accord with Jay for whom it is "precisely the proliferation of models of visuality that the antiocularcentric discourse, for all its fury against the ones it distrusts, tacitly encourages" (Jay 1994: 591). What Jay means as postmodern criticism might be seen to argue that the antidote to privileging any one visual order is a multiplicity of seeing, a dialectics of seeing: "it is better to encourage the multiplication of a thousand eyes, which, like Nietzsche's thousand suns, suggests the openness of human possibilities" (Jay 1994: 591).

Bal (1993) and Flynn (1993) respectively suggest the importance of many different ways of seeing and many different practices of reason, multiplying perspectives and proliferating points of view. In particular, Flynn asks if we do not need a gaze of reciprocity, generosity and friendship. Warnke (1993) adds the importance of an aesthetic education which likewise could multiply our perceptions, expand our horizons and deepen our moral vision (Levin 1993: 22). To these sentiments I would suggest we add the late work of Jung and archetypal psychology, for Jung at the end of his work envisioned the light of consciousness as having multiple intensities, composed of scintilla or sparks, like the stars in a night sky. For him the Self as an expression of the Primordial Man is not a vision of fixed essences but of multiple illuminations, radiating both as single monad but at the same time with many faces and many eyes (Jung 1947/54).

The multiplicity is radicalized in archetypal psychology in Hillman's polytheistic view. Both these and the postmodern ideas resonate with the end phase of the alchemical work imaged in the display of the *cauda pavonis*, an exquisite display of colors in the peacock's tail which heralds the illuminatory multiplicity of psyche.

The image indicates the restoration of the whole person not seen as a synthesis or sublation, or Hegelian uplifting, but, as Hillman put its, as a prolonged acceptance of a twilight state, a hesitancy that does not subsume all into a fixed position. This is echoed by Jung in his *Alchemical Studies* when he states:

> deeper insight into problems of psychic development soon teaches us how much better it is to reserve judgment. . . . Of course we all have an understandable desire for crystal clarity, but we are apt to forget that in psychic matters we are dealing with a process of experience, that is, with transformations which should never be given hard and fast names if their living movement is not to petrify into something static. The protean mythologem and the shimmering symbol express the process of the psyche far more . . . clearly than the clearest concept; for the symbol not only conveys a visualization of the process . . . it also brings a re-experiencing of it, of that twilight which we can learn to understand through inoffensive empathy, but which too much clarity dispels.
>
> (Jung 1942: 162–163)

A similar sentiment was also expressed by Bion, who stated:

> Instead of trying to bring a brilliant, intelligent, knowledgeable light to bear on obscure problems, I suggest we bring to bear a diminution of the light – a penetrating beam of darkness; a reciprocal of the searchlight. . . . The darkness would be so absolute that it would achieve a luminous, absolute vacuum. So that, if any object existed, however faint, it would show up very clearly. Thus, a very faint light would become visible in maximum conditions of darkness.
>
> (Bion 1974: 37)

The complexity of our times demands that we transcend simple one-sided judgments and enter into a broader vision, as well as to entertain many ways of imagining. From critics and debunkers Stern and Noll to classical analysts Edinger and von Franz, Jung has been seen as devil and saint, Eurocentric racist and compassionate wise man. The sheer range of evaluation testifies to the sense that Jung carries a multiplicity of mythical projections and perhaps for this reason is an exemplary modern man, a man at the crossroads of cultural transformation. He deserves to be seen with no fewer sensibilities than those he gave to us with which to see.

References

Adams, M .V. (1996) *The Multicultural Imagination*, London: Routledge.
Bal, M. (1993) "His master's eye," in D. Levin (ed.) *Modernity and Hegemony of Vision*, Berkeley, University of California Press.
Bion, W. (1974) *Brazilian Lectures*, Rio de Janiero: Imago Edition.
Brooke, R. (1991) *Jung and Phenomenology*, London: Routledge.
Corbin, H. (1978) *The Man of Light in Iranian Sufism*, Boulder, Col.: Shamhala.
Edinger, E. (1985) *Anatomy of the Psyche*, LaSalle, Il.: Open Court.
Flynn, T. (1993) "Foucault and the eclipse of the vision," in D. Levin (ed.) *Modernity and the Hegemony of Vision*, Berkeley, University of California Press.
Grumaldi-Craig, S. (1997), "Going black," in J. Hillman (ed.) *Haiti Spring* 61.
Haeffner, M. (1991) *The Dictionary of Alchemy*, London: The Aquarian Press.
Hillman, J. (1972) "An essay on Pan," J. Hillman and W. Roscher, Pan and the Nightmare, New York: Spring Publications.
—— (1978) "Therapeutic value of alchemical language," *Dragonflies: Studies in Imaginal Psychology*, all issues.
—— (1979) *Puer Papers*, Dallas: Spring Publications.
—— (1997a) "The seduction of black," in S. Marlan (ed.) *Fire in the Stone*, Wilmette, Il.: Chiron Publications.
—— (1997b) "The seduction of black", in J. Hillman (ed.) *Haiti Spring* 61.
—— and Roscher, W. (1972) *Pan and the Nightmare*, New York: Spring Publications.
Jay, M. (1994) *Downcast Eyes*, Berkeley: University of California Press.
Jung, C.G. (1942) "Paracelsus as a spiritual phenomenon," *CW* 13.
—— (1947/54) "On the nature of the psyche," *CW* 8.
—— (1953) "Psychology and Alchemy," *CW* 12.
—— (1955/56) "Mysterium Coniunctionis," *CW* 14.

—— (1962) *Memories, Dreams, Reflections*, New York: Pantheon Books.

—— (1967) "Alchemical Studies," *CW* 13.

Levin, D. M. (ed.) (1993) *Modernity and the Hegemony of Vision*, Berkeley: University of California Press.

—— (ed.) (1997) *Sites of Vision*, Cambridge, Mass.: The MIT Press.

Marlan, S. (ed.) (1997) *Fire in the Stone*, Wilmette, Il.: Chiron Publications.

Neumann, E. (1955) *The Great Mother*, Princeton: Pantheon Books.

Nye, A. (1993) "Assisting at the birth and death of philosophic vision," in D. Levin (ed.) *Modernity and the Hegemony of Vision*, Berkeley: University of California Press.

Ortiz-Hill, M. (1997) "C G Jung in the heart of darkness," in J. Hillman (ed.) *Haiti Spring* 61.

Papadopoulos, R. (1984) "Jung and the concept of the other," in R. Papadopoulos and G. Saayman (eds) *Jung in Modern Perspective*, Craighall, South Africa: A. D. Donker.

Tanizaki, J. (1977) *In Praise of Shadows*, Stoney Creek, Conn.: Leete's Island Books.

Tarnas, R. (1991) *The Passion of the western Mind*, New York: Ballantine Books.

Winnicott, D. (1964) Book review of *Memories, Dreams, Reflections*, by C. G. Jung, *The International Journal Psycho-Analysis*, 45, 450–5.

Warnke, G. (1993) "Ocular criticism and social criticism," in D. Levin (ed.) *Modernity and Hegemony of Vision*, Berkeley: University of California Press.

Part 3

THERAPEUTIC ISSUES

EDITOR'S INTRODUCTION

Freud once described the libido as those instincts subsumed under the term "love." Even if it is often reduced to sex, the vicissitudes of love make up a central theme in psychoanalysis, particularly, perhaps, in the works of Fairbairn, Klein, Guntrip, and Kohut. It is less thematic in the work of Jung, for whom *Eros* is taken up as "the feminine principle." Can love be a "feminine principle?" Only in the most abstract way, perhaps – one that hardly quickens the blood.

For Veronica Goodchild, in order to enter the mysteries of love we need to be conscious of its shadows and its intimate affiliation with *Chaos*. If we do this, she says, we find not the chaotic shadows of an obsessional *Logos* but a different kind of knowledge, a kind of knowing that is essential to human well-being. Further, considering that we are made of the stuff of the universe, we are lead to recognize that the love which sustains us, however intimately personal, is also a Love that is not peculiarly human. Here we enter the sacred mysteries.

If we follow Goodchild and place love at the thematic center of psychological life, then perhaps we need to find a different set of terms when we speak of those defining ideas of analytical psychology, such as consciousness, transformation, Self and individuation.

11

EROS AND CHAOS

The mysteries and shadows of love

Veronica Goodchild

In a love relation, as Jung once put it, you risk everything.
Marie-Louise von Franz

Yet to sing love, love must first shatter us.
H. D.

Prologue

From his early work, *Phenomenology of Perception* (1962) to his last, *The Visible and the Invisible* (1968) Merleau-Ponty worked at an archaeology of the perceptual world, that domain of experience which he called "*être sauvage*," wild being. His phenomenology was a return to beginnings, to those chaotic places which subtend the Cartesian dichotomy of subjective mind and objective world, to that landscape of experience where, as he said in "Eye and mind," the painter, for example, takes his body with him, not in order to know the world, but to love it (1964: 159–190). As a critique of that kind of "high altitude thought" which would survey the world from afar, his phenomenology always sought to restore the original dialogue between body and world. For the purposes of this essay it is important to remember that in the final analysis Merleau-Ponty understood that intertwining between the flesh of the body and that of the world to be one of desire, of eros, of love. If he conceived of that eros in primarily sexual terms, as the pivotal chapter on sexuality in *Phenomenology of Perception* indicates (1962: 154–173) we should not forget that in his last writings the chiasm or crossing between body and world was enlarged to the point that he was calling for a "psychoanalysis of nature," a call which makes sense only if one grants a fecund vitality which animates psyche and nature, only if one can imagine that Eros is the arc which holds the ensouled body and world together in an amorous embrace.[1]

Jung's psychology is also about the powerful force of Love. In the chapter entitled "Late thoughts," in *Memories, Dreams, Reflections*, Jung makes the following observations on Love:

> beside the field of reflection there is another equally broad if not broader area in which rational understanding and rational modes of representation find scarcely anything they are able to grasp. This is the realm of Eros . . . a god . . . whose range of activity extends from the endless spaces of the heavens to the dark abysses of hell; but I falter before the task of finding the language which might adequately express the incalculable paradoxes of love. Eros is a *kosmogonos*, a creator and father–mother of all higher consciousness . . . For we are in the deepest sense the victims and the instruments of cosmogonic "love" . . . something superior to the individual, a unified and undivided whole . . . . Love is his light and his darkness, whose end he cannot see. "Love ceases not." . . . If (man) possesses a grain of wisdom, he will . . . name the unknown by the more unknown, – *ignotum per ignotius* – that is, by the name of God.
>
> (1963: 353–354)

This essay attempts a phenomenology of the terrain of Love, especially in relation to the theme of Chaos, that place of wild being which phenomenology explored beneath the ordered regularity of Cartesian thinking. Guided by the spirit of phenomenology, especially that of Merleau-Ponty, and the work of Jung, especially with respect to his insights about love and its shadows, this essay is an exploration into those wild places where Love and its dark partner Chaos roam.

Introduction

Love is a mystery, a cosmic force, a divine ray that permeates the universe. Love is the quintessential archetype of the Self, an incalculable paradox that includes everything and its opposite, "sweetly bitter," as Sappho, that daring devotee of Aphrodite, writing some six hundred years B.C., describes the awesome force that visits from beyond, making us tremble, and yearn (Balmer 1984: 30). Love both transcends human consciousness, and yet is that God-factor that is the *sin qua non* of consciousness itself, the essence upon which all life, subtle and manifest, depends, whether we know it or not.

In the human realm, we are perhaps more familiar with love's pain, the failure of love, and its impossibility. Indeed, the consulting room of modern psychotherapy is full of the complaints and woundings of love's disappointments, its abandonments and rejections. Whole schools of psychotherapy are based on such failures of love, in one guise or another: incest problems (Freud), love made hungry (Fairbairn), inadequate mirroring or idealizing (Kohut), envy (Klein). These shadows of love are what we expect to confront in the consulting room. This is the dark *prima materia* into whose black soil the seed of the *lapis* is invisibly sown. Work on the parental complexes and personal shadow material is meant to clear the way towards healthy self-regard, adult sexuality, and the capacity for differentiated relationship and meaningful work, the implicit if not stated goals of most treatment. Freud says that we learn to love so that we won't fall ill. Fairbairn explicitly states that our search for a love relationship is the fundamental endeavor of our lives. Guntrip follows Fairbairn in emphasizing the centrality of our desire for love. Von Franz tells us that the famous physicist, Wolfgang Pauli, died a premature death from cancer because of his inability to surrender into love's embrace.

Yet most schools of psychoanalytic psychology continue to restrict themselves to the cure of symptoms within a personalistic frame. In this way such schools render an invaluable service to the child in the adult, in terms of healing early woundings, re-experiencing aborted transferences, and integrating split-off aspects of the personality, thereby allowing for the possibility of an authentic maturational process.

It was clearly Jung's view, however, that psychotherapy, in providing a container for the regressive movement of psychic energy, also allowed for the deep immersion of the ego – beyond its personal history – in the waters of the collective unconscious which would allow for the rebirth of the personality. For Jung, the whole analytic process was not so much about curing symptoms and enabling adaptation, but discovering through one's pain a link to the infinite, a re-situation of one's personal life within its sacred ground. This sacred ground is that "broader area," the "more unknown," the field of cosmogonic Love.

And what is it that so often happens in therapy, no matter what you think you are there for? An erotically charged transference develops, most likely in the void produced by an undeveloped capacity for relationship, and a simultaneous longing for such soul-to-soul union, for that which has not yet been experienced. But maybe it is erroneous to speak of such "causes;" perhaps the large field of love looks for any excuse to constellate itself, and what better opening than the intimate sharing of story and soul between two people.

In fact, there is such a great longing in the human soul for a true meeting with another, a meeting in which one knows the other, and one is known by the other, that the transference, and perhaps even the emergence of psychotherapy itself during this century, could be the search for this kind of mutual revelation, so grievously lacking for many in our time. It is perhaps notable that the rise of psychotherapy coincides, historically, with Nietzsche's famous phrase that "God is dead." The God of Love, not finding hospitable reception within the domain of Christianity, began looking for more favorable venues. Hillman writes:

> When we look back upon the past seventy years, or back yet further to the women in the hospitals of Paris and Nancy, we can see the

> psyche going to therapy in search of eros. We have been looking for love for the soul. That is the myth of analysis.
>
> (1972: 296–297)

On a darker note, of the "unethical" behaviors between therapist and patient, the literal sexual acting out of the transference is reported to be the most common, an abuse of Eros, who perhaps comes in the back door when the daimonic dimension of love's numen is too poorly appreciated, and we become possessed by its power shadow. Or is it that such transgressions also signal a deeper cultural disturbance at the heart of our world, that our neat and all too complacent personalistic, and even archetypal, psychological theories are helpless to address? The suppression of transpersonal love in the human sphere, and our inability to embody love, either individually or collectively, may lie behind its abuses. Similarly, two thousand years of Christianity have not exactly made us better lovers!

Actually, as the poet Rilke reminds us, love is a high achievement, belonging to maturity:

> To love is good, too: love being difficult. For one human being to love another: that is perhaps the most difficult of all our tasks, . . . the work for which all other work is but preparation. For this reason young people, who are beginners in everything, cannot yet know love: they have to learn it. . . . But learning-time is always a long, secluded time, and so loving, for a long while ahead and far on into life, is – solitude, intensified and deepened loneness for him who loves. Love is . . . a high inducement to the individual to ripen, to become something in himself, to become world, to become world for himself for another's sake, it is a great exacting claim upon him, something that chooses him out and calls him to vast things.
>
> (1954: 53–54)

Differentiation of self is a prerequisite for relationship, and this sort of refinement of self often requires lengthy periods of solitude, working the *prima materia* of one's own soul. As Lockhart writes: "The psyche always pushes for uniqueness because it is only in bringing uniqueness in relation to another unique nature that relationship is possible at all" (1987: 31). But Rilke goes beyond this, suggesting that love is a vocation that calls us out into the service of life. The ripening of character that emerges from such solitude is not for its own sake, but for the world's. We are called, not only to be in relationship with each other, but to celebrate the world, each in our own way. This is a claim made upon us as humans, that which differentiates us from the angel and the animal, as Rilke writes elsewhere, and the implication is that we are ethically bound to respond.

Rilke's attitude better seems to approach the vastness of love that Jung writes about in his autobiography. Jung's psychology is a psychology of the Self, that is, a psychology that devotes itself to the symbolic and mythic images, affective representations, and patterns of behavior associated with the faces of the divine in their many archetypal manifestations. In the realm of psychotherapy, the focus of attention is traditionally on how these Self images reveal themselves in the specific life, dreams, and fantasies of an individual person. But the Self cannot be reduced to psychology, or the practice of psychotherapy, because its "range of activity extends from the endless spaces of the heavens to the dark abysses of hell" (Jung 1963: 353). Perhaps Jung's reluctance to create Institutes, except as research facilities, lay in a real fear of dogmatizing psyche into a system, or reducing the Self to a heuristic concept in psychotherapy, much as has already happened in those training Institutes with a clinically pragmatic emphasis.

I wonder, too, if perhaps psychology has overburdened the human realm, especially with its prejudice of the soul as residing "within," and that until we find our way back out of our therapy cells into relationship with each other, and especially into union with the world, to find again our place as microcosm to macrocosm, such as in ancient times, we will continue to perpetuate a hubris whose dark shadow is the destruction that we are all too familiar with in modern times. The psyche is simply too large just for humans.

The love in the transference relationship is often experienced as arising out of a field much larger than the two mere mortals who must endure the onslaught. It is Jung and his colleague Marie-Louise von Franz who have most contributed to our understanding of the archetypal, transpersonal and transpsychic dimensions of this cosmic mystery. Hence their researches into the complex language of alchemy, still largely unread by many students of depth psychology. In Jung's essay, "The psychology of the transference" (1946: 163–323) he writes of the many transformations of love in the analytic process, using the rich and paradoxical imagery of the secrets of alchemy, as if our preoccupation with love, or perhaps we should say more accurately, love's preoccupation with us, lies disturbingly at the very heart and depth of earthly life. The therapy process can become the soulscape for an awareness of love and its dark shadows, its vicissitudes from instinct to spirit and back, and for the differentiation of feeling to embody and be made present, in the human sphere. Perhaps this is what it means to be both the victims and instruments of cosmogonic love, and, like Job, if we respond to the invitation to suffer the numinous affects and images of love and its woundings, we too, may be offered a glimpse of its divine face, and be graced with its power to transform the cells of our souls. This kind of transformation inevitably leads us back into the River of Life. As von Franz writes: "If we could see through all our projections down to the last traces, our personality would be extended to cosmic dimensions" (1980b: 14). The implication is that refinement of consciousness leads us out of a world divided, leads us out of psychology itself, into a cosmic synchronistic field, where psyche and matter, Self and Cosmos are One.

Nevertheless, such *coniunctio* or unitive experiences often first yield into painful chaotic states as an old order begins to break up and pass away.

Chaos-Order, Chaos-Eros

Chaos is usually linked in the west with order, or cosmos. Even in the dictionary, chaos is defined as "disorder" as opposed to the orderly, harmonious whole of the universe. Chaos, as undifferentiated, *massa confusa*, is usually that reality out of which a new form or organization is seen to arise, or more accurately, is crafted. In many myths, Chaos is the primordial substance that precedes the creation of the world by the God, or Goddess, and is the gaping void to which all destroyed worlds return. In Genesis I: i we read:

> In the beginning God created the heaven and the earth. And the earth was without form, and void; and darkness was upon the face of the deep. And the Spirit of God moved upon the face of the waters. And God said, "Let there be light:" and there was light.
>
> (King James translation)

In contemporary culture, chaos theory tends to delineate two major fields within itself: the "order-out-of-chaos" group, and the "hidden-order-within-chaos" group. (Hayles 1990: 9). Unquestioned by both groups is the assumption that order is somehow superior to chaos. The Jungian analyst, Van Eenwyk, who has elaborated the correspondences between Jung's theories (especially in relation to the symbol) and chaos research in his book *Archetypes and Strange Attractors* (1997), has primarily preserved chaos' relation to order with an unexamined assumption. Though at various places in his text he points to the essential component of relationship, eros, and the determining influence of conscious cooperation with the psyche, and he beautifully lays out the value of chaos in psychological life, he nevertheless maintains culture's bias toward linking chaos with order.

In the practice of psychotherapy, too, understanding, interpretation, and meaning, are often employed at the expense of experiencing with the patient empty and dissociative chaotic states. As Schwartz-Salant writes, here critiquing Jung and the practice of Jungian psychology: "the overall spirit of (Jung's) psychology is that knowledge exists which can put order into chaos" (1993: 1). He adds that although states of absence and the void are acknowledged by Jung – for example picture seven, the "Ascent of the Soul," in the *Rosarium Philosophorum* – Jung too quickly fills in such deep levels of the *nigredo* with knowledge about such states (ibid: 2). Schwartz-Salant suggests that most Jungians are trained to treat Jung's *nekyia* as their own, as if their job is to continue refining his *prima materia*, rather than plunging into such depths of chaos and despair themselves. By contrast, Schwartz-Salant proposes that a sane person's mad or psychotic parts, are "like the chaotic waters of mythology" and "they are always crucial to change and regeneration" (ibid.: 3).

Hillman too acknowledges that the Apollonic voice of reason and order that rules depth psychology's practice will have none of chaos, "those dark nights and confusions which are its nest" (1972: 99). But by refusing chaos, we are in danger of losing Eros, too. Eros "renews itself in affective attacks, jealousies, fulminations, and turmoils. It thrives close to the dragon" (ibid.: 99).

But I wonder if there is not something deadening about this order as opposed to chaos, and whether it reflects more our cultural bias spanning the past four hundred or so years: of control over the inanimate world by an all-powerful ego and a rational consciousness separated and distanced from both the larger cosmic fabric, and the deeper levels of psyche, of which we are in fact in intimate thread.

Marie-Louise von Franz writes:

> The God who fashions the world as a dead object is mostly found in civilizations which have a rather developed technical aspect . . . in which consciousness has already . . . developed as an independent power apart from the unconscious . . . [and] the Godhead is no longer imminent in the material world.
>
> (1975: 90)

She adds: "This process has reached its highest form in our civilization" (ibid.: 92).

Von Franz then relates a story called "The death of Chaos-Unconscious," (ibid.: 92–93) from a Chinese philosopher, in which two characters, Heedless and Hasty, wanted to be kind and shape Chaos into a beautiful, conscious being, but in so doing they killed him. In other words, molding chaos into consciousness and order can kill and destroy an essential aspect of creation. This story highlights the questionableness of human consciousness understood as enlightened order, certainly an element we can appreciate as we hover precariously on the edge of extinction, with environmental crises, terrorist attacks, uncontrollable and untreatable diseases, not to mention our personal and interpersonal limitations via our ignorance of potent psychological and cosmic forces – all this, with the acceleration of knowledge over the past several hundred years.

Now, consider this Orphic creation myth:

> Black-winged night, a goddess of whom even Zeus stands in awe, was courted by the Wind and laid a silver egg in the womb of

> darkness; and Eros whom some call Phanes was hatched from this egg and set the Universe in motion. Eros was double-sexed and golden winged and, having four heads, sometimes roared like a bull or a lion, sometimes hissed like a serpent or bleated like a ram.
>
> (Graves 1960: 30)

The myth suggests an intimate and mysterious connection between Chaos – here imaged as the "womb of darkness" – and Eros as the two great primordial forces of the cosmos – one that N. Katherine Hayles notes in her book, *Chaos Bound* (1990: 19), but does not pursue. Eros as the "golden-winged" also suggests his birth from Aphrodite, the "golden one," who, as Graves points out as the "['foam-born'] is the same wide ruling goddess who rose from Chaos and danced on the sea" (p. 49). Aphrodite, the one who according to the Homeric hymns is accompanied by "bright-eyed lions, bears, and quick insatiable panthers" (1960: 79), the one who stirs amritic longing in the loins of men, animals, and women. Here Chaos is the intimate companion of divine and chthonic Love.

It is both notable and grievous that Chaos retained its connection with order but lost its more vital relation with Love. Surely this is no accident. Love is dangerous and so is Chaos. Each evokes the image of the Other: our highest spiritual longings and our deepest earthly yearnings, and still more profoundly, the urge to unite these cosmic and human vibrations within the souls and cells of our bodies. These realities we either tend to disparage or not allow ourselves to long for enough. This is understandable: we reduce the body to biological drives and split off spirituality into ethereal realms. What gets avoided, perhaps out of an instinctual terror and awesomeness, is the *tremendum* of the daemonic powers of sexuality, and the numinosity of the chthonic realms, and the fundamental Otherness to the ego of these archetypal powers.

The nuance of this terror is already enfolded within the symbols of the myth. Our story links Eros with the theiomorphic forms of bull or lion, serpent, and ram. Of these, the bull, serpent, and ram, are among the animals associated with the god Dionysus. The Orphic mysteries themselves were concerned with the essential expressions of the Dionysian. Indeed, the founder of these mysteries was considered to be the mythic figure of Orpheus, the human incarnation of Dionysus, who "with his lute, made trees and the mountain tops that freeze, bow themselves when he did play." Dionysus is known as the "mad god," the god who dies and is ever reborn. Patron of music, drama, and intoxication, his rites abounded in wild ecstasy and dark terror, emotional excess and violent abandonment. These cathartic rituals and ceremonies aimed at integrating mankind's bestial violence and needy sexual desirousness into harmonious and socially acceptable ways. Those who refused devotion to Dionysus, were torn to pieces like Pentheus of Thebes, or otherwise met with terrible and terrifying deaths.

In the name of order and rationality, our culture tends to repress and designate as evil these uncontrolled and chaotic realms of Dionysus, thus endangering our environment with expressions of hate and hostility, and an incapacity to love. Our myth anticipates patriarchal terror of the dark unknown when it admits that "even Zeus stands in awe" of the goddess Night. The patriarchal ego prefers orderly progress, and predictable solar consciousness.

It must not be forgotten either, that Dionysus was primarily a god of women, and his rites were primarily women's rites. Our myth reconnects us to the lost Goddess and her Dionysian consort. In our western tradition, chaos has played the role of the Other, and has often been depicted as female, and has even been connected specifically with women's experience. Chaos as a system of non-linear dynamics draws our attention to this mostly marginalized feminine, especially in its cyclical, sensual, erotic, dark, rhythmic, and transformational dimensions. Such "dynamics" are eclipsed in the patriarchal ego's attachment to reasonable, linear, unchanging, ideals that delude us into thinking that we are protected from the overpowering and unpredictable, otherwise known as Life!

If we could tend to the instinctual domains of desire and aggression with the devotion and awareness accorded to the god of transformation, as in ancient times, a god linked with the awesome presence of the divine feminine, these unsettling archetypal energies could both be ritually expressed, inhibited, and contained, and be transformed into poetic and symbolic form, that is, into culture (Whitmont 1992). Orpheus stands as that mythic symbolic image that translates raw instinct into consciousness, longing into sacred song. He is that transcendent bridge between the daimonic and human worlds, that knows that chaotic violence is intimately connected with regeneration, creativity, and erotic love.

This enlightened "gnosis" of dark chaos' relation with the sweet and formidable aromas of love, is contained within the symbolic imagery of the golden-winged, androgynous Eros–Phanes–Aphrodite. The god(dess) comes before our visionary eye with glistening aura, a vast form containing the wisdom of earth secrets and instincts that long for rebirth into a radiant cosmos alive with Love. Until we find again appropriate religio-cultural channels for these transpersonal energies that move through our world and live in us as powerful affects seeking an individual ethical response, we will continue to destroy ourselves and dismember each other, like Pentheus, in ways, both individual and collective, that have become all too familiar today. And the great cosmic forces of Chaos and Eros will continue to degenerate into the shadowy and depotentiated forms of impotent cherubs smiling mindlessly on Christmas cards.

But even today, chaos theory cannot fully mask culture's secret longing for such a transformation that would reunite the range and complexity of human feeling within its archetypal matrix and mystery. Such longing breaks through in "strange attractors," and the "butterfly effect." Eros and Psyche, having perhaps been disappointed with their inadequate treatment in depth psychology, have fallen out of Spirit into Matter where once again, from their cosmic, transpsychic spheres, they approach life in the human realm.

Love as we know involves a fall, and chaos gives birth to this new creation, this fall into love. The word "chaos" itself attracts attention. ("Chaos Theory" for example is much more evocative than its proper scientific name, "non-linear dynamics!") It lures us out of our safely distanced modes of being and invites us to let our hair down, abandon ourselves to unthinkable and unthought thoughts, and wild spontaneous acts. Chaos leads us into an unfamiliar, undomesticated world, one that precedes a more cultivated and civilized mode, a forgotten place where, leaving daylight consciousness behind and its neat and tidy theories, we enter the confusion and dark abyss of all we have both intentionally and unavoidably put aside. Now the chasm of a world opens up, a world unformed, unredeemed, yet somehow brimming with secret life and inchoate possibility, a world as yet unknown and completely unpredictable. In this place we surrender to a destiny that we cannot imagine, much less impose.

Being thus poised at the edge of the void is echoed too in the first stirrings of Love. Sappho writes of it thus:

like a wind
crashing down
among oak trees
love shattered
my mind
(Friedrich 1978: 119)

Love takes us out of our mind with its neatly ordered arrangements, and our carefully constructed world comes completely unraveled. The daughter of Dione, goddess of the oak tree in which the amorous dove nests, takes us beyond limits of what we think we know and who we are, and fills us with loving inspiration that charges the circuitry of our bodies with an imagination of worlds unseen and longing for recognition and incarnation: "the synthesis of wild emotion and high sophistication" (Friedrich 1978: 123). In similar vein, H. D. writes of Achilles' response to Helen: "it was not that she was beautiful, but he stared and stared" (1957: 251).

A cosmic shudder moves through our bodies, and we fall into the terrors and panic engendered by this "sweetly bitter" potion. Every new deep love undoes us so, loosens our limbs, sets us aflame. When we fall under the spell of this cosmic mystery it is like falling through the cracks of a world into a new universe. A new birth occurs and a new creation comes into being, one that is almost immediately attacked from within and without. We are virginal again, we lose our tongues, become like an awkward teenager, not knowing what to say: voice stuttering, face blushing, forgetting, distracted, sweating, lips trembling. We become so unsure of ourselves, humbled by the Visitation. In our total vulnerability to love's arrows, everything opposite to love emerges. Every shade, every secret, every doubt has a light shined upon it once more. All our most despised aspects, our jealousy, envy, hatred, fears, parade themselves before love's eye. And the golden light of love around us attracts hatred and envy. The legions of disappointed ones, the unloved and the unlived in our environment, begin to try to undermine and spoil the bliss with poisonous tongue and venomous acts.[2]

Love is such a fateful factor in a life: we cannot make it happen, and life is meaningless and very lonely if it never comes into being. Love brings us close to the deepest feelings of which we are capable. We are never more vulnerable than when we love. Love takes us to the heights of cosmic bliss and simultaneously to the depths of passion and suffering. In this sense, more than anything else, it has the power to release us from the limitations of consciousness and reveal to us glimpses of the heart of the soul of the world, the divine reality at the "Hanabku," the cosmic center, where god and goddess are entwined in the profoundest and most playful, ritual erotic dance. Love brings life, reimagines life beyond transience to a glowing *unus mundus* where spirit and matter are one, united in the *anima mundi*, where mere mortals become the microcosm of the universal, and stars dance in the fabric of our form. Love leads us to our goal; love is our goal. As von Franz writes: "Whoever cannot surrender to this experience has never lived; whoever founders in it has understood nothing" (1980b: 142).

Dreaming the work

Not too long ago, I had the experience of the unleashing of a fierce range of affects that had a profoundly disturbing effect on me, and poignantly commented on this relation between chaos and love. An early dream commented on the situation:

> My daughter Sarah and I are together in NYC, in midtown Manhattan. Snakes begin to come out. First one, then another, then they start teaming out. At first I try to get rid of them, or kill them, but then I realize it's a hopeless task because there are so many of them. I look at the patterns of the snakes' bodies to determine if they are benign or poisonous. Mostly they are benign, but I know that there is one snake amongst them that is poisonous. I must be able to protect Sarah from that one. I am filled with a kind of anxiety and vigilance that is almost overwhelming to me.

Thrown out of the paradise of my daylight world, I am initiated into the

Hadean realm with the promise of underworld knowledge, and a different kind of treasure, one where the poison is also potentially the cure. My soul and body were gripped by what seemed like alien powers and affects that dislodged the status quo and invaded my consciousness. "The old order has to die," a voice kept reiterating. I felt my world shattering; I no longer knew myself; I could not eat or sleep. The descent into such a chaotic state felt as if it was destroying the fabric of being. I felt profoundly unlovable, deeply unacceptable to myself and others, embarrassed by my feelings and their intensity. I began to withdraw. What was being cracked open was a self that felt it had to merit and achieve its welfare, and that could not trust that she could be loved for who she is, an exposed self that wants to be safe in the knowledge that she is loved "for better or worse," a self that wants to surrender in trust to the love offered, and to the Love bestowed as Gift. It was as if proving myself and pleasing others were defenses against annihilation and total despair. Now I was being invited into what I feared most, and did not know it until then, into the absence, the void, the nothingness. Terror seized me, and an excruciating kind of vulnerability. Giving up succeeding, giving up control, I felt displaced, unknown to myself, and a deep loss and melancholy overtook me. A sense of dependency and fragility such as I had never known began to melt still frozen rocks around my heart. It is only the power of Love that can reveal such tenderness, such terror, of feeling.

Another dream ends as follows:

> Then an unknown man passes through my house. He has got lost and is looking for a town by the ocean that is actually near where we live, but I have never heard of it before. It is called "Gweu" or "Ghent," and we are looking at it on a map that reminds me of France. The man is somewhat surprised that I haven't been there yet, because this coastal village is meant to be so beautiful: one of the seven wonders of the world!

"Gweu" is the Indo-European root of the word chaos! So there is a spirit in the dream who is moving me in the direction of chaos, and supporting the dissolution of old ways of being. Ghent makes me think of Vermeer, and his paintings of women who are both close to light and darkness and who evoke a quiet, strong presence. These two images are brought together in the landscape of France, a country that has always been associated for me with love.

The collapse of the conscious attitude always feels like the end of a world, and we feel abandoned to the wild elements and forces of nature, dissolved back into original chaos. Von Franz writes: "The urge for individuation, as long as it is a natural inordinate urge, seeks impossible situations; it seeks conflict and defeat and suffering because it seeks its own transformation." She adds, "Sitting in Hell and roasting there is what brings forth the philosopher's stone" (1980a: 254).

Chaos is outlawed in cosmologies in the west, especially in our Judaeo-Christian tradition. It tends to be devalued as the unknown realm of nothingness and non-being outside the divine order. In much the same way, evil has been marginalized and divested of its reality as the *privatio boni*, not embraced as a power and force in itself. But what is excluded from the collective consciousness finds its way in underground and heretical movements. So in alchemy, chaos is the watery abyss, the loss of a familiar consciousness, the *prima materia*, the initial psychic and material situation where elements are separated and hostile to each other. It is an unredeemed leaden state that marks a hopeless loss of soul, a *solutio* in which our fixed attitudes begin their devastating dissolution. Yet this chaotic state is highly valued as containing divine but hidden sparks of Light, and thus it is an essential stage in the opus. It is comparable to that moment in Gnosticism where an awareness of homesickness, strangeness, alienation and secret longing, is the birth of the moment of the sojourner's travels back to the Alien God and the divine realms of light, the stirrings of a deep knowing that was once known but has been forgotten (Jonas 1963).

The alchemists recognized that in breakdown and desolation a new birth takes place. The *coniunctio* first takes place in the underworld, in the new moon, where there is no light, when we are in the deepest depression, and most alienated from ourselves, others, and life. It is only in these dark, vegetative, abysmal states that the *nigredo* can dissolve old structures that no longer accord with our soul's essence. Thus these states of deadness, withdrawal, and fragmentation, are essential to the rhythm of transformation. But we must be willing to sacrifice what we know, what we know about, and sink into the unfathomable realms of unknown experience. The true meaning of "to suffer" suggests this ability to tolerate both intense affects and their absence, to undergo and be subjected to an original experience as in an initiation rite. Knowledge, method, and theory can shield us from such daring originality, and therein lies their danger and their protection. William Blake writes that "our emotions are the influx of the Divine in the body," but we do need a body that is vital and strong enough to incarnate these subtle and piercing divine rays. In a letter written in 1953, Jung writes: "The clinical practice of psychotherapy is a mere makeshift that does its utmost to prevent numinous experiences" (1975: 118). The willingness to suffer intense emotion and the disorientation that accompanies it, IS the *sine qua non* of the experience of the *numinosum*, and of new spiritual levels from the world soul or transcendent archetypal realms that have never before been made conscious. In the anonymous medieval text, *The Cloud of Unknowing*, the author describes the fact that

> the closer the soul of the mystic gets to the Godhead the darker and more confused he becomes. Such texts say in effect that God lives in the cloud of unknowing and that one has to be stripped of every

> idea, every intellectual conception, before one can approach the light which is surrounded by darkness and utter confusion.
>
> (Von Franz 1980a: 208)

Submitting ourselves to chaos, allowing ourselves to be worked on by such mysterious cosmic vibrations, we are led to the borders of a Mystery, a revelation, a gnosis, that in its silence speaks more words than we ever imagined or dreamed. But this Voice which brings revelation, as the experience of the numinous, is, as Neumann observes, "always new," and "cannot be other than anti-conventional, anti-collective, and anti-dogmatic," so the "ego affected by it comes into conflict with the dogma and agencies of the dominant consciousness" (1989: 386). Heretics, mystics and poets are ostracized by their societies as their "new" understandings threaten the status quo and the interests of controlling groups. It is dangerous to be original, and the inertia of large collective forces conspires to oppress authentic experience. But we are already blinded by the light of our one-sided consciousness, and like the story the ancient Orphites tell, when the feminine spirit of God could no longer tolerate the light of God, she fell down into chaos, with sparks still clinging to her, from which place she tried to raise herself up again (von Franz 1980b: 170). Surely we are at such a moment when the soul of the matter is in need of restoration, and the mysteries of Life seek our vision and our passion, and we need to fall in love with the world again.

In a poem entitled *Duration of Childhood* Rilke muses:

> But the constellation
> of his future love has long
> been moving among the stars. What terror
> will tear his heart out of the track of its fleeing
> to place it in perfect submission, under the calm
> influence of the heavens?
>
> (Rilke 1989: 265)

Could the chaos of our world losing its way in breakdowns on all levels from the personal to the political signal that moment of terror, that moment of deadly peril where consciousness seeks its own destruction and dissolution? Perhaps this is to void a cultural "false self" and a deep disturbance felt at the heart of ourselves and our world. All our knowledge and differentiation that at times is of inestimable value borders, too, on a congealment of awareness that is in danger of destroying and devouring the Thou of the Other, the Thou of the World.

At this crisis point it is as if we must become a mystery to ourselves again, actually the mystery that we truly are; we must become again the One which I am not, the Stranger that I am, the Mystery that can never, and must not ever be "understood." Rather to become again, in our vertical axis as it were, the Orphan, the Star, the one who has no human heritage but only a divine destiny, the one who must be protected, and can only be lived, the seeming impossibility of which being the very condition that rallies the latent forces of our spontaneous and creative natures. At this threshold landscape, we must allow ourselves to fall into "fateful detours and wrong turnings," and with no small terror become aware that our calling as humans has no models, no methods: only the secret promise and hints of the voices, images, dreams, and energies, within, between ourselves and the other, and without in the world, that can never be wholly known, but nevertheless borne, inadequately perhaps but with full heart, making the imponderables and the Invisibles known through our fragile frames, giving body to that which requires our participation, and our witness, our sacrifice, and especially our love. In this sense we are no longer hero or heroine, and we must arrest ourselves away from our childhood state, becoming the mystical adept ensouling the world through a translation of original experience into a human text for which there is no script.

Responding thus out of the wholeness of who we are, and not out of isolated elements that are always in doubt, invites us into a subtle attending to the "awe inspiring guest who knocks at our door portentously" (Jung 1975: 590) now that the dominants of our culture have disintegrated, and we are floating on a sea of collective and individual insecurity and exploration. And who is this coming guest? Who is this soul figure, at once so destructive and creative? Perhaps this "sensing of a new dominant arising from the chaos of a world losing its way" (Lockhart 1987: 51) that Jung alludes to near the end of his life, is Love. Love, the incalculable, irrational, ungraspable, unanalyzable, impenetrable Mystery, the "creator and father–mother of all higher consciousness" (Jung 1963: 353).

Freud (1930), too, considers this possibility for the future. At the end of *Civilization and Its Discontents*, and towards the end of his life, speaking of man's instinct for aggression and self-destruction that "could now very easily exterminate one another to the last man" and which gives rise to "unrest . . . dejection . . . apprehension," speaks to the importance of Eros for the future. "And now it may be expected that the other of the two "heavenly forces," eternal Eros, will put forth his strength so as to maintain himself alongside of his equally immortal adversary" (Freud 1930: 105).

Love's story is born out of a dark, windy night, with a sliver of a silver moon crowned with glistening golden stars, and with the limitless watery abyss rising and falling to secret rhythms in deep harmony with the foamy cosmos.

Love, source of every living thing, delivers us into the *Xairos*, the meeting place of the worlds, the almost unbearable beauty of Presence, the place where spirit and matter transcend their differences and become One. This cosmic realm brings us into our full identity, embracing all of existence, including our dark and chaotic forces, and faces us with a fearsome, unapproachable mystery. Beyond a psychology of projections sustained by a world split in two, we enter the Temple of a cosmology of relations illumined by all of nature, and surrender into a devotional attitude that in rich simplicity inspires the artistry of a life. This landscape can never be understood or integrated: only deeply and playfully related to by responding to its hints and gestures and our loving regard.

Rumi writes in his poem, "What Hurts the Soul?":

> We tremble, thinking we're about to dissolve
> into non-existence, but non-existence fears
> even more that it might be given human form!
>
> Loving God is the only Pleasure.
> Other delights turn bitter.
>
> What hurts the soul?
> To live without tasting
> the water of its own essence.
>
> People focus on death and this material earth.
> They have doubts about soul-water.
> Those doubts can be reduced!
>
> Use night to wake your clarity.
> Darkness and the living water are lovers.
> Let them stay up together.
>
> When merchants eat their big meals and sleep
> their dead sleep, we night-thieves go to work.
> (Rumi 1994: 40)

Notes

1 A loving thank you to my husband, Robert Romanyshyn, who has deepened my own understanding of Jung's phenomenological approach to the psyche, with his scholarly background in phenomenological philosophy, particularly the work of Merleau-Ponty. I am especially grateful to Robert for his contribution to this opening paragraph.

2 Von Franz (1980b: 123). In writing of the case of two people who fall in love, von Franz warns of the "poisonous mistake" that people make by infecting others with their own doubts about a participation, by calling it a projection. For the lover, the other is the beloved, not a projection of the animus. Strictly speaking, a projection is only such when doubt arises, causing a disturbance in the field. I emphasize this point because these days the word projection is used often carelessly with the consequence of thoughtlessly hurting others. With von Franz, I believe we should exercise greater caution when we speak of projection.

References

Balmer, J. (1984) *Sappho: Poems and Fragments, Psychics*, NJ: Meadowlands Books.

Freud, S. (1930) *Civilization and Its Discontents*, New York: Doubleday Anchor Books.

Friedrich, P. (1978) *The Meaning of Aphrodite*, Chicago: University of Chicago Press.

Graves, R. (1960) *Greek Myths: 1*, Harmondsworth: Penguin Books.

Hayles, N. K. (1990) *Chaos Bound*, Ithaca and London: Cornell University Press.

H. D. (1957) *Selected Poems*, New York: Grove Press.

Hillman, J. (1972) *The Myth of Analysis: Three Essays in Archetypal Psychology*, Evanston, IL: Northwestern University Press.

Homeric Hymns (1970) trans. C. Boer, Chicago: Swallow Press.

Jonas, H. (1963) *Gnostic Religion*, Boston: Beacon Press.

Jung, C. G. (1946) "The psychology of the transference," *CW* 16: 163–323.

—— (1963) *Memories, Dreams, Reflections*, New York: Vintage Books.

—— (1975) *Letters, II*, Princeton: Princeton University Press.

Lockhart, R. A. (1987) *Psyche Speaks*, Wilmette, IL: Chiron Publications.

Merleau-Ponty, M. (1962) *Phenomenology of Perception*, trans. C. Smith, London: Routledge.

—— (1964) "Eye and mind," in *The Primacy of Perception*, trans. C. Dallery, ed. J. Edie, Evanston: Northwestern University Press.

—— (1968) *The Visible and the Invisible*, trans. A. Lingis, Evanston: Northwestern University Press.

Neumann, E. (1989) "Mystical man," in J. Campbell (ed.) *Mystic Vision*, Princeton: Princeton University Press.

Rilke, R. M. (1954) *Letters to a Young Poet*, New York: W. W. Norton & Co., Inc.

—— (1989) *The Selected Poetry of Rainer Maria Rilke*, trans. S. Mitchell (ed.), New York: Vintage International.

Rumi. (1994) *Say I Am You*, trans. J. Moyne and C. Barks, Athens, GA: Maypop.

Schwartz-Salant, N. (1993) "Jung, madness, and sexuality," in *Mad Parts of Sane People in Analysis*, Wilmette, IL: Chiron Publications.

Van Eenwyk, J. R. (1997) *Archetypes and Strange Attractors*, Toronto: Inner City Books.

Von Franz, M. L. (1975) *Creation Myths*, New York: Spring Publications.

—— (1980a) *Alchemy*, Toronto: Inner City Books.

—— (1980b) *Projection and Recollection in Jungian Psychology*, La Salle and London: Open Court.

Whitmont, E. C. (1992) *Return of the Goddess*, New York: Crossroad.

EDITOR'S INTRODUCTION

A central endeavour in phenomenological psychology has been to describe the open clearing that is the ontological ground of human existence, and thereby to undercut theoretical differences and approaches to understanding the structures of human existence, including the structures of human transformation. Mary Watkins's essay is a meditation on that ground, the opening of Being, where "Being" is not a personal capacity, as it is often (mis)understood in the humanistic tradition. Rather, Being is that moment of coming into Presence of both person and world in a single, liberating occurence. As Watkins argues, it is the liberation of Being that is the authentic call of human existence, a call which is itself healing. She also poses a challenge to phenomenology's customary preoccupation with individual persons and experiences and its generally unreflective complacency regarding the broader socio-political contexts in which personal experiences are constituted. In this way she outlines the possibility of understanding the work we do as psychologists as a genuinely "liberation psychology," in which the politics of that claim should not be neglected.

12

DEPTH PSYCHOLOGY AND THE LIBERATION OF BEING

Mary Watkins

Martin-Baro (1994), the Jesuit psychologist murdered by a Salvadorean death squad in 1989, called in his work for the creation of a "liberation psychology." I would like to begin to explore what depth psychology can contribute to such an undertaking. At the same time, I would like liberation psychology to challenge and help rework problematic aspects of depth psychology. Depth psychology can be seen as an effort which radically challenges dominant cultural paradigms of selfhood and reality. It can also be seen as reflecting, conserving, and perpetuating aspects of the cultural status quo that contribute to human suffering. It is a confusing mixture of oppressive and libertory practices and theories. It is a mixture which perhaps the lens of a psychology of liberation can help us begin to clarify, so that liberation of one level does not mitigate against but supports liberation on other levels.

Liberation psychology, borne from the inspiration of liberation theology, argues that psychology itself requires liberation before it can be a clear force for liberation. The first step in such a process is to situate itself as a discipline within a cultural and historical context. Only in this way can the implications of the values in its theories and practices for the maintenance or transformation of particular aspects of culture be articulated. For depth psychology this would require creating awareness of its historical and cultural roots in European and American experience, in largely middle- and upper-class, male, Judaeo-Christian experience. Liberation psychology would ask what the implications of these roots are, particularly when this psychology is applied to members of other groups. One central implication of these origins that liberation psychology critiques is that depth psychology has not adequately understood and articulated the relationship between socio/cultural/economic structures and individual suffering. The focus on intrapsychic dynamics and the dyadic transferential relationship between patient and therapist often neglects the relationship between cultural and individual pathology. Indeed, the underlying paradigm of self in American culture –

rooted as it is in the Enlightenment, Puritanism, and the rise of industrialism and capitalism – would have us each think we are individually responsible for our shortcomings, gifts, pain, and health. A more contextualized view of self would seek to articulate the interrelations between what we have cordoned off as internal/private and what we take to be public/social.

> psychology has for the most part not been very clear about the intimate relationship between an unalienated personal existence and unalienated social existence, between individual control and collective power, between the liberation of each person and the liberation of a whole people. Moreover, psychology has often contributed to obscuring the relationship between personal estrangement and social oppression, presenting the pathology of persons as if it were something removed from history and society, and behavioral disorders as if they played themselves out entirely in the individual plane.
>
> (Martin-Baro 1994: 27)

When we consider human development and individuation, too often we have seen these as processes located within the individual. One can work on one's own "development" without regard to the other, even while acting in ways that use or impede the other in his/her own development.

Third-World liberationists have rejected the term "development" for cultural and economic progress, for too often it implied adopting an economic system that required their oppression or their neighbor's. Liberation was chosen as a better term for the goal of cultural change, for it is relational, based on a paradigm of interdependence. The liberation of one is inextricably tied to the liberation of all. Perhaps liberation is also a better term for psychological development in a perspective that strives for the acknowledgment of interdependence.

In a psychology of liberation the term "the other" is as crucial as the term "the self." Openness to the revelation of the other is as necessary as openness to the liberation of one's own thoughts, feeling, and images. Liberation is a holistic term that urges us to consider economic, political, spiritual, and psychological liberation together. In its holism it helps us to resist thinking that one could be psychologically liberated or individuated while economically or culturally enslaved or curtailing of the freedom of others. It urges us to look at how psyche reflects these other levels of human existence.

I believe that at the heart of its methods depth psychology is a psychology of liberation, but that it has focused on psychological liberation without enough clarity on the total context that is needed for human liberation. Without maintaining awareness of this broader context, its impulse toward liberation can actually subvert its own goal. Cushman (1995) argues that when we question why in our time the interior or the psychological has been chosen as the backdrop for human concern and activity, we discover that it has allowed us to retreat from disappointment and disillusionment about the lack of community and tradition from which we suffer. I would add that this retreat to the psychological has also buffered us from our feelings of impotence and ineffectuality in creating the kinds of communities and social order that we most deeply desire to be homed by, and that we already know are more conducive to psychological well-being.

I would like first to turn to some of depth psychology's liberational methods, as exemplified in the work of some its major founders, and then explore the application of these to wider contexts. Because of the mixture of radical and conservative tendencies in each theory, one could choose other aspects of depth psychology to argue against the points I will make. I am choosing to articulate those threads which I see as most conducive to a psychology of liberation!

When we look at the basic methods the founders of depth psychology proposed to their patients to help them address their suffering, we find a common movement toward what could be called the liberation of being. This is so despite differing theoretical allegiances which led the masters to various interpretive schemas. The common impulse across depth psychologies to liberate being links depth psychology to perennial spiritual traditions across time. It also speaks to the particular configurations of suffering in our cultural–historical time that western depth psychotherapy has been committed to address and heal. By focusing on this aspect of therapeutic practice – the liberation of being – I hope first to clarify the ways in which depth psychology can contribute to a psychology of liberation, and then to address how it needs to widen its sensibility toward oppression and liberation, embracing the challenge of the globalization of psychology (Sampson 1989).

Depth psychology has cultivated ways of being with what has been oppressed and marginalized that are applicable to interpersonal and intercultural settings. As I outline where the impulse to the liberation of being is within the methods of the various schools of depth psychology, let us also examine the manner of being they are honing so that we can see its relevance to liberational practices on other levels of human existence.

The schools of depth psychology suggest the importance of being able to bracket a controlling ego-directed manner of being in order to allow the free occurring or autonomy of being. In their therapeutic endeavors one cannot get to where one is going directly, through discursive, logical thinking. Van den Berg (1971) argues that the historical emergence of a strong, bounded, masterful ego constellated the co-emergence of what is called the dynamic unconscious. The logical rationality of the ego has pushed emotion, intuition, and image into the shadows of the margin. Analytic technique calls these marginalized ways of knowing into the consulting room, radically redistributing power from the oneness of the ego to the voices of the many. Despite the theoretical disagreements between the principal schools of depth psychotherapy, each argues that healing can occur when the spontaneous movement of being – feelings, thoughts, words, images, or bodily energy – can arise without hindrance. Freud and Jung were intensely interested in the content of what arose through their methods of free association and active imagination, and much of their analytic, interpretive work focused on this content. I would like to suggest, however, that it is often the mode of being that allows this content to come forth that is most essential to healing efforts. Heard with the ears of a liberation psychology, it is the openness to retrieve from the process of marginalization that which has been rendered inferior and denigrated that is central to healing. This mode of allowing *what is* to arise, is as crucial interpersonally, culturally, and interculturally as it is to so-called intrapsychic phenomena.

Free association

For Freud, patient and doctor were involved in corollary movements of mind, whose aims were the liberation of thoughts, fantasies and memories from their repressed status. While highly valuing reason, he understood that what is extruded from consciousness makes itself known in symptoms and neurotic suffering. For this reason he sought to address consciousness that had become too narrowed by asking both patient and doctor to welcome the previously repressed/oppressed.

He instructed the patient to give voice to all thoughts, memories, and images which enter her mind, whether spontaneously arising or while associating to a dream fragment or symptom. She was to try to restrain from any conscious selection or censoring of thoughts, regardless of their being unpleasant or appearing ridiculous, irrelevant, or uninteresting. Through this "fundamental rule," as it was called, one was to report literally whatever "falls into the mind" (*Einfalle*). In free association a voluntary selecting of thoughts is gradually eliminated so that a different order, the order of the unconscious, can arise. In Freud's words, "when conscious purposive ideas are abandoned, concealed purposive ideas assume control of the current of ideas" (1900: 531). One abandons a "systematic and purposeful search with a known aim" to "an apparently blind and uncontrolled meandering" (Jones 1961:155). This meandering radically supplements the truth that the critical rationality of the ego can provide. He describes this meandering as requiring a "mobile attention," not unlike one's attention in a hypnotic state or while falling asleep.

The "critical faculty" leads us to "reject some of the ideas that occur to [us] after perceiving them, to cut short others without following the trains of thought which they would open up to [us], and to behave in such a way toward still others that they never become conscious at all and are accordingly suppressed before being perceived" (Freud 1900: 102). In its efforts at exclusion, it hides a fuller truth. By observing where resistance to free arising of thoughts occurred, Freud could inquire into the conflict over expression:

what is seeking to be expressed and what is seeking to prevent expression and why. In attending to this antithesis and intervening as a midwife of the repressed, healing was aided.

Freud would ask the patient to let himself go as you would do in a conversation which leads you from cabbages to kings, let ideas "emerge 'of their own free will' " (Freud 1900: 102). This "widening of consciousness" on the patient's part was aided by the atmosphere gifted by the therapist's own "evenly-hovering attention," which would attempt to avoid selecting things to focus on from the patient's material so that premature ideas of order were not superimposed on the free associations. Both doctor and patient were to avoid psychotherapy's becoming a scene for the discussion of the already known, instead of a place where mind begins to occur freely, as resistances are lifted through interpretation.

Liberation psychology urges us not to apply knowledge from one group to all other groups. As a praxis, it asks that we go alongside those we are trying to understand, to allow them to speak of their problems with their own voice. The psychologist is not to enter as an expert, but to act as a midwife to those who have been disempowered, so that they can begin to be the protagonists of their own history. In this we can hear Freud's connection between the process of extrusion and the origination of symptoms and suffering. His method of making room for the repressed/oppressed, welcoming it, and of allowing its own order and meaning to become apparent, rather than to be dictated to by the dominant ideology of the egos of the doctor and the patient are consistent with a psychology of liberation. On both cultural and intrapsychic levels such a practice radically revises and supplements the previous sense of truth.

Active imagination

After his break with Freud, Jung applied a widened conception of the fundamental rule to himself in an attempt to heal and understand himself: "Since I know nothing at all, I shall do whatever occurs to me" (1962: 173). From 1912–1917 he found himself building sand castles, hewing stones, painting mandalas, holding conversations with imaginal figures; that is, he allowed images to arise and tried to body them forth in his activities. In turning his attention to the flow of images, Jung met an imaginal figure, Philemon, whom he said taught him about the autonomy of the psyche. By this Jung meant that there are things in the psyche which we do not produce, things which have a life of their own (1962: 183).

The method of active imagination was proposed to liberate this autonomous life of images and figures, so that a relationship between the conscious and the unconscious could be formed. This dialogue between the conscious point of view with which one is habitually identified and the freely arising images provided not only for a compensation of conscious attitudes by unconscious ones, but for an interpenetration and gradual synthesis of the conscious and the unconscious.

"Moreover," said Jung, "this work [of active imagination] has a definite effect . . . whatever [one] has put into it works back on him and produces a change of attitude which I tried to define by mentioning the *non-ego-centre*" (1935: 173). The process of active imagination gradually moves the center of one's awareness from habitual identification with the ego, which is often one-sided, to a more central position where one is less severed from the various outposts of the personality. Indeed, Jung – and Hillman (1971) since – stressed the polycentered nature of psyche. Active imagination is a method that invites the specificity of each perspective to be articulated, particularly insofar as it differs from the ego's.

In active imagination, as in free association, one tries to stop the ways the ego tries to remain in control of psychic experience so that the spontaneous movement of thoughts and images can begin to emerge into awareness. It is this repositioning which, I believe, has a healing effect, regardless of the content of the imagery or thoughts. This is a crucial point. It is sometimes tempting for Jungian and archetypal therapists to become excessively focused on the imagery per se. Interest in imagery for its own sake can obscure the significance of having moved to a place of witnessing which invites the other, the marginalized, to appear. It is this stance that is capable of being curious about and interactive with what has been "foreign" that is a critical contribution of these methods to a psychology of liberation.

Jung's racism and anti-Semitism, as well as his suspicion of politics, would not seem to ally him with any "liberation" movement. However, his acknowledgment of and respect for psychic multiplicity, his articulation of imaginative dialogue (rather than interpretation) as a method for psychic transformation, and his vision of a place to stand amidst multiplicity that is not fettered by efforts at control and domination, are deeply in the spirit of a psychology of liberation. At times in his writings he clearly seemed to grasp the interpenetration of self and other, though his elaboration on greeting the other appears much more highly developed with respect to "interior" psychic realities.

Jung certainly had an interest in other cultures – African, Native American, Chinese, Indian – and he spoke of the necessity to respect them. He even studied these cultures in an attempt at cultural self-reflection. Nevertheless, he remained somewhat unclear concerning the limitations of his own Germanic, Christian and romantic roots, and of the conceptual colonialism that these roots tended to perpetuate. Moreover, his interest in the collective aspects of psyche, beneath differences, was keener than his interest in beginning to articulate a truly multicultural depth psychology.

Samuels (1993) in his ground breaking book, *The Political Psyche*, outlines how to map Jung's grasp of multiplicity onto the domain of cultural differences. Samuels's ideas are central to a depth psychology of liberation. He urges depth psychologists to work in an interdisciplinary fashion, acknowledging the limitations of a purely psychological point of view, so that phenomena can be grasped in their political and economic complexity, rather than having these domains reduced to psychology. He advocates the aligning of depth psychology with the powerless rather than the powerful (as Jung did), in order to use its psychological expertise to help articulate the experience of marginalized others. Such work aids in releasing such others from the stereotypes of the dominant culture. The analyst's goal is not to become an expert of ethnic and cultural differences, but "a mediator who enables the patient to experience and express his or her *own* difference" (Samuels 1993: 328).

Were the spirit of how Jung approaches intrapsychic experience fully lived out within analytical psychology, it could move it from Jung's fascination with the collective to a truly multicultural psychology, making room for the particularities of each specific Other (see Adams 1997). Here *depth* psychology could also refer to penetrating and articulating the depth of differences – interculturally, interpersonally, and intrapsychically.

Liberating the capacity to play

At the core of Winnicott's object relations psychotherapy was a questioning about how we get a sense of feeling alive and real, sensibilities fundamental to feeling our lives are worth living. In his attention to the early relationship between mother and child he observed how a baby can be made precociously to comply with her mother's needs and desires, in order to maintain a relationship with her. In doing so, however, the child distances from her own needs and desires, and loses a sense of connection with what freely arises in her own experience, be it desires, feelings, thoughts. This inhibition of the spontaneity that characterizes the aliveness of the person is, for Winnicott, synonymous with illness. It breeds a sense of futility and hopelessness. Psychotherapy, he argued, must then provide a space, a "holding place," in which it is safe enough for spontaneous experience, play, to arise. In this free arising there is awakened the pleasure of being alive, the foundation of psychic health.

The transition from ego-mindedness to a space in which images, thoughts, feelings, and bodily sensations might arise was the focus of Winnicott's psychotherapy. Indeed, for him, psychotherapy "has to do with two people playing together" (1971: 38). When playing is not yet possible, therapy is aimed at overcoming the blocks to play, so that the spontaneity of being can occur. Winnicott was clear that what mattered most about play was not its content, or the analyst's subsequent interpretations, but the state that characterizes play: "a near-withdrawal state," a state in which one can be surprised by oneself, a "non-purposive state."

Winnicott claimed that in play "one is free to be creative and [that] it is only in being creative that the individual discovers the [true] self" (1971: 55). Creativity is a "coming together after relaxation, which is the opposite of integration" (ibid.: 64). He might have a several-hour session with an adult, where she is free to lay on the floor, free to transition out of the ego mode of relating one's difficulties, into a transitional space in which being could freely occur. This spontaneous space is also a resting place, where the efforts of control, mastery, and knowing are relaxed. In it the mind can fall back into the body. When psyche and soma cease to be defensively split, one experiences what Winnicott described as the true self. This self collects together the details of the experience of aliveness, which yield a sense of realness.

The analyst must not scurry to create impressive interpretations, but clear the space so that the patient can surprise herself with an understanding that emerges. The capacity to play was superordinate to the capacity to know.

In Winnicott we find an allegiance not to thought, feelings, images or bodily experience per se, but to that state of being in which one's inherent liveliness can become the foundation of activity in the world. His dictum was clear, "After being – doing and being done to. But first, being" (1971: 85). That freedom in one of these areas – the movement of thoughts, images, bodily energy, playing – effects movement in the others is often experienced, and indicates how bifurcating our theories and approaches can be. One of the central values of liberation theology that a liberation psychology borrows is the emphasis on the promotion of life and the articulation of the historical and sociocultural conditions that mitigate against and those which liberate life and liveliness (Martin-Baro 1994: 26). Martin-Baro and Paulo Freire would agree with Winnicott that it is only in a context that promotes liveliness that true creativity can emerge, creativity which is necessary to the vitality of the culture, as well as the individual.

Winnicott's meticulous description of how a child precociously complies to a mother's needs and desires in order to be loved could have been the beginning of an object relations theory of how psychic structure complies to the dominant paradigms of the culture, even when this causes pathology. Despite an interest in culture as the "place" of transitional experience, he did not see the culture streaming into the child's identity through the mother's needs and desires, and in the very structuring of the infant–mother relationship. Karen Horney (1937) opened the window out of the reduction of most psychodynamics to the mother–child relationship by asking what is acting in a cultural way to create so many mothers with narcissistic and depressive suffering. This window keeps getting closed.

Winnicott sets up the facilitating conditions for feeling alive – for being – in his consulting room, but says little about how the culture – beyond the mother – can attempt to give these very qualities to children: safety, reliability, consistency, the making of time and space to receive the other, the refusal to dominate the other through our ideas for him, the understanding of the necessity for uncertainty and wandering for the birthing of meaning and liveliness. He did not have perspective on the cultural context of his own practice and theory. In effect, Winnicott describes the "facilitating environment" as a nuclear family with a mother as sole caretaker of a child, and he does not question this as the recent cultural–historical invention that it is. At least in his major writings, he does not discuss the profound effect of the rise of industrialism on family structure: its erosion of "extended" families, its removal of the father from the home, its creating material desire to propel a capitalist economy that structures much of the daily life of mother and children. He endeavored to support individual mothers, but without critically examining the social structures that most impacted on their mental health and, thus, on that of their children.

Perhaps, however, the method of how Winnicott worked with the constraining of being by compliance can have a wider application than he imagined. His individual therapy sought to illumine how such constraint arose in response to the demands of relationship and then to practice loosening this constraint within an area of safety, with the aims of liveliness, creativity, and meaning. Once we understand how broad are the forces to which we comply, Winnicott's work could have wider implications for healing. Without insight into the wider forces to which we comply, however, his work distorts the sources of our suffering, compromising our efforts to address them.

Phenomenology's practice of world-openness

Central to the practice of phenomenologically oriented psychotherapies is the understanding that psychopathology is a constriction away from *what is.* The analyst attempts to create an openness, a spaciousness, so that what the patient has extruded can gradually emerge into its own authentic presence (Boss 1963). The awareness of *what is* constitutes healing, as it alleviates the sufferings that arise from efforts to extrude, defend, and distort.

Charles Scott says that the "therapeutic occurs as one is able to welcome events" (1982: 159). The capacity to welcome events cuts across domains. It is as relevant in welcoming the being of the other as it is in allowing the multiplicity of ourselves. It is an openness toward things as they are, an "openness toward the forthcoming of hiddenness" (ibid.: 83). This openness requires that we suspend our ego-interests, intentions, and desires, with their relentless judgments. Such an openness corresponds to a liberation of being.

In a similar vein, Fromm – psychoanalyst, social critic, member of the Frankfurt critical theory group – argued that the rise of capitalism and industrialism created a cultural shift from an emphasis on being to having. Such a transition entailed a further strengthening of the ego and its capacities for control and mastery. This strengthening was won by disassociating from the broader base of psyche, body, nature, community, and the spiritual, until the autonomy of the ego became seen as a goal. The movements of mind that support such an ego involve copious comparisons between self and other, meticulous monitoring of issues of sufficiency, inferiority and superiority, a heightened critical and judgmental capacity, maintenance of power, control and autonomy.

All of the psychotherapeutic practices I have outlined above are effective in softening such an ego, and in creating a different mode of participation. Opinion, criticism, judgment, premature understanding, and interference are explicitly bracketed so that they do not limit the appearance of what has been cast out. Listening and dialogical interaction are the means of coming to know what has been extruded. Through dialogical interaction, as in active imagination, the other can effect the self, as much as the self can effect the other. Control and domination are supplanted by dialogue and understanding. These are powerful tools with which to participate interpersonally and interculturally. It is a potential legacy from depth psychology to community activism that I deeply treasure, and which I hope will find a greater scope of usefulness.

Liberation across domains: vignettes from psychotherapy, large-group dialogue, and "Theatre of the Oppressed"

Psychotherapy

I would like to highlight the attempt on the clinician's part to listen for issues of oppression and liberation across domains – the so-called intrapsychic, the spiritual, the interpersonal, and the cultural. To shift to an interdependent paradigm of self – where the well-being of one is understood to be dependent on the manner of relations with others, the invisibles, earth, community, culture and global interconnectedness – we must practice holding liberation of being in the widest and deepest ways possible.

The clinical vignette is of a type that will be familiar to psychotherapists, yet it offers a sense of how the liberation of being in one domain – in this case with a feeling of anger and an impulse to murder – can in time broaden to include the liberation of being in relationships with oneself, one's partner, children, and friends, in cultural understanding and community action.

Carolyn came to therapy at the age of thirty-nine, married, mother of three, exhausted, depressed, anxious, and obsessive. Her brother's recent death by alcohol had made it impossible to hide from her own suffering. She was no longer able to navigate daily life with as much defense and pretense.

It emerged in therapy that Carolyn's father practiced a destructive form of patriarchy, exercising his position with abusive power toward the mother and abusive sexuality with his daughter. Both were frightened of his over-ruling and rageful presence. He clearly felt his daughter's body was his own property, as reaching in to touch her breasts on her wedding day amply describes.

Her mother became progressively under the sway of alcoholism and was correspondingly unavailable to Carolyn. The father was openly promiscuous with other women, parading his sexual potency.

Carolyn was able to remember her first incident of escape into obsessive thinking. In late latency she saw her father kiss a woman in clear view of herself. For a moment she felt like killing him. Then she looked up. There were branches on the tree above him, and she began to count them meticulously. By the time I saw her twenty-seven years later, such counting formed a backdrop to her daily activities, enabling her to distance from her pain and confusion, while radically narrowing her field of vision. She would count each dish as it went into the dishwasher, each piece of laundry as it was being folded. She could not leave the house until a high level of order and cleanliness had been achieved. Even on Christmas Day she scurried between her children to throw away the wrappers from the presents as they were opened. Her job as a fitness instructor was also in part an effort to control the body, though her own body would not succumb, and often stopped her with multiple painful injuries.

She was preoccupied by what others wanted from her, taking great pains to please them. She reported a lack of sexual desire, and experienced intrusive imagery of her father during sexual activity. Even when masturbating she could not experience an orgasm as hers, but would find herself looking down at herself as she would during intercourse.

In therapy she was initially confused about what she herself thought and felt. In her other relationships she had taken refuge in being the respondent. Therapy by its very structure of turning attention to her challenged this passivity, and highlighted her inability to allow herself to arise freely in the presence of another. She was too frightened to lay down on the analytic couch and, at first, even to close her eyes. We explored her fantasies of what would happen if she were to do either of these. In her image the other – myself – would become larger and larger, dwarfing and controlling her almost to her extinction. Her vigilance was a clear attempt to defend herself from domination by the other. A dream expressed the intensity of her fear:

> I was in some doctor's office on a stretcher being held down. I can feel the scratchiness of his wool pants. He puts his finger in his pocket and told me to suck on it. Then he turns and his penis is erect and it is in my mouth through his pants. He has no face. I see him only from the waist down. Someone else is holding me down. I awake screaming.

Here the domination of sexual abuse is mapped onto the figure of the doctor. Laying down is utterly unsafe. In a state of need herself – being at the doctor's – her vulnerability is exploited for the doctor's pleasure. The situation overpowers her, holding her into the abusive and abrasive moment.

In another dream she angrily confronts her father and a lover of his. Helping her greet her spontaneous feelings of anger was the initial key to subsequent liberation of feelings, thoughts, images, bodily experiences – and, indeed, the world of other people.

In her relations with her parents she feigned cheerfuless, survived visits, censored the expression towards them of spontaneous feelings and thoughts, and rigidly maintained the schedule of contact by phone and visit that they had prescribed for her. Any deviation from this pattern provoked anger and rejection by her parents.

The re-emergence of anger – kept largely in check by her unexamined obsessive preoccupations – broke her ability to perform seamlessly the role of the grateful, happy daughter. As this role began to dissolve, it clarified how it had become generalized to other contexts – with friends, her church, her children's school. There too she had remained hidden from herself and others by organizing her activity around the needs and desires of the other. Her increasing lethargy and depression now viscerally felt connected to the degree that she had left herself out of these arrangements. But then who was she actually? What did she actually feel and think? The spaciousness in therapy that allows one to wait for feelings and thoughts was both anxiety provoking and greatly desired. Therapy allowed her to begin a practice of self-initiation rather than pure responsiveness: a self-initiation that arose from waiting patiently for her own thoughts, feelings, and desires to arise.

As she began to crawl out from under the expectations others had of her, she became increasingly aware of her expectations for those closest to her, particularly her husband. She became aware that she had needed him to be a solid mountain behind which to take refuge. When he ventured into the expression of his doubts, particularly regarding his work, she felt she wanted him to stop and resume his former pose as self-assured and certain. The evolution of the marriage, of her capacity to allow the other to arise freely, was utterly dependent on her awareness of the extent of constraint to which she had submitted. The more hardy her own contact with her truth and voice, the more she could allow him vulnerability and uncertainty.

As she became able to discuss the extent of sexual abuse in her experience, I encouraged her to join a sexual abuse group. Through deep listening to the others in the group, as well as having the courage to speak her own story, she came to understand the ways in which internalized destructive gender relations form some of the most intimate dimensions of psyche. This was critical to her growing interest in women's studies as a potential path of study and subsequent livelihood. As she focused on her role in the community, she was clear that the joyless taking on of responsibility which felt burdensome needed to be replaced by activities that enlivened her and those with whom she worked.

After two years of working together she came to therapy several days after Christmas. She had been determined to sit with her children as they joyously unwrapped their presents and to be present within the moment to the intensity of her feelings of their preciousness to her and her love toward them. Surrounded by torn paper, and scattered ribbons, she had been able to let Christmas morning arise in all its messiness!

In the climate of "managed care" in the USA, and the insurance companies' destruction of long-term psychotherapy, it is important to say that the release from depression for Carolyn could not be meaningfully won by drugs or short-term psychotherapy. Both would be a systemic re-enactment of abuse, overpowering her needs and desires by the system's desire for profit. The unfolding of being that has been tightly constrained can only happen in time, in safety, ultimately in a relationship that welcomes what is in the other and what arises in the "between" of the relationship.

A liberation of feeling was critical as an initial key to other liberations, but insufficient in itself. To liberate feeling alone would not help her see the relationship between her constriction of herself and her constriction of those close to her. It would not help her see into the relationship between her subjugation of herself and her father's subjugation of her, and into the history of gender relations in the culture that it mirrored. The practice of being open to her feelings and thoughts could be linked to the practices of being aware of her body and of being open to those close to her. As she became more familiar with the landscape of her own desires, and cognizant of the familial and cultural pressures that mitigated against their emergence, her sense of her future work shifted, from one which, in part, contributed to further control of the body to one which sought to understand further women in relation to culture.

Given that liberation in one domain can be broadened to include others, one can argue that depth psychologists could engage in work at any of these levels and hold it in such a way that broader liberation could be evidenced. I would like to give several examples of such work to nourish our therapeutic imagination. This broadening of the possible modes of intervention is necessary as the depth therapies are seriously eroded by economic pressures. Beyond this, however, is the necessity to liberate depth therapeutic practice itself from existing only in the consulting room. It is more possible to imagine ourselves working in different contexts as we understand how our paradigms of selfhood and the personal have constrained us into the present format of healing – mostly one on one, with a focus on what is conceived to be the personal.

Large-group dialogue

On community and intergroup levels the same qualities of being which are necessary for the free arising of personal being are in great need for cultural life. As we have become encapsulated into individualistic identities, preoccupied with our personal survival and well-being, the thought of the culture has become fragmented. Bohm (1996) proposed a large-group dialogue process to address this fragmentation. While one is encouraged to give voice to thoughts, one is urged not to overidentify with opinions, but rather to try to see the assumptions behind them. We hear a familiar language – one is not to defend an opinion or to attack that of another person. One sits more to the side and listens to the diversity which is present. Through such deep listening the group can begin to think together, with a foundation in the complexity of the issue at hand as voiced through the many present. The respectful, inquiring manner of presence with each other becomes more focal than particular content. The relevance of this attentional stance for the mediation and resolution of deep intergroup and intragroup conflict is clear. The defense of an idea without deep listening into assumptions and the competing ideas of neighbors is a form of oppression, particularly if one has power to impose the idea on others.

Recently, in an initial dialogue of a group of thirty-seven adult learners beginning in a graduate school context, each person had the opportunity to share something, most of which was relevant to the experience of beginning school again. For many group members – all of whom were Caucasian – beginning school was portrayed as exciting, as "coming home." A Mexican-American student offered his experience of entering an American elementary school, unable to speak English. He was given an older student as a translator. The translator refused to interrupt the teacher to ask if the boy could go to the bathroom. Unable to communicate this himself, and mindful of the school rule not to leave the classroom without permission, he finally wet his pants in full view of the other students. On another occasion his younger sister ran to him upset by something that had happened at school. The school-yard monitor separated them, sister crying, for there was to be no Spanish spoken at the school. Another Mexican-American student shared a similar experience where she was forbidden to speak Spanish with her closest friend while at school, and so was alienated and lonely among a sea of Anglo students. Later in the dialogue a Japanese student struggling with his difficulties being in an English-speaking classroom said simply, "I feel as though there is a huge boulder on my chest, and yet I must continue to walk." A Caucasian student from the South was moved to say that until that evening she had never heard directly the pain caused by prejudice and racism. Several women students shared their hope that they would be able finally to speak in a classroom, after their earlier school experience of being silenced and their childhood experiences of being sexually abused and silenced into secrecy. Several others offered their anxiety at needing to be perceived as highly capable, aware that this was already alienating them from others and causing them to dominate the classroom discussion.

Through such a dialogue process the experience of beginning school in midlife is opened up so that the memories and hopes brought to the common moment of beginning together can be heard in their depth and diversity. In the listening one hears the voices of internal conversations, the forging of fear and corrosive self-doubt through racism and sexism; one witnesses what is shared in the moment and the breadth of the differences that exist. That which has previously been exiled in similar settings is allowed presence.

Theatre of the oppressed and the liberation of desire

Paulo Freire, the founder of the Brazilian literacy movement and author of *Pedagogy of the Oppressed* (1989), describes a two-part process of liberation in a group setting. The first part, called conscientization, invites participants to describe their worries and concerns. Through a process of active inquiry the group searches for the relationship between a concern and the structure of cultural reality that creates it. In oppressive situations the structural dynamics are often obscured in order to preserve existing power relationships. The liberation of voices in the group and concerted examination of what is experienced challenge oppressive practices.

Once the relationship between personal suffering and cultural practice has been clarified, the group is able to engage in the second step, annunciation. In annunciation the members of the group, understanding the dynamics of their lived situation, can begin to imagine utopically how they deeply desire their situation to be transformed.

Augusto Boal (1995) has translated these principles into a theatre of the oppressed. Situations that cause suffering are enacted. The audience is released from passivity and enlisted to create dramatic solutions to the problems posed. In such theatre work those who are ordinarily dispossessed begin to rehearse alternative possibilities that can be incarnated in their world.

City At Peace is an arts project in Santa Barbara that works with youth effected by gangs, drugs and alcohol, dysfunctional families, lack of community and school responsiveness. The teenagers meet weekly to learn mediation and conflict resolution skills, to share their daily experience, and to translate their experience into the arts. One 16-year-old shared in her poetry her experience of her father's death on his job, caused by heavy machinery that was operated by a fellow employee who was drunk. The latter, though clearly at fault, was never reprimanded. She had never been given a chance to speak with this man. Her prose raged at the injustice of her father's death and her lack of opportunity even to talk to the man involved in her father's death. "But why not?" query members of the project. Might it be possible through a process of mediation to bring together Claire and her family with this man, so that each could be heard and the potential for reconciliation be given an opportunity? One of the group leaders shared the Quaker model of restorative justice, where just such a meeting between the perpetrator and the victim and the victim's family is enabled to occur through the court system, putting a personal face onto the event and allowing the chance for direct reparation and forgiveness, rather than abstract justice only. The group members are eager to help put such a system into place for Claire and others.

In another example, the students enact moments of racism they have experienced in their schools. The brawl is slowed down, so that each character is given a chance to voice his thoughts and feelings, and then his deeper desires regarding the divisions by which his life has been eroded.

The practice of nonviolent conflict resolution has enabled these young people to listen to each other. The quick and violent impulsivity of gang life is gradually supplanted by hearing into moments that would formerly have been experienced mainly in action. The liberation of being that the practice of deep listening affords, the liberation of being that the arts and theatre invite, leads into the liberation of desire for intergroup healing of hostilies.

A depth psychologist committed to the liberation of being might be found in the consulting room, the classroom, the teen theatre group, the prison or hospital, in an outdoor nature classroom, or in the office of a policy maker. In each of these sites the impulse toward the liberation of being can be nourished . . . if only we can hear and see the many levels of liberation that are needed and clarify the manner of their interpenetration. The basic stance of depth psychology – to call forth marginalized being, to respect the multiple voices which comprise truth, and to invite dialogue – can be practiced across the domains of the intrapsychic, interpersonal, intercultural, and ecological.

Such a depth psychologist would also be an interested cultural historian, able to situate her theories and practices. As Martin-Baro says,

> [this] does not mean throwing out all of our knowledge; what it supposes, rather, is that we will relativize that knowledge and critically revise it from the perspective of the popular majorities. Only then will the theories and models show their validity or deficiency, their utility or lack thereof, their universality or provincialism. Only then will the techniques we have learned display their liberating potential or seeds of subjugation.
>
> (Martin-Baro 1994: 28)

A depth psychological stance informed by such a view of liberation would align research in depth psychology not only with phenomenological and clinical approaches to the unfolding of meaning, but to a tradition of partcipatory action research which seeks to liberate through the practice of research, engaging those who expect to be subjects as collaborators and co-authors whose knowledge can provide the wisdom for interventions and their assessment. Since sociocultural and economic structures are understood to impact psychological structure and well-being, efforts at understanding these are critical to a more comprehensive depth psychology, a psychology which is meeting the world rather than shrinking from it in a defensive posture. Such a depth psychology can be a multicultural psychology. It can hold the beauty of its basic stance while penetrating and addressing the complexity of forces that undermine the liberation of being.

References

Adams, M. V. (1997) *The Multicultural Imagination: Race, Color, and the Unconscious*, London: Routledge.

Boal, A. (1995) *The Rainbow of Desire: The Boal Method of Theatre and Psychotherapy*, London: Routledge.

Bohm, D. (1996) *On Dialogue*, London: Routledge.

Boss, M. (1963) *Psychoanalysis and Daseinsanalysis*, trans. L. Lefebre, New York: Basic Books.

Cushman, P. (1995) *Constructing the Self, Constructing America: A Cultural History of Psychotherapy*, Reading, MA: Addison-Wesley.

Freire, P. (1989) *Pedagogy of the Oppressed*, New York: Continuum.

Freud, S. (1900/1953) "The Interpretation of Dreams," Standard Edition of *Complete Psychological Works of Sigmund Freud, Vol. IV*, trans. J. Strachey, London: Hogarth Press.

Fromm, E. (1976) *To Have or to Be*, New York: Bantam Books.

Hillman, J. (1971) "Psychology: monotheistic or polytheistic?" *Spring*, 193–208.

—— (1992) *We've Had A Hundred Years of Psychotherapy and the World's Getting Worse*, San Francisco: HarperCollins.

Horney, K. (1937) *The Neurotic Personality of Our Time*, New York: Norton.

Jones, E. (1961) *The Life and Work of Sigmund Freud*, New York: Basic Books.

Jung, C.G. (1935) "The Tavistock lectures", *CW* 18, 5–182.

Jung, C.G. (1962) *Memories, Dreams, Reflections*, New York: Pantheon Books.

Martin-Baro, I. (1994) *Writings for a Liberation Psychology*, Cambridge, MA: Harvard University Press.

Sampson, E. (1989) "The challenge of social change for psychology: globalization and psychology's theory of the person", *American Psychologist*, 44, 6, 914–921.

Samuels, A. (1993) *The Political Psyche*, London: Routledge.

Scott, C. (1982) *Boundaries in Mind: A Study of Immediate Awareness*, New York: Crossroads.

van den Berg, J. H. (1971) "Phenomenology and metabletics," *Humanitas*, VII, 3, 279–290.

Winnicott, D. W. (1971) *Playing and Reality*, London: Tavistock.

EDITOR'S INTRODUCTION

The Dutch have been pioneers in the development of phenomenological psychology, but much of their work is known only to scholars in the field, and even then only some of it is available in English. Professor Mook's discussion of Dutch contributions to the phenomenology of play and play therapy is thus an introduction for most of us to literature of which we may have only heard. The sense of easy affinity that Jungians might have in relation to these Dutch phenomenological studies on play is anticipated and felt by Mook. However, being especially sensitive to the epistemological traditions in which Jungian and phenomenological thought are situated, she does not blur significant differences between them. She draws on the phenomenological hermeneutics of Ricoeur and Gadamer to to find a rigorous way of maintaining the tensions between the radically descriptive style that has been the hallmark of Dutch phenomenology and the symbolic interpretations of analytical psychologists such as Dora Kalff. But she also points to a phenomenological hermeneutic approach that accommodates Jungian theory and interpretation while submitting them to hermeneutic epistemological criteria.

13

PHENOMENOLOGY, ANALYTICAL PSYCHOLOGY, AND PLAY THERAPY

Bertha Mook

Introduction

Existential phenomenology and analytical psychology have both made major contributions towards understanding the nature and the complexities of what it means to be a human being in the world. They can be seen as countermovements to the pervasive natural scientific viewpoint in mainstream psychology where human subjects are objectified and distanced from their own bodies, from others and from the things around them. Both movements aim to recover and understand the explicit as well as the implicit meanings of our lived experience situated in historical contexts. Yet they mostly remain apart since leading phenomenologists critiqued Jung's implicit ontology and epistemology as Cartesian in the tradition of nineteenth-century materialism and realism. Today, new post-Jungian developments in analytical psychology have led to theoretical shifts and a growing concern with ontological and epistemological issues.

Jung is known as a creative, insightful man who was guided primarily by inner experience. His central thesis was to reawaken a sense of soul in the world which he perceived was lost in modern life. Although Jung often referred to himself as a phenomenologist, his writings show that his understanding of phenomenology was naïve and that he lacked knowledge of its philosophy. He was also unclear about his own metatheoretical assumptions, and consequently his theoretical formulations are often confusing and at times contradictory. Brooke (1991) remarks that, on the one hand, Jung endorsed a natural scientific viewpoint in calling himself an empirical scientist and in seeing human beings as self-contained intrapsychic entities. On the other hand, his psychology became poetic as the relationship between himself and his subject matter was to a great extent a work of intuitive imagination, which he preferred to express in metaphors. Searching for the source and the foundation of our primordial experiences, he turned to pre-Enlightenment sources which led him to formulate his theory of personality, and in particular his concept of the collective unconscious and its archetypes. Despite the richness of Jung's theory, the problem remains that his poetic perspective has not been grounded in a systematic anthropology or methodology, and that his natural scientific tendencies still persist in analytical psychology today.

As Brooke points out, despite their justified critiques, most phenomenologists have seriously underestimated the value and richness of his analytical psychology. In explicating Jung's phenomenological and hermeneutic intentions as well as his Cartesian tendencies, Brooke's reading is successful in bringing phenomenology and analytical psychology closer together and in opening the door for a continuing dialogue between them. Central to his book lies the thesis that Jung's own writings go beyond the confines of his explicit theoretical position and reveal an understanding that is for the most part congenial to existential phenomenology. In moving towards a phenomenological analytical psychology, Brooke attempts to articulate Jung's major concepts into the language of existential phenomenology.

The unique contribution of existential phenomenology to analytical psychology lies primarily in overcoming the Cartesian separation of subject and world by providing an ontology and an anthropology of the human world as a network of meaningful relations. More specifically, the existential-phenomenology of Merleau-Ponty provides us with an embodied view of human existence and thus offers the possibility of fundamentally integrating the body and the psyche in meaningful patterns of human–world relatedness. His phenomenological studies of child psychology in particular throw light on the emergence and the expression of psychological life as fundamentally embodied and intertwined with the surrounding world. His philosophy of ambiguity embraces a continual exploration of the interrelatedness between the known and the lived, or the revealed and the concealed, and as such endorses the poetic and the metaphorical character of human life. Phenomenology also offers a rigorous methodology which aims to describe the meaning-structures of phenomena as they reveal themselves to consciousness. Analytical psychology in turn is challenging and potentially fruitful to an existential phenomenological psychology and psychotherapy. Its insights into the nature of the collective unconscious with its archetypes and primordial images, and the process of individuation with its patterns of psychological development and transformation, have led to a rich theory of personality that might deepen a phenomenological understanding. In the field of psychotherapy, Jung's methods of amplification and active imagination are congenial and important to a phenomenological approach as well. Key Jungian concepts could furthermore be submitted to a rigorous phenomenological and hermeneutic analysis.

In the 1950s a phenomenological and a Jungian approach to play therapy were developed relatively independent of each other yet strikingly similar in intent and focus. The existential phenomenological approach referred to as imagery-communication was originally developed by Langeveld (1955) and co-workers in Utrecht. With its emphasis on imaginative play and other creative expressions, it sought to develop a phenomenologically based therapeutic approach for children in contrast to the prevailing verbal psychoanalytic and humanistic therapies primarily developed for adults. Simultaneously, a Jungian play therapy approach referred to as sandplay was developed in Zurich by Kalff (1966), who showed a similar recognition of the primordial status of play and imagery in her therapeutic work. Both the original phenomenological and Jungian approaches to play therapy with children have been further developed and are today actively practised and in increasing demand (Hellendoorn 1988; De Domenico 1994).

Despite their similarities, phenomenological and Jungian therapies with children differ in their ontological and epistemological foundations, and consequently in their understanding and interpretation of the therapeutic relationship and the meaning of play and other imaginative expressions. More importantly, these major yet diverse approaches to child psychotherapy have never been brought into a fruitful dialogue with each other. In this chapter, I would like to explore the thesis that the existential phenomenological and the Jungian approaches to play therapy with children are mutually enriching and complementary in nature. The existential phenomenologically based approach referred to as imagery-communication will first be introduced. In particular, its concepts of play, images and symbols, and the role of understanding and interpreting imaginative play in therapeutic practice will be elaborated. The Jungian approach and its understanding of play, images, symbols and interpretation will subsequently be discussed in the light of Jung's theory of personality. The key phenomenon of play and the hermeneutic tension between phenomenological understanding and Jungian interpretation of therapeutic play will be addressed in the light of the phenomenological hermeneutics of Gadamer and Ricoeur. This will in turn open the door towards a phenomenological hermeneutic approach that could incorporate and build a bridge between the phenomenological and Jungian viewpoints in adhering to hermeneutic criteria for understanding, interpretation and validation.

Phenomenology and imagery-communication

The mode of child psychotherapy called imagery-communication draws on the existential phenomenological philosophy of Heidegger and Merleau-Ponty, the phenomenological psychology of Buytendijk and the pedagogical anthropology of Langeveld. Originally developed by Langeveld (1955), Vermeer (1955) and Lubbers (1971), it focuses on therapeutic communication through the imagery of play and other creative expressions.

From an existential phenomenological point of view, play is a way of being-in-the-world, a mode of world-relatedness where "world" refers to a horizon of meaning (Strasser 1963: 80). In her well-known existential phenomenological study of play, Vermeer (1955) applies and further develops Buytendijk's concept of play and of images. She reveals that play is characterized by an ambiguous dialectical structure anchored in the poles of fantasy and reality which in turn serve as a background to and as the boundaries of the playworld itself. Phenomenologists see the essence of play as a to-and-fro movement between the player and his or her playthings. Herein they endorse Buytendijk's (1932) early insight that the player does not only play with something but that the "something" also plays with him. Play furthermore has the character of imagery. For the playing child, the things of the everyday world change and show a different face. The child starts to play with the play-images that are evoked from and around his playthings in reality, and that draws him into their spell. Vermeer points out that a double-meaning structure unfolds between the created play-images and reality. For example, a table evokes the play-image of a house but remains at the same time a table in reality, or a slipper may become a doll's cradle but also remains a slipper. This double-meaning structure leads to an adaptive exchange of expectation and surprise and lends play its magical and exciting character. Buytendijk writes that the domain in which subject and object are related in play is the domain of images, of fantasy, of appearances, of symbols and of possibilities.

In her extensive study of the role and meaning of images in the theory and practice of imagery-communication, Kwakkel-Scheffer (1983) reviews the relevant literature in this field and the foundational contribution of Buytendijk. Images are defined by him as the appearance of the things around us in their pathic character. Herein he draws on the distinction made by Straus (1930: 82) between pathic and gnostic modes of perceptual relatedness to our world. The pathic mode involves an immediate communication with others and with things and evokes feelings as well as real and virtual movements. It is most characteristic of young children, who are open to change, flexible and tend to be flooded by ambiguities and possibilities. The gnostic mode includes more distance, is informed by knowledge and becomes stronger as the child matures. It is goal-directed, focused and more stable in character. In all acts of perception, both modes are operative in an interrelated fashion. Buytendijk describes the difference between the gnostic and pathic ways of perceptual relatedness to the world as one of grasping versus being grasped. The playing child is typically grasped by his playthings which appear to him in their pathic character and as such evoke play-images.

Based on Buytendijk's concept of images, Langeveld speaks of imaginative images as expressions of personal meanings of me-and-my world experiences where my relationship to my world is predominantly pathic in character. He sees these images as prereflexive figures of experience and as such primary to words. He further makes the valuable distinction between personal meanings expressed through images and open, shared meanings expressed through words. Phenomenologists in imagery-communication emphasize that the child expresses his personal meanings of his own person–world experiences through images which originate in unity with his world. These images are distinguished from fantasy images which are not or are barely related to reality.

A slightly different concept of images is introduced by Van Lennep (1958), who refers to image-making in drawings and other artistic products as a crystallization of experience. In imagery-communication, Lubbers (1971) adopts this definition and is most known for encouraging his child clients to express their problematic world in the concrete imagery of drawing, painting or clay figures and to develop an illusive world around it by narrating through the images. The therapist and client are seen as shaping this world together in a process referred to as "symmorphoses." The images the child client creates are often concealed and symbolic in character and may call for timely interpretation.

In the therapy playroom, raw materials such as sand, water and clay as well as the playthings themselves aim to evoke a pathic response in the child. The pathic mode of relatedness is most strongly involved in the touching and feeling of the substance of materials in the playroom. Inspired by Merleau-Ponty (1962), Vermeer speaks of sensopathic play where the touching and handling of raw materials leads to an interweaving of impressions, feelings and movements in the child. In this kind of body-play, the child is totally immersed in a sensopathic experience and images still remain implicit. For example, she may enjoy to shuffle the sand or splash in the water or pound the clay simply for her own enjoyment. The child's immersion-in-activity and the openness and flexibility of the situation can lead to endless possibilities. Images easily emerge as the shuffled sand becomes a mountain, the water a lake or the clay a ball or a pancake. By seeing, touching and feeling the surrounding recognizable playthings, the child responds to their appeal. The evoked play-images move her and impel her in turn to move with them. She easily surrenders to their call and is lured into their spell.

In their view of symbols, writers in imagery-communication tend to follow Rumke (1949/65), who sees symbols as the most adequate way for expressing a coherence that we do not yet know. We could say that symbols refer to our represention of things, events or happenings in our life-world that we do not fully comprehend. We need a pathic as well as a symbolic attitude to see and understand symbols for they reveal themselves to a subject who is open and receptive to his world. In the context of imagery-communication therapy, this applies both to the child and to his therapist (Kwakkel-Scheffer 1983). In his playful surrender, the child with a pathic relatedness to his play-world may express himself through symbolic images and in doing so, he reveals something to his therapist about his relationship to his world. The therapist in turn needs to assume a pathic and a symbolic attitude to grasp its possible meanings. Symbols reflect deeper meanings of the child's life and let the therapist participate in them.

From a phenomenological point of view, imagery-communication in play therapy thus involves the child's playing with images evoked in the concrete, intimate encounter with his playthings in the presence of his therapist. Together, they constitute a playworld filled with possibilities, expectations and surprises. Once the play is unfolding and the child moves into an imaginative playworld, imagery related to previous experiences and to new imaginings emerge. Herein the child's age and experience obviously play a role. For example, for a young child, a hobby-horse may evoke the image of riding-a-horse and he typically becomes immersed in the act of riding itself. For the older child, the same toy may evoke the same image of riding-a-horse which is then elaborated upon. He might play that after a long ride his horse needs a rest. He is tied to the leg of a table which serves as the image of a tree where the carpet serves as the image of grass for his food. Imaginative play becomes more differentiated and complex once themes are elaborated, different scenes are created and a landscape of events is configured in a play-narrative. Here, the playing child is usually moved by deeper feelings and the pathic involvement increases. In the example of the horserider, the child may imagine that he is a grown-up man who is riding through a forest. As the sun sets and the sky darkens, the rider is unexpectedly attacked by a wild animal which leads to a tense and emotion-filled struggle for survival. Once the rider is abandoned and about to die, the therapist may intervene by suggesting that his call for help has been heard which may lead to new imagery. The dying man is suddenly spotted by a helicopter and brought to the hospital. His family is informed, and upon arrival, learn that they nearly lost their beloved husband and father. In such imaginative complex imagery, the actual playthings remain involved and help to concretize and consolidate the playworld.

The therapist in imagery-communication, through play or other creative expressions, is an active participant and may be called upon by the child to be a co-player. In encountering the child, she fosters a pathic attitude in him by showing a pathic involvement herself. She uses her voice in rhythm and intonation to express feelings of expectation, surprise, encouragement and a scala of other emotions and attitudes. The therapist tries to bring the child to a mimesis, i.e. to a figurative and symbolic expression of problematic past or present experiences through the medium of creative imagery. In order to grasp and understand the child's personal meanings in imaginative play, the therapist is called upon to experience imaginatively his imagery in an analogous way. In the playworld, she respects the anonymity of the figures and happenings and accepts the child's meanings which she helps to explicate. At times, the imaginative playworld is relatively open and the child's meanings can be readily understood within the context of his life-world. At other times, the playworld widens and becomes increasingly complex. Figurative and symbolic figures may appear drawn from the child's personal life and his fantasies as well as from sources in the real world. Different and often conflicting themes may emerge and be tied together into a play-story. Meanings may be difficult to decipher as they are often concealed or obscured in symbolic images in which case interpretation is called for. At all times, the therapist facilitates the child's play by helping him to differentiate further emotionally loaded images and break through obstacles and barriers encountered in the playworld. This in turn opens the possibility for a different experiencing and a different outcome, a re-ordering of feelings, and a new integration of past and present experiences within the child's life-world.

A phenomenological approach to imagery-communication in play therapy emphasizes the importance of therapeutic understanding and verbalization of personal meanings attributed by the child to the created imagery. The therapist encounters the child client in his playworld and actively shares in his experiencing, which forms the fertile ground for her understanding. Although the problem of interpretation is recognized, the phenomenological approach as originally conceived does not elaborate upon it. This constitutes a significant difference with Jungian approaches to play therapy which are predominantly interpretative in character.

Jungian play therapy

Jungian therapeutic play has its roots in Jung's own play and art experiences. In contrast to Freud who devalued images as regressive and infantile, Jung (1962) embraced them as meaningful expressions of the human psyche. As is well known, Jung's break with Freud triggered a major personal and professional crisis which led him to embark on a journey into the unknown regions of his own unconscious in search of his personal identity. During these years of inner exploration, Jung yielded to powerful affects and strange visions that regularly flooded his consciousness. He would move into the affect, personify the images and dialogue with the encountered figures. Every morning, he sketched a mandala that corresponded to his inner experiences. Based on his personal experiences, Jung discovered that it was therapeutic to find the images hidden within strong emotions and that moving into the affect facilitates their revelation. He wrote: "To the extent that I managed . . . to find the images that were concealed in the emotions, I was inwardly calmed and reassured". And further: "As soon as the image was there, the unrest or the sense of oppression vanished. The whole energy of these emotions was transformed into interest in and curiosity about the image" (1962: 177). Jung would then typically dialogue with the imagery figures encountered and paint them to amplify further his experiences. He thus unwittingly created his well-known techniques of amplification and of active imagination.

In this highly significant period of his life, Jung recalled his turbulent childhood in which he was often plagued by anxiety dreams and frightening daytime visions. He also remembered his childhood passion for play and how it offered him a sanctuary in which he gained some sense of control and mastery. What is most amazing is that Jung at this time in his adult life returned to his former sanctuary of play in an attempt to recover the creative life he experienced as a child. As in his childhood, he began to build houses, castles and villages out of twigs and stones at the lakeshore, and afterwards he would draw and paint his play experiences. Recovering play and exploring his own images, dreams and fantasies resulted for Jung in powerful insights and discoveries that grounded his life work. In his words: "The years that I was pursuing my inner images were the most important of my life . . . the later details are only supplements and clarifications of the material that burst forth from the unconscious. . . . It was the *prima materia* for a life-time's work" (1962: 199).

Throughout his life, Jung continued to illustrate his dreams and other inner experiences through drawing, painting and carvings in stone. For him, play and the expressive arts remained primary media for exploring and giving shape to his inner world. He found that expression in tangible forms facilitated integration of unconscious material into conscious awareness. Through his own experiences, he came to see that the unconscious is not only a place for repressed emotions but more importantly, a source of healing and transformation. With Jung's rediscovery of the power of play, his continual involvement in the expressive arts, and his thorough familiarity with images and with active imagination, he can indeed be called a master at imagery-communication. Although Jung himself did not work with children, he enthusiastically endorsed the use of play and art in therapeutic practice.

Jung's unprecedented journey of personal healing, his clinical experience, his anthropological research and his reading of antiquity, mythology, symbolism and alchemy laid the foundations for his theory of personality and in particular for his original formulation of the collective unconscious with its archetypes. His discovery of primordial images as analogue motifs in myths, fairytales and dreams within and across human races gave shape to his belief in archetypes which he saw as inherited patterns of energy and potentialities. Archetypes in turn express themselves in images and mythological experiences that reveal transpersonal and ancestral wisdom and potentially help us to make sense out of our often incomprehensible experiences. Although Jung saw archetypes themselves as unknowable, he claimed that their images are knowable and have a fascinating and affective numinosity that set them apart from other images. For Jung, symbolic images are the natural language of the unconscious and the best expression of a relatively unknown "fact." Symbols act as a bridge between the conscious and the unconscious, between the familiar and the strange, the literal and the more abstract (Ryce-Menuhin 1992). Jung saw the archetype of the Self as the central organizing principle of the collective unconscious that strives toward fulfilment of our potential and towards the unity of personality. He found that the language of the Self is that of images, feelings, metaphors and symbols, and called it mythopoetic in contrast to the verbal, rational language of the ego. Contrary to existential phenomenologists, Jung attributed great importance to fantasy which he saw as "the mother of all possibilities" (Jung 1921/71: 52). For him, fantasy is an autonomous psychic function that bridges the subject and the object, the inner and the outer worlds and weaves all other psychic functions together in one living union. Jung saw the development of personality as a process of individuation in which the multiple characteristics within the person are integrated within the Self as the centre of psychological life.

For Jungian child analysts, a rich fantasy and imaginative play life suggest a lively Ego–Self communication (Neumann 1973). Play, dreams and fantasies are seen as the royal road to the unconscious. Play activates the healing function of the psyche which in turn awakens affects and prepersonal archetypal images that have a transforming effect on consciousness. Typical archetypal themes of childhood include the great mother, the eternal youth, the hero, the anima and the animus, the shadow, the trickster and the wise old man or woman. In contrast to Jung's belief that the integrative processes of individuation were limited to the second half of life, Fordham (1969) convincingly shows that the individuation process is already operative in early childhood.

Child analysts base their use of play and other creative expressions on Jung's personal healing journey, his regular return to self expression through play and art, and on his understanding of the psyche. As a group, they encourage the use of a variety of expressive techniques in order to evoke meaningful images and symbols within a therapeutic relationship. Herein they rely heavily on the creative function of the psyche to help their child patients gain access to their inner worlds in the presence of an analyst who honours and respects their play, art and similar mythopoetic expressions of the psyche.

As mentioned earlier, Kalff (1966) in the mid-1950s developed a specific form of Jungian play therapy called sandplay. At the time, it was enthusiastically embraced by Jung and became increasingly popular with children as well as with adult patients. Kalff was in turn inspired by Margaret Lowenfeld's "World Technique." As early as the 1920s, Lowenfeld presented her child patients with a metal tray half filled with mouldable sand and a box of varied miniature toys. The children called the box of toys "the world," and spontaneously made their "world pictures" in the sandtrays. A new technique was thus in the making and created by the children themselves (Bowyer 1970). In Jungian sandplay, the child or adult patient is offered a specially designed, small sandtray with dry and wet sand and hundreds of toy-sized miniatures. The latter represent human, animal, plant and mineral life, buildings for all purposes, vehicles for air, land and sea, prehistoric and fantasy animals, and historic and symbolic figures from eastern and western cultures. Most patients take about twenty to forty minutes to complete a sandtray. Coloured slides are taken of a series of sandtrays over time.

Jungian sandplay is seen as evoking the free feeling of play and imagination leading to an immediate, concrete expression of a world. The tactile experience of touching and moulding sand, and of handling a large variety of colourful objects made from different materials relaxes the patient and facilitates creative expression. Ryce-Menuhin (1992), a leading exponent of Jungian sandplay, sees it as the mirror of the psyche par excellance. He writes: " From a Jungian standpoint, sandplay mirrors the Eternal Child playing archetypal games" (p. 6). Kalff assumes that healing takes place first at a non-verbal level. In the silent holding presence of an analyst, sandplay is seen as allowing a creative regression that fosters and enables healing. Analysts often incorporate sandplay as a complement to verbal analysis to provide a non-verbal ritual in which patients can express images from their archetypal unconscious. It is conceived as a powerful medium in bypassing verbal defences and in intensifying and amplifying material from verbal analysis.

Most Jungian play analysts tend to be non-directive. The analyst is seen as offering a safe container or a free and protected space to her child clients. The establishment of a transference relationship is seen as essential and believed to activate the healing potential of the psyche and in particular the archetype of the Self. This allows concrete expression through images and symbols in play and other non-verbal media which in turn lead to building bridges between the Self and the ego and, consequently, between the inner and the outer world. In doing so, it facilitates psychological growth and fosters the processes of integration and individuation.

When working with play or art images, some Jungian therapists will address an imaginative figure directly as if it were real and a partner in the therapeutic dialogue. For example, in using spontaneous drawings, Allan (1988) emphasizes the importance of talking about the content of the drawing in the third person. Referring to one of his cases, he illustrates: "I notice you have drawn a big gorilla. I wonder what the gorilla is thinking . . . feeling . . . and planning to do next" (p. 96). Here the child and the therapist turn directly to a personified image for an indirect understanding of the child's world. It conveys a respect for the power of images in play therapy and can be seen as an application of Jung's technique of active imagination in therapeutic work with children. As Hillman notes, it recognizes the image "as a living intelligence" that can communicate a truth about the soul, as it can in ancient cultures (in Allan 1988/94: xx).

Interpretation in play therapy is usually approached with caution. The analyst is expected to have an elaborate knowledge of archetypal theory and of symbols as she aims to raise the content of the collective unconscious to consciousness in order to interpret its possible meanings. Jungian play therapists tend to keep verbal interpretations of symbolic imagery by and large to themselves. When interpretations are offered to the child patient, they are usually delayed till a series of sandplays, drawings or other creative expressions have been made. In Jung's method of synthetic interpretation, the leading or emotionally charged images are amplified and elaborated upon by exploring the patient's meanings as well as the analyst's meanings.

Epistemologically, Jungian interpretation tends to be rooted in a correspondence theory of truth, which implies a direct correspondence or relationship between interpretations and empirical reality, either in the psyche or the world. Interpretations are treated as hypotheses which are thought to be either "true" or "false." Jungian analysts are thus inclined to draw direct relationships between symbols in the child's play or art and what they are believed to signify in the psychic reality of the child. This mode of interpretation has been criticized by phenomenologists, who reject symbolic interpretations that are one-directional or overly general, as in both cases symbols are reduced to signs (Bachelard 1958/64). However, Jung himself and many play therapists realize that interpretation remains a complex matter, and that the meanings of symbols can only be approximately known. Effective interpretation can lead to a heightened awareness and a possible reuniting with the Self which in turn leads to renewal and transformation.

Towards a phenomenological hermeneutic approach

The existential phenomenological and Jungian analytic play-therapy approaches with children reveal a considerable degree of similarity despite their theoretical differences. Both approaches recognize the primordial and powerful role of images in representing meanings, and see play as the child's natural language for expressing and exhibiting his world. Both also use active imagination in the therapeutic dialogue and in creatively confronting and working through psychological tensions and barriers. Being actively involved in the child's imaginative play and indirectly dialoguing with the child through his created play and art images are actually a key technique in imagery-communication that seems to have developed independently of Jung.

The fundamental theoretical differences between the phenomenological and Jungian approaches can be traced to their epistemological view of the subject–object relationship which in turn shapes their understanding of personality and of play therapy. The existential phenomenological stance of seeing the person and her world as inseparably interwoven forms the foundation for a view of play as an embodied mode of being-in-the-world and of images as the appearance of things around us in their pathic character. Here imaginative play in a therapeutic context calls for a therapeutic understanding of the child's personal meanings in the context of his life-world. Fantasy is de-emphasized and seen as a passive and withdrawn form of relatedness. For the Jungians, on the other hand, with their intrapsychic focus and their natural scientific epistemological leanings, fantasy is of utmost importance, and play becomes an overly subjective phenomenon. Images are primarily seen as symbolic expressions of the unconscious archetypes and archetypal activity, and as such they reveal common and universal meanings albeit tailored to the child's individual life circumstances. The analyst in turn aims to interpret the hidden, symbolic meanings revealed in the child client's play or art. These key differences once again raise the question of the meaning of play and the role of understanding versus interpretation in play therapy.

In addressing the question of play and the hermeneutic tension between phenomenological understanding and Jungian interpretation of images and symbols in play therapy, we will turn to the phenomenological hermeneutics of Gadamer and Ricoeur. These authors have extended the object of hermeneutic understanding and interpretation beyond written texts to include play, art and verbal dialogues. Herein they have in principle opened the door towards a phenomenological hermeneutic approach to play therapy. In his ontological concept of play, Gadamer (1960/89) succeeds in moving beyond previous psychological theories in establishing play as an autonomous phenomenon in its own right. In his theory of interpretation, Ricoeur (1969/74, 1981/89) bridges the gap between understanding and interpretation in revealing that they are different phases of the same process. In doing so, he moves beyond previous dichotomous views between understanding and interpretation that have so plagued the field of psychotherapy (Mook 1994). Applying these hermeneutic contributions to phenomenological and Jungian play therapies will enable us to start crossing over previous divides and bring these disciplines closer together in a potentially fruitful and mutually enriching way.

In recent developments, Lubbers (1988) took the initiative of integrating imagery-communication as a basic principle within a broader phenomenological hermeneutic approach. Herein he has expanded his earlier method of narrating through imagery and gives more weight to the role of language and interpretation. A hermeneutic approach in practice implies that both therapist and child enter the hermeneutic circle of question and answer and together search for the "most probable" interpretation of the child's problematic life-world.[1] With rich clinical illustrations, Lubbers effectively demonstrates the power and usefulness of his approach. Informed and inspired by the ongoing work of Lubbers, the writings of Gadamer and Ricoeur, and my own extensive clinical experience, I believe that a phenomenological hermeneutic approach to play therapy is not only possible but eminently suitable for understanding and interpreting the meaning of children's expressions through words and imagery (Mook 1991, 1994).

In his invaluable writings on play, Gadamer (1960/89) anew illuminates this foundational human phenomenon. Where previous phenomenologists focused on the reciprocal relationship between the player and his play object, Gadamer goes a step further in asserting the primacy of play over the player. He points out that play itself masters the player and draws him into its spell, and that this absorption of the player into his play frees him from the burden of reality. In the medial movements between the player and his play object, ever new configurations are created that order the play and lend it its particular structure. Gadamer sees this structure of play as an autonomous whole that rises above the subjectivity of the player and above the reality of his world. He stresses that the function and sole purpose of play is to represent its own meanings. In his words: "In the representation of play, what *is* emerges. In it is produced and brought to light what otherwise is constantly hidden and withdrawn" (p. 101). In other words, Gadamer sees the representation of play as revelatory and recognizes its essence as truth. As such, play is ontologically prior to the player. The player in turn discovers his own self-presentation in his play by subordinating himself to it and listening to what it has to say. In the therapeutic context, we could say that the imaginative play of a child has a story to tell to the child and his therapist as it reveals meanings about the child and his life-world that were previously concealed. We will attempt briefly to illustrate this viewpoint by turning to a clinical case vignette.

Mary, age seven, was referred for play therapy because of increasingly difficult "acting-out" behaviour and defiance of authority at home and at school. Six months earlier she and her three older siblings had tragically lost both their beloved parents in a fatal car accident. The family had been close-knit and very religious. During her first session, Mary appeared initially cheerful and expressed her belief that her parents are now very happy because they are in heaven and are listening to the singing of angels. She denied any feelings of loss or sadness and refused to talk about it any more. In the sandbox, she started to shuffle the sand and soon a small heap of sand was transformed in a big mountain. At its foot, she built a whole village with many houses, a school, a church and other public buildings, and landscaped it with trees and parks. In several scenes, she acted out peaceful family and village life with loving and caring relationships between parents and children. Suddenly her mood changed and she seriously announced that the mountain was actually a volcano but it had been dormant for "hundreds of years." Now it had suddenly come alive and in the dark of night started to pour out lava. With mounting intensity, she played out how the lava reached the houses of the sleeping villagers and how it destroyed everything in its blazing fury, leaving only devastation and destruction in its wake. Overcome with shock, she abruptly left the scene.

This play starkly contrasts with Mary's conscious belief about the loss of her parents and reveals in a dramatic fashion the magnitude of the devastating pain and loss brought upon her. Her imaginative play brings her suffering to light through primordial images that speak on the one hand of safe, secure and loving family relationships and a peaceful village life, and on the other hand of unexpected, traumatic devastation by means of cosmic forces beyond the control of human beings. The play reflects a world that is not only personal but also familial and communal, and that expresses as such personal as well as commonly shared meanings. The play also harbours universal meanings in its symbolic imagery of fire and cosmic disaster. It speaks of what the player cannot say, and through the power of its images, begins to reveal to the child and her therapist what needs to be known and worked through in order to help this child come to terms with the unspeakable tragedy that befell her.

With Gadamer, the key question of the meaning of play achieves a new focus and a new horizon. In its emphasis on the primacy of play over the player, it warns that we lose the essence of play if we reduce it to overly subjective explanations. It hence poses a direct challenge to the Jungian viewpoint. At the same time, it challenges the phenomenological position by saying that the meanings revealed in play reach beyond the child's personal meanings of his life-world and may include commonly shared and universal meanings. In its revelatory character, play can be seen as bringing to awareness what is not yet known, or what was previously unconscious, as long as the unconscious is seen as world-related and rooted in sedimented layers of lived experience. Imaginative play in therapy thus calls on both the child and the therapist to listen to what it has to say in that it reveals its primordial meanings and its own truth, beyond the child's or the therapist's level of awareness. These meanings may be obscure and symbolic, and may call for depth interpretation.

In phenomenological hermeneutics, the concepts of understanding and interpretation are seen as closely related in that interpretation always involves understanding and understanding always has an interpretative dimension. Ricoeur agrees with Gadamer that understanding is always based upon an existential pre-understanding and as such is rooted in history and tradition. To understand is to grasp and be grasped by the meaning of a text as a whole. In his novel theory of interpretation, Ricoeur (1981/89) does not only incorporate the process of understanding but also that of explanation. Returning to the epistemological questions raised by Dilthey, he argues convincingly that Dilthey's dichotomy between explanation and understanding as the respective methods of the natural versus the human sciences is not tenable and has created a great deal of confusion. He emphatically rejects this dichotomy and resolves the problematic in his novel theory of interpretation which involves both understanding and explanation as a dialectic within one hermeneutic circle. Ricoeur points out that this dialectic is already present in a dialogical situation when we explain something to someone so that he can understand.

In Ricoeur's theory of interpretation, the first phase of understanding involves a naive grasp of the text as a whole that takes into account the multiplicity of meanings and the potential horizons that can be actualized in different ways. The second phase involves a more sophisticated sense of understanding that is supported by explanatory procedures. Explanation calls for a degree of distantiation. Here the reference to reality is temporarily suspended and the sense of the text as a whole is subjected to explanatory hypotheses to unfold a range of propositions and reveal possible depth meanings which in turn point to a possible world. The process of interpretation involves the dialectic of distantiation and appropriation where the former enlarges the horizon of the text and the latter the horizon of the reader. In appropriation, the reader makes that which was initially alien his own and thus enlarges his self-understanding, which is the goal of hermeneutics. This goal is similar to that of psychotherapy where the therapist aims to make the unknown known or the unconscious conscious in order to increase the client's understanding of himself.

In the light of the writings of Gadamer and Ricoeur, a child's imaginative play can be seen as a figurative and symbolic expression that constitutes a text and calls for interpretation. In a hermeneutic approach to play, the relationship to the world of the play-text takes precedence over the relationship to the world of the player. We find in both Gadamer's concept of play and in Ricoeur's theory of interpretation an initial displacement of the subject who is subsequently reintroduced in a more modest role as all interpretation culminates in appropriation. In imaginative play, as in narrative fiction, the child can be seen as carrying out imaginative variations on reality which is kept at a distance and metamorphozed in the process. In the spirit of Ricoeur, we could indeed say that the world of play explodes the world of the player. The power of imaginative play lies in this metamorphosis and redescription of reality.

A hermeneutic approach to interpretation in play therapy can be seen as a bridge between the existential phenomenological and Jungian approaches in that it enables us to incorporate the tension between phenomenological understanding and Jungian interpretation in one theory of interpretation. Within this perspective, both therapeutic approaches are involved in the processes of understanding within interpretation but their focus differs. The first phase of understanding is mostly operative in the phenomenological approach of imagery-communication where the therapist aims to understand the child's personal meanings. The second phase, which involves a more comprehensive process of understanding and draws on explanatory procedures, can be seen as operating mainly in a Jungian analytic approach where the analyst aims to uncover symbolic depth meanings that extend beyond the personal world of the child to commonly shared and universal meanings.

In interpreting the text of Mary's play, for example, a phenomenological understanding reveals the child's personal meanings of being totally overwhelmed and devastated by the magnitude of the tragedy that befell her in the dramatic loss of both her parents. In the eruption of the volcano and its destruction of everybody and everything around it, Mary imaginatively extends her personal tragedy to a whole community of people and shows us at the same time how her former familial and communal embeddedness have been fundamentally destroyed. At a deeper level, the play seems to point to symbolic depth meanings that may call for Jungian explanatory hypotheses. The therapist is faced with the challenge of interpreting the possible meanings of the ever-powerful symbolic images of fire, death and cosmic disaster which, in Jungian terms, are archetypal and rooted in our collective unconscious. What do they mean in this particular play and how do these meanings relate to Mary's life-world? A Jungian interpretation might suggest that Mary's play is an attempt to re-create a safe world in view of her own powerful "volcanic" feelings that threaten to devastate her world *for a second time*. Thus the volcano is no longer only an image of the devastation of her life-world but a psychological image of her archetypal shadow that she aims to control through a denial of her unspeakable grief. Such a partial interpretation may explain at least to some extent her continuing anxiety and denial. At the same time, it exemplifies the one-sidedness of a Jungian interpretation.

In the practice of a hermeneutic approach to play therapy, the therapist and the child are both active participants in that they enter the hermeneutic circle together and within this dialogical structure, contribute to the creation of an imaginative play narrative as well as to its understanding and interpretation. In a stance of receptive openness, the therapist should let herself be grasped by the play as a whole and be open to its horizon of possible meanings. If called for, symbolic meanings could be submitted to Jungian explanatory hypotheses within the hermeneutic circle of question and answer. In their therapeutic dialogue, the therapist should let her perspective of understanding be shaped and modified by the child's perspective such that the fusion of their mutual horizons of meaning will culminate in a new understanding and move the therapeutic process forward.

The difficult question of the validity of interpretation needs to be further addressed. In discussing the question of truth and verification in psychoanalysis, Ricoeur (1981/89) points out that the truth claim made by psychoanalysis lies in increasing the patient's self-recognition by helping him overcome the distortions that have led to his misunderstanding. As this takes place within a verbal dialogue between therapist and patient, we are dealing with a "saying-true" to oneself and to the other (p. 265). A similar truth claim could be made by phenomenological and Jungian therapists. We could add that in play therapy with children, we are not only dealing with a "saying-true" but also with a "doing-true" in reference to the child's play actions, and that both truth claims seek to be reconciled in a play-story. Such truth claims are narrative in character as we are dealing with self and other recognition in the contexts of stories or texts, and call for the use of narrative criteria. In the practice of play therapy, the therapist applies the text-in-context principle of hermeneutics, and the narrative criteria of coherence and consistency within and between texts. This means that in the interpretation of imaginative play, all partial insights and explanatory fragments need to be verified within the play-text as a whole in a coherent and consistent manner. Once understood as a whole, the play text should be seen in the contexts of other plays, art products and therapeutic dialogues and finally in the context of the child's real life-story. For in play therapy, be it phenomenological or Jungian, the therapist enables the child to tell his story that needs to be told, and to build and rebuild out of the fragments of a distorted life a new and coherent narrative that is intelligible and recognizable for himself and for others. Understanding in play therapy can thus be said to have a narrative character and partial explanatory statements need to be integrated in a narrative structure of interpretation.

From a hermeneutic perspective, existential phenomenological and Jungian analytic play therapy approaches can be fruitfully brought together under the umbrella of a human science that is philosophically grounded in phenomenological hermeneutics, and methodologically in a hermeneutic circle wherein the interpretation of texts are validated by narrative criteria of truth. Such an approach can provide the Jungians with an epistemological foundation that is consistent with Jung's phenomenological and hermeneutic intentions, his emphasis on meaning rather than facts, and on understanding rather than explanation (Brooke 1991). It will counteract the remnants of Cartesian thinking in analytical psychology and may help to overcome persisting theoretical confusions and ambiguities. A narrative model can be seen as congenial to the Jungians with their emphasis on the imaginal and metaphorical nature of the psyche, and their therapeutic intent to construct a coherent and intelligible narrative of the Self out of fragments of unconscious experiences that are brought to light in the course of successful analysis. Adhering to narrative truth, rather than to their customary correspondence theory of truth, will make it possible for Jungian analysts to verify symbolic and archetypal depth hypotheses within a hermeneutic circle of interpretation. This mode of interpretation will be more acceptable to phenomenologists and could in turn add depth and density to their understanding of the unconscious and the role of common and universal meanings in human life.

Truth and validation in psychotherapy, and in play therapy in particular, remain a complex matter for they demand that we articulate not only the interrelationships between therapeutic theory and practice, but also their intricate relatedness to hermeneutics and narrative. In this chapter, we have only made a beginning with this momentous task and aimed to show that it is pregnant with possibilities for the future development of play therapy.

Note

1 The term "most probable" is used by Lubbers in following Hirsch's (1976) epistemological hermeneutics. However, the term is admittedly awkward because

it seems to smuggle in once again the correspondence theory of truth and the assumption of a real, empirical ground to meaning. The term suggests that interpretations are still hypotheses, softened from "true" or "false" to "probable." As I shall argue later, perhaps it is preferable to say that the "best" interpretation is the one that best links together the concrete facts and images into a coherent narrative, and that the veracity of the interpretation is to be found in terms of human meaning rather than in terms of empirical measures. In this way a consistently hermeneutic sensibility can replace an outdated and ultimately untenable "epistemological hermeneutics." For this critique of Hirsch see Madison (1988).

References

Allan, J. (1988/94) *Inscapes of the Child's World*, Dallas: Spring Publications.

Bachelard, G. (1958/64) *The Poetics of Space*, Boston: Beacon Press.

Brooke, R. (1991) *Jung and Phenomenology*, New York: Routledge.

Bowyer, R. (1970) *The Lowenfeld World Technique*, Oxford: Pergamon.

Buytendijk, F.J.J. (1932) *Het Spel van Mens en Dier*, Amsterdam: Kosmos.

De Domenico, G. (1994) "Jungian play therapy techniques," in K.J. O'Connor and C.E. Schaeffer (eds) *Handbook of play therapy*, Vol. 2, New York: Wiley.

Fordham, M. (1969) *Children as Individuals*, New York: G.P. Putnam's Sons.

Gadamer, H.G. (1960/89) *Truth and Method*, New York: Crossroads.

Hellendoorn, J. (1988) "Imaginative play techniques in psychotherapy with children," in C.E. Schaeffer (ed.) *Innovative Interventions in Child and Adolescent Therapy*, New York: Wiley.

Hirsch, E.D. (1976) *The Aims of Interpretation*, Chicago: University of Chicago Press.

Jung, G. (1921) "Psychological Types," *CW* 6.

Jung, G. (1962) *Memories, Dreams, Reflections*, New York: Pantheon Books.

Kalff, D.M. (1966) *Sandspiel*, Zurich: Rascher Verlag.

Kwakkel-Scheffer, J.J.C. (1983) *Beelden in woorden*, Lisse: Swets & Zeitlinger.

Langeveld, M.J. (1955) "Bevrijding door beeldcommunicatie," *Nederlandsche Tijdschrift van de Psychologie*, 2, 443–455.

Lubbers, R. (1971) *Voortgang en Nieuw Begin in de Opvoeding*, Gent: Van Gorcum.

Lubbers, R. (1988) *Psychotherapie Door Beeld en Begripsvorming*, Nijmegen: Dekker & Van de Vegt.

Madison, G. (1988) *The Hermeneutics of Postmodernity*, Bloomington: Indiana University Press.

Merleau-Ponty, M. (1962) *The Phenomenology of Perception*, trans. C. Smith, London: Routledge.

Mook, B. (1991) "The significance of hermeneutics to child psychotherapy," *Journal of Psychiatry and Neuroscience*, 16, 3, 182–187.

Mook, B. (1994) "Therapeutic play: from interpretation to intervention," in J. Van der Hellendoorn, R. Kooij, and B. Sutton-Smith (eds) *Play and Intervention*, Albany: SUNY Press.

Neumann, E. (1973) *The Child*, New York: Putnam's Sons.

Ricoeur, P. (1969/74) *The Conflict of Interpretations*, Evanston: Northwestern University Press.

Ricoeur, P. (1981/89) *Hermeneutics and the Human Sciences*, Cambridge: Cambridge University Press.

Rumke, H.C. (1949/65) *Karakter en aanleg in verband met het ongeloof*, Amsterdam: Ten Have.

Ryce-Menuhin, J. (1992) *Jungian Sandplay*, London: Routledge.

Strasser, S. (1963/80) *Phenomenology and the Human Sciences*, Atlanta Highlands: Humanities Press.

Straus, E. (1930/82) *Man, Time and World*, Pittsburgh: Duquesne University Press.

Vermeer, E. (1955) *Spel en Spelpaedagogische Problemen*, Utrecht: Byleveld.

Van Lennep, J. (1958) *Beleving en verbeelding in het tekenen*, Amsterdam.

EDITOR'S INTRODUCTION

John Haule discusses something that is central to Jungian analysis but is almost entirely part of the oral tradition. For that reason alone it is a fascinating study. It concerns the questions of subjectivity, consciousness, authority, and agency in therapeutic work, and shows that the center of gravity for each of these terms is shifted – from ego to Self. What Ricoeur argued with regard to Freud's theory is clearly illustrated here with regard to Jungian therapeutic praxis: that subjectivity, consciousness, and reflection are no longer mutually implicated. The clinical significance of Haule's chapter therefore reaches beyond Jungian analysis, through psychotherapy more generally, to questions about anthroplogy: the structure of human self-understanding and interaction.

Haule's approach is unique in this volume as his method is an empirical phenomenology of verbal accounts of what it means to "analyze from the Self" (or to be analyzed like that!). Consistent with a research tradition that was pioneered at Duquesne University, but has also been developed at Rhodes University, Haule appropriates Husserl's *eidetic* method of "free imaginative variation" in a concrete, empirical way. He analyzes the essential structures of the experience of "analysis from the Self" that are described in these first-hand verbal accounts. This paper is thus a good example of descriptive, empirical phenomenology.

14

ANALYZING FROM THE SELF: AN EMPIRICAL PHENOMENOLOGY OF THE "THIRD" IN ANALYSIS

John Ryan Haule

Introduction

Jung often spoke of his approach to psychotherapy as "analyzing from the Self", to which he contrasted "prestige analysis," based on persona, and "ego-centered analysis," driven by a fear of the unconscious. This chapter explicates "analyzing from the Self" phenomenologically by attending to reports from Jung's close associates and students who speak of the uncanny way he addressed their deepest issues directly. Three dimensions of *Mitwelt* are distinguished within the analytic *temenos*: (a) the social adaptation and inauthenticity of the persona field, (b) the critical reality-testing in the interaction between two egos, and (c) the imaginal "gathering" of the Self field.

The expression "analyzing from the Self" is nowhere to be found in Jung's *Collected Works*. Yet if we pay attention to those who knew Jung personally, who analyzed with him, and who trained in the early days of the Zurich Institute when Jung was still alive, we find that the notion of "analyzing from the Self" expresses something essential about how Jung understood his unique contribution to the therapeutic enterprise. This chapter takes its data from what might be called the "oral tradition" in Jungian studies, what Jung's close associates have to tell us about their meetings with him, how he influenced them, and what it was like to engage with him, Self-to-Self. Such accounts enable us to distinguish three modes of analytic discourse: (a) that which proceeds from the Self, (b) that which is dominated by persona, and (c) that which relies heavily upon the discriminations of the ego.

Experiencing the self in analysis: First person reports

Reports from Jung's patients and students

In his essay, *Reflections on Professional Deformation*, Robert Stein (1988: 151–61) recounts five meetings he had with Jung on the topic of "analyzing from the Self." In the first, Stein has an analytic hour with Jung to which he has brought a list of questions, but Jung is "in an expansive mood" and just "rambles on," never giving the young American a chance to speak. Stein discovers, however, that Jung is addressing all of his concerns. It is a profound encounter and Stein goes away "elated and overwhelmed." The second meeting takes place in a seminar where Jung devotes nearly two hours to answering a question Stein has submitted. Stein experiences Jung as the "Great Man," who humbly refuses to identify with the Great Man archetype. Furthermore, Stein accurately anticipates every word Jung says. It is an ecstatic encounter, and Stein is inflated for hours afterwards until an "*enantiodromia*" sets in leaving him depressed for weeks. The third meeting also takes place in a seminar, where Jung speaks of the necessity for the analyst to be "natural, spontaneous, open, vulnerable, and unprotected by the professional persona." An Italian candidate asks whether this sort of procedure will not enable the shadow to enter the analytic field. Jung responds immediately, "Well, of course!" There is a moment of embarrassed silence, and then the seminar begins to chuckle over the foolishness of the question.

Disappointed that there was little talk of these matters in the courses and supervision he was receiving at the Zurich Institute, Stein transferred to the London Institute. There, again, he was disappointed and complained to his supervisor that there was too much of ego in the London approach. His supervisor responded, "Well, Jung may be able to trust the Self, but most of us have to rely on our ego." Shaken, Stein returned to Zurich and arranged a meeting with Jung: "With great passion I told him of my fear that the London school was moving regressively back into traditional Freudian ego psychology. He was very supportive, reassuring me that there was nothing to fear because in time the Self would win out."

By the end of his training in Zurich, Stein found himself far removed from "the ego-centered world" and totally committed "to serving the life of the soul." He was worried that he was too poorly adapted to the extraverted world he had to return to in the United States, and addressed a question to Jung in a seminar: "How can an individual carry this new spirit of individuation back into a world that has no adequate vessels to contain it? Do we not need, as Jesus said, new bottles for the new wine?" Jung "responded irritably and cruelly by saying that I would not have asked such a question if I had understood the concept of the Self; and for good measure, to really put me in my place, he made sure to let me know that in Biblical times they used wine-skins, not bottles."

Some thirty years later, Stein was still wrestling with this shadowy and unfeeling response from Jung and had arrived at a few conclusions of his own. Surely his book *Incest and Human Love* (Stein 1973/84) is one attempt to come to grips with "analyzing from the Self." He gives another in the article I have been summarizing, an incident in which he and his analysand both fall asleep during an analytic hour and the analysand has a dream which transforms the analysis. The burnt-out businessman realizes that he has been in analysis in order to dispose of his depression so that he can get on with his old life as he had envisioned it before he became depressed. The dream tells him that he is in analysis in order to discover his soul, that he has to relinquish his old life and learn to live a life centered in soul.

Although Stein's struggle with the notion of "analyzing from the Self" is more complete than most, many of those who knew Jung personally have similar stories to report. Marvin Spiegelman, for instance, tells of a final meeting he had with Jung in 1959, upon his graduation from the Zurich Institute. At first the two of them had nothing to say to one another and fell silent.

> Then [Jung] began to speak, from out of himself somewhere. He spoke of his own life. Throughout all this apparent soliloquy, I was totally present too and I had the experience, subsequently reported by others also, that Jung was "speaking to my condition," and addressing himself to all my problems, fears, concerns, and deep desires. Most of all, it was an experience of Self speaking to Self.
>
> (Spiegelman 1982: 87–9)

In the documentary film *Matter of Heart* (Whitney and Whitney 1983), Hilde Kirsch tells of an analytic session she had in 1960, when Jung was 85. She told him only the first half of her very long dream out of respect for his age and health. Then, "He just started to talk." At first she failed to see the relevance of what he was saying; but, "Then suddenly he said, 'Oh, that is as if you dream' and he told me the second part of my dream which I hadn't told him." Mrs Kirsch comments: "It was really as if he was always in, inside of your unconscious and not trespassing, but because he has been whatever one was, and so he knew how to be there." In the same film, Liliane Frey-Rohn tells of a similar event:

> You could come into his room in analysis, and he was just speaking about the dreams you had the night before, last night, not knowing them, but he was, he was involved. He was so transparent for people, and that was the fascinating thing in the relationship with Jung. Therefore, everybody who knew Jung had the feeling he speaks one's own language.

There are many such stories, but in some of them we hear more of the subjective state of Jung's analysand. For example the Australian, Rix Weaver, speaks of an interview that began with some small talk about her native continent. Then Jung asked her if there was something she wished to ask:

> All thoughts of dreams left me and my question surprised me, appearing as it seemed, of its own accord. "What," said I, "is the difference between me and that table?" In the company of the Great Man it seemed as if I was aware on a different level of the oneness of all things.
>
> (Weaver 1982: 91–5)

Jane Wheelwright's encounter with Jung in the 1930s is even more dramatic.

> It was hard going with Jung because, once in his presence, one felt as though all the surrounding matter had turned into whizzing molecules. Everything there seemed to be moving, melting, changing forms. Everything stirred. Reality blurred, conversation happened unplanned. I felt someone, not me, spoke through me and someone not Jung was speaking through him. There was also the feeling of being swept into the depths of a perilous, dangerous underworld but since Jung had descended into this strange world and emerged so could I. In his presence I did not register on the difference of our statures! An archetype had taken over? Whatever it was, it seemed to be creating before my eyes and ears and senses a model of the changed person I was meant finally to become. Trying the new me on me, so to speak. Equally strange was Jung. Instead of being the doctor who cures you, he was allowing himself to be equally affected. . . . Two people were caught in a vice [*sic*] that was forcing them to undergo an important rearrangement of themselves that had significance – some meaning far beyond them.
>
> (Wheelwright 1982: 97–105)

Jung's experience of the self in analysis

Now that we have a fairly vivid feel for what it was like to be Jung's patient in an analysis from the Self, we might wonder how such events felt to him. His English friend, Eddy Bennet, gives us an overview, paraphrasing what Jung told him in 1950:

> He had learned never to start an interview beyond a few pleasantries – "How are you?" – but to wait for the patient because the instincts,

> the archetypes, lie in between and we don't know what may be there. But at times in conversation some topic occurs to him for no apparent reason, and he talks about it and finds it is just the right thing. For instance the other day he began talking to a woman doctor about his African tour and snakes, and wondered why he was telling her all this; then it turned out to be absolutely relevant for he discovered that she was deeply interested in these things. So we wait and the instincts guide us.
>
> (Bennett 1985: 25)

In this passage Jung seems to be telling us he is acting in a largely unconscious manner when these marvelous events occur. Such an impression is strengthened when we consider what he said to Swiss journalist, Emil Fischer (Fischer 1977: 166): "If someone were to ask me: What are you thinking just now? – I wouldn't know. I think unconsciously."

This impression is made more explicit in the story Jung often told about his one-session success with a young school teacher from the bucolic Canton of Solothurn who suffered a terrible insomnia. He started by telling her that falling asleep was just a matter of letting herself go, like the sail of a boat that simply goes with the wind. As this first ploy earned him a blank stare, Jung went on to describe the feel of the wind, water, and tiller, hoping to draw her into an imaginative and emotional experience of the wind. But the next thing he knew, he was humming a lullaby about a boat on the Rhine that his mother used to sing. By the end of the session, he was rocking her in his arms as he softly crooned. In an interview with journalist Georges Duplain, Jung hints at how he experienced this session:

> How was I to explain to [her doctor] that I had simply listened to something within myself? I had been quite at sea. How was I to tell him that I had sung her a lullaby with my mother's voice? Enchantment like that is the oldest form of medicine. But it all happened outside my reason: It was not until later that I thought about it rationally and tried to arrive at the laws behind it. She was cured by the grace of God.
>
> (Duplain 1977: 419)

What rational sense Jung must have made of incidents like this is suggested in the notes Marion Baynes made at a talk Jung gave to the students of the Zurich Institute in 1958. Other talks, recorded by other students, agree with these notes – even to the choice of words Jung used. Clearly it was a favorite theme for him in his last decade, in which he described the Self which may come to presence between analyst and analysand as "the Great Man, the 2,000,000-year-old Man."

> Analysis is a long discussion with the Great Man – an unintelligent attempt to understand him. Nevertheless, it is an attempt, as both patient and analyst understand it. . . . Work until the patient can see this. It, the Great Man, can at one stroke put an entirely different face on the thing – or anything can happen. In that way you learn about the peculiar intelligence of the background; you learn the nature of the Great Man. You learn about yourself against the Great Man – against his postulates. This is the way through things, things that look desperate and unanswerable. The point is, *how are you yourself going to answer this*? . . . The unconscious gives you that peculiar twist that makes the way possible.
>
> (Baynes 1977: 360–1)

If there is a difference between the Great Man and the Self – and I doubt there is – it would lie in the fact that Jung speaks of only one Great Man present between analyst and analysand. This is made even more explicit in a gesture he made to Professor Charles Boudouin of Geneva (Boudouin 1977: 80) as early as 1934 to indicate the "mutual unconscious communication and penetration [that] appears to take place" between therapist and patient: "With brief, firm gestures he touched first my forehead, then his own, and thirdly drew a giant circle with his hand in the space between us; . . . 'In short, one doesn't dream here, and one doesn't dream here, one dreams there.' "

Jung sometimes spoke of Self as though it were a private possession, each of us having a Self deep within our psyche, distinct from ego but nevertheless not completely unconscious. Clearly "soul," "Great Man," and "Self" can be used interchangeably to refer to the unitary state experienced in an "analysis from the Self." Furthermore, this notion of a personified superior being which comes to presence between therapist and patient is no mere theoretical abstraction for Jung. For, as he told the students at the Zurich Institute: "If you take the unconscious intellectually, you are lost. It is not a conviction, not an assumption. It is a *Presence*. It is a *fact*. It is *there*. It *happens*."

Analyzing from the self: a summary

If we summarize all these "oral tradition" reports on Jung's analyzing from the Self, we arrive at a fairly clear picture of "analyzing from the Self." Jung wanders off on a soliloquy, following a vague "hunch," which he describes as "listening within." He does not know where he is going with his monologue, but proceeds "unconsciously." Evidently further hunches make themselves known as he talks, and he follows them as well. When this procedure is successful, he finds that he is "closing in" on issues of central importance to his analysand. He describes his own subjective conditions for this hunch-driven monologue as speaking "spontaneously," while he "holds himself open, vulnerable, and unprotected by his professional persona." He is unconcerned by the possibility that his "shadow may enter" the interaction with his patient – apparently believing that if the analysand feels cruelly treated, this is what the Great Man requires. The Great Man is neither Jung himself nor the patient, but a Third direction-giving "Presence." It is the Self or soul, as an unconscious spirit which guides the process. Sometimes the Great Man may be conceived as an unconscious factor within Jung himself, to which he "listens." At other times the Great Man is understood to be the patient's Self or potential wholeness which he is addressing. But most frequently the Great Man is experienced as a Third partner who is within neither partner but rather dwells in the space between them both. Alternately it is described as the "background" against which they meet and in dialogue with which they come to understand themselves in a new and more adequate manner.

While all this is going on, the patient is deeply affected. The world of habitual, everyday consciousness dissolves into "whizzing molecules." The patient no longer knows who she is: "What is the difference between me and that table?" She has the sense that neither she nor Jung is directing the interaction; rather "someone, not she," is speaking through her, and "someone, not Jung," is speaking through him. Sometimes this altered state of consciousness is described as a Self-to-Self encounter, and sometimes as directed by a Third agent, a "2,000,000 year-old Man." It is an "overwhelming" experience which may result in "elation," "inflation," or a "cruel" belittlement. The patient often feels that her mind is being "read." Jung tells her the second half of the dream she withheld from him, or he starts right in speaking as though he had witnessed her untold dreams of the night before. She feels "transparent," a subjective condition that sometimes is experienced as gratifying and sometimes as a dangerous descent into "a perilous underworld."

A phenomenological description

The language Jung and his associates are using in these accounts has a distinctly mythological and metaphysical character. Nevertheless, in contrast with most of Jung's published writings, these reports from the "oral tradition" of Jungian psychology have an experience-near flavor that lends itself very well to the language and style of a phenomenology that scrutinizes our "lifeworld." Although each of us constructs a lifeworld as an individually unique project, we encounter it as an unexamined given. Generally we enter analysis when our life has become burdensome and our perspective too limiting. In this context, neurosis represents an opportunity. Our discomfort leads us to a psychoanalytic set of heuristic questions. What *is* the life project we are living? Is there any possibility of altering it? What compelling interests and potential satisfactions have been systematically excluded and lie ready for discovery and implementation?

Analyzing from the ego

As a dialogue deliberately focused on problems inherent in the patient's lifeworld, analysis might well be conceived as the work of two "egos," two conscious/preconscious subjects engaged in a discourse designed to expose potential freedoms that have been lurking beneath the seeming "givens" of the patient's life. Looked at this way, the patient finds his life depressing, conflicted, and guilt-ridden because he has taken things for determined and immutable that actually might well be opened to critical reflection. There are actions he might take – if only the possibility of doing so would occur to him, if certain unexamined "givens" were only brought to light as the unwarranted assumptions they have always been.

Such an ego-to-ego dialogue is a deliberate enterprise based upon what the patient already knows about his lifeworld and what the analyst can uncover that is presently unknown but ready-to-be-known. The analyst is on the look-out for unconscious pseudo-philosophies in the patient's view of himself and of the life he is living, unrecognized rigidities that take the form of inflexible propositions. These may be identified by the flat tone with which they are uttered, a tone of voice that reveals a semi-conscious "internal monologue" by which the patient maintains his lifeworld as the freedom-denying structure it has become. The patient says, in effect, "My boss, my wife, my mother, is just like all the rest." Or, "I do my best to handle my life with integrity, and this is the trap it leads to." Upon hearing such unexamined statements from the patient, the analyst knows a "complex" has appeared in the ego-to-ego dialogue, a feeling-toned proposition characterized by resignation, rage, or sentimentality.

The patient has alluded to one of the unexamined conditions that limits his egohood. For ego, above all, is the conscious agency for establishing what is real and working out strategies for negotiating it. In the face of a "complex," or inflexible "internal monologue," the patient has ceased to "test" reality. He has fallen victim to an habitual and automatic theme, the "possession by a complex," that unconsciously establishes unwarranted limits to his freedom.

Analyzing from the ego is a subtle practice based on reality-testing. By posing questions the patient has failed to ask himself: "In what way is your boss like all the rest"; "how does integrity become a trap?" The analyst tests the reality of what has been grasped of the patient's lifeworld by opening questions that have not been posed and exposing implications that have been taken for granted. In this process the patient is induced to open up the closed and automatic responses that limit the free subjectivity of his potential egohood. Analyzing from the ego strives to restore to the domain of free and reality-testing subjectivity those issues that have unconsciously been closed off. In the course of this work, the patient becomes more fully the ego he has potentially always been. He participates more and more fully, freely, and competently in the ego-to-ego dialogue. Fewer and fewer automatic interruptions occur, as the patient's freedom to test the propositions limiting his lifeworld grows.

Analyzing from the persona

Jung advocated a style of analysis "unprotected by the professional persona" in which the shadow was very likely to appear. In some accounts, he made no attempt to hide his disgust for those who practice "prestige psychology," "satisfying their vanity by preaching [his ideas] to others" (von Franz 1975: 6) instead of letting them "silently change their lives" (Hannah 1976: 323). From this we may gather that "prestige" analysis is characterized by the therapist's identification with the role of analyst – as one who possesses a saving doctrine and perhaps has even been touched personally by Jung himself. In hiding behind such a professional persona, the analyst maintains a position outside of and above the patient's struggles. Such an approach perpetuates the fiction that the analyst is a person of high prestige and great power who may be able to "heal" neurotic individuals by teaching them what they need to know.

Analyzing from the persona, however, must be more than a rite of self-glorification on the part of the analyst. If some sort of therapy really takes place, if the patient is changed and returns to her life with a sounder and more adequate attitude, consciousness must have been raised; work must have been done. To clarify the nature of this work, we cannot stop short with the usual description of persona as a mask we don – a kind of false self to hide behind in our dealings with the social world. Surely it may be that, but it is more. It is a dimension of our lifeworld. Persona is the strategy we pursue to adapt to and negotiate the world of "collective consciousness." Our social/cultural life together as human beings, citizens of a certain nation, and members of whatever sub-societies we may inhabit, affects us – for the most part unconsciously – as a field of influence. When the ideas, assumptions, and feeling values of society act upon us unconsciously, our experience is somewhat analogous to that of iron filings that arrange themselves along the invisible lines of force in a magnetic field. Without acknowledging it, *we* think what "everybody" thinks.

Our lifeworld is never free of the influences of a persona field that demands conformity, promises prestige, and threatens us with marginalization and disdain. To the extent that we are conscious of persona-field influences as dystonic to our own lifestyle and values, we may struggle against them in an effort to give our lifeworld an individual integrity which is related to but not simply governed by the persona field. In every case, "my persona" is my unique stance toward and strategy for negotiating the persona field that influences us all.

From this perspective, neurosis is experienced as the discomfort we suffer from a conflict between the semi-conscious demands of the persona field and the personal requirement we innately feel to construct a unique lifeworld of personal authenticity. "Analyzing from the persona" is an interpersonal endeavor designed to make conscious this conflict over "prestige" issues. It is a dialogue which takes up the issue of the patient's lifeworld construction as a stance toward the persona field. Nevertheless, it is not necessarily a superficial endeavor, for consciousness raising *vis-à-vis* the persona field is never complete as long as the deeper integrity of the patient's lifeworld remains unaddressed.

This deeper dimension of the patient's life is largely comprised of what Jung calls "shadow," that aspect of her lifeworld that has remained unlived or lived sporadically through unconscious compulsions because it conflicts with the "prestige" she has been seeking in her inadequate attempts to strategize an adaptation to the persona field. Analyzing from the persona is, therefore, a dialogue that makes conscious the task of finding a stance and a strategy for negotiating the persona field. The patient finds an "ego," an agency of free choice midway between the requirements of persona-field adaptation and her disturbing and shadowy resistances to an inauthentic quest for social prestige. The shadowy resistances are brought to awareness and revalued as preliminary attempts to construct a unique, satisfying, and authentic lifeworld.

Analyzing from the Self

While ego- and persona-centered analyses may each be described as a dialogue between two people in which the analysand's experience, frustrations, and neurotic dead ends form the subject matter of the exchange, analyzing from the Self is a different sort of thing. In the dialogues we have described, the patient has taken time out from his everyday life to reflect upon it. Nevertheless, his life outside of the analytic meetings is the central issue, something like the "text" that the analytic dialogue strives to interpret. The patient reports upon his extra-analytic lifeworld and engages the analyst in a thematizing dialogue that seeks to make sense of his experience in order to open up the issues that he has unconsciously closed off or ignored.

The analytic Mitwelt

In analyzing from the Self, by contrast, the subject matter derives primarily not from the patient's life outside of the analytic meetings but from experiences that occur uniquely in the therapeutic encounters themselves. These analytic rendezvous take place within a kind of joint lifeworld in which analyst and analysand participate as equals. (Wheelwright: "Two people were caught in a [vise] that was forcing them to undergo an important rearrangement of themselves that had . . . some meaning far beyond them.")

In Jungian language, we might call this joint lifeworld a *temenos*, a sacred space "cut off" [*temno*] from the profane world, in which numinous events occur that are virtually unthinkable outside of the analytic temple. In attending to this jointly lived *temenos*, Jung refers to the lifeworld's capacity for intimacy and mutuality, its participation in a *Mitwelt*, a co-world, a single world lived in a shared manner.

By analogy, we might consider the nuclear family as the distinctive *Mitwelt* into which each of us has been born and within which we initially discover ourselves as unique individuals. The familial *Mitwelt* is in each case encountered by the child as simply "the world." Later, as the child finds extra-familial playmates and schoolrooms of peers under the direction of a teacher, she begins to notice that the familial *Mitwelt* is only one jointly lived world among many. She encounters a collision between lifeworlds – no doubt disturbing and gratifying by turns – that forces her to intensify the work of constructing a unique lifeworld of her own.

Later still, when she falls in love, she discovers a *Mitwelt* of a different kind – not one that has pre-existed her entry, but one that comes into existence in that numinous moment when she finds herself drawn into the eyes of her future lover. From this moment onward, she finds that her life has been gloriously "rearranged." The most important dimension of her lifeworld is now that region where it overlaps and dissolves into a oneness with the lifeworld of her lover. This newly forming erotic *Mitwelt* becomes her primary concern, even her obsession; it becomes the meaning-giving context wherein she and her lover reveal themselves and discover one another as their interactions jointly build a single shared world. Furthermore, the erotic *Mitwelt* she shares with her lover opens up new depths in her appreciation of herself so that her own lifeworld is enhanced. She returns to her everyday life renewed and deepened.

In similar fashion, the analytic *Mitwelt* is an intense realm of experience shared between analyst and analysand which begins the moment the two individuals meet. Like a personal lifeworld, it takes on an objective quality all its own and is constructed – for the most part unconsciously – by every move and countermove of the interaction. It is a world set apart, a *temenos*, which is entered at the beginning of each analytic session and exited at the end. Nevertheless, like the erotic *Mitwelt* just described, it has lasting effects upon the individual lives of the two participants. What takes place in the analytic *Mitwelt* is a process of disclosure and discovery, in which each participant's self-consciousness is broadened and deepened by the events, ordinary and numinous, that unfold.

Although every analysis – like every human relationship – builds its own unique *Mitwelt* through the rituals of choosing a place and hour set apart wherein the matters discussed and the intimacies shared are quite distinct from the affairs of everyday, an analysis that proceeds from the Self values that *Mitwelt* differently from other kinds of therapy. In analyses that center upon ego and persona, the *Mitwelt* itself remains in the background as the unacknowledged context for an interaction that reviews the patient's life-world as it is lived outside of the analytic *temenos*. An analysis which centers on the Self, however, makes the analytic *Mitwelt* alone the focus of its concern. The shared life of the participants becomes both the context and the content of the interaction. Analysis is, in this case, not so much a time and place set apart for reflection upon the analysand's neurotic issues as they manifest somewhere else but rather constitutes the here, the now, and the whole of their attention. In an analysis from the Self, the therapeutic *Mitwelt* obtrudes to the forefront and comes to presence as the living matter and the central issue of the work.

Transparency and the Self field

In an analysis from the Self, the *Mitwelt* makes itself felt as a dissolution of the everyday into "whizzing molecules," where one's habitual identity as an "ego" is "rearranged," and one is impressed above all by the oneness of all things. Here one's conscious and relatively consistent subjectivity is relativized in a manner not unlike what occurs under the influence of the persona field. One's impressions are drawn – as iron filings by a magnet – into a new and ego-dystonic configuration. But while the ideas, expectations, and values of the persona field are anything but unfamiliar, belonging as they do to public consensus, the unsettling and disorienting effects of a *Mitwelt* centered in Self may be as unfamiliar as an alien cosmos.

We might refer to this realm of experience as the *Self field*, suggesting by the word *field* the widely reported experience of encountering extraordinary impressions that feel as though they have been invisibly "induced," and by the word *Self* that numinous sense of oneness that attends our entry into an analytic *Mitwelt* that is truly "other" and more comprehensive than our everyday experience. In *Jung and Phenomenology*, Brooke (1991) offers us a language to name and articulate the two orders of subjectivity that Jung has called "ego" and "Self." The ego – or self-conscious subject – "appropriates" a world and makes it his own, while the Self more-or-less unconsciously "gathers" a world of much greater scope. Our Self is always out in front of our ego, gathering more than can ever be appropriated, assembling the unified background within which the foreground of our appropriated lifeworld constitutes a selection of favored memories, ideas, impressions, feelings, and the like. Compared with the appropriated world and the quality of "mine" that attends its subjectivity, the world gathered by the Self represents the implicit and rarely appreciated wholeness of our lifeworld as well as a subjectivity of improbable breadth and coherence.

Entry into a Self field subjects both parties to a dissolution of their appropriated lifeworlds. For both participants, the foreground of an habitual world-construction and ego-identity fades into a comprehensive background of numinous significance and sometimes terrifying otherness that is nevertheless in some sense "ours." The sharp clarity of world-appropriating egohood is overshadowed by a fuzzy and almost mystical awareness. The boundaries and limits of mainstream psychotherapy are lost. Analyst and analysand find themselves "transparent" to one another, just as their habitually limited worlds of experience have become transparent to a "background" that belongs to neither of them: "Not in my head, nor in your head, but there between us." They are encompassed by a *Mitwelt* of overwhelming extent, significance, and disorienting realness.

When Jung urges his students to be "natural, spontaneous, open, vulnerable, and unprotected by the professional persona," he is recommending that the analyst relinquish the two most familiar dimensions of every lifeworld: the appropriated world that is in each case "mine" and the persona field that involuntarily pulls us into line with what "everybody believes." Instead, Jung reports that he "listens within" and "thinks unconsciously." He favors a kind of "letting be" wherein he holds himself open for whatever may unexpectedly come to presence – an attitude very similar to what Heidegger (Heidegger 1968) and Meister Eckhart (Eckhart 1981) before him called *Gelassenheit.* It is a sort of "active passivity": "active" in the sense that it is a stance voluntarily assumed; "passive" in the sense that it eschews every kind of expectation and preordained therapeutic task, save for the anticipation that something unexpected will appear; and "active," again, in the sense that what comes to presence must be "taken up" – taken seriously no matter how irrational it may seem – and articulated. Even this active move of taking up and articulating remains "passive" in the sense that Jung does not know *why* he begins to "speak of Africa and snakes," to hum a lullaby, or peevishly to insist that in biblical times wine-skins were used rather than bottles.

In the spirit of *Gelassenheit*, Jung begins a soliloquy. If it were the usual sort of "internal monologue" by which each of us inadvertently maintains the inflexible and complex-ridden structure of our lifeworld, his speech would be heard as the idiosyncratic ramblings of a crotchety old man. But it is not. His analysands report "Jung was speaking to my condition, and addressing himself to all my problems, fears, concerns, and deep desires." He tells them the dreams they had withheld from him. While speaking from "out of himself," he explores their depths. His monologue is simultaneously both "his" and "theirs." Thus in an analysis from the Self, what comes to presence is a *Mitwelt* where Self encounters Self. When two appropriated worlds have dissolved into an encompassing realm of profound and disturbingly alien mutuality, "my" concerns are also "yours." Amidst "whizzing molecules," "two people undergo an important rearrangement of themselves that has some meaning far beyond them."

The 2,000,000-year-old Man

When Jung refers to the "background" of the *Mitwelt* he shares with a patient in an analysis from the Self as "the 2,000,000 year-old Man," he is making four separate claims: (a) the *Mitwelt* itself acts with a discernible intentionality so that it comes to presence as a Third agent; (b) because this agent is described as two million years old, the perspective of the "Third" extends far beyond the personal experience of himself or his analysand and encompasses the entire experience of the human race; (c) when he speaks of the 2,000,000-year-old Man in English, he uses the impersonal pronoun, *it*, implying that this agency is entirely impersonal; and (d) it is always *the* 2,000,000-year-old Man, suggesting that it is the same impersonal Third agency that comes to presence as a guiding force in every analysis that proceeds from the Self.

In the Self field an impersonal agency is discernible that manifests an intentionality the analyst can use as a guide. Clearly this is Jung's doctrine familiar to us as the intrapsychic Self which gathers a world much more comprehensive than any one of us is able to appropriate as "my" lifeworld. In the intrapsychic doctrine, consistently developed from *Symbols of Transformation* (Jung 1912/52) onward, "my" Self gathers a world which is revealed to me through fragmentary intimations (such as dreams, synchronicities, and waking fantasies often having a numinous character) that can be meaningfully assembled as the "personal myth" which connects "my" individual destiny with that of the human race, revealing a transcendent dimension to my personal lifeworld.

The oral tradition of the two million year-old Great Man – which apparently begins after the writing of *The Psychology of the Transference* (Jung 1946) in the mid-1940s – extends this doctrine to the meeting of analyst and analysand in the therapeutic *temenos*. Here, the Great Man which gathers an encompassing world of mythic significance is neither "my" Self nor "your" Self, but "ours." Furthermore, the Great Man functions as an inductive field, drawing memories and fantasies into presence which are likely to have an irrational and arbitrary character when viewed from the perspective of either individual's appropriated world. Nevertheless, when these are taken seriously, they are found to have a profound significance for both parties sharing the analytic *Mitwelt*.

If individuation (the goal of intrapsychic life) be construed along the lines that form the theme of "Two essays in analytical psychology" (Jung 1928), we could articulate the process phenomenologically as follows. Individuation is the appropriation of a lifeworld which hews a course midway between the adaptive pressures of the persona field and the mythic potentials of the Self field. Psychic life becomes a quirky, idiosyncratic "individualism" when it ignores these two forms of collective influence and is likely to lead to the dead end of neurosis, a one-sided isolation both from the social life of the present and from the timeless mythic realities of the human race. Alternatively, when our construction of a lifeworld *identifies* with the images and aspirations that come to presence through the fields either of the persona or of the Self, one becomes an impersonal stereotype of a human being, completely devoid of personal authenticity.

In the doctrine of the Great Man, individuation has been extended to the analytic *Mitwelt*, where the field-like forces of persona and Self are felt jointly. When Jung urges his students to be "unprotected by the professional persona," he recommends that they maintain a distance between themselves and the office of therapist and healer; for this would lock them into the persona field, where the analyst enters the therapeutic *Mitwelt* to "heal" and the analysand to "be healed." When limited by this power differential, analyst and analysand never leave the sphere of what has been appropriated as "mine," so that what is "ours" is never allowed to come to presence. To allow the Self field to come to presence, Jung urges his students to be "natural, spontaneous, open, and vulnerable." As analysts, we are to enter the therapeutic *Mitwelt* without presuppositions and in the unknowing spirit of *Gelassenheit*. Without predetermined goals, we are simply to be attentive to whatever comes to presence.

Hence the analyst's role in an analysis from the Self avoids the pitfall of "therapy as usual" by (a) refusing to accept the therapeutic task as expected by our public consensus and (b) maintaining a non-knowing expectancy (*Gelassenheit*) that is receptive to what the Self field may bring to presence. There is a third task and a third danger – namely that the analyst may identify with the Great Man and assume the role of a wise guru who has all the answers. How precarious a balance this may be – to speak the wisdom of the Great Man and yet never to believe one is the Great Man – may be intuited from Robert Stein's clumsy formulation: "Jung was the Great Man, but he refused to identify with the Great Man archetype." Jung's own account, as recalled by Marion Baynes, is much clearer: "Analysis is a long discussion with the Great Man – an unintelligent attempt to understand him. . . . You learn about yourself against the Great Man – against his postulates." Thus the analyst's third task is to take on the role of a listener who receives "It, the Great Man, the peculiar intelligence of the background," as the Third agent in their dialogue. The analyst assumes an attitude that implicitly asserts: "I'm not the Great Man, and you're not the Great Man. We have come together to hear what the monumental background has to tell us both." By taking a stance midway between the inductive forces of the persona field and of the Self field, the analytic partners may be guided along a course we might call "the joint individuation process of the therapeutic *Mitwelt*."

Analyzing from the self and humility

As a practicing Jungian analyst, I have found the writing of this essay to be a profoundly humbling experience. For, naturally enough, I have been led to ask myself again and again, "What is the style of analysis that I practice?" It has been easy to recognize my own work in the descriptions I have provided of analyses that proceed from the ego or from the persona. But do I ever analyze from the Self? Do I ever practice the one kind of analysis that Jung took to be distinctively his own contribution to the psychotherapeutic enterprise? If not, how dare I continue to call myself a Jungian and not simply admit that I deserve all the opprobrium that comes of being a "prestige psychologist," preaching Jung's ideas to others?

I was ready to accept a very depressing verdict about my place in the Jungian world when a whole series of humiliating incidents came to mind. I recalled moments in my work when I had not a clue as to what was going on, when I thought I had no right to call myself an analyst – or indeed a therapist of any kind. I felt the analysis had gotten hopelessly stuck and I was simply biding my time until things would simply change of their own accord. Surprisingly, they sometimes did so, and I felt the two of us (my analysand and I) had escaped failure by the merest fluke. I could see no hand I had played in our recovery. I was simply a bumbling fool who had been saved "by the grace of God." It has taken some time during the writing of this chapter before it occurred to me that "by the grace of God" is precisely how Jung describes a successful turn in an analysis that proceeds from the Self. I conclude from this that analyzing from the Self is probably always a humbling experience. The non-knowing of *Gelassenheit* is subjectively experienced as stupidity and unworthiness. The genius of Jung lay in his ability to trust his stupidity.

When we listen to the oral tradition wherein Jung's disciples tell us of Jung's greatness in being a conduit for the wisdom of the Great Man, we invariably identify with them in their "transference projection" onto Jung as the Old Wise Man of Zurich. When they entered a Self field shared with Jung, they assumed – very much in line with their idealizing projection – that Jung had some extraordinary talent for inducing an experience of the Self field. But in Jung's own experience, he had no idea *why* he suddenly began "to speak of Africa and snakes" or to hum a lullaby. He simply fell into an unconscious state. "What was I thinking just now? I wouldn't know. I think unconsciously." Very likely from his perspective, it was the analysand who "induced" a Self field the moment she entered the room.

This resonates with my experience. On all those humiliating occasions when I found myself supremely stupid and incompetent, I secretly wondered whether my analysand's unconsciousness had "induced" this thick-headedness into the field between us. I was led to wonder about "psychic contamination" and the worst sort of *participation mystique*. Alternatively, when the analysis accomplished something in spite of me, I was prone to give my analysand all the credit. She evidently was possessed with extraordinary psychic powers and had "induced" the Self field that had guided us both. Perhaps our narcissism as Jungian analysts – with all the grandiosity and impotence that flows by turns from it – stems from our aspiration someday to be like Jung rather than accept the more likely and humbling alternative that Jung may have been more like us than we care to admit.

References

Baynes, M. (1977) "A talk with students at the institute," in W. McGuire and R. F. C. Hull (eds), *C.G. Jung Speaking*, Princeton: Princeton University Press.

Bennet, E.A. (1985) *Meetings with Jung*, Zurich: Daimon.

Boudouin, C. (1977) "From Charles Boudouin's journal: 1934," in W. McGuire and R.F.C. Hull (eds), *C.G. Jung Speaking*, Princeton: Princeton University Press.

Brooke, R. (1991) *Jung and Phenomenology*, London: Routledge.

Duplain, G. (1977) "On the frontiers of knowledge," in W. McGuire and R. F. C. Hull (eds), *C.G. Jung Speaking*, Princeton: Princeton University Press.

Eckhart, M. (1981) *Meister Eckhart: The Essential Sermons, Commentaries, Treatises, and Defense*, trans. and introduced by E. Colledge and B. McGinn, New York: Paulist.

Fischer, E.A. (1977) "On creative achievement," in W. McGuire and R.F.C. Hull (eds), *C.G. Jung Speaking*, Princeton: Princeton University Press.

Hannah, B. (1976) *Jung: His Life and Work, A Biographical Memoir*, New York: G.P. Putnam's Sons.

Heidegger, M. (1968) *Discourse on Thinking*, trans. J. M. Anderson and E. H. Freund, New York: Harper and Row.

Jensen F. (ed.), (1982) *C. G. Jung, Emma Jung, and Toni Wolff*, San Francisco: The Analytical Psychology Club of San Francisco.

Jung, C. G. (1912/52) "Symbols of Transformation," *CW* 5.

—— (1928) "Two essays in analytical psychology," *CW* 7.

—— (1946) "The Psychology of the Transference," *CW* 16.

McGuire, W. and R. F. C. Hull (eds), (1977) *C. G. Jung Speaking*, Princeton: Princeton University Press.

Spiegelman, J. M. (1982) "Memory of C. G. Jung," in F. Jensen (ed.), *C.G. Jung, Emma Jung, and Toni Wolff*, San Francisco: The Analyical Psychology Club of San Francisco.

Spiegelman, J.M. (ed.) (1988) *Jungian Analysts: Their Visions and Vulnerabilities*, Phoenix: New Falcon.

Stein, R. (1973/84) *Incest and Human Love: The Betrayal of the Soul in Psychotherapy*, Dallas: Spring Publications.

—— (1988) "Reflections on professional deformation," in J.M. Spiegelman (ed.), *Jungian Analysts, Their Visions and Vulnerabilities*, Phoenix: New Falcon.

Von Franz, M.-L. (1975) *C.G. Jung: His Myth in Our Time*, trans. W.H. Kennedy, New York: C.G. Jung Foundation.

Weaver, M.I.R. (1982) "An interview with C.G. Jung," in F. Jensen (ed.), *C.G. Jung,*

Emma Jung, and Toni Wolff, San Francisco: The Analytical Psychology Club of San Francisco.

Wheelwright, J. (1982) "Jung", in J. Ferne and S. Mullen (eds) *C.G. Jung, Emma Jung, Toni Wolff: a Collection of Remembrances*, San Francisco: The Analytical Psychology Club of San Francisco.

Whitney, M. and Whitney, M. (1983) *Matter of Heart*, a Michael Whitney–Mark Whitney Production, sponsored by the C. G. Jung Institute of Los Angeles.

INDEX